Communications in Computer and Information Science 2988

Rationale
The CCIS series is devoted to the publication of proceedings of computer science conferences. Its aim is to efficiently disseminate original research results in informatics in printed and electronic form. While the focus is on publication of peer-reviewed full papers presenting mature work, inclusion of reviewed short papers reporting on work in progress is welcome, too. Besides globally relevant meetings with internationally representative program committees guaranteeing a strict peer-reviewing and paper selection process, conferences run by societies or of high regional or national relevance are also considered for publication.

Topics
The topical scope of CCIS spans the entire spectrum of informatics ranging from foundational topics in the theory of computing to information and communications science and technology and a broad variety of interdisciplinary application fields.

Information for Volume Editors and Authors
Publication in CCIS is free of charge. No royalties are paid, however, we offer registered conference participants temporary free access to the online version of the conference proceedings on SpringerLink (http://link.springer.com) by means of an http referrer from the conference website and/or a number of complimentary printed copies, as specified in the official acceptance email of the event.

CCIS proceedings can be published in time for distribution at conferences or as post-proceedings, and delivered in the form of printed books and/or electronically as USBs and/or e-content licenses for accessing proceedings at SpringerLink. Furthermore, CCIS proceedings are included in the CCIS electronic book series hosted in the SpringerLink digital library at http://link.springer.com/bookseries/7899. Conferences publishing in CCIS are allowed to use our online conference service (Meteor) for managing the whole proceedings lifecycle (from submission and reviewing to preparing for publication) free of charge.

Publication process
The language of publication is exclusively English. Authors publishing in CCIS have to sign the Springer CCIS copyright transfer form, however, they are free to use their material published in CCIS for substantially changed, more elaborate subsequent publications elsewhere. For the preparation of the camera-ready papers/files, authors have to strictly adhere to the Springer CCIS Authors' Instructions and are strongly encouraged to use the CCIS LaTeX style files or templates.

Abstracting/Indexing
CCIS is abstracted/indexed in DBLP, Google Scholar, EI-Compendex, Mathematical Reviews, SCImago, Scopus. CCIS volumes are also submitted for the inclusion in ISI Proceedings.

How to start
To start the evaluation of your proposal for inclusion in the CCIS series, please send an e-mail to ccis@springer.com

Ricardo Baptista · Bárbara Barroso ·
António Coelho · María Luz Castro Pena ·
Carla Sousa
Editors

Videogame Sciences and Arts

15th International Conference, VJ 2025
Maia-Porto, Portugal, December 4–5, 2025
Proceedings

Springer

Editors
Ricardo Baptista
IPMaia
Maia, Portugal

Bárbara Barroso
Instituto Politécnico de Bragança
Bragança, Portugal

António Coelho
Faculdade de Engenharia
Porto, Portugal

María Luz Castro Pena
University of A Coruña
A Coruña, Spain

Carla Sousa
Universidade Aberta, LE@D
Lisbon, Portugal

ISSN 1865-0929 ISSN 1865-0937 (electronic)
Communications in Computer and Information Science
ISBN 978-3-032-31641-7 ISBN 978-3-032-31642-4 (eBook)
https://doi.org/10.1007/978-3-032-31642-4

This Springer imprint is published by the registered company Springer Nature Switzerland AG
The registered company address is: Gewerbestrasse 11, 6330 Cham, Switzerland

Preface

The 15th International Conference on Videogame Sciences and Arts (Videojogos 2025) was held on December 4–5, 2025, at the *Instituto Politécnico da Maia* (IPMaia), in Maia, within the Porto Metropolitan Area, Portugal. Organized by IPMaia in collaboration with the *Sociedade Portuguesa de Ciências dos Videojogos* (SPCV), the conference continued to consolidate its role as an international forum for the presentation and discussion of current research, creative practice, and applied innovation in the broad and evolving field of videogame sciences and arts. To ensure this cohesive path, all submitted short and full papers were subjected to a double-blind peer review process, with an average of three reviews per contribution.

Videojogos 2025 brought together researchers, educators, designers, developers, artists, and industry professionals from diverse disciplinary backgrounds. As in previous editions, the conference fostered dialogue across technological, artistic, educational, cultural, and societal perspectives, reaffirming the status of videogames not only as entertainment products, but also as complex computational systems, cultural artifacts, pedagogical media, and spaces of social expression. This plurality of perspectives was clearly reflected in the 20 contributions, including two short papers, selected for this volume from 26 submissions.

The papers collected in this volume can be meaningfully framed into four broad thematic strands. The first, Serious Games, Gamification, and Applied Play, brings together contributions addressing the design and critical understanding of game-based approaches in contexts such as education, financial literacy, media literacy, mental health, and intergenerational inclusion. Across these works, a common concern emerges with the meaningful use of game structures and motivational dynamics, not merely as instruments for engagement, but as frameworks capable of supporting reflection, learning, behavioral change, and social participation.

A second strand, Accessibility, Inclusion, and Human-Centered Design, highlights the importance of designing games and interactive systems that are more inclusive, more adaptable, and more responsive to diverse users and contexts of use. The contributions in this area examine questions such as accessible content creation, AI-generated audio descriptions for blind and visually impaired users, and design frameworks grounded in usability, pedagogy, and participatory or user-centered approaches. Taken together, these papers show that accessibility and inclusion are not peripheral concerns, but central dimensions of quality, relevance, and innovation in contemporary game research and development.

The third strand, Artificial Intelligence, Procedural Generation, and Computational Approaches to Play, reflects the field's growing technical sophistication. The papers gathered under this theme address machine learning, reinforcement learning, procedural generation, computational modelling, and data-driven approaches to gameplay, content generation, and interactive behavior. Importantly, these contributions do not frame technical development as an end in itself; rather, they demonstrate how computational methods may serve design exploration, emergent storytelling, expressive systems, and new forms of interaction, analysis, and creative experimentation.

A fourth strand, Game Studies, Cultural Memory, and Critical Perspectives, brings together papers that approached videogames as cultural, historical, and discursive objects. These contributions examine issues such as gender representation, identity, social imaginaries, memory, local production histories, collecting practices, and the broader cultural narratives that surround play and digital media. In doing so, they underscore the importance of critical, interpretive, and historiographical perspectives for understanding the role of games in contemporary culture and for situating game research within wider debates in the humanities and social sciences.

Taken as a whole, the volume testifies to a field that continues to expand simultaneously in methodological breadth, technical depth, and societal relevance. One of the most significant features of the works presented at Videojogos 2025 lies precisely in their capacity to connect domains often treated as separate: engineering and criticism, design and pedagogy, computation and culture, experimentation and reflection. The result is a body of work that not only documents current developments in videogame research but also illustrates the richness of the questions currently redefining the field.

All submissions included in the conference program were subject to peer review by members of the Program Committee and external reviewers. Editorial decisions were based on relevance to the conference themes, originality, scholarly and/or technical quality, and clarity of presentation. The papers selected for this volume represent a curated cross-section of the research presented at Videojogos 2025 and reflect the scientific and thematic diversity that characterized the conference.

As volume editors, we would like to express our sincere gratitude to all authors for their submissions and for the quality of their work. We are equally indebted to the members of the Program Committee, both Scientific Chairs and Committee reviewers, the keynote speakers, the session chairs, and the organizing team, whose dedication, expertise, and generosity were essential to the success of this edition. We also gratefully acknowledge the institutional support of IPMaia and the continued contribution of SPCV to the strengthening of this conference series and of the wider research community it serves.

We hope that this volume offers readers a meaningful and representative overview of current work in videogame sciences and arts. Beyond documenting the outcomes of Videojogos 2025, it reflects a field that is increasingly interdisciplinary, critically engaged, and socially aware – one that continues to expand the range of questions it addresses.

March 2026

Ricardo Baptista
Bárbara Barroso
António Coelho
María Luz Castro Pena
Carla Sousa

Organization

General Chair

Ricardo Baptista	Instituto Politécnico da Maia, Portugal

Program Committee Chairs

António Coelho	University of Porto, Portugal
Bárbara Barroso	Polytechnic Institute of Bragança, Portugal
María Luz Castro Pena	University of A Coruña, Spain

Program Committee

Alan Carvalho	FATEC São Caetano do Sul, Brazil
Ana Veloso	University of Aveiro, Portugal
Anna Unterholzner	ITI/LARSyS, Portugal
Anabela Marto	Polytechnic Institute of Leiria, Portugal
André Pereira	KTH Royal Institute of Technology, Sweden
Andreas Theodorou	Umeå University, Sweden
Alexander Dockhorn	Gottfried Wilhelm Leibniz University Hannover, Germany
Carla Sousa	Universidade Aberta, Portugal
Eduarda Abrantes	Polytechnic Institute of Leiria, Portugal
Eva Oliveira	Polytechnic Institute of Cávado and Ave, Portugal
Frutuoso Silva	University of Beira Interior, Portugal
Filipe Luz	Lusófona University, Portugal
João Dias	University of Algarve, Portugal
Jorge López Moreno	Rey Juan Carlos University, Spain
Leonel Morgado	Open University, Portugal
Liliana Vale Costa	University of Aveiro, Portugal
Luís Reis	University of Porto, Portugal
Maria Carmen Juan	Polytechnic University of Valencia, Spain
Mário Vairinhos	University of Aveiro, Portugal
Micael Sousa	University College Dublin, Ireland
Markus Wiemker	TH Köln – University of Applied Sciences, Germany

Mustafa Can Gursesli	Tampere University, Finland
Nelson Zagalo	University of Aveiro, Portugal
Óscar Mealha	University of Aveiro, Portugal
Patrícia Gouveia	University of Lisbon, Portugal
Paulina Tsevetkova	Bulgarian Academy of Sciences, Bulgaria
Pedro Cardoso	University of Porto, Portugal
Phil Lopes	Lusófona University, Portugal
Riccardo Fassone	University of Turin, Italy
Roberto Ribeiro	Polytechnic Institute of Leiria, Portugal
Rui Nóbrega	NOVA University Lisbon, Portugal
Rui Prada	Instituto Superior Técnico, Portugal
Ruth Contreras Espinosa	University of Vic, Spain
Terhi Marttila	ITI/LARSyS, Portugal
Teresa Romão	NOVA University Lisbon, Portugal
Valter Alves	Polytechnic Institute of Viseu, Portugal
Salma Elsayed	Abertay University, UK
Wolfgang Mueller	University of Education Weingarten, Germany

Contents

Serious Games, Gamification, and Applied Play

Through the Lens of Play: Directions for Reframing Gamification and Serious Games ... 3
Angelica Cunha dos Santos, Virgínia Fernandes Mota, and Emanuel Felipe Duarte

Gamification for Media Education: A Systematic Literature Review of Effectiveness, Challenges, and Platform Design Priorities ... 15
Ana Filipa Oliveira, Carla Sousa, Ana Lamy, Catarina Regra, and Viviana Fernandes

The Impact of Gamification on Engagement in a Financial Literacy App ... 31
Ricardo Carvalho, Rui Prada, Carla Pacheco, Guilherme Pires, and Francisco Oom

Applying Gamification via *PlayNwhere* for Intergenerational Inclusion: A Case Study of Sanofi's "*Jornada De Gerações*" ... 44
Alvaro Marcos Antonio de Araujo Pistono and Ricardo José Vieira Baptista

"I Ended up not Playing More...": A Design Model to Support Completion of Narrative Serious Games for Mental Health ... 56
Dalila Martins, Nelson Zagalo, and Ana Patrícia Oliveira

Designing a User-Centered Educational Serious Game on Camilo Castelo Branco ... 68
Gonçalo Castro, Edgar Pereira, and Rui Carreira

Accessibility, Inclusion, and Human-Centered Design

AI-Generated Audio Descriptions: An Empirical Evaluation with Blind and Visually Impaired Users ... 83
D. Alves Araújo

An Accessible Sketch-Based Framework for 3D Plant Model Generation ... 89
Ana Martins, Anabela Marto, Rita Ascenso, Roberto Ribeiro, Nuno Rodrigues, and Alexandrino Gonçalves

In-Game Behaviour Expression Using Dynamic Key Bindings 101
Samuel Gomes, Carlos Martinho, and João Dias

Artificial Intelligence, Procedural Generation, and Computational Approaches to Play

Playing Hex and Counter Wargames Using Reinforcement Learning and Recurrent Neural Networks 109
Guilherme Palma, João Dias, and Pedro A. Santos

Conditional Latent Diffusion Models for Controlled Terrain Generation 123
Margarida Amaro, João Dias, and Pedro A. Santos

From Play to Plot: Sifting Emergent Stories Through Clustering Heuristics 135
Miguel Belbute and Carlos Martinho

Wait, It's All Dynamical Systems? Always Has Been: Toward Precisely yet Intuitively Designing Ludonarrative Ergodicity 148
Pratama Wirya Atmaja, Darlis Herumurti, Sylvester Arnab, Hadziq Fabroyir, and Petros Lameras

Game Studies, Cultural Memory, and Critical Perspectives

Unveiling Hidden Pioneers: Carla Vieira Faria's Legacy in Portuguese Digital Game History 169
Luciana Lima and Maria Júlia Vieira

From Pitch to Pixel: Portuguese Football, Identity, and the Microhistory of *Elifoot* 184
Ivan Barroso and Filipe Luz

Aloy's Challenge to Gender Stereotypes in Contemporary Video-Game Narratives 196
Maria Júlia Vieira, Dalila Martins, Pedro Cardoso, and Luciana Lima

The Rhetoric of Contagion in Digital Games: Depiction, Symptomatology, and Social Measures Across 16 Games 210
Liliana Vale Costa and Nelson Zagalo

Video Games as Mirrors, Refuges, and Stages: A Reflexive Thematic Analysis of Self-image in the Digital Era 226
Carla Sousa, Mustafa Can Gursesli, Amanda Cei Santos Pirola, Ana Filipa Oliveira, Juho Hamari, and Mirko Duradoni

Gamified Labubu: Exploring the Psychological Factors of Adult Play in Brazil and Finland 242
Katriina Heljakka, Letícia Hara Takahama Tagliacollo, and Jorge Luís Ferreira Abrão

Game Consumption in Ludic Spaces: A Chronotopic Approach 255
Lizbeth Kanyat

Author Index 271

Serious Games, Gamification, and Applied Play

Through the Lens of Play: Directions for Reframing Gamification and Serious Games

Angelica Cunha dos Santos[1], Virgínia Fernandes Mota[1,2], and Emanuel Felipe Duarte[1(✉)]

[1] Instituto de Computação, Universidade Estadual de Campinas, Campinas, Brazil
a290207@dac.unicamp.br, virginia@teiacoltec.org, emanuel@ic.unicamp.br
[2] Colégio Técnico, Universidade Federal de Minas Gerais, Belo Horizonte, Brazil

Abstract. As computing becomes increasingly ubiquitous, efforts to integrate play and game-like features into more aspects of everyday life have focused primarily on gamification and serious games approaches. We argue that these approaches often neglect the essence of play as an emergent, situated, and culturally embedded phenomenon, reducing it to a set of transferable mechanics such as badges, points, or leaderboards. Furthermore, the strong influence from behavioral psychology can introduce theoretical-methodological inconsistencies, particularly when these approaches are situated within third-wave HCI research, where human experience, context, and meaning-making are central concerns. By critically examining these tensions through the lenses of play theory and third-wave HCI, we highlight how the instrumentalization of play risks reinforcing conditioning and transmission-learning models, rather than constructivist approaches that value autonomy and plurality. In this essay, we aim to foster reflection and discussion, proposing a reframing of gamification and serious games research towards promoting more meaningful, plural, and theoretically coherent engagements with play.

Keywords: Play Theory · Gamification · Serious Games · Third-Wave HCI

1 Introduction

The act of playing – as in children playing, acting in a play, playing an instrument, playing a digital game and so on – is characterized as something intrinsically human and social [4,18], and even political [11]. As computing advances become increasingly ubiquitous, it seems natural to want to "borrow" successful game characteristics for purposes beyond entertainment. Efforts to bring play and game-like features to more aspects of everyday life beyond entertainment have focused primarily on the concepts of *gamification* and *serious games*. In gamification, typical game elements such as scoring, badges, and leaderboards are applied in different, initially non-game contexts as a strategy to promote more

R. Baptista et al. (Eds.): VJ 2025, CCIS 2988, pp. 3–14, 2027.
https://doi.org/10.1007/978-3-032-31642-4_1

engagement among users [31]. Serious games, on the other hand, are games with an explicit primary purpose that differs from entertainment, typically with an educational and/or simulation emphasis [1].

Both gamification and serious games have become widespread in areas such education, healthcare, marketing and workplace productivity. While we acknowledge their widely reported potential to engage users and enhance learning outcomes, critiques have also emerged. Scholars have pointed out that these approaches often rely on reductive understanding of games, privileging reward structures and external motivators over the more complex and situated qualities of play [3,24,30]. In doing so, these approaches risk instumentalizing play, transforming it into a means of control, surveillance or efficiency rather than an end itself. Moreover, this instrumentalization is not culturally neutral: it reflects and reproduces broader social and political dynamics [13,22].

In this essay, we argue that any analysis of gamification and serious games must foreground play not as a set of transferable mechanics but as an emergent phenomenon: lived, situated, plural and culturally embedded. We further contend that neglecting this perspective reveals theoretical-methodological inconsistencies in both fields. Building on classical definitions of play, as well as on more recent critical perspectives, we seek to reframe gamification and serious games through alternative directions more aligned with contemporary values of freedom, experience, autonomy and representation. We guide our analysis on basis of the following two research questions:

Research Question 1: How an emergent and situated perspective on play could inform gamification and serious games approaches?

Research Question 2: What theoretical-methodological inconsistencies may arise from gamification and serious games approaches, and how can they be reframed?

The remaining of this paper is structured as follows. Section 2 offers a critical discussion of play as an emergent phenomenon and examines how it can be applied to gamification and serious games. Section 3 addresses theoretical and methodological inconsistencies in these fields and considers how they might be reframed. Finally, Sect. 4 concludes by outlining future directions and possibilities for research and design.

2 Play as an Emergent Phenomenon

The theme of the first critique we will address is the very essence of play, or lack thereof. It is possible to argue that common elements in "gamified" systems (points, badges, leaderboards *etc.*) are not essential features of games [3,5,24]. Gamification approaches, therefore, tends to appropriate mostly elements considered superfluous, leaving aside more significant qualities of mechanics, gameplay, narrative, aesthetics *etc.* We argue that when we focus on games as technical products with features to be catalogued and replicated, we may fail to recognize that what really matters is the emergent phenomenon that surrounds them when people are involved: play. A similar argument can be made towards serious games, which often defy their very characterization as games when they deprive players of their autonomy. Serious games are often "played" out of obligation in educational, therapeutic, and other contexts, and often fail to produce experiences that players consider pleasurable [28].

Revisiting seminal works on play, such as Johan Huizinga's *Homo Ludens* [18] and Roger Caillois' *Man, Play and Games* [4], we can highlight aspects that seem to be neglected in gamification and serious games approaches. For instance, Huizinga [18, p. 13] presents formal characteristics for games and the act of playing, such as: being a free (as in freedom) activity, disconnected from material interest, and that promotes the formation of social groups. These characteristics feel immediately incompatible with an ever-increasing emphasis on guidance and accumulation (of points, badges, "knowledge" *etc.*) in gamified systems and serious games. In turn, the continuum proposed by Caillois [4, p. 13], with the complementary opposites of *paidia* (something free, carefree, improvised) and *ludus* (something structured, arbitrary, imperative), is particularly of interest, especially if we consider that gamification approaches and serious games are more easily classified as *ludus*, while the counterpart *paidia* seems more neglected in computational systems. *Ludus* alone is not sufficient to allow play to emerge and be sustained.

This critique is not new, as seen in Smith *et al.'s* [26] call for "paidia-based gamification", which seeks to reintroduce more open and improvisational forms of play into education settings, and in Thibault and Hamari's [30] attempt to reappropriate gamification by emphasizing playful experiences rather than instrumentalized mechanics. The concepts of Gameful Design and Gameful Experience propose a learning design inspired by the subjective qualities of play, rather than by its external mechanics alone [8]. The aim is to create environments that foster experiences similar to real games, with a focus on authentic and meaningful engagement. The playification approach follows the same logic by valuing spontaneous ludic experiences, free from fixed goals, scores, or rewards [20]. It is illustrated in a physical rehabilitation context in which participants received only auditory signals without explicit instructions or predefined objectives. The interpretation of these signals emerged through the interaction between the participants and the therapist. This form of engagement recalls Huizinga's concept of the "magic circle", in which play creates a symbolic space separate from the utilitarian purposes of real life, sustained by internal rules and the freedom of participants to act [18].

While these contributions highlight important directions, we feel that further developments are still needed. Recent work has revisited the very concept of play, reframing it around issues of representation and diversity in contemporary game design [22]. Their argument expands classical conceptions of play, traditionally centered on formal or structural characteristics, by integrating cultural and political perspectives that acknowledge who plays, how they play, and whose experiences are made visible or marginalized in digital games. This perspective reinforces our claim that play should be understood as a plural and culturally situated phenomenon rather than a universal or value-neutral one. Therefore, it challenges gamification and serious games approaches that treat play as generic and transferable mechanism, detached from social and cultural contexts.

Similarly, phenomenological approaches to digital game have foregrounded embodiment, intentionality and the socio-cultural contexts in which play emerges. Mota and Duarte [21] argue that digital play cannot be reduced to a set of predefined mechanics or outcomes, but rather unfolds though players' perceptual, emotional and embodied engagement with game environments. This perspective situates play within the third wave of HCI (Human-Computer Interaction), which enphasizes experience, meaning-making, and context. Such idea complements our discussion by showing that neglecting play as a phenomenological phenomenon leads to theoretical and methodological inconsistencies in gamification and serious games.

From this standpoint, overlooking play in gamification and serious games represents not only a design limitation but a theoretical–methodological inconsistency, as these approaches tend to reduce games to transferable mechanics rather than recognizing play as a lived, plural, and culturally situated phenomenon.

2.1 Towards Applying Play on Gamification and Serious Games

To advance this discussion, we propose starting points to better understand and discuss play as an emergent phenomenon. By shedding light on how play is being neglected in gamified systems and serious games, we can start to think about how these areas of research can be approached through different lenses. The discussion, however, should not adopt any static or hegemonic definition of play. The very concept of play we presented should not be taken as universal or final, as it remains narrowly understood through Global North Western lenses – privileging structured, rule-based forms and overlooking its cultural specificity and expressive plurality. Therefore, we should not only look at how gamified systems and serious games can benefit from play, but also keep on discussing play itself from other cultural, political, social lenses.

Different definitions of play and its essence can create more engaging and meaningful gamified experiences. Play, then, can serve as a conceptual guiding principle, highlighting intrinsic motivators (challenge, autonomy *etc.*), promoting socially significant interactions, and inspiring flexible mechanics that value exploration and creativity over simply compliance with predetermined rules or accumulation of rewards. Therefore, towards applying play on gamification and serious games we need to take into account:

- **Situated and phenomenological experiences**: gamified design should account for how users experiences interactions – their perceptions, emotions, meaning-making, embodiment, social contexts – ensuring that challenges and rewards resonate with lived experiences, in line with the third wave of HCI (which we will further address in the next section).

- **Sociocultural relevance**: by integrating cultural and social dimensions into game mechanics and narratives, systems can create experiences that reflect and accommodate users' backgrounds and values, fostering engagement and meaning as emergent qualities of the interaction, instead of only as predetermined qualities of a digital product.
- **Balance exploration and structure**: Following Caillois' distinction between *paidia* and *ludus*, it is possible to combine some degree of free exploration with the presence of structured objectives, allowing users to experiment, discover and learn creatively, without having to give up on purpose (*e.g.*, specific learning objectives or goals).

Therefore, directly answering our first research question, by considering these listed aspects, we believe that gamification and serious games approaches can move beyond only borrowing "successful" game mechanics (points, badges, leaderboards *etc.*). By leveraging the richness of play as an emergent phenomenon, gamification and serious games approaches could be more situated instead of "static" or imposing, valuing sociocultural aspects and allowing the exercise of autonomy and freedom, without losing a specific desired purpose. However, to ensure that such reorientations are consistent with contemporary understandings of human experience and learning, it is necessary to reflect on the underlying theoretical–methodological implications, as we discuss next.

3 Theoretical-Methodological Inconsistencies

The theme of the second critique we will address is theoretical-methodological compatibilities, or lack of thereof. It is possible to argue that serious games and gamification approaches commonly share a strong influence from behavioral psychology (also known as behaviorism, the shaping of behavior through conditioning) in their efforts to promote engagement and training [14,19]. In summary, "desired" user behaviors can be incentivized through rewards (*e.g.*, points, achievements, or leaderboards) for specific actions associated with that behavior, and "undesired" behaviors can be punished (in subtle or explicit ways) or even not be made available at all. This raises a substantial problem that needs awareness and discussion: the behaviorist theoretical-methodological background for cognition and learning contrasts with other backgrounds more recently adopted in HCI research, such as phenomenology [16], constructivism [27] and embodied cognition [15], in what is often labeled as "third-wave" HCI [2,9,17]. While behaviorism emphasizes learning as a process of controlled conditioning, where the mind and subjective experience are irrelevant in face of observable behavior, third-wave HCI backgrounds emphasize aspects such as subjective experience, sense-making through action and perception, the relationship between body and environment, and the free construction of knowledge. We highlight that paradigmatic inconsistencies are bound to arise when gamification and serious games approaches are employed without a proper understanding of their theoretical-methodological implications.

A particularly problematic manifestation of this tension appears in educational and training contexts. Works on gamification and serious games often claim that these approaches can "transmit" or "facilitate the transfer of knowledge", suggesting that the application of game elements inherently enhances learning outcomes. However, this perspective is implicitly aligned with a model of education and an understanding of the learning process in which knowledge is viewed as an object that can be simply passed from one to another, a transmission model. Such assumptions disregard the constructive nature of knowledge. As Paulo Freire argued [12, p. 46], knowledge is not something that can be deposited by teachers into passive learners as empty vessels, but rather something that is constructed together through dialogue, overcoming the teacher-student dichotomy. Therefore, besides a behaviorist stance, by treating knowledge as something that can be delivered through predetermined goals, points, badges, or rewards for specific behaviors, gamification and serious games risk reinforcing passive and oppressive learning models that do not promote autonomy and free thinking.

As discussed in Sect. 2, neglecting play as an emergent, situated and plural phenomenon contributes to these inconsistencies. This observation resonates with broader critiques in the literature. Taken together, the chapters *The Ludification of Culture* [23] and *Why Fun Matters: In Search of Emergent Playful Experiences* [10] in *Rethinking Gamification* [13] highlight how gamification is often reduced to quantifiable mechanics detached from emergent, cultural and experiential dimensions. The former emphasizes the socio-cultural implications of what has been called ludification of culture, warning that the increasing reliance on game logic is never neutral. The latter stresses that what makes games engaging is not a pre-designed feature but an emergent quality arising from improvisation, social interaction and context. Both critiques align with our argument that gamification and serious games, when grounded in behaviorist or transmission-based models of learning, risk stripping play of its autonomy and spontaneity, turning it into an instrument for external goals rather than a lived, meaningful experience.

The emphasis on external motivations and measurable goals in gamification and serious games directly contradicts Huizinga's [18] notion of the "magic circle", which defines play as a free and spontaneous act. When play becomes instrumentalized for educational, therapeutic, or corporate purposes, it loses its symbolic autonomy. In education, for example, students often engage in tasks mechanically to obtain rewards, thereby reducing cognitive engagement with the content [8,25]. In serious games, similar mechanisms may lead participants to focus on extrinsic success indicators (such as scores, ranks, and completion rates) rather than on experiential learning. This tendency emerges from the lack of methodological guidelines [6]. Gamification and serious games based on external control replace freedom and exploration with functionality and performance, integrating play into systems of productivity and dissolving its boundary from the "real world." The result is a mechanical, predictable, and instrumentalist experience.

This critique echoes Bogost's [3] view of gamification as an empty corporate rhetoric that uses the vocabulary of games to mask mechanisms of manipulation and surveillance. DeWinter [7] extends this argument by drawing a parallel between gamification and classical Taylorism: both seek to control, measure, and optimize human activity, transforming play into an extension of capitalist logics of productivity. While Taylorism disciplined bodies through time and motion studies, gamification disciplines attention and motivation through data-driven metrics. Yet, presented under the aesthetic of play, it creates an illusion of freedom and engagement that conceals its managerial function. As a counterpoint, Thibault [29] proposes "punk gamification" as a critical reappropriation of these practices. Drawing inspiration from the punk movement, this approach embraces aesthetic disobedience, creative imperfection, and non-functionality as forms of resistance to corporate control. It advocates for gamified and serious game experiences that may provoke discomfort, irony, or reflection rather than obedience and optimization. Such experiences reassert play as voluntary, imaginative, and free—a phenomenon that emerges from lived experience rather than imposed structures.

In summary, the theoretical-methodological inconsistencies identified across current approaches to gamification and serious games reveal a persistent tension between behaviorist principles and the promotion of autonomy, between transmission-oriented models of learning and the constructive nature of knowledge, and between the instrumentalization of play for productivity and the preservation of freedom and spontaneity. When play is treated merely as a mechanism of behavioral conditioning or knowledge delivery, its potential is constrained, reducing complex human experiences to measurable outputs. Recognizing these contradictions is essential to move beyond reductionist applications of game logics and toward frameworks that value experience, creativity, and autonomy as central to meaningful engagement.

3.1 Towards Theoretical-Methodological Reframings

In a capitalist society where metrics and quantitative results are the norm, there is a persistent pressure to instrumentalize play as a means to optimize engagement, productivity, and learning outcomes. As widely reported in the literature, gamification and serious games are powerful tools in promoting the improvement of such metrics. However, their application is not neutral: It can reinforce logics of control and surveillance, as the logic of play can be appropriated by economic and institutional interests. Moreover, these very metrics should be questioned, as they often fail to account for the inherently subjective and diverse ways in which individuals perceive and perform play. For instance, what is meaningful or engaging for one person may be ineffective for another – and this is not something we need to get rid of, but something that should be welcomed: different forms of play. Theoretical-methodological alignment, therefore, requires gamification and serious games to be approached through alternative directions more aligned with contemporary values of freedom, experience, and autonomy.

For a theoretical-methodological reorientation to be possible, it is necessary to understand the game as a situated cultural practice, with aesthetic, social, and affective dimensions, which is not limited to the logic of reward and measurement. Just as Fuchs *et al.* [13] argue, the gamification of culture should not be confused with the quantification of behaviors through extrinsic mechanics; this implies reducing the game to a tool of control, emptying its critical and experiential potential. Thus, gamification design must incorporate the plurality of the game, with its unpredictability, emergent nature, and social and historical context, as constitutive elements, not as noise to be eliminated.

Proposals such as "punk gamification" [29] present themselves as a provocative alternative to corporate appropriation and instrumentalization of games. By valuing imperfect aesthetics, non-functionality, and subjective expression, this approach invites a repositioning of games as a political practice, resisting standardization and utilitarian logic. This approach is similar to the third wave of HCI, which values subjective experience, embodiment, sociocultural context, and the construction of meaning through interaction. Similarly, the perspectives of Gameful Design [8] and Playification [20] propose player-centered experiences capable of stimulating autonomy, curiosity, and a sense of belonging, aligning them with constructivist learning models. Therefore, towards answering our second research question, we need to reframe gamification and serious games by addressing their theoretical-methodological inconsistencies through the following directions:

- **Constructivist and phenomenological perspectives:** When designing serious games and gamified experiences, it is important to consider that knowledge is not transferred or conditioned, but rather constructed. Participants should be allowed to attribute meaning to the interaction based on their own experience. The design must encourage reflection and situated learning, in which context is an active part of cognition.
- **Play and its plurality:** The journey must be designed to allow the player to explore, interact with other players, and the environment. It must allow room for error, learning, and creativity, allowing the player to experiment without being bound by right and wrong, or inflexible fixed goals. The rules can be negotiable, and the game can accommodate pauses, retreats, and unforeseen trajectories, without mechanical penalties.
- **Decentralization of progress**: When designing a serious game or gamified application, progress and rewards should not be solely external/extrinsic, but rather something that emerges from the game being played and the learning journey being taken, making engagement intrinsic. Other forms of mediation, such as self-assessment, observation of interactions, and listening to participants, should be considered.
- **Politically Conscious Design:** Gamification can alter people's behavior and value views, so design must be ethical, political, and also aware of its social role. To achieve this, its ideological implications must be made clear, and a space for reflection and criticism must be provided.

To directly answer our second research question, we see two main theoretical-methodological inconsistencies that commonly arise from gamification and serious games approaches: 1) the homogenization of learning through behaviorist and transmission-oriented models is inconsistent with constructivist approaches that value plurality and the learners' agency; and 2) the instrumentalization of play for productivity (or other extrinsic motivations) is inconsistent with its spontaneity and freedom. Therefore, to reframe these issues, design must move beyond neutrality and efficiency, considering users as active agents with interpretive and emotional capacities. It must include pedagogical practices where humans can learn collaboratively, based on their experiences, and develop critical autonomy. Reframing gamified experiences, therefore, requires rethinking its epistemological foundations and the values that support it, promoting a situated, ethical practice committed to freedom, reflection, and agency.

4 Conclusion

In this paper we have argued about problems we identify in current gamification and serious games approaches that are strongly present in HCI research communities and forums. Our argument revolves around two main points: 1) although these approaches are based on games (in the sense that they try to "borrow" deemed successful game characteristics), they seem to neglect the central phenomenon surrounding these artifacts: the emergence of play; and 2) these approaches inherently bring with them theoretical-methodological implications that are not aligned with more contemporary values such as freedom, experience, and autonomy, causing inconsistencies and furthering agendas that researchers may not be aware of, or may even disagree completely.

By shedding light on the subject and fostering reflection and discussion, our aim is to provoke researchers into looking at alternative directions for gamification and serious games research and applications. When play is acknowledged as an emergent phenomenon, and theoretical-methodological approaches are carefully considered and their implications accounted for, we believe that researchers have a sufficient starting point for either revisiting and redefining these approaches of gamification and serious games, or for proposing new approaches.

4.1 Directions for Future Work

This study highlights gaps in the theoretical and methodological approaches to gamification and serious games that warrant further investigation. One key direction is the incorporation of phenomenological and embodied perspectives. Future research could examine how players' subjective experiences, bodily engagement, and situated interactions shape the emergence of play. A second direction concerns decolonial and culturally plural approaches. Existing frameworks often reflect dominant Global North epistemologies and overlook diverse cultural practices and understandings of play. Finally, studies should explore design frameworks integrating ethical, political, and relational considerations, supporting autonomy, co-authorship, and experimentation while resisting instrumentalization, surveillance, and standardization. By engaging these perspectives, future research can expand understandings of play as an emergent, relational, and culturally situated phenomenon, challenging dominant assumptions underpinning contemporary gamification and serious games research.

Acknowledgments. This study was financed, in part, by the São Paulo Research Foundation (FAPESP), Brasil, Process Number #2024/16790-5; by the Universidade Estadual de Campinas (UNICAMP), Brasil, FAEPEX grant #2356/24; and by the Coordenação de Aperfeiçoamento de Pessoal de Nível Superior (CAPES), Brasil, Finance Code 001.

Disclosure of interests. The authors have no competing interests to declare that are relevant to the content of this article.

References

1. Abt, C.C.: Serious Games. Viking Press, New York (1970)
2. Bødker, S.: When second wave hci meets third wave challenges. In: Proceedings of the 4th Nordic Conference on Human-computer Interaction: Changing Roles, NordiCHI '06, pp. 1–8. ACM, New York (2006). https://doi.org/10.1145/1182475.1182476
3. Bogost, I.: Why Gamification is Bullshit. In: The Gameful World: Approaches, Issues, Applications. The MIT Press (2015). https://doi.org/10.7551/mitpress/9788.003.0005
4. Caillois, R.: Man, Play, and Games. The Free Press, Los Angeles (1961)
5. Chorney, A.I.: Taking the game out of gamification. Dalhousie J. Interdisc. Manag. **8**(1) (2012). https://doi.org/10.5931/djim.v8i1.242
6. Dallaqua, M.F., Nunes, B., Carvalho, M.M.: Serious games research streams for social change: critical review and framing. Br. J. Edu. Technol. **55**, 460–483 (2023). https://doi.org/10.1111/bjet.13404
7. deWinter, J., Kocurek, C.A., Nichols, R.: Taylorism 2.0: gamification, scientific management and the capitalist appropriation of play. J. Gaming Virtual Worlds **6**(2), 109–127 (2014). https://doi.org/10.1386/jgvw.6.2.109_1
8. Dichev, C., Dicheva, D., Angelova, G., Agre, G.: From gamification to gameful design and gameful experience in learning. Cybern. Inf. Technol. **14**(4), 80–100 (2015). https://doi.org/10.1515/cait-2014-0007
9. Duarte, E.F., Baranauskas, M.C.C.: Revisiting the three hci waves: a preliminary discussion on philosophy of science and research paradigms. In: Proceedings of the 15th Brazilian Symposium on Human Factors in Computing Systems, IHC '16. Association for Computing Machinery, New York (2016). https://doi.org/10.1145/3033701.3033740
10. Fizek, S.: Why fun matters: in search of emergent playful experiences. In: Fuchs, M., Fizek, S., Ruffino, P., Schrape, N. (eds.) Rethinking Gamification, pp. 273–287. meson press (2014)
11. Flanagan, M.: Critical Play: Radical Game Design. MIT Press, Cambridge (2009)
12. Freire, P.: Pedagogia da Autonomia: Saberes Necessários à Prática Educativa. Paz e Terra (2021), originally published in 1996

13. Fuchs, M., Fizek, S., Ruffino, P., Schrape, N.: Rethinking Gamification. Meson Press (2014)
14. Gardiner, B.: How gamification took over the world (2024). https://www.technologyreview.com/2024/06/13/1093375/gamification-behaviorism-npcs-video-games/
15. Gibson, M.: Embodied cognition, body coherence, and immersion in non-euclidean virtual reality. In: Proceedings of the 16th Conference on Creativity & Cognition, C&C '24, pp. 25–29. Association for Computing Machinery, New York (2024). https://doi.org/10.1145/3635636.3664628
16. Glöss, M.: New perspectives for phenomenology in interaction design. In: Proceedings of the 13th Nordic Conference on Human-Computer Interaction, NordiCHI '24. Association for Computing Machinery, New York (2024). https://doi.org/10.1145/3679318.3685404
17. Harrison, S.R., Tatar, D.G., Sengers, P.: The three paradigms of hci. In: Alt. Chi. Session at the SIGCHI Conference on Human Factors in Computing Systems, pp. 1–18. ACM, San Jose (2007)
18. Huizinga, J.: Homo Ludens: A Study of the Play-element in Culture. Routledge & K. Paul, Abingdon (1949)
19. Linehan, C., Kirman, B., Roche, B.: Gamification as behavioral psychology. In: The Gameful World: Approaches, Issues, Applications. The MIT Press (2015). https://doi.org/10.7551/mitpress/9788.003.0006
20. Márquez Segura, E., Waern, A., Márquez Segura, L., López Recio, D.: Playification: the physeear case. In: Proceedings of the 2016 Annual Symposium on Computer-Human Interaction in Play, CHI PLAY '16, pp. 376–388. Association for Computing Machinery, New York (2016). https://doi.org/10.1145/2967934.2968099
21. Mota, V.F., Duarte, E.F.: Phenomenology and digital games: perspectives on why and directions on how. In: Phenomenological Concepts and Methods for HCI Research @ INTERACT (2025)
22. Mota, V.F., Duarte, E.F.: Revisiting and reframing play: towards incorporating representation and diversity in contemporary game design. In: Darin, T., Rios, K., Cruz, G., Tórtoro, L., Ricca, D. (eds.) Interaction and Player Research in Game Development, pp. 19–28. Springer, Cham (2025). https://doi.org/10.1007/978-3-032-01426-9_2
23. Raessens, J., Fuchs, M., Fizek, S., Ruffino, P.: The ludification of culture. Presented at the Rethinking Gamification (2014)
24. Robertson, M.: Can't play, won't play (2010). https://kotaku.com/cant-play-wont-play-5686393
25. Silva, J., et al.: Ética e ia na sala de aula: Relato de experiência com o jogo ai-audit em disciplinas de computação. In: Anais do XXXIII Workshop sobre Educação em Computação, pp. 397–407. SBC, Porto Alegre (2025). https://doi.org/10.5753/wei.2025.8108
26. Smith, A., Fernández Galeote, D., Legaki, N.Z., Hamari, J.: Gamified metacognitive prompts in a higher education flipped classroom. In: Proceedings of the 26th International Academic Mindtrek Conference, Mindtrek '23, pp. 95–107. Association for Computing Machinery, New York (2023). https://doi.org/10.1145/3616961.3616990
27. Smith, J.: Constructivism in computer science education. In: Proceedings of the 53rd ACM Technical Symposium on Computer Science Education, SIGCSE 2022, vol. 2, p. 1171. Association for Computing Machinery, New York (2022). https://doi.org/10.1145/3478432.3499203

28. Spiel, K., Gerling, K.: The purpose of play: how hci games research fails neurodivergent populations. ACM Trans. Comput.-Hum. Interact. **28**(2) (2021). https://doi.org/10.1145/3432245
29. Thibault, M.: Punk gamification. In: Koivisto, J., Hamari, J. (eds.) Proceedings of the 3rd International GamiFIN Conference. CEUR Workshop Proceedings, vol. 2359, pp. 58–69. CEUR-WS.org, Levi (2019). https://ceur-ws.org/Vol-2359/
30. Thibault, M., Hamari, J.: Seven points to reappropriate gamification. In: Spanellis, A., Harviainen, J.T. (eds.) Transforming Society and Organizations through Gamification, pp. 11–28. Springer, Cham (2021). https://doi.org/10.1007/978-3-030-68207-1_2
31. Walz, S.P., Deterding, S.: An introduction to the gameful world. In: The Gameful World: Approaches, Issues, Applications. The MIT Press, Cambridge (2015). https://doi.org/10.7551/mitpress/9788.003.0001

Gamification for Media Education: A Systematic Literature Review of Effectiveness, Challenges, and Platform Design Priorities

Ana Filipa Oliveira[1], Carla Sousa[3(✉)], Ana Lamy[1], Catarina Regra[2], and Viviana Fernandes[2]

[1] Lusófona University, CICANT, Lisbon/Porto, Portugal
ana.filipa.oliveira@ulusofona.pt
[2] School of Psychology and Life Sciences (EPCV), Lusófona University, Lisbon, Portugal
[3] Universidade Aberta, Laboratory of Distance Education and eLearning, Portugal, Lisbon, Portugal
carla.mira@uab.pt

Abstract. Gamification has become a prominent pedagogical strategy in formal education, integrating game design elements into learning environments. Its application in media education, particularly for fostering media literacy, news literacy, and information literacy, is of increasing societal importance given the challenges of misinformation, polarisation, and digital citizenship. However, evidence in this area remains fragmented, with limited synthesis of effective practices and implementation challenges. This Systematic Literature Review (SLR) examines empirical evidence on gamification in formal education with a focus on media education, aiming to identify effective practices, explore their impact on learning outcomes, and explore challenges, success factors, and design priorities for platforms. Following PRISMA 2020 guidelines, a systematic search was conducted across several databases, covering 2015–2025 with 32 studies met the inclusion criteria. Data extraction captured bibliographic details, contexts, gamification strategies, outcomes, and implementation factors. The most frequently applied strategies were points and scoring (74.2%), immersive and visual tools (51.6%), and leaderboards (35.5%). Media and Information Literacy (MIL) represented the dominant outcomes (68.8%), followed by motivational and affective factors (21.9%) and emergent literacies such as AI and data literacy (9.4%). Most studies (75.0%) reported positive effects, though inclusivity was explicitly addressed in only 15.6% of cases. Findings highlight the potential of gamification to promote both engagement and critical literacies, while also revealing methodological limitations, small-scale samples, and limited attention to diversity.

Keywords: Gamification · Media Education · Media Literacy · News Literacy · Educational Technology

R. Baptista et al. (Eds.): VJ 2025, CCIS 2988, pp. 15–30, 2027.
https://doi.org/10.1007/978-3-032-31642-4_2

1 Introduction

The integration of gamification into education has gained substantial attention over the past decade, as educators and researchers increasingly explore the potential of game-based elements to enhance learning outcomes, motivation, and engagement. Gamification is broadly defined as the use of game design elements in non-game contexts to influence behaviours, foster engagement, and support learning processes [1]. In education, gamification typically involves the incorporation of points, badges, leaderboards, narratives, and interactive challenges into traditional or digital learning environments to stimulate learners' intrinsic and extrinsic motivation [2].

In this expanding domain, media education and media literacy hold a notably significant role. Media literacy, frequently broadened to encompass news literacy and information literacy, provides learners the essential skills to access, assess, and create media in a thoughtful and socially responsible manner [3,4]. In an era marked by increasing issues related to disinformation, polarisation, and the ethical application of digital technology, enhancing media literacy through creative pedagogical methods has emerged as a societal imperative [4–6]. Gamification might, therefore, present possible solutions to these difficulties by developing immersive, motivating, and contextually relevant learning experiences, thereby rendering the abstract principles of media critique and verification more accessible to varied learner demographics.

Notwithstanding the potential of gamification, the current knowledge base exhibits various drawbacks. Prior reviews have investigated the general effectiveness of gamification in education [7–9], although limited attention has been given to its implementation in the specialised fields of media education, media literacy, and news literacy. Research primarily concentrates on either the technological implementations of gamification or its psychological effects within expansive educational contexts, neglecting the design and application of gamification methods to enhance critical literacies in formal educational environments [10]. Moreover, whereas several research emphasise beneficial effects on student engagement and learning results, the evidence is fragmented and frequently inconsistent across various educational levels and cultural contexts [11,12]. This dispersion muddles the ability of educators, legislators, and platform developers to ascertain the most effective gamification practices and the conditions under which they can be practically applied.

The societal significance of approaching these disparities is substantial. Digital citizens need not only fundamental technical skills but also the capacity to critically traverse intricate information landscapes [13,14]. Integrating gamification into curricula centred on media and news literacy can equip educational systems with the motivational support and cognitive resources necessary for learners to combat misinformation, engage responsibly with media, and participate effectively in democratic processes.

This Systematic Literature Review (SLR) therefore seeks to consolidate and critically evaluate existing empirical evidence on gamification practices within formal educational contexts, with a specific emphasis on media education.

The review maps current practices, synthesises evidence on their effectiveness, and identifies both challenges and enabling factors that shape implementation. In doing so, it also highlights opportunities for improving gamification platforms to better support educators and learners in diverse contexts. This study clarifies how gamification might enhance educational achievements and promote broader societal objectives, particularly media literacy, democratic engagement, and fair access to learning opportunities.

The overarching aim of this SLR is to synthesise current evidence on the use of gamification in formal education, with a particular emphasis on media education. The review intends to map effective practices, evaluate their impact on learning outcomes, and examine the challenges and opportunities for their implementation, in order to inform the development of gamified platforms and tools that better support educators and learners in diverse contexts. To address this aim, the review is guided by four research questions:

- RQ1. What are the most effective gamification practices currently used in education, with a focus on media education in formal contexts, and how can they be integrated into gamification platforms?
- RQ2. How does gamification enhance learning outcomes (including media and information literacy[MIL]), engagement, and motivation, and what evidence supports these effects?
- RQ3. What are the key challenges and success factors in implementing gamification across different educational contexts, and how can platforms address these?
- RQ4. What features or improvements should gamified platforms and tools prioritise to better support educators and learners in diverse settings?

2 Method

2.1 Eligibility Criteria

Studies were eligible for inclusion if they described the practical application of gamification in formal educational contexts, such as schools, universities, or structured training programmes. Eligible materials focused on peer-reviewed real-world implementations, including case studies, projects, initiatives, training courses, and educational programmes. The included studies should be published or implemented between 2015 and 2025, to ensure fitting to contemporary pedagogical and technological challenges.

To be included, materials were required to report on gamification practices that addressed at least one educational goal, such as news literacy, media literacy, STEM, language learning, or other curricular objectives. In addition, eligible records had to present a clear description of the gamification practices, methodologies, or implementation processes to allow for meaningful synthesis.

2.2 Information Sources and Search Strategy

The search strategy drew on a combination of bibliographic databases, registers, and grey literature sources to ensure comprehensive coverage. Four main sources were consulted: *IEEE Xplore*, the *ACM Digital Library*, *Education Resources Information Center* (ERIC), and *ResearchGate*.

Searches were carried out on the 4th of March 2025. *IEEE Xplore* was searched across all available metadata, while the *ACM Digital Library* and *ERIC* were searched at the full-text level, with *ERIC* restricted to peer-reviewed material. *ResearchGate* was consulted through an unstructured search of research projects and outputs to capture potentially relevant grey literature not indexed in formal databases. The time frame for all searches was limited to publications and implementations between 2015 and 2025.

In total, these searches yielded 954 records (*IEEE Xplore* = 26; *ACM Digital Library* = 672; *ERIC* = 256), with an additional set of potentially relevant studies identified via *ResearchGate*. No restrictions were placed on geography at this stage, though only materials available in English were considered for inclusion.

In the search process, boolean operators were used to combine key concepts relating to gamification, education, and media literacy. The following core query was applied, with adaptations to suit the syntax of each database:

> (gamification) AND (education OR "formal education" OR school) AND ("media literacy" OR "news literacy" OR "information literacy") AND (initiative OR project OR "training course" OR programme OR intervention)

Where available, database filters were applied according to the inclusion criteria. In *IEEE Xplore*, searches were conducted across all metadata fields; in the *ACM Digital Library* and *ERIC*, the search was extended to the full text of records, with *ERIC* limited to peer-reviewed outputs. *ResearchGate* was searched in an unstructured manner, using equivalent keywords, to identify grey literature and project documentation not captured by the other databases.

2.3 Selection Process

The selection process was conducted in line with the inclusion and exclusion criteria established for this review, ensuring that retained studies addressed the overarching aim and research questions. Screening and eligibility decisions were applied in an increasingly detailed manner.

First, the initial searches were conducted by an experienced scholar with expertise in game-based learning, who was also responsible for the first stage of title and abstract screening. This process was carried out in constant iteration with a second experienced scholar specialising in media literacy, to ensure conceptual alignment with both domains of the review.

Following this stage, four junior scholars carried out the eligibility assessment of full-text reports. This was conducted under continuous discussion and supervision with the two experienced scholars, who provided guidance in cases of uncertainty and ensured consistency in the application of the criteria. Discrepancies were resolved through discussion until consensus was reached.

No automation tools were used in the selection process.

2.4 Data Collection Process, Data Items, and Synthesis Method

Data collection followed the same team structure and logic as the selection process. Four junior scholars extracted data from the included reports under the supervision of two experienced scholars with expertise in game-based learning and media literacy. Discrepancies were resolved through discussion and consensus, and no automation tools were used. All information was organised in a structured Excel file prepared for the review.

For each study, data items included bibliographic details, information on the educational context, descriptions of the gamification practices employed, and reported outcomes. Particular attention was given to effects on media literacy, news literacy, or broader educational goals, as well as to learner engagement and motivation. Additional information on implementation challenges, success factors, participant characteristics, and features or recommendations for gamification platforms was also extracted, where available.

All extracted quantitative variables were analysed using descriptive statistics, which allowed for the summarisation of key patterns across studies. Qualitative information was examined through critical content analysis procedures, enabling the identification of recurrent themes, challenges, and recommendations [15]. Results were tabulated in a structured Excel file and organised in relation to the overarching categories of practices, learning outcomes, implementation factors, and platform features.

3 Results

The systematic search yielded 965 records, with 954 from electronic databases and 11 from registers. After removing 227 duplicates, 738 records were screened, and 684 were excluded based on inclusion criteria. Full-text retrieval was sought for 55 reports, but one was unobtainable, leaving 54 for eligibility assessment. Among these, 22 were excluded: 10 for being secondary or conceptual studies, 4 for lacking gamified applications, 7 for irrelevance to media or information literacy, and 1 for being unavailable in English.

Ultimately, 32 studies met the inclusion criteria and were retained for the final review. The full selection process is summarised in the the flow diagram (Fig. 1), based on PRISMA's flow diagram [48].

3.1 Characteristics of the Studies

The full set of studies included in this SLR ($N = 32$) has a total composed sample of 4164 participants ($M = 143.6$; $SD = 178.3$), ranging from 10 in the

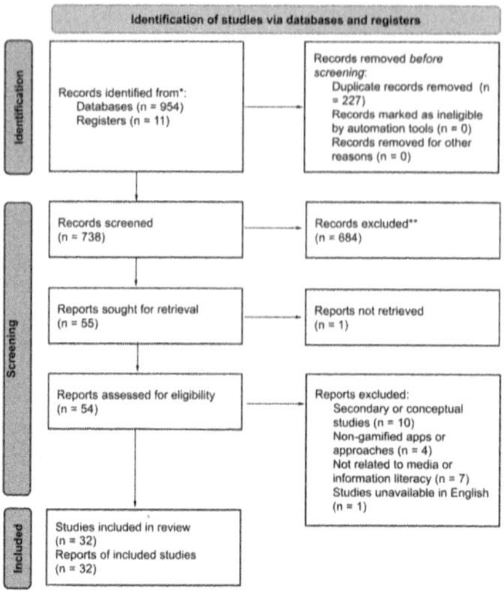

Fig. 1. PRISMA flow diagram summarising the search and selection process for studies included in the review ($N = 32$).

Table 1. Overview of studies' main characteristics ($N = 32$)

Study	Year	Sample (N)	Methodological Approach/Gamification Assessment
Ahmad et al. [18]	2021	229	Quantitative; pre and post with control group (experimental)
Alam et al. [19]	2023	223	Mixed methods; pre and post intervention
Alnuaim [20]	2024	168	Quantitative; pre and post with control group (experimental)
Arifin and Setiawan [21]	2022	40	Qualitative; post intervention
Ashley [22]	2019	40	Mixed methods; pre and post intervention
Baha'i et al. [10]	2016	76	Quantitative; performance and post intervention
Bai et al. [23]	2022	49	Mixed methods; pre/post with performance assessment
Bioglio et al. [24]	2019	472	Mixed methods; pre and post with control group
Capecchi et al. [25]	2024	217	Quantitative; post intervention
Fahlevi et al. [26]	2024	23	Mixed methods; post intervention
Gramß [27]	2019	216	Quantitative; post intervention
Hinterreiter et al. [28]	2024	121	Mixed methods; pre/post with control group
Isanoa-Sinche & Llerena-Izquierdo [29]	2023	40	Quantitative; pre and post intervention
Jeon et al. [17]	2021	882	Quantitative; pre and post with control group
Kilhoffer et al. [30]	2023	27	Qualitative; not specified
Molnár et al. [31]	2022	n/a	Quantitative; performance during intervention
Morais et al. [32]	2022	95	Quantitative; post intervention
Ng et al. [33]	2024	68	Mixed methods; pre/post with control group
Palalas & Wark [34]	2017	39	Qualitative; performance and post intervention
Pek & Koh [35]	2021	51	Qualitative; pre/post with performance assessment
Roslan et al. [36]	2023	269	Quantitative; post intervention
Ruiz [37]	2024	107	Quantitative; pre and post intervention
Rzabayeva et al. [38]	2024	60	Quantitative; pre/post with control group
Saenboonsong & Poonsawad [39]	2024	63	Mixed methods; performance + post intervention
Seaborn et al. [40]	2017	76	Mixed methods; performance and post intervention
Sime et al. [41]	2020	329	Mixed methods; pre/post with performance assessment
Suartama et al. [42]	2023	78	Mixed methods; pre/post with performance assessment
Sukmana et al. [43]	2022	n/a	Mixed methods; media/platform analysis
Tang & Singha [44]	2024	n/a	Qualitative; post intervention
Tiede et al. [45]	2022	28	Quantitative; pre/post with performance assessment
Toledo et al. [16]	2022	10	Mixed methods; pre and post intervention
Zainuddin [46]	2023	68	Mixed methods; pre/post with control group

approach of Toledo et al. [16] and 882 in the study developed by Jeon et al. [17]. The main characteristics of each study are systematised in Table 1.

The 32 studies in the review used a wide range of methods, including quantitative, qualitative, and mixed methods approaches. Quantitative designs predominated, frequently utilising pre- and post-test measures, with or without control groups, to evaluate the impact of gamification interventions (e.g., Ahmad et al. [18]; Jeon et al. [17]; Rzabayeva et al. [38]). Mixed-methods studies were also significant, integrating performance data with surveys or qualitative feedback to assess both quantifiable results and experiential aspects of gamified learning (e.g., Alam et al. [19]; Bai et al. [23]; Sime et al. [41]). A limited number of studies employed exclusively qualitative methodologies, primarily concentrating on post-intervention reflections, performance observations, or platform analysis (e.g., Arifin and Setiawan [21]; Sukmana et al. [43]; Tang and Singha [44]).

Assessment methods primarily included pre/post-intervention measures and performance evaluations with some incorporating control groups to enhance causal assertions (e.g., Bioglio et al. [24]; Hinterreiter et al. [28]). Others depended on post-intervention surveys or qualitative feedback to gain insights into motivation, engagement, and learner perceptions (e.g., Gramß [27]; Palalas and Wark [34]).

3.2 Gamification Strategies

A common thread in the studies was the usage of points, scores, and leaderboards as basic mechanics. These components were consistently employed to promote competition and monitor learner advancement, manifesting in contexts from digital learning environments [30,38], to more intricate platforms incorporating dashboards and real-time feedback [21]. Points and rankings were frequently integrated with badges and rewards, forming multifaceted motivational frameworks designed to maintain learner engagement over time [19,20,22]. Although these mechanics are well-established in gamification, their prevalence in various educational contexts indicates that they continue to serve as a standard approach for reinforcing achievement and promoting perseverance.

Numerous studies integrated narrative and scenario-based components to facilitate contextualized and immersive learning experiences. Role-playing mechanics, narratives, and the incorporation of avatars or characters were applied to enhance identification and emotional engagement with the content [36,37,44]. Interventions aimed at enhancing MIL frequently employed real-world scenarios and problem-based tasks, providing learners with opportunities to engage in critical thinking in authentic contexts [26,27]. These strategies show a move away from models that are only competitive and toward designs that include experiential and situated learning. This makes gamification fit better with educational goals.

A third strand of practice includes feedback and collaborative tools, which were seen as important learning aids in all the different implementations. Quizzes, challenges, and progress-tracking systems all had feedback loops built in so that learners could keep track of how they were doing and change their strategies [35,39,46]. Team-based activities, forums, and cooperative modules made it easier for people to work together, which is like the social aspect of gamification [21,28,43]. These designs strengthened both autonomy and social engagement by combining personalised performance indicators with peer interaction. This shows a balanced approach to skill development and motivation.

In a more quantitative and data-driven approach, the different strategies were categorised. Firstly, in a non-mutually exclusive manner, the frequency of each strategy was coded, as represented in Table 2.

Table 2. Total of categorised gamification strategies (N articles = 32; N categorised strategies = 124)

Categorised strategies	n	%
Points and scoring	23	74.2
Immersive and visual tools	16	51.6
Leaderboards and competition	11	35.5
Narrative and story	10	32.3
Quizzes and tests	9	29.0
Challenges and missions	9	29.0
Feedback and progress tracking	9	29.0
Badges and achievements	8	25.8
Simulation and real-world scenarios	6	19.4
Collaboration and social learning	6	19.4
Gamified environment and platform	2	6.5
Dashboards and tools	1	3.2
Other strategies	14	45.2

Note. Percentages were calculated considering the total sample ($N = 32$), to represent the significance of each strategy in the overall SLR.

As a second lens, each paper was categorised considering its main gamification approach, resulting in the distribution presented in Table 3.

Moreover, gamification strategies were also classified as shallow or deep, considering the level to which they structurally changed each learning programme, and according to Santos [47] proposal. In this sense. Most of them represented shallow gamification strategies ($n = 7$; 21.88%)

3.3 Learning Outcomes and Gamification Effectiveness

Each study was classified considering its main learning outcome(s), following three labels: (1) MIL-driven; (2) other emergent literacies (e.g., AI, big data,

Table 3. Main categorised gamification strategies of each article ($N = 32$)

Category	n	%
Points and scoring	9	29.0
Immersive and visual tools	8	25.8
Quizzes and tests	4	12.9
Narrative and story	2	6.5
Feedback and progress tracking	2	6.5
Badges and achievement markers	2	6.5
Collaboration and social learning	1	3.2
Challenges and missions	1	3.2
Gamified environment and platform	1	3.2
Leaderboards and competition	1	3.2

cybersecurity); and (3) affective and motivation-driven. The categorisation of learning outcomes reveals that most gamified educational interventions ($n = 22$; 68.75%) are primarily geared toward promoting MIL, including digital citizenship, critical literacy, and related competencies. Affective and motivational outcomes, such as engagement, interest, and learner confidence, were central in seven studies (21.88%), reflecting the importance of emotional and behavioural factors in sustaining learning. A smaller but emerging subset ($n = 3$; 9.38%) addressed emergent literacies, including AI, data literacy, and cybersecurity, highlighting the evolving relevance of these topics in formal education.

Nevertheless, it is important to note that these categories are not always mutually exclusive. For instance, AI and algorithmic literacies are often intertwined with broader MIL frameworks. However, for analytical clarity, and to map the mentioned emerging trends, each study was assigned a single dominant category based on its primary learning focus.

Regarding the effectiveness of the gamified interventions, most studies' conclusions pointed towards positive impacts on the targeted learning outcomes (n = 24; 75.0%). Nevertheless, three studies (9.4%) mentioned that the results highly varied between learners, while in two studies (6.3%), results did not support gamification's effectiveness. Furthermore, in three studies (9.4%), effectiveness was not specifically discussed.

3.4 Inclusion and Diversity Within Gamification Approaches

Most studies ($n = 27$; 84.4%) did not explicitly explore how diversity and inclusivity aspects were considered when developing and implementing the gamified approaches to media education. Nevertheless, this was a concern expressed - through different lenses - in five studies (15.6%). In this subsample, attention was directed towards addressing socio-economic, linguistic, and ability-related barriers in gamified education. Gamification was applied to enhance digital competencies among educationally disadvantaged employees in low-skilled occupations, illustrating its potential to workforce inclusion [28]. Similarly, the use of text-to-speech and interactive eBooks demonstrated measurable benefits for young children with language impairments and limited digital experience, highlighting the relevance of accessibility technologies in reducing literacy gaps [31]. Other interventions focused on structurally excluded populations, such as adult literacy learners, where gamification was integrated into mobile and cross-platform solutions to meet the specific needs of this group [35]. Inclusivity was also framed through the lens of demographic and contextual adaptability, with evidence suggesting that gamification can be effectively employed across diverse student populations regardless of age or academic background [21]. Furthermore, the potential of immersive technologies, such as VR and AR, to enhance learning opportunities for learners with disabilities was explicitly recognised [33].

4 Discussion

This review synthesised 32 empirical studies on gamification in formal education with an emphasis on media education, media literacy, and news literacy. Overall, the findings reinforce previous evidence suggesting that gamification can be an effective pedagogical approach to foster engagement, motivation, and knowledge acquisition [4,7,8,10,11]. At the same time, the results extend the current state of knowledge by mapping how specific gamification strategies intersect with literacy outcomes, showing that while points and scoring remain the most dominant approach, immersive and visual tools, narrative elements, and feedback loops are increasingly being adopted to support critical literacies.

Although gamification is increasingly promoted in educational contexts, its implementation in media education is still comparatively overlooked relative to wider educational settings. Most of the research in the sample emphasised literacy-related outcomes, especially MIL, while also recognising motivational and affective advantages. This dual focus suggests that gamification has the capacity not only to stimulate student interest but also to scaffold critical thinking skills in relation to complex information environments, a dimension of increasing societal urgency considering disinformation and polarisation [13,14,49]. However, the results revealed that inclusivity and diversity are seldom addressed in systematic ways, with only a small subset of studies explicitly considering disadvantaged groups or accessibility needs.

Regarding effective practices and integration into platforms (RQ1), the findings highlight that points and scoring systems, although prevalent, are often combined with complementary strategies such as feedback loops, storylines, or immersive technologies to enhance depth of learning. Studies that connected gamification to real-world scenarios, such as fact-checking exercises or news assessments, proved particularly effective in advancing media literacy skills, aligning with earlier research that stresses the importance of contextualised learning [50,51]. For platform design, this suggests that effective gamification should move beyond simplistic competition-based models and embed authentic problem-solving and narrative features. In terms of effects on learning outcomes

(RQ2), engagement, and motivation, the synthesis revealed robust evidence that gamification enhances engagement and motivation, echoing trends found in previous meta-analyses [51]. More importantly, positive outcomes were also documented for knowledge acquisition and competency development, particularly in areas of media and digital literacy. However, effectiveness varied between learners, suggesting that gamification does not work uniformly across populations. These variations highlight the need for adaptive systems that personalise challenges, feedback, and pacing to sustain learner engagement while accommodating diverse abilities and backgrounds [12].

Regarding challenges and success factors (RQ3), the review shows that most studies did not explicitly address diversity or inclusivity in the design and implementation of gamified approaches to media education, with only 15.6% of the sample doing so. This represents a key challenge in the field, as the lack of systematic attention to inclusivity limits the potential of gamification to reach disadvantaged or under-represented learners. When inclusivity was considered, success factors were evident. For example, gamification was employed to build digital competencies among low-skilled workers [28] or to adapt mobile learning tools for adult literacy learners [35]. In these cases, gamification was not only motivational but also responsive to specific socio-economic and linguistic barriers. Furthermore, evidence from some interventions suggests that gamified learning experiences are effective across demographic groups, independent of variables such as age or degree major [21], highlighting their adaptability in diverse educational settings. Another success factor emerging from the evidence was the use of immersive technologies such as VR and AR, which were explicitly identified as promising for learners with disabilities [33]. Taken together, the results suggest that while challenges remain in mainstreaming inclusivity, successful implementation is facilitated when gamification is adapted to learner diversity, integrated with accessibility tools, and designed in alignment with the socio-cultural and technological realities of target populations.

In terms of platforms' characteristics (RQ4), data suggests that platforms and tools should prioritise flexibility, allowing educators to combine points and leaderboards with narrative, immersive, and collaborative tools. Personalisation features, accessibility functions (like text-to-speech or multimodal interfaces), and integration with real-world problem-solving tasks emerged as critical enhancements. Future platforms and tools should also embed analytics to provide real-time feedback, enabling adaptive learning while supporting educators in tracking literacy development.

4.1 Limitations and Future Directions

Several limitations were identified in the evidence base. First, most studies were small-scale, which limits generalisability. Only a minority used rigorous experimental designs with control groups, while many relied on post-intervention surveys or qualitative accounts, raising concerns about causality that can impact some in-depth conclusions. Second, inclusivity and accessibility were rarely considered explicitly, leaving open questions about gamification's effectiveness and implementation for learners with disabilities, linguistic minorities, socio-economically disadvantaged groups, and different formal, non-formal, and informal learning environments.

The review process also has limitations. Only English-language materials published between 2015 and 2025 were included, potentially excluding relevant studies in other languages. Also, while multiple reviewers participated in screening and data extraction, risk of bias was not formally quantified across studies.

Future research should conduct larger, multi-site studies employing rigorous experimental designs (e.g. randomized controlled trials, longitudinal follow-ups) explore inclusivity through participatory co-design approaches, and examine gamification's long-term impacts on sustained literacy outcomes. Theoretically grounded studies exploring mechanisms through which game elements influence learning would strengthen knowledge of gamification's effectiveness.

Acknowledgments. This work was developed on the scope of *NewsArcade@Classroom - Seriously Play the News in the Classroom!*, funded by the European Union's Creative Europe Media Programme. Views and opinions expressed are however those of the authors only and do not necessarily reflect those of the European Union or EACEA. Neither the European Union nor the granting authority can be held responsible for them [Project Reference: 101186092].

Disclosure of Interests. The authors declare no competing interests in the development of the present SLR.

References

1. Nacke, L.E., Deterding, S.: The maturing of gamification research. Comput. Hum. Behav. **71**, 450–454 (2017). https://doi.org/10.1016/j.chb.2016.11.062
2. Hamari, J., Koivisto, J., Sarsa, H.: Does gamification work? – a literature review of empirical studies on gamification. In: 47th Hawaii International Conference on System Sciences (HICSS), pp. 3025–3034. IEEE, Waikoloa (2014). https://doi.org/10.1109/HICSS.2014.377
3. Hobbs, R.: Media literacy foundations. In: Hobbs, R., Mihailidis, P. (eds.) The International Encyclopedia of Media Literacy, 1st edn., pp. 1–19. Wiley (2019). https://doi.org/10.1002/9781118978238.ieml0063
4. Suárez-Perdomo, A., Garcés-Delgado, Y., Arvelo-Rosales, C.N.: Systematic review on adolescents' construction of media literacy in educational settings. Rev. Educ. (2025). https://doi.org/10.1002/rev3.70048
5. Wang, A., Burdina, G.: Developing students' creative thinking using innovative education technologies. Interact. Learn. Environ. 1–11 (2023). https://doi.org/10.1080/10494820.2023.2184390
6. Kendrick, M., Early, M., Michalovich, A., Mangat, M.: Digital storytelling with youth from refugee backgrounds: possibilities for language and digital literacy learning. TESOL Q. **56**(3), 961–984 (2022). https://doi.org/10.1002/tesq.3146
7. Ratinho, E., Martins, C.: The role of gamified learning strategies in student's motivation in high school and higher education: a systematic review. Heliyon **9**(8), e19033 (2023). https://doi.org/10.1016/j.heliyon.2023.e19033

8. Oliveira, W., Dantas Scaico, P., Hamari, J., Li, Z., Shi, L.: The effects of gamification on students' flow experience. J. Comput. Assist. Learn. **41**(5), e70120 (2025). https://doi.org/10.1111/jcal.70120
9. Krath, J., Schürmann, L., von Korflesch, H.F.O.: Revealing the theoretical basis of gamification: a systematic review and analysis of theory in research on gamification, serious games and game-based learning. Comput. Hum. Behav. **125**, 106963 (2021). https://doi.org/10.1016/j.chb.2021.106963
10. Li, M., Ma, S., Shi, Y.: Examining the effectiveness of gamification as a tool promoting teaching and learning in educational settings: a meta-analysis. Front. Psychol. **14**, 1253549 (2023). https://doi.org/10.3389/fpsyg.2023.1253549
11. Huang, R., et al.: The impact of gamification in educational settings on student learning outcomes: a meta-analysis. Educ. Tech. Res. Dev. **68**(4), 1875–1901 (2020). https://doi.org/10.1007/s11423-020-09807-z
12. Luo, Z.: Gamification for educational purposes: what are the factors contributing to varied effectiveness? Educ. Inf. Technol. **27**(1), 891–915 (2022). https://doi.org/10.1007/s10639-021-10642-9
13. Hamayel, H.J., Hawamdeh, M.M.: Methods used in digital citizenship: a systematic literature review. J. Dig. Educ. Technol. **2**(3), ep2207 (2022). https://doi.org/10.30935/jdet/12520
14. Dass, M.A., Kumar, M.P.M.P.: Critical digital citizenship: a scale development and validation study. Int. J. Technol. Des. Educ. **35**(4), 1493–1513 (2025). https://doi.org/10.1007/s10798-024-09960-z
15. Pope, C., Mays, N., Popay, J.: Synthesising Qualitative and Quantitative Health Research: A Guide to Methods. McGraw-Hill Education, Buckingham (2007)
16. Toledo, W., Louis, S.J., Sengupta, S.: NetDefense: a tower defense cybersecurity game for middle and high school students. In: IEEE Frontiers in Education Conference (FIE), pp. 1–6. IEEE, Uppsala (2022). https://doi.org/10.1109/FIE56618.2022.9962410
17. Jeon, Y., Kim, B., Xiong, A., Lee, D., Han, K.: ChamberBreaker: mitigating the echo chamber effect and supporting information hygiene through a gamified inoculation system. Proc. ACM Hum.-Comput. Interact. **5**(CSCW2), 472:1–472:26 (2021). https://doi.org/10.1145/3479859
18. Ahmad, A., Zeeshan, F., Marriam, R., Samreen, A., Ahmed, S.: Does one size fit all? Investigating the effect of group size and gamification on learners' behaviors in higher education. J. Comput. High. Educ. **33**(2), 296–327 (2021). https://doi.org/10.1007/s12528-020-09266-8
19. Alam, M.I., Malone, L., Nadolny, L., Brown, M., Cervato, C.: Investigating the impact of a gamified learning analytics dashboard: student experiences and academic achievement. J. Comput. Assist. Learn. **39**(5), 1436–1449 (2023). https://doi.org/10.1111/jcal.12853
20. Alnuaim, A.: The impact and acceptance of gamification by learners in a digital literacy course at the undergraduate level: randomized controlled trial. JMIR Ser. Games **12**, e52017 (2024). https://doi.org/10.2196/52017
21. Arifin, Z., Setiawan, B.: Utilising gamification for online evaluation through Quizizz: teachers' perspectives and experiences. World J. Educ. Technol. Curr. Issues **14**(3), 781–796 (2022). https://doi.org/10.18844/wjet.v14i3.7278
22. Ashley, C.: Improving information literacy through gamification: fantasy brand leagues. Mark. Educ. Rev. **29**(2), 107–112 (2019). https://doi.org/10.1080/10528008.2019.1610332

23. Bai, S., Hew, K.F., Gonda, D.E., Huang, B., Liang, X.: Incorporating fantasy into gamification promotes student learning and quality of online interaction. Int. J. Educ. Technol. High. Educ. **19**(1), 29 (2022). https://doi.org/10.1186/s41239-022-00335-9
24. Bioglio, L., Capecchi, S., Peiretti, F., Sayed, D., Torasso, A., Pensa, R.G.: A social network simulation game to raise awareness of privacy among school children. IEEE Trans. Learn. Technol. **12**(4), 456–469 (2019). https://doi.org/10.1109/TLT.2018.2881193
25. Capecchi, S., et al.: A gamified platform to support educational activities about fake news in social media. IEEE Trans. Learn. Technol. **17**, 1765–1779 (2024). https://doi.org/10.1109/TLT.2024.3410088
26. Fahlevi, A.R., et al.: Integrating big data concepts into education through RPG games: a study using agile methodologies. In: IEEE 2nd International Conference on Electrical Engineering, Computer and Information Technology (ICEECIT), pp. 366–371. IEEE, Jember (2024). https://doi.org/10.1109/ICEECIT63698.2024.10859671
27. Grams, D.: Media competence: enabling for digitization. In: IEEE Global Engineering Education Conference (EDUCON), pp. 1212–1215. IEEE, Dubai (2019). https://doi.org/10.1109/EDUCON.2019.8725053
28. Hinterreiter, S., Spinde, T., Oberdörfer, S., Echizen, I., Latoschik, M.E.: News Ninja: gamified annotation of linguistic bias in online news. Proc. ACM Hum.-Comput. Interact. **8**(CHI PLAY), 1–29 (2024). https://doi.org/10.1145/3677092
29. Isanoa-Sinche, M., Llerena-Izquierdo, J.: Towards a meaningful experience on the use of digital educational resources and media created at Ardora. In: IEEE Seventh Ecuador Technical Chapters Meeting (ECTM), pp. 1–5. IEEE, Ambato (2023). https://doi.org/10.1109/ETCM58927.2023.10308988
30. Kilhoffer, Z., et al.: "How technical do you get? I'm an English teacher": 44th IEEE Symposium on Security and Privacy, SP 2023. Proceedings of the 44th IEEE Symposium on Security and Privacy, pp. 2032–2049 (2023). https://doi.org/10.1109/SP46215.2023.10179333
31. Molnar, G., et al.: Possibilities and challenges of monitoring and evaluating digital education in electronic environments from a pedagogical and technological perspective. In: IEEE 20th Jubilee World Symposium on Applied Machine Intelligence and Informatics (SAMI), pp. 000069–000072. IEEE, Poprad (2022). https://doi.org/10.1109/SAMI54271.2022.9780733
32. Morais, J., Simoes, J., Lourenço, J., Lopes, S.F.F.: Perceptions on gamification towards cybersecurity literacy: social sustainability of educative projects. Revista EDaPECI **22**, 63–77 (2022). https://doi.org/10.29276/redapeci.2022.22.318247.63-77
33. Ng, D.T.K., Xinyu, C., Leung, J.K.L., Chu, S.K.W.: Fostering students' AI literacy development through educational games: AI knowledge, affective and cognitive engagement. J. Comput. Assist. Learn. **40**(5), 2049–2064 (2024). https://doi.org/10.1111/jcal.13009
34. Palalas, A., Wark, N.: Design principles for an adult literacy mobile learning solution. In: Proceedings of the 16th World Conference on Mobile and Contextual Learning (mLearn 2017), pp. 1–8. ACM, New York (2017). https://doi.org/10.1145/3136907.3136934
35. Pek, S.E., Koh, J.H.L.: Team formation using character-based gamification: effects on online teamwork experience during COVID-19. In: 16th International Conference on Computer Science & Education (ICCSE), pp. 247–252. IEEE, Lancaster (2021). https://doi.org/10.1109/ICCSE51940.2021.9569643

36. Roslan, R., Ayub, A., Ghazali, N., Zulkifli, N., Latip, S., Abu Hanifah, S.: Investigating factors that affect the continuance use intention among higher education learners towards a gamified m-learning application. J. Inf. Technol. Educ. Res. **22**, 97–128 (2023). https://doi.org/10.28945/5080
37. Gil Ruiz, P.: Gamification as a methodology to enhance analytical and sustainable engagement on social media. Disc. Educ. **3**(1), (2024). https://doi.org/10.1007/s44217-023-00074-7
38. Rzabayeva, D., Kassymova, G., Pratama, H.: The role of gamification in promoting digital literacy: bridging the gap between fun and learning, **144** (2024). https://doi.org/10.31643/2024.20
39. Saenboonsong, S., Poonsawad, A.: The development of students' creative problem-solving skills through learning model in a gamification environment together with cartoon animation media. J. Educ. Learn. **13**(2), 138 (2024). https://doi.org/10.5539/jel.v13n2p138
40. Seaborn, K., Fels, D., Bajko, R., Hodson, J.: Gamifying the media classroom: instructor perspectives and the multidimensional impact of gamification on student engagement. Int. J. Game-Based Learn. **7**, 22–49 (2017). https://doi.org/10.4018/IJGBL.2017100102
41. Sime, J.-A., Themelis, C., Arapoglou, Y., Marantou, A., Theodoridou, K.: Designing a social exploration MOOC - visual literacies: exploring educational practices and technologies. J. Open Flexible Dist. Learn. **24**(2), 15–27 (2020). https://doi.org/10.61468/jofdl.v24i2.377
42. Suartama, I.K., Simamora, A.H., Susiani, K., Suranata, K., Yunus, M., Tisna Ms, G.D.: Designing gamification for case and project-based online learning: a study in higher education. J. Educ. E-Learn. Res. **10**(2), 86–98 (2023). https://doi.org/10.20448/jeelr.v10i2.4432
43. Sukmana, R.N., Pradinda, A.J., Suharsono, T.N., Gunawan, Laluma, R.H.: Gamification implementation in the learning media for waste separation. In: 16th International Conference on Telecommunication Systems, Services, and Applications (TSSA), pp. 1–5. IEEE, Lombok (2022). https://doi.org/10.1109/TSSA56819.2022.10063908
44. Tang, H., Singha, M.: A mystery for you: a fact-checking game enhanced by large language models (LLMs) and a tangible interface. In: Extended Abstracts of the CHI Conference on Human Factors in Computing Systems, pp. 1–5. ACM (2024). https://doi.org/10.1145/3613905.3648110
45. Tiede, J., Treacy, R., Grafe, S., Mangina, E.: Fostering learning motivation of students with reading and spelling difficulties by an AR-enhanced gamified educational app for literacy learning. In: IEEE Games, Entertainment, Media Conference (GEM), pp. 1–6. IEEE, St. Michael (2022). https://doi.org/10.1109/GEM56474.2022.10017825
46. Zainuddin, Z.: Integrating ease of use and affordable gamification-based instruction into a remote learning environment. Asia Pac. Educ. Rev. **25**(5), 1261–1272 (2024). https://doi.org/10.1007/s12564-023-09832-6
47. Santos, P.A.: Deep gamification of a university course. In: Conference Proceedings SciTecIN, vol. 15 (2015)
48. Page, M.J., et al.: The PRISMA 2020 statement: an updated guideline for reporting systematic reviews. BMJ **372**, n71 (2021). https://doi.org/10.1136/bmj.n71
49. Savage, S., Oliver, E., Gordon, E., Tutton, L.: Addressing social polarization through critical thinking: theoretical application in the "Living Well With Difference" course in secondary schools in England. J. Soc. Polit. Psychol. **9**(2), 490–505 (2021). https://doi.org/10.5964/jspp.7037

50. Khaldi, A., Bouzidi, R., Nader, F.: Gamification of e-learning in higher education: a systematic literature review. Smart Learn. Environ. **10**(1), 10 (2023). https://doi.org/10.1186/s40561-023-00227-z
51. Sailer, M., Homner, L.: The gamification of learning: a meta-analysis. Educ. Psychol. Rev. **32**(1), 77–112 (2020). https://doi.org/10.1007/s10648-019-09498-w

The Impact of Gamification on Engagement in a Financial Literacy App

Ricardo Carvalho[1,2,3(✉)], Rui Prada[1,3], Carla Pacheco[3], Guilherme Pires[2], and Francisco Oom[2]

[1] Instituto Superior Técnico, Universidade de Lisboa, Lisbon, Portugal
{ricardolncarvalho,rui.prada}@tecnico.ulisboa.pt
[2] Paynest, Lisbon, Portugal
{g.pires,f.oom}@paynest.com
[3] INESC-ID, Lisbon, Portugal
carla.pacheco@inesc-id.pt

Abstract. Financial literacy remains a persistent global challenge. Building on evidence that gamification can enhance motivation, this study examines a gamified redesign of Paynest's financial literacy app, which had previously shown low participation in its quiz section. A web-based prototype was developed with two conditions: a baseline reproducing the existing app and a gamified condition incorporating progression paths, checkpoints, and a redesigned coin system. A total of fifty-eight participants consented to take part in the study and were assigned to one of the conditions, which they could access for seven consecutive days. Engagement was quantified from logged user interactions on the platform, and the perceived experience was assessed with the validated GAMEFULQUEST questionnaire. Results showed that participants using the gamified condition submitted more quiz responses on average (5.42 vs. 3.64), though not significantly different, progressed further within categories, and reported higher perceived guidance and accomplishment. However, reduced autonomy corresponded to lower playfulness and immersion, although these differences were not statistically significant, and the design did not lead to measurable improvement in retention. Overall, the structured progression enhanced perceived competence and depth of engagement, but sustaining participation may require greater autonomy and habit-forming mechanisms.

Keywords: Gamification · Financial literacy · User engagement

1 Introduction

Financial literacy can be defined as "the knowledge of basic economic and financial concepts, as well as the ability to use that knowledge and other financial skills to manage financial resources effectively for a lifetime of financial well-being" [9, p. 12]. Despite its importance for both everyday management and

R. Baptista et al. (Eds.): VJ 2025, CCIS 2988, pp. 31–43, 2027.
https://doi.org/10.1007/978-3-032-31642-4_3

long-term planning, global levels of financial literacy remain low [11]. To address this challenge, Paynest, a Portuguese fintech, integrated a financial literacy module into its employer-supported app, offering quizzes and educational resources to employees. However, despite incorporating some basic gamification features, the app has struggled to sustain user engagement.

Gamification, which can be described as the integration of game design elements into non-game contexts [5], has been shown to improve motivation and promote behavior change across multiple domains [6,14]. Building on this evidence, this work investigates whether adding gamification elements, such as structured progression, can increase engagement and retention in the app. To this end, the study began by analyzing the current version of the app, examining usage data and conducting a user survey to identify key limitations in design and engagement. Based on these findings and research on gamification design, a new solution was proposed introducing structured progression, checkpoints, and a redefined coin system. The new solution was evaluated through a controlled study with fifty-eight participants, who were randomly assigned to either the baseline or the gamified version of the prototype for seven days. Engagement was tracked through interaction logs, and perceived experience was assessed using the GAMEFULQUEST questionnaire [8]. The study highlights both the potential and the limitations of gamification for promoting engagement in financial literacy learning.

2 Related Work

Gamification has been applied in a wide range of domains, with evidence that it can increase engagement, persistence, and learning outcomes when designs are carefully implemented [6,14]. Its effectiveness, however, depends not only on the presence of game elements but also on the psychological mechanisms that these elements trigger [13]. A core theoretical foundation is Self-Determination Theory (SDT), which links motivation to the needs for autonomy, competence, and relatedness [4]. In gamified systems, mechanics like progression and feedback support competence, meaningful choices foster autonomy, and social interaction enhances relatedness. SDT also distinguishes between intrinsic motivation, driven by enjoyment and growth, and extrinsic motivation, driven by rewards or pressures. While extrinsic incentives such as points or badges can increase short-term engagement, long-term participation typically relies on intrinsic reinforcement. Other perspectives complement this view: Flow Theory emphasizes balancing challenge and skill for deep engagement, and Goal-Setting Theory stresses the importance of clear objectives and feedback. Overall, gamification is most effective when designs integrate these principles to nurture both intrinsic and extrinsic motivation [10].

Applications of gamification to financial literacy remain limited but provide promising evidence. Progress tracking and goal-setting in personal finance apps have been shown to enhance perceptions of competence and autonomy, leading to greater adoption and satisfaction [2]. Gamified savings platforms can enable participants to exceed their initial savings targets by leveraging immediate feedback and symbolic rewards [7]. Interactive goal-setting and financial visualizations have been found to strengthen self-awareness and improve self-control in spending decisions [3]. Research also indicates that user characteristics influence effectiveness. Novice users appear to respond more strongly to extrinsic incentives such as monetary rewards, whereas experienced users benefit more from social and competitive features [1]. Gamification can also reinforce positive financial attitudes and planning habits, though its effects are weaker among individuals already confident in their financial management skills [12].

Together, these findings suggest that gamification has the potential to support financial literacy by enhancing competence, structuring goals, and providing meaningful feedback. However, existing interventions are often short-term, limited to narrow user groups, and raise ethical concerns when designs rely too heavily on extrinsic incentives rather than empowering users.

3 Preliminary Studies

Current Solution Description. As previously mentioned, a core component of Paynest's product is its financial literacy modules, with the main offering being a Quiz Section covering four categories: Finance, Investments, Savings, and Taxes. The main screen (Fig. 1a) displays the categories, each linking to its list of quizzes (Fig. 1b). Each quiz card is labeled either "New" if the user has not yet attempted it, or with the user's best score if it has been completed. Each quiz consists of 10 questions and provides immediate feedback after each answer, as shown in Fig. 1a. After completing a quiz, users are redirected to a results (Fig. 1d) page that shows how many questions were answered correctly and how many coins were earned. Currently, users receive 10 coins for each correct answer. The system accounts for previous attempts, meaning that if a user scored 5 correct answers (50 coins) on the first try and 6 correct answers on the second, only the difference (10 coins) is awarded. However, this mechanism is not clearly communicated, as the results page displays the number of correct answers and coins as if it were the first attempt, which can cause confusion. On the results page, only users who score below 60% are prompted to retry the quiz; otherwise, they are redirected back to the main Quiz page. Finally, the coins currently serve no functional purpose beyond being displayed at the end of each quiz and on the Quiz Home page.

Usage Metrics. At the time of writing, Paynest offered 26 quizzes, yet only about 16% of eligible users had completed one. Among these users, the average number of quizzes completed was 3.02, with quartile values of $p_{25} = 1$, median $= 1$, and $p_{75} = 3$. This distribution indicates that most users completed very few quizzes, with only a minority showing sustained participation.

User Survey. To better understand how users perceive the financial literacy offerings, an online survey was distributed to employees of 14 client companies.

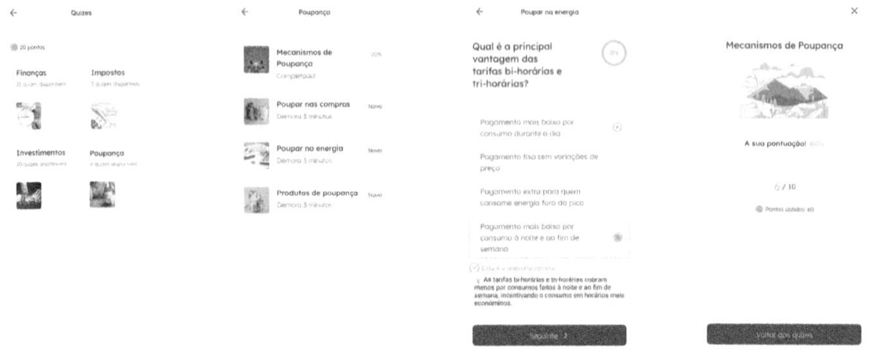

(a) (b) (c) (d)

Fig. 1. Screens from Paynest's app: (a) home page, (b) category page, (c) quiz page, (d) quiz result page.

Of 298 people invited, 23 responded. Although the small sample size limits generalization, some clear patterns emerged. Participants appreciated the diversity of content and the immediate feedback from quizzes but described the coin system as meaningless and confusing, and they criticized the fixed length of 10 questions. The most common barrier to adoption and continued use was lack of time. Several respondents also highlighted the need for more dynamic and interactive formats, such as simulators or shorter materials, to make the experience more engaging and accessible. Additionally, participants mentioned that because these topics can be complex, they would need to dedicate focused time to engage with the app, suggesting that clearer guidance on where to start could help facilitate engagement.

4 Solution

Building on the survey results and the limitations identified in the current system, this solution introduces a structured progression system with locked categories, levels within each category, and checkpoint quizzes that revisit earlier content. The coin system has been redesigned to make progression transparent and meaningful, allowing users to unlock new content while receiving clearer feedback on their performance. By defining in advance which quizzes serve as suitable entry points, the design aims to reduce users' uncertainty about where to begin and to better scaffold the progression of difficulty across topics. The quiz component was intentionally kept exactly the same as in the baseline version to isolate the effect of the new progression system.

The design assumes that the lack of structure and progression in the baseline version contributes to early disengagement. Without clear entry points or goals, users may begin with quizzes of inappropriate difficulty and have little incentive to return, as there is no sense of ongoing or pending progress to motivate them.

In contrast, a sequenced path with explicit goals, intermediate checkpoints, and consistent feedback is expected to enhance perceived competence and sustain engagement over time.

On first entry to the gamified condition, users are greeted with a short dialog inviting them to select an initial category and receive 70 coins (Figs. 2a, 2b). They can then browse each category, viewing the full list of locked quizzes identified only by their titles (Fig. 2c). When ready, they can commit to a category by spending 50 coins to unlock it (Fig. 2d).

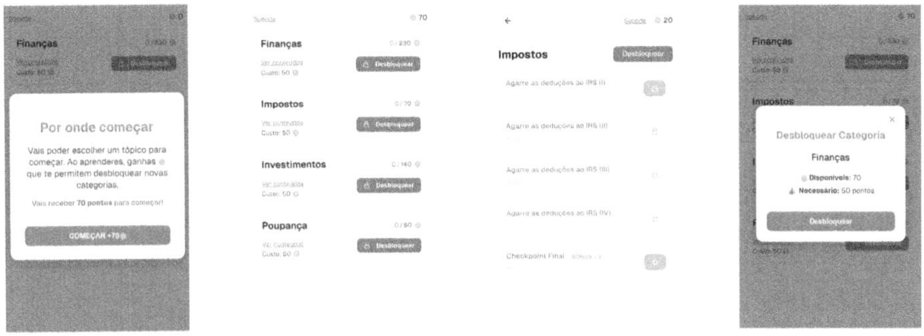

(a) (b) (c) (d)

Fig. 2. Screens from the developed solution: (a) welcome popup, (b) categories initial view, (c) locked category view, (d) popup to unlock category.

This design creates a balance between autonomy and commitment: users may choose their starting point, but once a category is unlocked, the system nudges them to continue advancing within it before exploring others. While this reduces overall freedom, the expectation is that guiding learners to progress in depth within a topic will improve focus and consistency. The main page displays (Fig. 3a) progress for each category, reinforcing a sense of advancement. Within each category (Fig. 3b), only the first level is initially unlocked, and quizzes were ordered using Paynest's performance data and content dependencies, progressing from introductory to more advanced financial concepts. To unlock the next level, the user must answer at least 60% of the questions correctly. The response page (Fig. 3c) shows the current result, previous best score, and earned coins, making both progress and coin calculation clearer.

A further enhancement is that upon unlocking a new level, the response page presents an additional step with a button that directs users to the next quiz (Fig. 3d). This transition helps maintain focus and momentum, minimizing disengagement between levels. Another central addition is the use of checkpoint quizzes, inserted approximately every three to five quizzes depending on category length. Checkpoints are also 10 questions long, consolidate earlier material, are visually emphasized, and award triple coins compared to regular quizzes. The rationale is that they can enhance both extrinsic and intrinsic motivation: extrinsically, the higher coin multiplier provides a salient incentive to reach these milestones, while intrinsically, recalling previous content reinforces mastery and competence, encouraging continued progression. These checkpoints set clear goals in the learning path. Together, the introduced design elements create a learning experience that combines extrinsic incentives with intrinsic reinforcement, while keeping users focused on their progress within a coherent path.

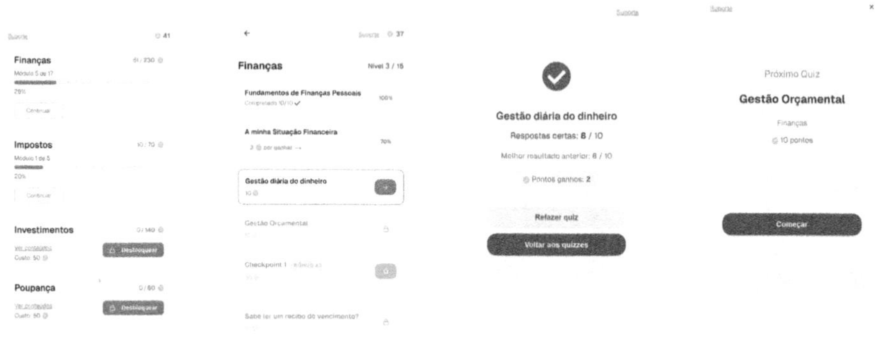

(a) (b) (c) (d)

Fig. 3. Screens from the developed solution: (a) main page with progress indicators, (b) ongoing category page, (c) response improvement, (d) new level step.

5 Evaluation

5.1 Procedure

To evaluate the developed solution, a web-based application was implemented with two experimental conditions: a baseline replicating the existing quiz section and a gamified version incorporating the progression system described above. Sixty participants were recruited through online invitations using a convenience sampling approach and were randomly assigned to one of two versions. Two did not complete consent, leaving fifty-eight valid participants who could access their assigned version for seven consecutive days. Assignment was slightly skewed toward the gamified condition (2:3 ratio) to increase data for that group. On first access, participants were directed to a consent page outlining the study's purpose, duration, and procedures, including the scope of data collection (interactions, progress, and questionnaire responses). Data were handled securely and pseudonymously under GDPR compliance, stored for up to three years, and deletable upon request. Participation was voluntary, with the right to withdraw at any time. After providing consent, participants were automatically redirected to their assigned version of the application. Because the study lasted seven days and relied on a web solution rather than a native app, participants received scheduled email communications: a welcome message at enrollment, reminders on days two and four, and a final message linking to the closing questionnaire. The emails were the exact same for both conditions.

5.2 Metrics

The evaluation followed a mixed methods design, combining objective usage metrics with subjective self-reports using a questionnaire. This approach enabled both behavioral engagement and participants' perceptions of the gamified experience to be analyzed in a complementary way.

Usage Data. To objectively measure the impact of the solution, a logging system was implemented to record all user actions on the platform, including page arrivals, button clicks, authentication events and quiz responses. Each log entry stored the timestamp, user ID, event name, and event properties. All data were treated pseudonymously, with users identified only by the randomly generated ID.

Several metrics were measured:

- **Engagement:** total, average, and quartile distribution of quiz responses per user.
- **Depth of progression:** completion percentage within categories (e.g., 3 of 5 quizzes = 60%).
- **Exploration:** number of distinct categories with responses per user and the distribution of activity across them.
- **Retention:** number of distinct days with quiz responses per user during the study period.
- **Scores and difficulty:** average quiz difficulty and user scores, including and excluding retries or checkpoint quizzes.
- **Continuation behavior:** proportion of users proceeding directly to the next quiz from the result page.

Questionnaire. To complement behavioral data, participants completed the Gameful Experience Questionnaire (GAMEFULQUEST) [8], a validated instrument for assessing perceived gamefulness across seven dimensions: accomplishment, challenge, competition, guidance, immersion, playfulness, and social experience. Items were rated on a 7-point Likert scale (1 = Strongly Disagree, 7 = Strongly Agree). The questionnaire was implemented via the EUSurvey platform, ensuring GDPR-compliant, EU-based data storage, and was automatically sent to participants by email on the seventh day of the study.

5.3 Hypotheses

Hypotheses were defined for the main constructs of engagement, progression, exploration, retention, and perceived experience, with other metrics analyzed exploratorily.

- **H1 (Engagement):** Gamified users will, on average, submit more quiz responses than baseline users, as the combined game elements support competence needs and provide clearer short-term goals.
- **H2 (Depth of progression):** Gamified users will complete a higher proportion of quizzes within categories, since the progression design limits cross-category movement while checkpoints sustain goal-oriented engagement.
- **H3 (Exploration):** Baseline users will engage with more distinct categories, as the absence of structural constraints allows greater autonomy and free exploration.
- **H4 (Retention):** Gamified users will show higher day-to-day persistence, driven by visible goals and progress cues.
- **H5 (Perceived experience):** Gamified users will report higher *Guidance* and *Accomplishment*, as the structured path specifies where to begin and how to advance, with points and checkpoints reinforcing achievement.

6 Results

Engagement. As shown in Table 1, participants in the gamified condition submitted on average 5.42 quiz responses compared to 3.64 in the baseline condition. Quartile distributions indicate that participants in the gamified version showed higher upper-range activity levels than those in the baseline condition, suggesting greater overall participation. Four participants in each condition explored the app but submitted no quiz responses. However, a Mann–Whitney U test showed no statistically significant difference between modes ($U = 477.5$, $p = .31$), indicating that H1 was not supported despite a positive trend.

Table 1. Engagement per mode. Mean Resp. indicates the average number of responses per user. Q1, Median, and Q3 indicate the 25th, 50th, and 75th percentiles of the number of responses per user.

Mode	Users	Total Resp.	Mean Resp.	Q1 Resp.	Median Resp.	Q3 Resp.
Gamified	33	177	5.42	2	3	8
Baseline	25	91	3.64	1	2	5
Total	58	268	4.60	–	–	–

Depth of Progression. As shown in Table 2, gamified users generally advanced further within categories than Baseline users. Normality tests (Shapiro–Wilk, $p < 0.05$ for all categories) indicated non-normal distributions, so Mann–Whitney U tests were applied to all comparisons. In *Finanças*, completion was significantly higher for gamified users (50.5% vs. 22.3%, $p = 0.016$). A similar but non-significant trend appeared in *Poupança* (81.3% vs. 59.4%) and *Investimentos* (38.3% vs. 26.5%). Only in *Impostos* did Baseline users progress further

(40.0% vs. 20.0%), though this result is based on very small samples and should be interpreted with caution. Overall, H2 was partially supported, with significant improvement in one category and consistent trends in others. An interesting finding is that users often delayed unlocking new categories until reaching a checkpoint or fully completing the current one, even when they already had enough coins. Across eight recorded unlock events, users held an average of 129 points despite only 50 being required to unlock new content. Additional analysis showed that many participants paused at or after completing checkpoints, indicating that these moments acted as meaningful milestones.

Table 2. Average completion per category (% of quizzes completed per user who interacted with that category) by mode, with Mann–Whitney U test results. The first column shows total quizzes per category (checkpoint quizzes in parentheses). Gamif. = Gamified, Basel. = Baseline.

Category	Quizzes	Gamif. avg.	Gamif. n	Basel. avg.	Basel. n	p-value
Finanças	12 (+3)	50.5%	14	22.3%	16	**0.016**
Poupança	3 (+1)	81.3%	8	59.4%	14	0.140
Impostos	4 (+1)	20.0%	3	40.0%	5	**0.022**
Investimentos	7 (+2)	38.3%	9	26.5%	8	0.882

Exploration. As shown in Table 3, participants in the baseline condition submitted quiz responses in a higher number of categories on average (2.05 vs. 1.17). Quartile distributions indicate that most gamified users remained within a single category (Q1 = Q3 = 1), while Baseline users typically reached at least two (median = 2, Q3 = 3). Eleven participants in the Baseline group submitted quiz responses in two or more categories, compared to only five in the gamified group. Accordingly, H3 was supported. This difference reflects the design's structural constraints more than user preference: exploration was limited by progression rules, whereas the baseline condition allowed freer movement across categories.

Table 3. Number of distinct categories in which users submitted quiz responses, by mode. Columns show the average, quartiles, users with ≥2 categories, and maximum observed values.

Mode	Avg. categories	Q1	Median	Q3	Users ≥ 2 cat.	Max
Gamified	1.17	1	1	1	5	2
Baseline	2.05	1	2	3	11	4

Retention. As shown in Table 4, the majority of participants were active on only one day (29 in the gamified condition and 21 in the baseline condition). A smaller subset engaged on at least two days (7 vs. 6), and only a few continued for three or four days (3 and 3 in the gamified condition vs. 2 and 1 in the baseline condition, respectively). Given the larger number of participants in the gamified condition, this difference becomes even less pronounced. According to the predefined metrics, retention remained low in both conditions and showed no significant improvement in the gamified condition, and therefore H4 was not supported. These findings highlight the need for stronger habit-forming mechanisms, such as streaks, recurring goals, and more effective notification strategies, to maintain user engagement over time.

Table 4. Number of users with responses on at least one, two, three, or four distinct days by mode.

Mode	1+ days	2+ days	3+ days	4+ days
Gamified	29	7	3	3
Baseline	21	6	2	1

Scores and Difficulty. As shown in Table 5, participants in the gamified condition achieved higher scores despite encountering quizzes of greater average difficulty (4.71 vs. 3.16). Condition (1), which includes all responses, indicates superior performance in the gamified condition. Although retries were available in both conditions, they occurred exclusively in the gamified condition and yielded particularly high scores (average 9.9 across 13 responses). Furthermore, checkpoint quizzes also produced elevated averages (9.25 across 32 responses) due to their repetitive nature. To control for these effects, a second calculation was conducted excluding both retries and checkpoint quizzes; this is reported as condition (2) in Table 5. Even after this adjustment, participants in the gamified condition maintained higher average scores than those in the baseline condition. Non-normality (Shapiro–Wilk, $p < 0.05$) led to the use of Mann–Whitney U tests, which confirmed significant differences in both cases ($p = 0.001$ and $p = 0.046$).

Table 5. Comparison of average quiz difficulty and scores by mode. (1): all responses including retries and checkpoints; (2): excluding retries and checkpoints.

Mode	Avg. difficulty (1)	Avg. score (1)	Avg. score (2)
Gamified	4.71	8.77	8.59
Baseline	3.16	8.09	8.09

New Result Page. As shown in Table 6, across 167 visits to the *quiz result page*, 136 users (81%) chose to continue directly to the next quiz, while only 31 exited the flow. Continuation rates were particularly high when the next quiz was a checkpoint (93%) compared to regular quizzes (79%). These data indicate that the redesigned result page effectively sustained engagement by facilitating seamless transitions between quizzes, while checkpoint quizzes further reinforced this effect by serving as motivational milestones within the progression path.

Table 6. User actions on the quiz result page by next quiz type.

Next quiz type	Continue	Leave
Checkpoint	28	2
Regular	108	29
Total	136	31

Table 7. GAMEFULQUEST dimension scores per mode (1–7 Likert scale). Abbreviations: Accomp. = Accomplishment, Comp. = Competition, Guid. = Guidance, Playf. = Playfulness, Social. = Social Experience.

Mode	Accomp.	Challenge	Comp.	Guid.	Immersion	Playf.	Social.
Gamified	5.95	5.07	4.95	5.90	3.92	4.78	3.92
Baseline	5.16	5.09	4.27	5.10	4.32	5.21	4.08
p-value	**0.017**	0.964	0.145	**0.008**	0.447	0.263	0.750
Cronbach's α	0.86	0.85	0.85	0.88	0.92	0.89	0.90

GAMEFULQUEST. Questionnaire responses were obtained from 23 participants (12 in the gamified condition and 11 in the baseline condition) out of the full study sample. Internal consistency was high across all dimensions, with Cronbach's alpha values exceeding 0.85. Normality for each dimension and condition was verified using the Shapiro–Wilk test, and all distributions satisfied this assumption ($p > 0.05$), allowing the use of independent-samples t-tests. As shown in Table 7, participants in the gamified condition reported significantly higher *Guidance* ($p = 0.008$) and *Accomplishment* ($p = 0.017$) scores compared to those in the baseline condition, indicating that the structured progression and checkpoint system enhanced perceived clarity and competence. The remaining dimensions did not differ significantly between modes ($p > 0.05$), although the mean values followed consistent trends: lower *Playfulness* and *Immersion*, reflecting the reduced autonomy of the structured path compared to the freer exploration of the baseline version. This illustrates the competence–autonomy trade-off: the solution enhanced clarity and progress but limited opportunities for self-directed discovery. Interestingly, despite gamified users reaching higher quiz difficulties on average (4.71 vs. 3.16), perceived *Challenge* levels ($p = 0.964$) did not increase, suggesting that the progression may have effectively scaffolded the difficulty curve. Overall, H5 was supported, as gamified users reported higher perceived guidance and accomplishment.

7 Conclusion

This study examined the impact of introducing progression paths, coins, and checkpoints into a financial literacy system. Results showed that the gamified version led to more quiz responses on average (5.42 vs. 3.64), though not significantly different, deeper engagement within categories, and stronger perceptions of guidance and accomplishment, confirming the value of structured progression for supporting competence. However, these benefits came with trade-offs: reduced autonomy corresponded to lower playfulness and immersion, although these differences were not statistically significant. Moreover, gamification did not lead to a measurable improvement in retention. Overall, H2, H3, and H5 were supported, while H1 and H4 were not.

These findings should be interpreted with caution. The sample was relatively small, slightly unbalanced across conditions, covered only a short seven-day period, and participants were not controlled for prior knowledge or motivation. Although the statistical tests used are robust to unequal group sizes, the smaller Baseline group reduces power, and some observed differences were not statistically significant. In addition, the progression path was not based on a validated pedagogical structure, and self-reported measures may be affected by bias.

In sum, the structured progression design increased perceived competence and depth of engagement but did not sustain participation, suggesting that future iterations should combine progression with greater autonomy and habit-forming features to support long-term use. Future work should employ larger and more balanced samples, extend the study duration to strengthen statistical reliability, and further examine additional progression and engagement mechanisms to better understand how design choices influence sustained participation.

Acknowledgments. This research forms part of the R&D project *FinTechGaming: Promoção da Literacia Financeira através do Gaming*, promoted by Paynest Portugal, Lda, in collaboration with INESC-ID, financed under the Portugal 2030 program through the FEDER fund (Project No. 18441, Operation Code: COMPETE2030-FEDER-01480500) and co-funded by the European Union. This work was also supported by national funds through Fundação para a Ciência e a Tecnologia (FCT) with reference UIDB/50021/2020 (DOI: 10.54499/UIDB/50021/2020).

Disclosure of Interests. The authors have no competing interests to declare that are relevant to the content of this article.

References

1. Bayuk, J., Altobello, S.A.: Can gamification improve financial behavior? The moderating role of app expertise. Int. J. Bank Market. **37**(4), 951–975 (2019)
2. Bitrián, P., Buil, I., Catalán, S.: Making finance fun: the gamification of personal financial management apps. Int. J. Bank Market. **39**(7), 1310–1332 (2021)
3. Cen, J.L.A.: Financial Literacy through Gameful Design. Master's thesis, University of Waterloo (2021)

4. Deci, E.L., Ryan, R.M.: Self-determination theory. Handb. Theories Soc. Psychol. **1**(20), 416–436 (2012)
5. Deterding, S., Dixon, D., Khaled, R., Nacke, L.: From game design elements to gamefulness: defining "gamification". In: Proceedings of the 15th International Academic MindTrek Conference: Envisioning Future Media Environments, pp. 9–15 (2011)
6. Hamari, J., Koivisto, J., Sarsa, H.: Does gamification work?-A literature review of empirical studies on gamification. In: 47th Hawaii International Conference on System Sciences, pp. 3025–3034. IEEE (2014)
7. Hashim, N., Scopelliti, I., Steinmetz, J.: Gamification can help consumers reach their saving goals (2021)
8. Högberg, J., Hamari, J., Wästlund, E.: Gameful experience questionnaire (GAMEFULQUEST): an instrument for measuring the perceived gamefulness of system use. User Model. User-Adap. Inter. **29**(3), 619–660 (2019)
9. Hung, A., Parker, A.M., Yoong, J.: Defining and measuring financial literacy (2009)
10. Krath, J., Schürmann, L., Von Korflesch, H.F.: Revealing the theoretical basis of gamification: a systematic review and analysis of theory in research on gamification, serious games and game-based learning. Comput. Hum. Behav. **125**, 106963 (2021)
11. OECD: OECD/INFE 2023 International Survey of Adult Financial Literacy. OECD Business and Finance Policy Papers 39, Paris (2023). https://doi.org/10.1787/56003a32-en
12. Pal, A., Indapurkar, K., Gupta, K.P.: Gamification of financial applications and financial behavior of young investors. Young Consum. **22**(3), 503–519 (2021)
13. Sailer, M., Hense, J.U., Mayr, S.K., Mandl, H.: How gamification motivates: an experimental study of the effects of specific game design elements on psychological need satisfaction. Comput. Hum. Behav. **69**, 371–380 (2017)
14. Xi, N., Hamari, J.: Does gamification satisfy needs? A study on the relationship between gamification features and intrinsic need satisfaction. Int. J. Inf. Manage. **46**, 210–221 (2019)

Applying Gamification via *PlayNwhere* for Intergenerational Inclusion: A Case Study of Sanofi's "*Jornada De Gerações*"

Alvaro Marcos Antonio de Araujo Pistono[1] and Ricardo José Vieira Baptista[2](✉)

[1] INESC TEC, Porto, Portugal
[2] IPMAIA, Maia, Portugal
rbaptista@ipmaia.pt

Abstract. This paper presents a case study on the implementation of the "*Jornada de Gerações*" (Generations Journey) initiative at Sanofi, co-developed with *Fábrica de Cursos* using the *playNwhere* gamification platform. The initiative was designed to address ageism in the workplace, a bias that undermines collaboration, knowledge transfer, and innovation. The programme sought to strengthen organisational culture by fostering intergenerational inclusion and supporting Sanofi's diversity and inclusion agenda. The programme was accessible to all staff, including factory workers beyond office roles. The intervention was structured as a gamified learning journey involving teams, each composed of four participants from different age groups. Teams engaged in challenges designed to stimulate reflection on stereotypes, promote empathy, and reinforce collaboration across generations. A key innovation was the customisation of *playNwhere*, which enabled tailored team registration and integrating three themed games. Each game highlighted a different dimension of the issue: recognising age-related prejudice, exploring the benefits of intergenerational collaboration, and showcasing Sanofi's initiatives for employees aged 50 +. The platform's browser-based accessibility ensured seamless participation across devices, reducing barriers that might discourage older employees. Data from platform analytics and participant reflections indicated strong engagement, with a 96% completion rate. The study concludes that gamified interventions such as the "*Jornada de Gerações*" can serve as powerful tools to address workplace ageism and promote inclusion. It offers practical insights into the design of intergenerational training initiatives and points to implications for future research, particularly the use of mixed-method evaluations and scalability to other dimensions of workplace diversity.

Keywords: Gamification · Serious Games · Intergenerational inclusion · Corporate training · Workplace diversity · Learning Experience Platforms (LXPs)

1 Introduction

Workplace diversity is increasingly recognised as a strategic asset for innovation and organisational resilience. Organisations that integrate employees from diverse backgrounds—spanning gender, ethnicity, abilities, and generations—are better positioned

R. Baptista et al. (Eds.): VJ 2025, CCIS 2988, pp. 44–55, 2027.
https://doi.org/10.1007/978-3-032-31642-4_4

to adapt to complex challenges and foster inclusive cultures [13]. Despite these benefits, however, ageism remains one of the least addressed forms of workplace bias. Age-related stereotypes often undermine collaboration, hinder knowledge transfer, and create divisions between younger and older employees, limiting the potential of intergenerational teams [9].

To counteract these challenges, organisations have increasingly sought more experiential and engaging training formats. Traditional lecture-based models often fail to influence behaviours or attitudes in a lasting way. In contrast, gamification and serious games embed learning objectives into interactive and playful environments that stimulate motivation, reflection, and collaboration. Research demonstrates that these approaches enhance learner engagement and strengthen behavioural outcomes by providing active, situated experiences that go beyond passive knowledge transfer [12].

Against this backdrop, Sanofi[1] launched the "*Jornada de Gerações*" (Generations Journey) in partnership with *Fábrica de Cursos*[2], leveraging the *playNwhere*[3] platform [8] to design and deliver a gamified learning journey focused on intergenerational inclusion. The initiative structured teams with participants from different age groups, encouraging problem-solving while reflecting on generational diversity.

This paper presents a case study of the "*Jornada de Gerações*", examining its design, implementation, and outcomes. Specifically, it aims to demonstrate how gamified interventions can help address ageism, foster intergenerational collaboration, and contribute to broader diversity and inclusion agendas in corporate learning. The remainder of this paper is organised as follows: Sect. 2 reviews the theoretical background on gamification, serious games, and learning platforms; Sect. 3 outlines the methodology adopted; Sect. 4 details the case description; Sect. 5 discusses findings and limitations; and Sects. 6 and 7 provide conclusions and future directions.

2 Theoretical Background

2.1 Gamification in Corporate Learning

Gamification, defined as the application of game elements in non-game contexts, has become a widely used strategy in corporate and educational learning environments. A meta-analysis reported in [10] demonstrated that gamification produces significant positive effects on cognitive, motivational, and behavioural outcomes, particularly when it incorporates social interaction, immediate feedback, and engaging narratives.

In corporate contexts, gamification has been applied across several areas of training:

- Socio-emotional competencies such as leadership, teamwork, and communication;
- Compliance and safety, using missions to reinforce regulatory standards;
- Technical training, accelerating processes such as the integration of new technologies;
- Onboarding, transforming induction programmes into interactive journeys;

[1] Sanofi is a global pharmaceutical company.

[2] Fábrica de Cursos is a Brazilian company specialising in corporate learning solutions.

[3] *playNwhere* is a gamified LXP platform that enables the creation of gamified learning paths, serious games, and learning-reinforcement plans (https://playnwhere.ai/V14).

- Sales and customer service, employing gamified competitions to reinforce desired behaviours.

These practices make learning more appealing by embedding mechanics such as points, rankings, missions, and microlearning formats accessible via mobile devices. Systematic reviews also confirm that gamification enhances learner motivation and improves acceptance of digital platforms [14]. Furthermore, accessible, browser-based design reduces technical barriers and broadens participation. Nevertheless, the literature emphasises that effects can be heterogeneous and may diminish over time, highlighting the importance of aligning game elements with organisational culture and learning goals [10].

2.2 Serious Games and Inclusion

Serious games, defined as interactive systems with explicit real-world learning goals, extend beyond gamification by providing immersive experiences that foster reflection and behavioural change. They have increasingly been used to promote diversity, equity, and inclusion (DEI). A systematic review reported in [11] found that accessibility remains underexplored but is crucial, as inclusive design significantly expands participation for learners with cognitive, motor, or sensory limitations.

These games have proven effective in addressing complex issues such as gender bias, cultural diversity, disability inclusion, and ageism. As reviewed in [15], serious games in inclusive business contexts provide safe environments for participants to explore dilemmas and test strategies for collaboration. Within corporate training, such interventions sensitise employees to multiple dimensions of diversity while aligning with broader organisational inclusion strategies.

Their effectiveness stems from their experiential nature: by placing participants in simulated roles, these games promote emotional engagement and perspective-taking, outcomes that are difficult to achieve with traditional training formats. Feedback mechanisms, progression systems, and structured debriefings further reinforce attitudinal and behavioural change [10].

Although originally developed in higher education, active and experiential methods have been shown to effectively address age-related prejudice, as illustrated in [3].Their findings resonate with broader practices in corporate learning, where experiential approaches are increasingly adopted to confront biases and foster intergenerational inclusion.

2.3 Platform Advantages: *playNwhere*

To realise the full potential of gamification and serious games, flexible and inclusive platforms are essential. *PlayNwhere*, developed by *Fábrica de Cursos*, exemplifies a gamified Learning Experience Platform (LXP) designed for the rapid implementation of interactive learning solutions. Its browser-based design eliminates the need for downloads, promotes accessibility, and reduces technical barriers—a fundamental aspect of supporting employees of all ages [11].

The system includes intuitive authoring tools that allow trainers to design modules with points, leaderboards, narratives, and collaborative challenges without requiring advanced programming skills. It also provides analytics features that enable managers to track performance, identify learning gaps, and adapt content in real time—an approach consistent with recent research emphasising the role of data-driven learning strategies [14].

Those aspects were decisive for Sanofi in choosing *playNwhere* as the platform for its initiative. Moreover, the support provided by *Fábrica de Cursos* was essential for understanding the platform's specificities and developing a customised solution tailored to the organisation's needs.

In addition to these strengths, *playNwhere* was selected over more traditional learning management systems and generic LXP solutions because these alternatives did not offer team-based mechanics aligned with Sanofi's requirements, integrated gamified challenges, or the degree of visual and functional customisation required for the company's intergenerational initiative. While platforms such as Moodle or mobile-focused microlearning tools allow for content delivery, they typically lack embedded collaborative game structures and require substantial development effort to replicate the interactive dynamics needed for this programme.

In summary, the literature demonstrates that gamification and serious games consistently deliver positive impacts on engagement and learning. Platforms such as *playNwhere* provide the technical conditions necessary to scale these strategies effectively, fostering not only knowledge acquisition but also meaningful cultural and organisational transformation.

3 Methodology

This study adopts a mixed-methods descriptive case study design, drawing on secondary data from project reports, platform analytics, and qualitative documentation generated during the implementation of the programme. A case study approach was deemed appropriate given its capacity to capture the complexity of a single organisational intervention and to examine phenomena situated within real workplace contexts, where the boundaries between the intervention and its environment are not clearly defined [17]. This is particularly relevant in studies involving intergenerational collaboration and inclusive organisational practices, domains in which prior research has highlighted the importance of understanding the social dynamics that shape participation and behavioural outcomes [16].

3.1 Participants

The intervention engaged a total of 111 teams, each deliberately composed of four participants drawn from different age groups. This design choice aimed to maximise intergenerational interaction, ensuring that younger and older employees had the opportunity to collaborate directly. Previous research highlights that intergenerationally mixed teams can reduce stereotypes and foster mutual learning in workplace contexts [9]. Participants represented a broad spectrum of professional roles within Sanofi, reflecting the company's commitment to inclusive learning. The programme was accessible to all employees, including factory workers, thereby ensuring participation beyond office-based staff.

3.2 Intervention Design

The programme was structured as a gamified learning journey delivered entirely through the *playNwhere* platform. Teams engaged in a series of challenges designed to promote empathy, cooperation, and awareness of generational diversity in the workplace. The structure combined individual missions with collaborative tasks, including team formation, encouraging both personal reflection and collective problem-solving. Game mechanics such as points, badges, and leaderboards were integrated to stimulate motivation and provide feedback, aligning with best practices in gamified learning where a balance of competition and cooperation reinforces engagement.

3.3 Data Collection and Measures

Data were collected primarily from platform analytics and project documentation. Key metrics included completion rates, frequency of logins, and progression across challenges. Team-level performance scores were also recorded, allowing comparisons across groups.

The main indicators of interest were:

- Completion rate: the proportion of participants and teams who successfully completed all assigned challenges.
- Engagement level: frequency and intensity of participation, measured through platform log data.

3.4 Data Analysis

Quantitative indicators were summarised using descriptive statistics to capture overall patterns of engagement and completion. Observations from facilitators and project managers were also incorporated to contextualise the quantitative data. This triangulation of system-generated analytics and managerial documentation strengthens the reliability of the findings [4].

In sum, the methodological design sought to align with the programme's objectives: to evaluate the effectiveness of a gamified intervention in promoting intergenerational inclusion. By combining team-based design, quantitative metrics, and documented managerial insights, the study provides a comprehensive account of the "*Jornada de Gerações*" initiative.

4 Case Description

4.1 The Challenge: Ageing Workforce and Ageism

Sanofi recognised that age-related bias, or ageism, can undermine organisational inclusion and innovation. With a workforce spanning multiple generations, the company identified the need to create opportunities for employees of different ages to collaborate, share experiences, and challenge stereotypes. The "*Jornada de Gerações*" initiative was therefore conceived as an interactive, gamified programme designed to strengthen empathy, teamwork, and awareness of intergenerational diversity.

4.2 Design and Implementation

The intervention was structured in several phases:

Team Registration (Pre-event): One week before the official start, employees were invited to form and register their teams on the *playNwhere* platform. Each team was required to consist of four members, with deliberate inclusion of participants from different age groups. To facilitate this process, the platform was personalised with a customised registration module specifically designed for intergenerational teams. This feature ensured that the inclusion of multiple generations was mandatory during team formation. The registration period not only enabled logistical organisation but also served as an early stage of team-building, encouraging participants to reflect on generational diversity before the gamified journey began.

Participation in Gamified Activities (Main Event): The core of the programme consisted of a three-day sequence of interactive challenges delivered through *playNwhere*. For this purpose, three existing games within the platform were visually and thematically personalised to reflect Sanofi's corporate identity and the theme of ageism. The games featured customised characters representing the four generations currently present in the workplace, along with visual elements aligned with Sanofi's branding. Certain game parameters, such as time restrictions for responding to challenges, were also adapted to the target audience, ensuring an appropriate balance between engagement and accessibility across age groups. The mechanics integrated points, badges, leaderboards, and narrative elements contextualised around workplace scenarios of intergenerational interaction. These adaptations allowed participants to experience the challenges in a setting that was both realistic and meaningful. The browser-based, mobile-accessible format ensured seamless participation across devices, reducing technical barriers and enabling employees of all age groups to engage fully. This design choice not only promoted inclusivity and diversity but also aligned with evidence that gamified online strategies achieve stronger outcomes in organisational learning when accessibility and usability are explicitly prioritised [7].

The first challenge was designed to introduce participants to the core concepts of ageism in the workplace. Structured as a knowledge-based activity, the game presented scenarios and questions that encouraged employees to identify and reflect upon stereotypes, misconceptions, and discriminatory behaviours related to age. Its primary purpose was to foster awareness by providing participants with foundational knowledge about age-related bias, thereby preparing them for deeper engagement in the subsequent challenges. Figure 1 shows the start page of this game.

The second challenge focused on highlighting workplace scenarios in which intergenerational collaboration could generate significant value but is often hindered by prejudice or stereotypes. The activity required teams to work together across generational lines, confronting the barriers that prevent the full utilisation of diverse perspectives and skills. Its purpose was to emphasise the practical benefits of intergenerational teamwork while drawing attention to the subtle ways in which bias can undermine collaboration. The entry screen of Game 2 is shown in Fig. 2.

Fig. 1. Game of the day 1: "*Desmistificando o Etarismo: Um novo olhar*" (Demystifying Ageism: A new perspective)

Fig. 2. Game of the day 2: "Força das Gerações: Trabalho em equipe com profissionais de várias gerações" (Strength of Generations: Teamwork with professionals from different generations)

A clearer illustration of the challenges faced by the teams can be drawn from one of the interactive scenarios used in the Day 2 game. In this activity, participants were confronted with questions related to the practical implications of intergenerational collaboration at Sanofi, requiring them to evaluate alternative responses and select the option that best aligned with the organisation's inclusion principles. For example, one scenario asked teams to identify the main benefit of working across generations, contrasting a correct option—highlighting the enrichment of solutions and innovation through diverse perspectives—with an incorrect choice that promoted age-based competition. Upon selecting an answer, the system provided immediate feedback explaining the reasoning behind the correct response and reinforcing how intergenerational collaboration contributes to employee well-being, productive teamwork, and improved outcomes for patients. This structure encouraged teams to reflect collectively on misconceptions and to integrate Sanofi's values into their decision-making during the game.

The third challenge was designed to present and reinforce Sanofi's programmes focused on generational inclusion and the development of employees aged 50 and above. By engaging with interactive scenarios, participants became familiar with initiatives aimed at valuing senior professionals and leveraging their expertise within the organisation. This final activity underscored the strategic role of age diversity in fostering innovation and sustainability in corporate contexts. The entry screen of Game 3 is shown in Fig. 3.

Awards and Recognition (Post-event): At the conclusion of the three days, the most successful teams were recognised through a structured rewards ceremony. Rankings were automatically generated online through customised leaderboards, allowing the identification of winning teams directly from platform data. Prizes were awarded

Fig. 3. Game of the day 3: "Iniciativas que transformam: Os programas da Sanofi sobre inclusão geracional e desenvolvimento de talentos 50 +" (Transformative Initiatives: Sanofi's programmes on generational inclusion and the development of 50 + talent)

for points scored. Research indicates that recognition and symbolic rewards can significantly enhance the long-term impact of gamified interventions by reinforcing positive behaviours—for example, according to [2], "online instructors have primarily used them to motivate students' learning and acknowledge their achievements by timely rewarding specific learning behaviour or performance."

Analysis and Reflection (Follow-up): Following the event, data from the platform were analysed to assess participation and completion rates, as well as patterns of engagement across teams. Facilitators and project managers also provided feedback, emphasising the effectiveness of the gamified approach in stimulating intergenerational dialogue. The triangulation of analytics and feedback provided actionable insights for refining future initiatives and confirmed the intervention's alignment with Sanofi's inclusion strategy [4].

4.3 Outcomes

The "*Jornada de Gerações*" generated several notable outcomes that highlight both the scale of participation and the depth of engagement. A total of 111 teams were registered. In total, 444 employees enrolled, of which 400 actively accessed the platform to begin the activities.

Participation remained consistently high throughout the event:

- 96.5% of those who started (n = 386) completed the first day's game.
- 87.2% (n = 349) continued into the second day.
- 80.3% (n = 321) participated on the third day.
- Ultimately, 79.5% (n = 318) completed the entire learning path.

The gamified design also included competitive dynamics that further stimulated engagement. Tournament results varied significantly, with team scores ranging from 6,200 to 370,798 points. The specially customised leaderboards for the initiative automatically ranked teams and individuals, enabling transparent recognition during the awards ceremony.

In the team rankings, the highest-scoring group reached 848,749 points, while the fourth position achieved 781,876 points, reflecting a high level of competitiveness across the event.

In the individual rankings, the leading participant reached 370,798 points, while the fourth position registered 251,889 points.

As feedback, the project manager reported, "The game was a success!".

On the whole, the intervention had a positive organisational impact, reducing generational bias, reinforcing intergenerational collaboration, and contributing to a culture of continuous learning. Taken together, these results illustrate how a carefully designed, gamified intervention can achieve both high participation and meaningful behavioural and cultural change in a corporate setting.

5 Discussion

The "*Jornada de Gerações*" initiative underscores the advantages of gamified interventions in corporate learning. The high participation and completion rates observed mirror findings from the literature, where gamification has consistently been shown to improve motivation and engagement. As noted in [1], gamification has the potential to enhance motivation and engagement through the affordances of game elements such as points, badges, and leaderboards. This reflects how the design of our intervention—combining points, challenges, and rankings—successfully engaged employees across generational groups.

Furthermore, by deliberately structuring teams with members from different age cohorts, the initiative encouraged direct intergenerational collaboration. This is consistent with the findings reported in [6], which indicate that "gameful experiences exert a significant positive influence on… Affective commitment towards the company" (p. 6). In our case, this commitment was not only to Sanofi as an organisation but also to colleagues of different generations, fostering empathy and teamwork.

Another relevant dimension of our design relates to flow and emotional engagement. Research shows that well-structured gamification balances challenge and skill, thereby increasing persistence and learning outcomes. As noted in [5], gamification has been found to influence psychological outcomes such as enjoyment, flow, and intrinsic motivation. The balance of competition and cooperation in "*Jornada de Gerações*", combined with visual personalisation and narrative framing, supported such flow experiences across the three-day programme. Importantly, the use of time restrictions in the games was deliberately intended to sustain engagement and to facilitate participants' immersion in a state of flow, making the experience more dynamic and psychologically engaging.

In practice, the intervention also highlighted the benefits of accessibility and scalability. Because *playNwhere* is entirely browser-based and mobile-friendly, it removed technical barriers and ensured that employees of all ages and digital literacy levels could participate seamlessly. Finally, recognition through symbolic rewards contributed to motivation and a sense of accomplishment. Leaderboards and rankings, automatically generated by the platform, reinforced team identity and appreciation of collective effort. According to [6], gameful strategies strengthen team identity development and knowledge sharing among employees, aligning with the observed outcomes of our case study.

Taken together, these findings suggest that gamification, when thoughtfully designed, can contribute meaningfully to inclusion and cultural transformation. It provides not only a framework for delivering learning content but also for reshaping how employees perceive and interact with one another across generational boundaries.

5.1 Limitations

Despite its promising outcomes, this case study presents several limitations that must be acknowledged.

First, the study relied primarily on secondary data sources, such as platform analytics and project reports, together with descriptive measures. While these provide valuable insights into participation and outcomes, they do not allow for strong causal inferences about the long-term effects of the intervention.

A second limitation concerns the absence of a control group. Without comparison to employees exposed to traditional training formats, it is difficult to determine whether the observed outcomes can be attributed exclusively to the gamified intervention or might have arisen from other contextual factors.

Furthermore, although participation levels were high, the study did not examine in depth the dynamics of interaction within teams.

Another important limitation relates to the lack of longitudinal monitoring, which prevents understanding whether improvements in intergenerational collaboration persist over time or decline once the novelty of gamification diminishes.

Recognising these constraints is essential for situating the findings within the broader literature and for interpreting the results with appropriate caution.

6 Conclusions

The "*Jornada de Gerações*" initiative at Sanofi, implemented through the *playNwhere* platform, provides compelling evidence of how gamification can be harnessed to foster meaningful inclusion and engagement in corporate settings. By intentionally forming intergenerational teams and guiding them through an immersive, collaborative journey, the programme succeeded in reducing barriers linked to age-related stereotypes and encouraging dialogue across generations. The exceptionally high participation and completion rates illustrate not only the attractiveness of gamified learning environments but also their capacity to sustain motivation over time.

Beyond engagement metrics, the initiative contributed to cultural transformation by positioning intergenerational collaboration as a central organisational value. The use of a flexible, browser-based platform further highlighted the practical benefits of accessibility and rapid deployment, which are critical in contemporary workplaces characterised by hybrid and geographically dispersed teams. Importantly, the programme was designed to be accessible to the entire workforce, including factory floor employees, thereby ensuring that participation was not restricted to office-based staff but extended across the organisation.

In conclusion, the case of Sanofi shows that gamification, when strategically aligned with organisational goals and supported by effective technology, can become a scalable and impactful approach for addressing issues such as ageism, while simultaneously strengthening corporate culture and learning outcomes.

Building on these findings, the following directions may guide future research and practice.

6.1 Future Work

Despite its promising outcomes, this case study presents several limitations that must be acknowledged.

Although promising, this case study represents an early step in exploring the potential of gamification for intergenerational inclusion. Several directions for future research and practice may be pursued:

- Quantitative evaluations: Future studies should incorporate pre- and post-intervention measures of attitudes towards ageism, using validated psychometric instruments, as well as longitudinal tracking to assess whether behavioural change is sustained over time.
- Comparative designs: Research could compare gamified interventions with traditional training methods or other digital learning formats, in order to isolate the specific contribution of gamification to learning and cultural outcomes.
- Qualitative insights: In-depth interviews and focus groups would provide richer accounts of participants' experiences, exploring how employees from different generations perceive and interpret the gamified learning journey.
- Scalability and transferability: Future initiatives might expand the model to address other themes of organisational inclusion, such as gender, disability, or cultural diversity, thereby testing its adaptability to varied contexts.
- Integration with microlearning and blended formats: Embedding short, gamified modules within wider blended learning strategies could reinforce key messages and ensure continuous engagement, while also enabling personalisation of learning paths.

By exploring these avenues, researchers and practitioners can deepen their understanding of the role of gamification in organisational development and develop interventions that are both engaging and evidence-based.

References

1. Alsawaier, R.S.: The effect of gamification on motivation and engagement. Int. J. Inf. Learn. Technol. **35**(1), 56–79 (2018). https://doi.org/10.1108/IJILT-02-2017-0009
2. Chen, M., Zhao, M., Pan, Z., Pan, Q., Bonk, C.J.: Investigating the impact of gamification components on online learners' engagement. Smart Learn. Environ. **11**, 47 (2024). https://doi.org/10.1186/s40561-024-00336-3
3. Cheung, K., Leung, A.Y.M., Xie, H.: Eliminating ageism in higher education: an intergenerational participatory co-design approach to inclusive digital education. Educ. Gerontol. **49**(5), 263–277 (2023). https://doi.org/10.1080/03601277.2023.2187107
4. Creswell, J.W., Poth, C.N.: Qualitative Inquiry and Research Design: Choosing Among Five Approaches, 4th edn. Sage Publications (2018)
5. Koivisto, J., Hamari, J.: The rise of motivational information systems: a review of gamification research. Int. J. Inf. Manag. **45**, 191–210 (2019). https://doi.org/10.1016/j.ijinfomgt.2018.10.013

6. Manske, J.: Gamification in the workplace: Enhancing employee engagement through gameful experiences. J. Innov. Manag. Digitalization **3**(1), 01 (2024). https://doi.org/10.56578/jimd030101
7. Nieto-Escámez, F.A., Roldán-Tapia, M.D.: Gamification as online teaching strategy during COVID-19: a mini-review. Front. Psychol. **12**, 648552 (2021). https://doi.org/10.3389/fpsyg.2021.648552
8. playNwhere. (n.d.). playNwhere. Accessed 17 Sept 2025. https://edtech.playnwhere.com/
9. Posthuma, R.A., Campion, M.A.: Age stereotypes in the workplace: common stereotypes, moderators, and future research directions. J. Manag. **35**(1), 158–188 (2009). https://doi.org/10.1177/0149206308318617
10. Sailer, M., Homner, L.: The gamification of learning: a meta-analysis. Educ. Psychol. Rev. **32**(1), 77–112 (2020). https://doi.org/10.1007/s10648-019-09498-w
11. Salvador-Ullauri, L., Acosta-Vargas, P., Luján-Mora, S.: Web-based serious games and accessibility: a systematic literature review. Appl. Sci. **10**(21), 7859 (2020). https://doi.org/10.3390/app10217859
12. Schrader, C.: Serious games and game-based learning. In: Zawacki-Richter, O., Jung, I. (eds.) Handbook of Open, Distance and Digital Education, pp. 1255–1268. Springer, Heidelberg (2023). https://doi.org/10.1007/978-981-19-2080-6_74
13. Shore, L.M., Cleveland, J.N., Sanchez, D.: Inclusive workplaces: a review and model. Hum. Res. Manag. Rev. **28**(2), 176–189 (2018). https://doi.org/10.1016/j.hrmr.2017.07.003
14. Simsek, E., Karakus Yilmaz, T.: A systematic review of the effects of gamification in online learning environments on learning outcomes. Open Praxis **17**(1), 59–75 (2025). https://doi.org/10.55982/openpraxis.17.1.692
15. Speelman, E.N., Rodela, R., Doddema, M., Ligtenberg, A.: Serious gaming as a tool to facilitate inclusive business: a review of untapped potential. Curr. Opin. Environ. Sustainabil. **41**, 31–37 (2019). https://doi.org/10.1016/j.cosust.2019.09.010
16. Yin, R.K.: Case Study Research and Applications: Design and Methods, 6th edn. Sage Publications (2018)

"I Ended up not Playing More…": A Design Model to Support Completion of Narrative Serious Games for Mental Health

Dalila Martins(✉), Nelson Zagalo, and Ana Patrícia Oliveira

DigiMedia, Department of Communication and Art, University of Aveiro, Aveiro, Portugal
{dalilamartins,nzagalo,apoliveira}@ua.pt

Abstract. Despite their potential many serious games (SG) suffer from low completion rates due to disengagement. This study proposes a Design Model aimed at enhancing player engagement in narrative SGs to support full game completion and to ensure the delivery of intended messages. The Model builds on analysis of case studies of entertainment and mental health-focused SGs; analysis of user reviews on Steam, and interviews with game designers and mental health professionals. Thematic analysis revealed six key principles for sustaining player engagement: Narrative Experience, Emotional and Mental Involvement, Player Actions and Choices, Objectives and Social Context, Accessible Gameplay, and Visual and Sound Atmosphere. The Model was implemented in a workshop involving professionals from psychology and game design, who applied the Model in the conceptual development of a mental health-focused SG. In addition, two interviews were conducted with two game designers from a renowned AAA company, in which the relevance of the Model was discussed. The results indicated that the Model was well structured, practical, and could be effective in the design of any SG. It is very similar to the elements that any game designer considers when designing an entertainment game. However, it also reveals some opportunities for improvement, particularly in the use of the Model in contexts with less funding, for example. By understanding and applying these principles, designers can better support player motivation and completion, thereby enhancing the educational and therapeutic value of SGs in the mental health domain.

Keywords: Serious Games · Game Design · Mental Health · Finalisation · Design Models

1 Introduction

Play is an innate activity that allows human beings to learn and grow, so a well-designed game should promote engagement and learning [1]. However, if a player gives up, they will not continue to learn from it [2]. One of the main objectives of SGs is to be able to reproduce the experiences that are achieved with entertainment games, in which the rules, aesthetics and narrative work exclusively to maintain the player's interest [3]. It is therefore necessary to understand in greater detail how engagement is produced, in

R. Baptista et al. (Eds.): VJ 2025, CCIS 2988, pp. 56–67, 2027.
https://doi.org/10.1007/978-3-032-31642-4_5

addition to interest, taking into account the personal preferences and behaviour of players in particular [4]. The diversity of personalities makes it impossible to guarantee that a game will be considered fun by all players [5], so their response to it is also individual [6]. In fact, it is estimated that only 10% to 30% of players complete a game [7] and there are countless justifications for this dropout, from switching to a new game [7]; its length [7]; the imbalance of flow [8] or decreased attention [9]. That said, game designers are increasingly interested in understanding how the game's sequence of events affects game progression and narrative pacing. In the case of SGs, this factor has even more impact, as they are often created for educational purposes, resulting in games that are considered boring and unstimulating by players [10]. With this in mind, we propose the creation of a Design Model for optimal player engagement in SGs. The Model aims to support the design of SGs, in the conceptualization phase, capable of captivating the player to the end. It consists of six principles and 23 sub-principles that promote the initial moment of designing narrative SGs in light of the salient elements of entertainment games. To demonstrate the applicability of the Model, we focus on the specific domain of SG for mental health. This decision is grounded in the increasing recognition of Health SGs as powerful tools to encourage behavioral change and self-management of chronic conditions [11]. In particular, mental health SGs are seen as promising artefacts for emotional awareness, self-regulation, and reducing stigma [12]. By applying the Model to SGs for mental health, we aim not only to refine its utility but also to contribute to a deeper understanding of the mechanisms that keep players involved until the intended message is fully delivered. In addition, two interviews were conducted with two game designers from an AAA company (which cannot be disclosed for confidentiality reasons) to discuss the relevance of the Model, in order to understand whether it was close to what a game designer needs when designing a game and what improvements could be implemented.

In addition, the problem of games not being completed is something that is still little discussed both in academia and in the industry, so it is necessary to understand what keeps players going and what motivates them to reach the end, both in an entertainment game and in an SG. It is believed that this Model contributes to bringing SG closer to the transformative potential of digital entertainment, while expanding its social and therapeutic effectiveness.

The Design Model is primarily aimed at the Portuguese gaming industry, which has been evolving over time [13] and already includes companies dedicated to developing SG as commercial products [14, 15]. However, it can also be applied in indie companies or in an academic context.

With regard to the structure of this article, it begins with a literature review, followed by the methodology, data analysis and model development. The way in which it was applied is presented, as well as the discussion surrounding its relevance, and finally conclusions are drawn regarding the topic.

2 Literature Review

2.1 Narrative in Games

The narrative in games refers to the sequence of events that unfolds during the gaming experience: "When we talk about stories, plots or narratives in video games, we are referring to a succession of programmed events that the player must perform in a specific order" [16]. [17] distinguishes three fundamental types of narrative structure in games: **(i) Linear Narrative:** common in older games or in titles strongly rooted in stories, where the narrative progression follows a defined line. This approach is effective in creating emotional impact but reduces player freedom. **(ii) Branched Narrative:** used in games, where the player's decisions affect the unfolding of the story and its multiple endings. **(iii) Emergent Narrative:** Characteristic of sandbox games, where the narrative emerges from the interaction between systems and player choices. Narrative design is a complex task that requires structuring, such as balancing the other elements that are part of the game's design. Some authors highlight concerns to be aware of when designing: (i) [18] suggest that the story should be integrated organically into the gameplay, in order to avoid excessive separation between cutscenes and interaction; (ii) [19] considers thematic and tonal consistency to be important, i.e., narrative elements should be in tune with the game mechanics, visual aesthetics, and player objectives in order to create a coherent and immersive experience. Finaly, (iii) [20] emphasizes the importance of an environment in which the player can act. This perspective emphasizes the importance of player agency as a central pillar in the construction of the narrative experience.

Narrative Serious Games Models. In recent years, several authors have proposed formal design methodologies to guide the development of SG [21]. However, most of these approaches emerge from academia, where the SG sector remains relatively small. Consequently, many frameworks are more abstract and less practical than traditional game design methodologies, which are industry-driven and market-oriented [22].

Among the most cited, [23] developed the DPE (Design–Play–Experience) framework, which structures SG design across four layers: learning, storytelling, gameplay, and user experience, while integrating design, play, and experiential dimensions, with technology as the underlying foundation. More recently, [24] proposed a web-based, collaborative framework composed of 23 blocks, organized into five categories (context and objectives, game design, mechanics, learning design, and evaluation). This model allows multiple visualizations, such as the game learning view, project view, and systemic view, thereby connecting learning and game mechanics within an iterative process. [25] extended this perspective by presenting a stakeholder-centred framework that integrates requirement analysis, implementation planning, and elements such as learning objectives, mechanics, narrative, interface, user experience, and evaluation. Its novelty lies in the validation of the structure through expert review, which confirmed its effectiveness for stakeholder management in SG design. Despite these contributions, the literature still shows a lack of narrative-oriented SG design models inspired by entertainment games, which could provide richer and more engaging frameworks for serious applications.

found the model easy to understand; they found the principles well defined and clear: 4 (n = 7) and 5 (n = 1); the implementation examples provided effectively helped to understand the application of the model: 4 (n = 4) and 5 (n = 1); the majority also agreed that the model helps to integrate mental health aspects into the game: 4 (n = 4) and 5 (n = 3) and, that the model facilitates idea generation for game design: 4 (n = 5) and 5 (n = 2). Also, the SWOT analysis carried out at the time of the workshop showed that in terms of strengths the model facilitates cooperation between professionals and systematises all the elements needed to realise an idea in a cohesive way and the categorical and systematised division is well done. In terms of opportunities, these only related to the logistics of the workshop. The weaknesses pointed out had to do with the identification of strategies only related to resources typical of AAA games, which in the eyes of the participants can condition the feasibility of smaller projects and, in terms of threats, they named the lack of balance between various elements of the model (some principles are more complex than others) and the complexity of the Model can lead to the creation of games that necessarily require a lot of monetary resources. Recommendations also included building a quick start guide for the model in a compact and self-explanatory way and integrating examples of independent productions.

In addition to the workshop, interviews were conducted with game designers from AAA company to understand whether the principles and sub-principles present in the Model are indeed relevant when designing games. Considering the secrecy surrounding AAA companies and the difficulty in obtaining interviews, it was decided to conduct semi-structured interviews, characterised by their informality, with four questions: (1) What considerations do you think are relevant to the Model presented? (2) As a game designer, how do you usually think about all these principles when designing a game? (3) Do you think the Model should follow a hierarchical structure so that some principles stand out more than others? (4) Do you think there is any principle or sub-principle missing from the Model or that something should be changed?

The interviewees recognised the usefulness and comprehensiveness of the Model, highlighting its ability to cover key design concerns. They considered that the hierarchy of principles is unnecessary, given that their relevance depends on the type and stage of the project. However, one of the interviewees suggested integrating "player actions and choices" into the principle of "accessible gameplay" and pointed out the absence of sub-principles dedicated to the form of representation of serious content. The other interviewee reinforced that, at a high level, the Model contemplates in a simple and structured way the vast majority of dimensions that guide the work of a game designer, even though some sub-principles could gain autonomy.

6 Conclusion

This research sought to tackle one of the main challenges that games can suffer from and that, in the case of SGs, can affect the objective of the game, namely the high rate of players giving up. In this way, a Design Model was constructed that promotes sustained involvement until the game is completed, with a special focus on mental health. This concern is not just a question of usability or entertainment, but of communicative effectiveness, especially when it comes to games with educational or therapeutic purposes.

To build this Model, the DBR methodology was adopted, and it was analysed case studies, collected and analysed user comments on the Steam platform and it was conducted interviews with game designers and mental health professionals, where it was possible to identify patterns and recurring themes related to player engagement. Thematic analysis of these sources led to the definition of six fundamental principles.

These principles are interconnected and operationalised through sub-principles, allowing for their practical application in the design process. The Model was applied through a practical workshop with the participation of eight professionals (game designers and mental health experts) in which participants used the Model to co-design a mental health SGs. The results of the workshop demonstrated the practical usefulness and clarity of the Model: participants considered the principles to be well-defined and easy to understand; the Model was seen as a facilitator of interdisciplinary collaboration and was also valued for its ability to systematise the elements needed to design SGs with an emotional and social impact. However, important limitations were identified, which are useful for future improvements to the Model, such as: the perception that some proposed strategies are more in line with big-budget (AAA) games, which may limit their applicability in independent production contexts or with reduced resources; the complexity of the model may represent an obstacle for beginners or projects with short deadlines and the need for a quick start guide and concrete examples of independent games was pointed out as a desirable improvement. In the case of interviews with two game designers from AAA, it was found that the Design Model does indeed follow the principles used in entertainment game companies and clearly covers all the elements necessary for the idealisation of a game. However, the Model could be even more comprehensive with some integration between principles or autonomy from other sub-principles. These observations point to clear paths of evolution: making the Model more scalable, adaptable to different production realities and more accessible to varied user profiles. In addition, integrations and disintegrations between principles and sub-principles should be reviewed. It should be noted that the Design Model has not yet been validated, so for the next steps it is important that validation be carried out to obtain even more feedback and be reformulated.

Thus, this study not only offers an important theoretical contribution to the field of SGs and gamification in mental health, but also provides a practical and relevant tool that can support stakeholders in creating meaningful experiences. This Model stands out for its emphasis on game completion and player engagement, critical factors for the success of any game. Furthermore, it is differentiated by its empirical basis, built from an analysis of elements that work well in entertainment games and can be transposed into SGs. This combination of theoretical foundation, industry feedback, and collaborative applicability between interdisciplinary areas (game designers and psychologists) positions the Model as a relevant and useful tool, capable of responding to the limitations observed and mentioned in many SGs. By reinforcing the link between emotional engagement, narrative design and social impact, the Model proposed here represents a breakthrough in building games that not only entertain but transform.

Acknowledgments. This work was supported by FCT - Fundação para a Ciência e Tecnologia, I.P. by project reference 2022.14590.BD and DOI identifier: https://doi.org/https://doi.org/10.54499/2022.14590.BD.

References

1. Vygotsky, L.S.: Play and its role in the mental development of the child. Int. Res. Early Child. Educ. **3**(2) (2016). www.marxists.org/archive/vygotsky/works/1933/play.htm
2. Karumbaiah, S., Baker, R.S., Shute, V.: Predicting quitting in students playing a learning game. In: Proceedings of 11th International Conference on Education Data Mining, EDM 2018 (2018)
3. M. S. D. Vasconcellos and G. C. Atella, 'As Várias Faces dos Jogos Digitais na Educação', *Informática Na Educ. Teor. Prática*, vol. 20, no. 4 dez, pp. 203–218, 2017
4. Almeida, F., Simoes, J.: The role of serious games, gamification and industry 4.0 tools in the education 4.0 paradigm. Contemp. Educ. Technol. **10**(2), 120–136 (2019). https://doi.org/10.30935/cet.554469
5. Piton, A., Blom, P.M., Spronck, P.: Exploring peak-end effects in player affect through hearthstone. In: 21st International Conference on Intelligents Games Simulation GAME- 2020, no. January, pp. 51–56 (2020)
6. Kosiński, J., Szklanny, K., Wieczorkowska, A., Wichrowski, M.: An analysis of game-related emotions using EMOTIV EPOC. In: Proceedings of the 2018 Federated Conference on Computer Science and Information Systems, FedCSIS 2018, pp. 913–917. Institute of Electrical and Electronics Engineers Inc. (2018). https://doi.org/10.15439/2018F296
7. Richards, A.: Why most people don't finish video games. The Independent. https://eu.indeonline.com/story/news/2020/06/27/why-most-people-dont-finish-video-games/113368900/
8. Gee, J.P.: What video games have to teach us about learning and literacy. Comput. Entertain. **1**(1), 20 (2003). https://doi.org/10.1145/950566.950595
9. Lorenz-Spreen, P., Mønsted, B.M., Hövel, P., Lehmann, S.: Accelerating dynamics of collective attention. Nat. Commun. **10**(1), 1759 (2019). https://doi.org/10.1038/s41467-019-09311-w
10. Dele-Ajayi, O., Sanderson, J., Strachan, R., Pickard, A.: Learning mathematics through serious games: an engagement framework. In: Frontiers on Education Conference FIE, pp. 1–5. IEEE (2016)
11. Sharifzadeh, N., et al.: Health education serious games targeting health care providers, patients, and public health users: scoping review. JMIR Serious Games **8**(1), e13459 (2020). https://doi.org/10.2196/13459
12. Gómez-León, M.I.: Serious games to support emotional regulation strategies in educational intervention programs with children and adolescents: systematic review and meta-analysis. Heliyon **11**(4), 42715 (2025)
13. AICEP. Gaminghub impulsiona indústria de videojogos. Gaminghub impulsiona indústria de videojogos. Accessed 24 Sept 2025. https://www.portugalglobal.pt/noticias/2024/dezembro/gaminghub-impulsiona-industria-de-videojogos/
14. Nonagon. Cereal Games is the first alumni company of Go-On Incubator. Accessed 24 Sept 2025. https://nonagon.pt/en/cereal-games-is-the-first-alumni-company-of-go-on-incubator/
15. nobox. Nobox. nobox. Accessed 24 Sept 2025. https://nobox.pt/
16. Egenfeldt-Nielsen, S., Meyer, B., Sorensen, B.: Serious Games in Education: A Global Perspective. Aarhus Universitetsforlag (2011)
17. Schell, J.: The Art of Game Design: A book of lenses, 3rd New edn. Taylor & Francis Ltd. (2020)
18. Adams, E., Rollings, A.: Andrew Rollings and Ernest Adams on Game Design. New Riders (2003)
19. Rouse III, R.: Game Design Theory & Practice, 2a Edição. Wordware Game Developers Library (2005)

20. Murray, J.: Hamlet on the Holodeck: The Future of Narrative in Cyberspace. Simon and Schuster (1997)
21. Serious Games Society. Tools and methods for SG design. Serious Games Society. Accessed 27 Sept 2025. https://seriousgamessociety.org/tools-and-methods-for-sg-design/
22. Guardiola, E., Czauderna, A.: Merging Gameplay and Learning in Educational Game Design: The Gameplay Loop Methodology in Antura and the Letters (2018)
23. Winn, B. (ed.): The Design, Play, and Experience Framework. In: Handbook of Research on Effective Electronic Gaming in Education. IGI Global (2009). https://doi.org/10.4018/978-1-59904-808-6
24. Jaccard, D., Suppan, L., Sanchez, E., Huguenin, A., Laurent, M.: The co.LAB generic framework for collaborative design of serious games: development study. JMIR Serious Games **9**(3), e28674 (2021). https://doi.org/10.2196/28674
25. Bunt, L., Greeff, J., Taylor, E.: Enhancing serious game design: expert-reviewed, stakeholder-centered framework. JMIR Serious Games **12**(1), e48099 (2024). https://doi.org/10.2196/48099
26. Y. Kim, S. Hong, and M. Choi, 'Effects of Serious Games on Depression in Older Adults: Systematic Review and Meta-analysis of Randomized Controlled Trials', *Journal of Medical Internet Research*, vol. 24, no. 9, 2022
27. Burguillo, J.C.: Using game theory and Competition-based Learning to stimulate student motivation and performance. Comput. Educ. **55**(2), 566–575 (2010). https://doi.org/10.1016/j.compedu.2010.02.018
28. Van Laer, T., Ruyter, K., Visconti, L., Wetzels, M.: The extended transportation-imagery model: a meta-analysis of the antecedents and consequences of consumers' narrative. J. Consum. Res. **40**(5), 797–817 (2014)
29. Bruckman, A.: Can educational be fun?. In: Game Developers Conference 99' (1999). https://faculty.cc.gatech.edu/~asb/papers/bruckman-gdc99.pdf
30. Camps-Ortueta, I., González-Calero, P.A., Quiroga, A., Gómez-Martín, P.P.: Measuring preferences in game mechanics: towards personalized chocolate-covered broccoli, pp. 15–27 (2019). https://doi.org/10.1007/978-3-030-34644-7_2
31. Disalvo, B.: Pink boxes and chocolate-dipped broccoli: bad game design providing justifications for reluctant learners. In: Games+Learning+Society Conference (2015). https://www.researchgate.net/publication/316636723
32. Susi, T., Johannesson, M., Backlund, P.: Serious Games-An Overview (2007)
33. Czauderna, A., Guardiola, E., Lux, J.D., Budke, A.: How insights into entertainment games can improve the design of educational games on complex societal problems. In: Proceedings of the European Conference on Games-based Learning, pp. 170–177. Dechema e.V. (2021). https://doi.org/10.34190/GBL.21.119
34. Gee, J.P.: What would a state of the art instructional video game look like? Innov. J. Online Educ. **1**(6), 1–6 (2005)
35. Arena, D.: Commercial Video Games as Preparation for Future Learning. Stanford University, Stanford (2012)
36. Nordine, J.C.: Motivating calculus-based kinematics instruction with super mario bros. Phys. Teach. **49**(6), 380–382 (2011). https://doi.org/10.1119/1.3628271
37. Vella, K., Peever, N., Klarkowski, M., Ploderer, B., Mitchell, J., Johnson, D.: Using applied games to engage mHealth users: a case study of MindMax. In: CHI PLAY 2018 - Proceedings of the 2018 Annual Symposium on Computer-Human Interaction in Play, pp. 523–534. Association for Computing Machinery (2018). https://doi.org/10.1145/3242671.3242686
38. Fitzgerald, M., Ratcliffe, G.: Serious games, gamification, and serious mental illness: a scoping review. Psychiatr. Serv. **71**(2), 170–183 (2020). https://doi.org/10.1176/appi.ps.201800567

39. Mahar, I.: Nobody Wins When Horror Games Stigmatize Mental Illness. Kotaku. Accessed 13 June 2024. https://kotaku.com/nobody-wins-when-horror-games-stigmatize-mental-illness-912462538
40. Mandryk, R.L., Birk, M.V.: Toward game-based digital mental health interventions: player habits and preferences. J. Med. Internet Res. **19**(4), 6906 (2017). https://doi.org/10.2196/jmir.6906
41. Fleming, T.M., et al.: Serious games and gamification for mental health: current status and promising directions. Front. Psychiatry **7**, 232141 (2017). https://doi.org/10.3389/fpsyt.2016.00215
42. Brezinka, V.: Computer games supporting cognitive behaviour therapy in children. Clin. Child Psychol. Psychiatry **19**(1), 100–110 (2014). https://doi.org/10.1177/1359104512468288
43. Carras, M., et al.: Commercial video games as therapy: a new research agenda to unlock the potential of a global pastime. Front. Psychiatry **8**, 297915 (2018)
44. Russoniello, C.V., Fish, M., O'Brien, K.: The efficacy of casual videogame play in reducing clinical depression: a randomized controlled study. Games Health J. **2**(6), 341–346 (2013). https://doi.org/10.1089/g4h.2013.0010
45. Krebs, R.E., Lembens, A.: Developing key ideas to teach "Acids" & "Bases" in upper secondary schools. In: Project-Based Education and Other Activating Strategies in Science Education XVIII (2021). https://www.researchgate.net/publication/351712029
46. Braun, V., Clarke, V.: Thematic Analysis: A Practical Guide. SAGE, London; Thousand Oaks, California (2022)

Designing a User-Centered Educational Serious Game on Camilo Castelo Branco

Gonçalo Castro[1], Edgar Pereira[1], and Rui Carreira[1,2,3,4](✉)

[1] Maia Polytechnic Institute, Maia, Portugal
rcarreira@ipmaia.pt
[2] N2i Research Centre, Maia Polytechnic Institute, Maia, Portugal
[3] UNICES Research Centre, University of Maia, Maia, Portugal
[4] LIACC - Artificial Intelligence and Computer Science Laboratory, University of Porto, Porto, Portugal

Abstract. This paper presents the development of an educational serious game focused on the life and works of Camilo Castelo Branco, created during a curricular internship at Maia's Public Library. The game was designed to engage young audiences with Portuguese literary heritage through interactive storytelling and playful mechanics. Thus, the project incorporated iterative feedback and educational design principles, partially guided by user-centered design methodologies. This case study explores the development process, technical challenges, and pedagogical considerations, highlighting the potential of serious games in cultural education.

Keywords: Serious games · Educational game design · Camilo Castelo Branco · Cultural heritage · Game-based learning · User-centered design

1 Introduction

The integration of digital games into educational environments has gained increasing relevance as a tool for promoting engagement, motivation, and cultural literacy. This paper presents the development of an educational game focused on the life and works of Camilo Castelo Branco, one of Portugal's most iconic literary figures. The project was carried out during the curricular internship of two students at Maia's Public Library, as part of the Multimedia Production and Digital Games level 5 program at the Polytechnic Institute of Maia (IPMAIA).

The main objective of the internship was to design and implement a game that could serve as a pedagogical resource for young audiences while visiting or planning to visit the library, encouraging them to explore Portuguese literature through interactive storytelling and playful mechanics. In addition, the virtual recreation of the library enabled an alternative way of getting to know and navigating the building.

The game was developed using Unity and other multimedia tools such as Blender and Photoshop, combining narrative design, character development, and programming to create an immersive experience centered on Camilo's biography and literary legacy.

R. Baptista et al. (Eds.): VJ 2025, CCIS 2988, pp. 68–79, 2027.
https://doi.org/10.1007/978-3-032-31642-4_6

Although the project was not fully guided by a user-centered design methodology, users were involved throughout the process and several principles of educational game design were applied, including accessibility, narrative coherence, and age-appropriate content. The game's structure, dialogues, and visual elements were also iteratively refined based on feedback from library staff and informal testing sessions. This report outlines the development process, technical challenges, and pedagogical considerations involved in creating the game, and reflects on its potential as a cultural and educational tool.

2 Literature Review

Gamification research primarily concentrates on either the technological implementations of gamification or its psychological effects within expansive educational contexts, neglecting the design and application of gamification methods to enhance critical literacies in formal educational environments [14]. Moreover, whereas studies demonstrate benefits for student engagement and learning results, the evidence is fragmented and frequently inconsistent across various educational levels and cultural contexts [15, 16]. Serious games have been widely explored as educational tools that combine entertainment with learning objectives. Meta-analyses indicate that they can enhance knowledge acquisition, motivation, and retention compared to traditional methods, although their effectiveness strongly depends on the alignment between game mechanics and pedagogical goals [1, 2, 4]. However, several authors warn that results are also conditioned by contextual factors such as the time allocated for gameplay, learners' digital literacy, and the integration of games into formal curricula [4]. This highlights the risk that games may become superficial experiences if not properly embedded within educational frameworks, and in addition, limited attention has been given to gamification in literary works.

Thus, methodologies such as User-Centered Design (UCD) [12] and Design Thinking [5, 13] have gained prominence in the development of such games, emphasising the importance of tailoring game mechanics and content to the needs and preferences of target users.

In the health sector, serious games have been shown to increase learners' confidence and performance [3]. Nevertheless, the heterogeneity of studies limits definitive conclusions [4, 6]. This variability suggests that serious games are not universally effective and must be adapted to the target audience, the learning objectives, and the way content is designed. This reflection is particularly relevant to our project, which also faces the challenge of translating complex literary content into accessible and engaging gameplay experiences.

In the field of cultural heritage, serious games are valued for their ability to foster engagement and awareness. Location-based experiences and interactive narratives have been shown to make history and culture more accessible [7, 8]. Furthermore, immersive technologies such as virtual reality can increase emotional involvement, but challenges remain in terms of accessibility, usability, and production costs [9]. Recent reviews also emphasize that many heritage projects remain at prototype stage and lack rigorous evaluation [10, 11].

Despite the extensive literature on serious games in health and cultural heritage, applications related to literary heritage are virtually nonexistent. Existing research does not present significant studies in this area, which confirms the need for innovative initiatives. Our game aims to contribute to filling this gap by valuing the memory of Camilo Castelo Branco and proposing a replicable model for other authors and their literary works.

3 Methodology

This project was developed during the curricular internship of two students at Maia's Public Library, as part of the Multimedia Production and Digital Games level 5 program at the Polytechnic Institute of Maia (IPMAIA). Its primary objective was to design and implement an educational serious game that introduces young audiences to the life and works of Camilo Castelo Branco through interactive storytelling and immersive gameplay.

The methodology followed a structured and iterative approach, divided into seven main phases adapted from Design Thinking [5] and UCD approaches, namely Planning and training, Conceptualization and Narrative Design, Cultural Impact, Technical Development, User Experience and Accessibility, Iteration and Feedback, and Documentation and Reflection.

Overall, the development process incorporated iterative feedback and informal testing, aligning with best practices in serious game design. Thus, the game aims to bridge the gap between cultural heritage and digital literacy, offering a playful yet informative experience for library visitors.

4 Results and Discussion

As described in the previous section, the internship was divided into the seven main phases which are presented in the following subsections.

4.1 Planning and Training

The internship began by the elaboration of a Game Design Document (GDD) draft in order to better guide the game development process which was progressively updated throughout the project. The interns also engaged in historical research on Camilo Castelo Branco, gathering biographical data and literary references to ensure cultural accuracy in the game's content. Additionally, a survey was distributed via Google Forms to gather insights into user preferences regarding game genres, visual styles, and interaction mechanics. The results obtained informed design decisions and helped align the game with the expectations of the target audience. The majority of the 17 participants were young adults, which may influence preferences toward more complex or narrative games (see REF _Ref210832093 \h * MERGEFORMAT Fig. 1).

The results shown in Fig. 2 suggest a limited familiarity with the author, reinforcing the importance of developing educational approaches that introduce his life and literature in an engaging way.

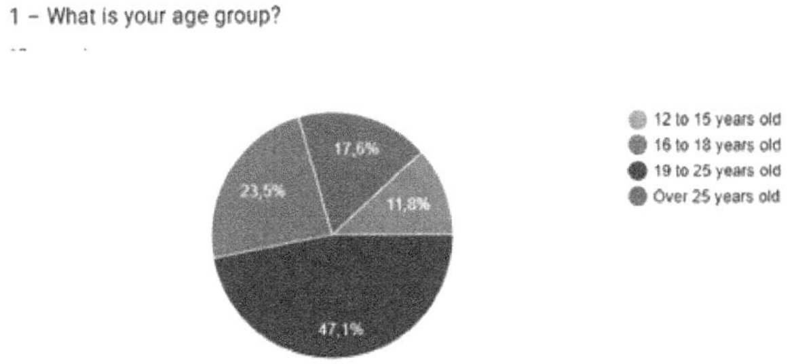

Fig. 1. Age group

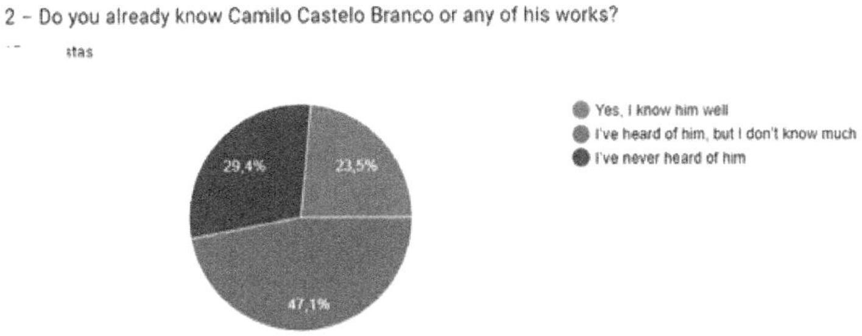

Fig. 2. Knowledge about Camilo Castelo Branco

4.2 Conceptualization and Narrative Design

Based on the users' feedback, the game concept was inspired by Camilo's biography and literary legacy. As can be seen in Fig. 3 and Fig. 4 the results supported the choice of a narrative exploration approach, and respondents are particularly interested in exploring the author's life story, while also valuing additional cultural and literary insights. A narrative framework was thus developed, featuring a fictional journey where players interact with characters and events from Camilo's life. The storyline was structured around key milestones, such as his early education, romantic relationships, and major works like *"Amor de Perdição"*.

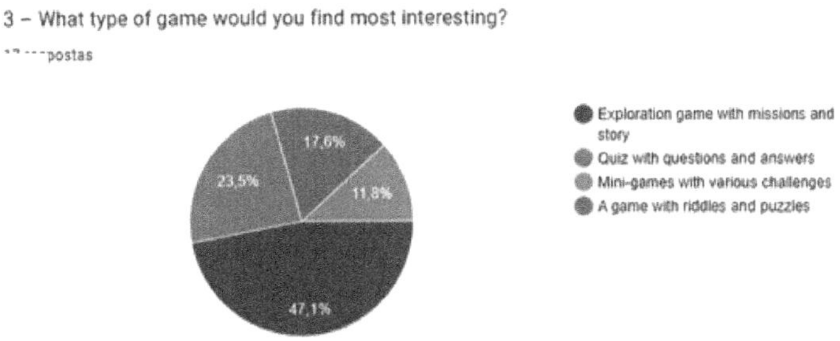

Fig. 3. Type of game respondents' preferences

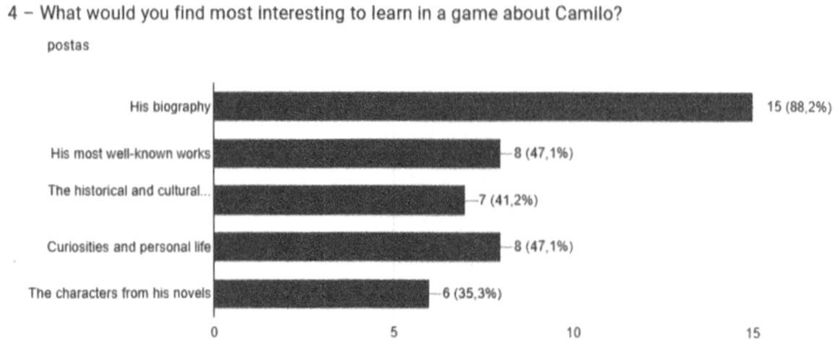

Fig. 4. Most interesting topics to learn in a game about Camilo Castelo Branco

A branching dialogue system was implemented to allow players to make choices that influence the progression of the story. These interactions were crafted to reflect the emotional tone and historical context of Camilo's life, while maintaining accessibility for younger audiences. Characters such as Camilo himself, Teresa, Simão, and various Non-Player Characters (NPCs) were designed with distinct personalities and roles, contributing to a dynamic and engaging narrative flow.

The game includes missions inspired by literary scenes, such as locating Teresa in a convent or delivering secret letters to Simão, which mirror the dramatic tension found in *"Amor de Perdição"*. These quests were designed to blend educational content with gameplay mechanics, encouraging players to learn through exploration and decision-making.

Dialogues were written with attention to historical authenticity and emotional depth, incorporating quotes, references, and fictionalized exchanges that evoke the spirit of Camilo's writing. Optional conversations with secondary characters enrich the narrative world and offer additional insights into the cultural and social context of 19th-century Portugal.

Overall, the narrative design serves as a bridge between literature and interactivity, transforming static historical content into a living experience. It reinforces the educational goals of the project while providing players with agency and emotional engagement.

4.3 Cultural Impact

The development of an educational game centered on Camilo Castelo Branco represents a meaningful contribution to the promotion of Portuguese cultural heritage through digital media. By transforming literary content into an interactive experience, the project bridges the gap between traditional education and contemporary digital engagement, offering a novel approach to cultural dissemination.

Camilo Castelo Branco is a central figure in Portuguese literature, known for his prolific output and emotionally charged narratives. However, his works are often perceived as distant or inaccessible by younger audiences. This game seeks to revitalize interest in Camilo's legacy by presenting his biography and literary themes in a format that resonates with modern learners. Through immersive storytelling, interactive dialogues, and exploratory gameplay, players are invited to engage with historical content in a way that is both educational and entertaining.

The project also contributes to the broader mission of public institutions such as Maia's Public Library, which aims to foster cultural literacy and community engagement. By integrating the game into the library's educational offerings, the initiative supports informal learning and encourages visitors to explore literature beyond traditional formats. The inclusion of real-world locations, such as a virtual recreation of the library itself, further strengthens the connection between digital and physical cultural spaces.

Moreover, the game aligns with national efforts to celebrate the bicentennial of Camilo Castelo Branco's birth (Fig. 5 shows his Biography), providing a timely and relevant resource for cultural programming. It demonstrates how multimedia tools can be leveraged to honor historical figures and make their stories accessible to new generations. The project serves as a model for how technology can be used to preserve and promote cultural identity, reinforcing the value of serious games in heritage education.

Fig. 5. Biography and cover of a book written by Camilo Castelo Branco

4.4 Technical Development

The game was built using Unity, with 3D models created in Blender and 2D assets designed in Photoshop. The development included:

- Level design: Three main environments were created—a virtual recreation of Maia's Public Library, an exterior cityscape, and two literary-inspired settings based on *"Amor de Perdição"* (respectively see Fig. 6, Fig. 7, Fig. 8 and Fig. 9). In addition the gameplay can be seen here: https://drive.google.com/file/d/1MiA6sq-vbiuFVKx_YTW4-GF3fjkmXcFi/view?usp=share_link.
- Programming: Custom scripts were written to handle player movement, item collection, dialogue interactions, and quiz mechanics.
- Audio integration: Background music, ambient sounds, and voice effects were added to enhance immersion.

Fig. 6. Virtual recreation of Maia's Public Library

Fig. 7. Exterior cityscape

Fig. 8. "Amor de Perdição" Story Scene

Fig. 9. "Amor de Perdição" Story Scene 2

4.5 User Experience and Accessibility

Designing an educational game for a diverse audience requires careful attention to usability and accessibility. Throughout the development process, several design choices were made to ensure that the game could be intuitively navigated by users with varying levels of digital literacy and gaming experience.

The interface was structured around simple visual hierarchies, with menus and options presented in a simplified layout (see Fig. 10). Interactive elements such as buttons, dialogue panels, and quiz prompts were designed with high contrast and readable fonts to enhance visibility. A dedicated instructions page (see Fig. 11) was included to explain game mechanics and controls, allowing users to familiarize themselves with the gameplay before engaging with the narrative.

Fig. 10. Main menu

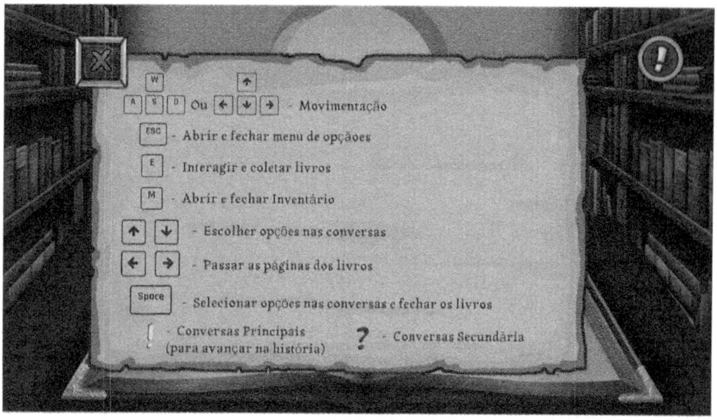

Fig. 11. Instructions manual

Customizable sensorial features were also considered during development based on user feedback. As can be seen in Fig. 12, camera sensitivity could be adjusted via the options menu, enabling smoother navigation for players with different preferences or motor abilities. Audio settings allow users to control background music and sound effects independently, supporting a more personalized experience. The game was tested informally with users of different age groups, and feedback led to refinements in menu structure, interaction flow, and visual aesthetics.

These design decisions reflect a commitment to inclusive game development, ensuring that the educational content is not only engaging but also accessible to a broad audience. Future iterations of the game could benefit from formal usability testing and the integration of additional accessibility standards, such as text-to-speech support or alternative input methods.

Fig. 12. Options menu

Fig. 13. Dialogue screen

4.6 Iteration and Feedback

Although formal usability testing was not conducted due to time constraints, informal feedback was collected from library staff, peers, and friends. This input led to several refinements:

•Simplification of interface elements for better navigation (such as reflected in the dialogue screen in Fig. 13).

•Adjustment of difficulty levels in quizzes and puzzles.

•Enhancement of narrative detail and historical accuracy in dialogues.

4.7 Documentation and Reflection

Throughout the internship, detailed documentation was maintained, including weekly activity logs, technical notes, and reflective analysis. A narrative script was drafted to guide the storytelling structure, and code snippets were annotated to explain key functionalities. These materials were compiled into the final GDD and served as the foundation for this scientific article.

5 Conclusion

The development of an educational game centered on Camilo Castelo Branco intended to represent a meaningful intersection between cultural heritage and digital media. Conducted during a curricular internship at Maia's Public Library, the project aimed to create an engaging and pedagogically valuable experience for young users, using interactive storytelling and game mechanics to promote literary awareness.

Throughout the development process, key principles of educational game design were applied, including narrative coherence, age-appropriate content, and iterative refinement based on stakeholder feedback. The project included participatory and responsive design practices that contribute to a more accessible and engaging final prototype, which tries to explore the potential of serious games as tools for cultural education in public institutions. It offers a playful yet informative approach to learning, capable of capturing the interest of younger audiences while preserving the richness of Portuguese literary history. Nevertheless, some limitations were identified, namely the inability to follow a fully structured approach around UCD or Design Thinking due to time constraints. Thus, future research could include structured usability testing, broader audience engagement, and the integration of accessibility features to enhance inclusivity. This would enable achieving the intended replicable model for other literary works.

This project not only fulfilled the academic requirements of the internship but also contributed to the broader discourse on the role of digital media in education. It highlights the value of combining technical skills with cultural sensitivity and sets the stage for future initiatives that leverage game-based learning to promote heritage and literacy.

References

1. Backlund, P., Hendrix, M.: Educational games – are they worth the effort? A literature survey of the effectiveness of serious games. In: 2013 5th International Conference on Games and Virtual Worlds for Serious Applications (VS-GAMES), pp. 1–8 (2013)
2. Clark, D.B., Tanner-Smith, E.E., Killingsworth, S.S.: Digital games, design, and learning: a systematic review and meta-analysis. Rev. Educ. Res. **86**(1), 79–122 (2016)
3. Azevedo, L., Costa, R., Pereira, E., Carreira, R.: Senior-centered cognitive training serious game design. In: Gaspar, P.M., Cueva Lovelle, J.M., Mentenegro-Marín, C., Guarda, T. (eds.) Health Technologies and Demographic Challenges. ICDTHT 2025. Springer Proceedings in Business and Economics, pp 45–54. Springer, Cham (2025). https://doi.org/10.1007/978-3-031-94901-2_4
4. Wouters, P., van Nimwegen, C., van Oostendorp, H., van der Spek, E.D.: A meta-analysis of the cognitive and motivational effects of serious games. J. Educ. Psychol. **105**(2), 249–265 (2013)
5. Brown, T., et al.: Design thinking. Harvard Bus. Rev. **86**(6) (2008)
6. Kyaw, B.M., et al.: Virtual reality for health professions education: systematic review and meta-analysis by the Digital Health Education Collaboration. J. Med. Internet Res. **21**(1), e12959 (2019)
7. Anderson, E.F., McLoughlin, L., Liarokapis, F., Peters, C., Petridis, P., De Freitas, S.: Serious games in cultural heritage. In: Proceedings of the 10th International Symposium on Virtual Reality, Archaeology and Cultural Heritage, pp. 29–48 (2010)

8. Mortara, M., Catalano, C.E., Bellotti, F., Fiucci, G., Houry-Panchetti, M., Petridis, P.: Learning cultural heritage by serious games. J. Cult. Herit. **15**(3), 318–325 (2014)
9. Bekele, M.K., Pierdicca, R., Frontoni, E., Malinverni, E.S., Gain, J.: A survey of augmented, virtual, and mixed reality for cultural heritage. J. Comput. Cult. Herit. **11**(2), 1–36 (2018)
10. Marques, B., Faria, J., Silva, F.: Serious games for cultural heritage: a review of trends and challenges. Digital Appl. Archaeol. Cult. Herit. **28**, e00337 (2023)
11. Lopez-Menchero Bendicho, V.M., Grande, A., Gaitatzes, A.: Serious games and gamified experiences for cultural heritage: a systematic review. Virtual Archaeol. Rev. **15**(30), 1–16 (2024)
12. Seif El-Nasr, M., Carstensdottir, E., John, M.: Designing Serious Games. MIT Press (2026). ISBN: 9780262049986. https://mitpress.mit.edu/9780262049986/designing-serious-games/
13. Zhang, Y., Chen, J.: Using design thinking in educational game design: a case study of pre-service teacher experience. In Blended Learning: Re-thinking and Re-defining the Learning Process, pp. 253–263. Springer, Heidelberg (2021). https://doi.org/10.1007/978-3-030-80504-3 21
14. Li, M., Ma, S., Shi, Y.: Examining the effectiveness of gamification as a tool promoting teaching and learning in educational settings: a meta-analysis. Front. Psychol. **14**, 1253549 (2023). https://doi.org/10.3389/fpsyg.2023.1253549
15. Huang, R., et al.: The impact of gamification in educational settings on student learning outcomes: a meta-analysis. Educ. Tech Res. Dev. **68**(4), 1875–1901 (2020). https://doi.org/10.1007/s11423-020-09807-z
16. Oliveira, W., Dantas Scaico, P., Hamari, J., Li, Z., Shi, L.: The effects of gamification on students' flow experience. J. Comput. Assist. Learn. **41**(5), e70120 (2025). https://doi.org/10.1111/jcal.70120

Accessibility, Inclusion, and Human-Centered Design

AI-Generated Audio Descriptions: An Empirical Evaluation with Blind and Visually Impaired Users

D. Alves Araújo(✉)

Faculty of Fine Arts and Faculty of Engineering, University of Porto, Porto, Portugal
aj@alvesjunior.com

Abstract. Smartphone apps now give blind and visually impaired (BVI) users quick access to AI tools that generate audio descriptions of objects, photos, and artworks (Lavric et al., 2024). Yet these outputs often stray from recommended guidelines and can include hallucinated details. To test their reliability, a master prompt referencing a description standard was submitted to six popular chatbots, and the results were voiced in European Portuguese with Google AI Studio. Thirteen descriptions were created for two works: Van Gogh's The Starry Night, compared against MoMA's expert version (*The Starry Night, MoMA*, n.d.), and a newly designed image inspired by H.G. Wells's The Time Machine. Twenty-five BVI participants evaluated the recordings in three sessions with varied exposure orders. While some chatbot descriptions were clear and useful, listeners also noted redundancy, unnatural translations, and factual errors. The results show both the potential of AI to scale description production and the risks of inaccuracy without human oversight.

Keywords: Audio Description · Artificial Intelligence · Blind and Visually Impaired

1 Introduction

Audio description (AD) enables BVI audiences to access visual culture by translating images into spoken language. Beyond film and television, museums and galleries increasingly rely on AD to broaden participation in the arts. As Josélia Neves argues, multi-sensory approaches are central to describing artworks in ways that go beyond simple visual transcription, requiring sensitivity to language, structure, and audience diversity (Neves 2012, n.d.). Yet producing high-quality AD remains labor-intensive and dependent on trained specialists. In parallel, large language models (LLMs) have become widely available through mobile applications, enabling BVI users to instantly generate descriptions of photographs, products, and artworks. These tools promise scalability but also raise concerns: recent research shows that AI models can engage in "scheming," producing misleading or inaccurate outputs that undermine reliability (OpenAI, 2025) and reports from advocacy organizations stress that automated solutions must be tested against accessibility standards before adoption (RNIB, 2023, n.d.). To date,

R. Baptista et al. (Eds.): VJ 2025, CCIS 2988, pp. 83–88, 2027.
https://doi.org/10.1007/978-3-032-31642-4_7

however, little empirical evidence exists on how AI-generated AD compares with expert practice from the perspective of end-users. This study contributes to filling that gap by systematically evaluating AI-generated descriptions with BVI participants. Using both quantitative ratings and qualitative feedback, the analysis examines clarity, accuracy, informativeness, engagement, and emotional resonance, while also considering contextual factors such as exposure order and audio duration. By combining numerical data with user insights, the study provides an evidence-based perspective on the potential and risks of AI-generated AD in cultural accessibility.

2 Methodology

2.1 Participants

Twenty-five adults participated, recruited through ACAPO, Portuguese Association of the Blind and Partially Sighted: 15 self-identified as blind or with significant vision loss, and 10 as low-vision or partially sighted (ACAPO, 2025). Ages ranged from 26 to 78 years (mean = 51.2, SD = 15.4). Demographic information included gender, age band, prior AD experience, and vision status.

2.2 Materials and Procedure

Two artworks anchored the study. Vincent Van Gogh's "The Starry Night" (1889) provided a known reference point (Brown, 2019), a Post-Impressionist masterpiece most AI systems would recognize from their training data (Fig. 1).

Fig. 1. The Starry Night by Vincent Van Gogh

The second image was created specifically for this study using Sora AI: a hyperrealistic photograph depicting a scene from H.G. Wells's The Time Machine (2025).

This stimulus allowed us to test whether AI could handle previously unseen content. Six AI systems were tested: three premium services (ChatGPT Pro 4.0, Claude Pro Opus 4, Gemini 2.5 Pro) and three free alternatives (DeepSeek, Perplexity, Qwen). Each received an identical master prompt incorporating recommended standard guidelines. Each AI generated descriptions for both artworks using its optimized prompts. The resulting descriptions were converted to European Portuguese using Google AI Studio's text-to-speech (Google AI Studio, n.d.), maintaining consistency in voice and delivery across all conditions (Fig. 2).

Fig. 2. The Time Machine by D. Alves Araújo and Sora AI.

2.3 Exposure Order

Participants were assigned to one of three blocks:

- Block A (n = 8): Claude – Starry Night (09:49); Claude – Time Machine (10:12); **Break**; MoMA – Starry Night (05:05).
- Block B (n = 9): Perplexity – Starry Night (06:00); Gemini – Time Machine (06:25); MoMA – Starry Night; **Break**; Perplexity – Time Machine (04:27); Gemini – Starry Night (06:00).
- Block C (n = 8): ChatGPT – Time Machine (02:49); DeepSeek – Starry Night (03:30); MoMA – Starry Night; Qwen – Time Machine (03:27); **Break**; ChatGPT – Starry Night (02:41); DeepSeek – Time Machine (02:58); Qwen – Starry Night (03:59).

2.4 Measures

After each description, participants rated five dimensions on a 1–5 Likert scale: clarity, accuracy, informativeness, engagement, and emotional resonance. A composite score was calculated as the mean across these items. Open-ended comments were also collected. Descriptive statistics were computed, with Welch's t-tests (Bobbitt, 2019) applied for group comparisons. Qualitative data from open comments were thematically analyzed to contextualize quantitative results.

3 Results

3.1 Quantitative Findings

The numbers paint a clear hierarchy, but the story they tell is more complex than simple rankings suggest. MoMA's expert description achieved 4.04/5 overall, establishing the quality benchmark. Among AI systems, Gemini led with 3.56, performing consistently across both artworks. Claude (3.44) and Perplexity (3.42) formed a middle tier, while ChatGPT (3.31) and Qwen (3.19) showed greater variability. DeepSeek's 2.69 average disguises a more dramatic story, acceptable performance for "The Starry Night" (3.63), but catastrophic failure with "The Time Machine" (1.75). The engagement dimension exposed AI's greatest weakness. While clarity and informativeness scores clustered around 3.5, engagement consistently lagged. MoMA achieved 3.88; no AI system exceeded 3.30. This gap proved decisive; preference scores correlated most strongly with engagement ($r = 0.82$, $p < .001$), not accuracy or completeness (Tables 1 and 2).

Table 1. Mean Ratings by Description Source (1–5 scale)

Source	Clarity	Objectivity	Informativeness	Engagement	Preference	Overall Mean
MoMA	4.04	4.12	4.20	3.88	4.00	4.04
Gemini	3.61	3.73	3.82	3.30	3.36	3.56
Claude	3.50	3.44	3.72	3.22	3.33	3.44
Perplexity	3.52	3.48	3.64	3.18	3.30	3.42
ChatGPT	3.31	3.44	3.50	3.06	3.25	3.31
Qwen	3.25	3.31	3.44	2.88	3.06	3.19
DeepSeek	2.88	2.81	2.69	2.44	2.63	2.69

Table 2. Comparative Performance Across Artworks

Chatbots	Starry Night Mean	Time Machine Mean	Difference
ChatGPT	3.50	3.13	−0.37
Claude	3.61	3.28	−0.33
DeepSeek	3.63	1.75	−1.88
Gemini	3.59	3.53	−0.06
Perplexity	3.47	3.38	−0.09
Qwen	3.38	3.00	−0.38

3.2 Qualitative Insights

Findings show that AI-generated ADs can perform comparably to expert descriptions, but their reception depends heavily on presentation. The combination of quantitative and qualitative evidence suggests three main conclusions:

1. AI Parity with Experts: Aggregated AI systems matched MoMA's expert AD on clarity and informativeness. Participant praise for Perplexity and Gemini underlines AI's ability to produce accessible, structured outputs when concise.
2. Order and Context Effects: Ratings of MoMA's AD shifted dramatically across blocks, despite identical content. Qualitative remarks confirmed that prior exposure and fatigue altered perception: listeners judged later descriptions against what they had already heard.
3. Length and Style Balance: Longer descriptions, especially Claude's, were consistently criticized as dense and overwhelming. Participants recommended focusing on visual details over historical context. Conversely, some welcomed contextual notes (e.g., Van Gogh's health), showing a tension between brevity and narrative depth.
4. Divergent Expectations for Emotion: Comments revealed no consensus on emotional tone. While some valued poetic engagement, others found it distracting. This divergence highlights the need for customizable AD outputs, allowing users to select between more factual or expressive narration.

3.3 Limitations

- Language Specificity: Testing only in Portuguese may not reflect performance in other languages.
- Artwork Sample: Two artworks cannot represent the full diversity of visual art.
- Delivery Method: TTS may have influenced perception independent of description quality.
- Temporal Factors: AI capabilities evolve rapidly; results reflect a specific moment in technological development.
- Participant Pool: Regional recruitment may not represent global diversity in preferences.

4 Conclusion

The promise of AI-generated audio description remains partially unfulfilled. Current technology can assist but not replace human expertise in creating meaningful cultural access. The gap between Gemini's 3.56 and MoMA's 4.04 might seem small on a five-point scale, but it represents the difference between adequate information transfer and genuine cultural participation. The BVI participants in this study didn't just evaluate descriptions; they illuminated what meaningful access requires. Their feedback reminds us that audio description is more than a technical challenge; it's a human service requiring empathy, cultural awareness, and narrative skill. AI can handle the technical aspects; humans must supply the humanity. As these tools proliferate through consumer apps, the stakes increase. BVI users are already encountering AI descriptions daily, often without knowing their source or accuracy. This study suggests we need standards, oversight, and continuous dialogue between developers, describers, and users. The goal isn't to gate-keep technology but to ensure it serves rather than misleads those who depend on it. Future work: Larger, counterbalanced studies with matched durations are needed to disentangle length from style effects. Additional expert baselines across artworks would strengthen comparisons. Adaptive AD systems, where users can toggle between concise, detailed, or emotive versions, may address divergent preferences while ensuring inclusivity.

Acknowledgments. The author would like to express sincere gratitude to João Fernandes, President of ACAPO, and to all the volunteers whose participation and valuable insights were fundamental to the empirical evaluation of this study.

References

Bobbitt, Z.: Welch's t-test: When to Use it + Examples. Statology (2019). https://www.statology.org/welchs-t-test/

Brown, F.: 10 most famous paintings. CNN (2019). https://www.cnn.com/style/article/most-famous-paintings

Google AI Studio. (n.d.). Accessed 30 Sept 2025. https://aistudio.google.com/

Lavric, A., Beguni, C., Zadobrischi, E., Căilean, A.-M., Avătămăniței, S.-A.: A comprehensive survey on emerging assistive technologies for visually impaired persons: lighting the path with visible light communications and artificial intelligence innovations. Sensors (Basel, Switzerland) **24**(15), 4834 (2024). https://doi.org/10.3390/s24154834

Neves 2012. (n.d.). Accessed 23 Sept 2025. https://www.researchgate.net/publication/271099098_Multi-sensory_approaches_to_audio_describing_the_visual_arts

OpenAI. Accessed 15 Sept 2025. https://openai.com/index/detecting-and-reducing-scheming-in-ai-models/

RNIB, 2023. (n.d.). RNIB. Accessed 23 Sept 2025. https://www.rnib.org.uk/professionals/research-and-data/reports-and-insight/exploring-ai-generated-audio-description-can-emerging-technologies-help-expand-access-to-broadcast-media/

The Starry Night, MoMA. (n.d.). The Museum of Modern Art. Accessed 23 Sept 2025. https://www.moma.org/audio/playlist/3/4289

An Accessible Sketch-Based Framework for 3D Plant Model Generation

Ana Martins, Anabela Marto, Rita Ascenso, Roberto Ribeiro(✉), Nuno Rodrigues, and Alexandrino Gonçalves

Computer Science and Communication Research Centre, School of Technology and Management, Polytechnic University of Leiria, 2411-901 Leiria, Portugal
roberto.ribeiro@ipleiria.pt

Abstract. Designing unique and accurate 3D plant models is often a complex task, typically requiring expert tools and time-consuming manual work. This work explores a sketch-based modelling approach that allows users to create diverse plant structures through intuitive 2D input, without the need for external hardware or sensors. This can be particularly useful in scenarios where specific or fictional plants must be represented and no pre-existing models are available. Drawing inspiration from both single-sketch and multi-sketch systems, we propose a hybrid workflow that supports the generation of branches and leaves with minimal constraints on plant type. Our system interprets user-drawn strokes to guide a structured modelling pipeline, including convex hull construction, swept surface branch modelling, and B-spline-based leaf generation. Additional features such as normal maps, level-of-detail (LoD) control, and 3D model variations are included to enhance visual fidelity and creative possibilities. The user interface was designed to reflect this workflow, focusing on clarity and control. This article outlines the conceptual design of the system and sets the stage for its future implementation and evaluation.

Keywords: Sketch to 3D · Blender · 3D Plant Modelling · 3D Generation · 2D to 3D

1 Introduction

The creation of unique and accurate 3D plant models remains challenging in the field of computer graphics, primarily due to the structural complexity of plants and the manual effort involved. As a result, publicly available plant models are scarce and often reused across virtual environments. The capacity to generate three-dimensional plant models from straightforward inputs, such as sketches or photographs, without the necessity for specialised hardware, presents a more inclusive and innovative alternative.

The present study investigates the use of sketch-based modelling for the intuitive definition of plant structures, building on previous single- and multi-sketch techniques [1–3]. It proposes a framework with a streamlined interface and

R. Baptista et al. (Eds.): VJ 2025, CCIS 2988, pp. 89–100, 2027.
https://doi.org/10.1007/978-3-032-31642-4_8

features such as normal maps, level-of-detail control, and automatic generation of multiple variants to enhance creative flexibility.

The framework targets creators of virtual environments who require custom or fictional plant species, offering a practical tool for design and prototyping. Planned user testing with at forty participants will assess usability via the System Usability Scale (SUS) and efficiency through task completion times.

The remainder of this paper is organized as follows: Sect. 2 reviews existing plant generation approaches. Section 3 introduces the proposed framework and workflows. Section 4 details the planned technologies and development steps, and Sect. 5 concludes with future work.

2 Related Work

Three-dimensional plant modelling is a growing research area with applications in agriculture [4], plant monitoring [5,6], scientific visualization [7], landscape design [8–10], and immersive virtual environments [11]. Existing methods include rule-based systems [12,13], visual-based techniques using photographs or sketches, and sensor-enhanced approaches [14–18]. A recent systematic review [19] summarizes these techniques, and software tools such as SpeedTree, xFrog, TheGrove3D, and TreeIt further support efficient, botanically informed 3D plant creation.

2.1 Systematic Review

Following the Preferred Reporting Items for Systematic Reviews and Meta-Analyses (PRISMA) guidelines, this study conducted a focused systematic review of methods that generate 3D plant models solely from photographs or sketches, excluding techniques that require specialised hardware or sensors.

Searches were carried out in Web of Science, Scopus, Springer, and IEEE Xplorer databases, using a robust search key developed through an initial exploratory phase. The review included 21 studies, from which two main approaches were identified: tree generation from photographs and sketch-based modelling.

Photographic tree generation predominated (1995–2021) [20–31], with three studies also incorporating sketch inputs. These works mainly aimed to reconstruct real tree structures, employing 2D-to-3D skeletonization pipelines with modular separation of foliage and branches, and often assessed visual realism, though formal evaluation metrics were uncommon. Sketch-based modelling methods (2005–2008) [1–3] followed a modelling-oriented workflow with pre-modelling steps, user interaction, and user interface (UI) support, producing 3D meshes while lacking automation, evaluation metrics, or system performance reporting. Together, these categories highlight a gap between mature photographic reconstruction techniques and earlier, less automated sketch-based approaches.

2.2 Sketch-Based Modelling Approaches

Aligned with the focus of this work, we conducted a detailed analysis of sketch-based modelling approaches, represented by only three studies published between 2005 and 2008. This small and dated body of research reveals a clear gap in recent developments, suggesting that freehand sketch-based techniques without the use of external sensors or tools remain largely under-explored.

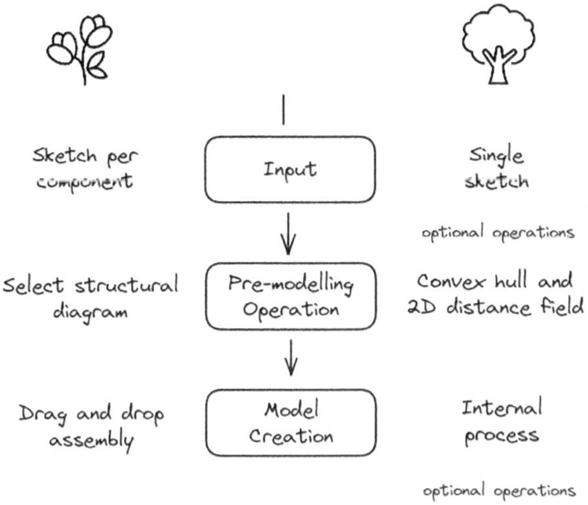

Fig. 1. Comparison of the process steps identified in each approach.

We carried out an initial analysis of the modelling process, illustrated in Fig. 1, which allowed us to identify commonalities in the workflow and categorize the different approaches into two main types:

- **Multi-sketch-based flower modelling** [1,2]: This approach uses an iterative process, with one sketch per flower component. Users select structural diagrams and manually assemble the model through drag-and-drop operations, allowing flexibility through multiple user-drawn inputs. It provides a strong basis for creating accurate flower models and was successfully tested with an executable version (see Fig. 2), while botanical terminology in the interface enhances intuitiveness. However, the interface requires prior familiarity, as the documentation is non-English and navigation relies heavily on icons.
- **Single-sketch-based tree modelling** [3]: This method starts with a single sketch of the entire tree, including branches and leaves, and automatically generates the 3D model. Pre-modelling operations, such as convex hull construction and 2D distance field computation, support the process, with optional editing providing additional flexibility. The workflow is highly automated, reducing user interactions, and botanical terminology helps enhance

realism, for example by maximizing the distance between branches. On the downside, implementation details for leaf generation are limited, described only as a "loop stroke".

(a) Target flower (b) Modelled Flower

Fig. 2. Flower modelling results using the executable from [1].

To better understand the differences between approaches, we conducted a detailed analysis of their implementation strategies and technologies (summarized in Table 1). Although we contacted the original authors for source code to gain further insights, no responses were received. Based on the available information, the modelling process generally involves shaping individual plant components before assembling the complete model. In the multi-sketch approach, our analysis focused on flower components (sepals, petals, and stems) due to their structural similarity to branches and leaves, aligning with the goal of developing generalized plant models.

It is noteworthy that the earliest multi-sketch method [1] provided a foundational basis for subsequent studies. The single-sketch technique [3] adapted its stem modulation method to shape branch curves, while a subsequent multi-sketch study [2] extended the framework with a merging algorithm for generating solid, waterproof models.

3 Framework Design

The proposed framework is designed to generate 3D plant models directly from freehand sketches provided by the user, without the need for supplementary input from devices such as sensors. Building on the comparative analysis of existing approaches, it selectively integrates features from prior methods to offer a flexible, intuitive, and generalizable modelling solution. To illustrate its functionality, we present two distinct usage scenarios and detail the corresponding design workflows.

Table 1. Implementation strategies and technologies used in the analysed approaches. Operations marked with an asterisk (*) are optional.

Process Step	[1] Multiple Sketch (07/2005)	[2] Multiple Sketch (04/2008)	[3] Single Sketch (08/2007)
Drawing Method	Flower components (parts)	Flower components (parts)	Tree structure (whole)
Drawing Operation(s)*	—	—	• Cut & erase stroke/branches • Define detailed shape of branches
Pre-Components Modelling Operation	—	—	3D convex hull construction
Components Modelling Operation(s)	• Petal & sepal: B-spline surface • Stem: energy-minimization curve reconstruction	• Petal & sepal: B-spline surface • Stem: energy-minimization curve reconstruction	• Child branch: length, angle and 2D distance field • Branch curves: depth modulation
Pre-Model Modelling Operation	Structural diagram choice	Structural diagram choice	—
Model Modelling Operation	Flower assemble (drag & drop) and fine-tune	Flower assemble (drag & drop), fine-tune and merging algorithm	Merge the two 3D trees, rotating one by 90°
Post-Modelling Operation(s)*	—	—	• Branch multiplication & propagation • Leaf arrangement • Reproduce 3D model from overall sketching

3.1 Initial Workflow

Building on the approaches discussed in Sect. 2.2, as well as the comparative overview in Fig. 1 and Table 1, we combined elements from both methodologies to propose a generalized and efficient workflow from the initial sketch to the generation of a 3D plant model. Users begin by creating a 2D sketch of the whole plant [3], while incorporating leaf generation alongside structural modelling [1,2]. Once the sketch is complete, the model can be generated with a single button click [3]. To enhance control and realism, leaf curvature can also be specified [1].

3.2 Use-Case Scenarios

All analysed approaches operate as stand-alone applications. In contrast, this work emphasizes usability and integration with modern 3D modelling environments, addressing the limitations of outdated, isolated tools. Blender was selected as a potential integration scenario due to its open-source nature, widespread adoption, and continuous enhancement of modelling features, which can handle post-modelling operations such as branch scaling, rotation, and texture assignment through its native tools. In comparison, the stand-alone scenario would require the implementation of these steps within the application itself.

3.3 UI Prototypes

Based on the proposed workflow and usage scenarios, we designed an initial user interface (UI) prototype for the two scenarios. Taking inspiration from previous approaches involving the handling of components through multiple panels [1,2], we decided to include a panel for each component in our UI.

Branch Panel. The Branch panel (see Fig. 3) allows users to sketch the overall branch structure, with brush size controlling branch thickness. Each new stroke is automatically connected to the existing structure and saved in real time, following the single-sketch approach [3].

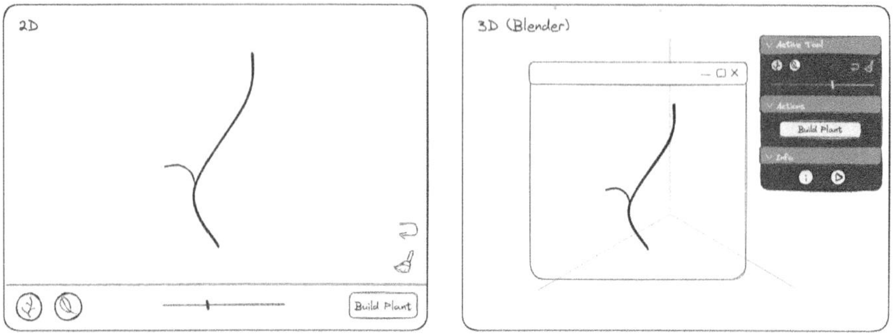

(a) Stand-alone application (b) Blender add-on

Fig. 3. Branch panel design.

Leaf Panel. The Leaf panel (see Fig. 4) enables users to draw individual leaf strokes and define the required curvature. To capture additional modelling information and increase flexibility, the panel includes a checkbox to indicate if the leaf is being viewed from the side or front and a selection box titled "# Leaves Added" to specify if a single or multiple leaves are being added. Once the parameters have been set, the leaf data can be stored by clicking the "Save" button.

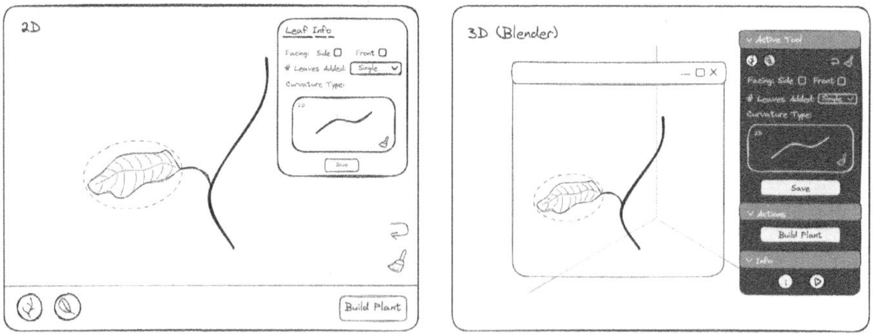

(a) Stand-alone application (b) Blender add-on

Fig. 4. Leaf panel design.

Additional Features. To address the usability limitations identified in the multi-sketch executable [1], two additional UI elements have been added: an information button ('i'), which provides a step-by-step guide to the modelling process, and a video button (an arrow icon), which plays a tutorial demonstrating how to use the application. The framework also supports optional operations, including undoing a stroke using the *Ctrl+Z* shortcut or the left-looping arrow button, and erasing all strokes with a button resembling a broom.

4 Framework Implementation

Based on the described scenarios and workflow, the Blender add-on approach was chosen for its broad usability and to leverage Blender's built-in 3D modelling tools, and the project will be implemented in Python, the language used for Blender add-ons.

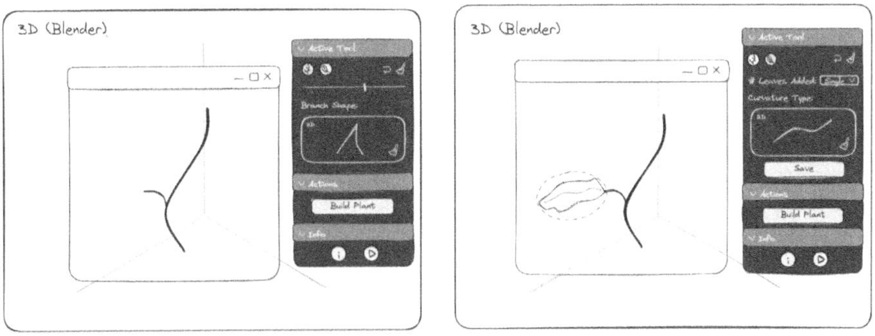

(a) Branch panel design (b) Leaf panel design

Fig. 5. Blender add-on revised design for implementation.

We selected the most suitable technologies from those discussed in Sect. 2.2 and adapted the UI design and workflow steps accordingly. The updated interface, shown in Fig. 5, introduces an optional feature in the "Branch" panel for drawing the branch shape, inspired by [3]. In the "Leaf" panel, the frontal/side checkbox was removed, as it is incompatible with the chosen leaf generation method, and each leaf is now represented by three strokes instead of an arbitrary number.

4.1 Detailed Workflow

The following steps outline the detailed workflow for the planned implementation, highlighting the technology choices and approach of each stage. For each stage, we explain the rationale behind the chosen methods and tools, and how these contribute to the modelling process.

1. **Initial Sketch** [1–3]
   The process begins with the user drawing a complete 2D sketch representing the overall structure of the plant, including both branches and leaves.
2. **Start Model Generation** [3]
   The initiation of the internal process of converting a sketch into a model is prompted by the selection of the *"Build Plant"* button.
3. **Convex Hull Construction** [3]
   Inspired by the pre-modelling step in [3], a 2D convex hull is first generated from the user's sketch, followed by the creation of a 3D convex hull to define the spatial boundary of the plant structure.
4. **Trunk and Main Branches Projection** [3]
   The initial strokes are projected onto a base plane at a fixed depth ($y = 0$). A 2D distance field is then computed to maximise the spacing of branches within the 3D convex hull. After determining the new positions, the branches are projected from their start points to the updated end points, resulting in an evenly distributed, planar branch layout within the 3D space.
5. **Child Branch Projection** [3]
   For each child branch, the process involves:
   (a) Calculating branch length
   (b) Determining branching angle
   (c) Using a 2D distance field to infer the y-coordinate
   (d) Projecting the branch into 3D space
6. **Branches Modelling** [1,2]
   Although two of the reviewed studies used depth modulation with energy minimisation for modelling branch curves, the reference article describing this method was unavailable. Given the available development time, it was decided that swept surfaces, as proposed in [2], represented a more practical alternative. Each branch is defined by a 2D stroke and brush size, as well as an optional user-drawn shape, which enables variation in thickness and curvature across branches.
7. **Leaves Modelling** [1,2]
   As mentioned in Sect. 2.2, the multi-sketch method provides a more detailed modelling process for leaf components (sepals and petals). Consequently, its approach is considered more suitable for guiding the modelling process. Leaves are therefore generated using B-spline surfaces, guided by three user-drawn 2D strokes (two outer contours and one inner line), as well as the drawn curvature type. Although the multi-sketch approach allows for either two or three strokes (e.g. using only two for petals), as we are not modelling petals, our method always assumes three strokes. In cases where leaf positions overlap, we intend to determine their depth order in the final model based on the drawing sequence, with leaves drawn most recently rendered on top.
8. **Normal Maps**
   To enhance realism and reduce manual effort, a set of predefined normal map presets (such as bark and leaf textures) are available to users. These

maps may be generated using well-known tools like CrazyBump[1], xNormal[2], or ShaderMap[3].

9. **Level-of-Detail (LoD) Variations**
Implementing multiple levels of detail (LoD) is essential for balancing visual fidelity with computational performance, especially when dealing with large quantities of plant models. By offering adjustable LoDs, users can customize the complexity of each model to suit the specific needs of their target scenario. One notable tool for vegetation optimization is Simplygon[4], which offers features such as billboard cloud generation and has been integrated into Blender as an add-on. However, its use is limited by licensing, as it has not been freely available since January 2017. Given the choice of Blender add-on scenario, this framework can leverage Blender's built-in modifiers, such as Remesh and Decimate, to generate multiple LoD versions of the generated model.
10. **3D Model Variations**
Visually distinct variations of the final 3D plant model are created by making small adjustments to the saved generation parameters, offering users greater creative freedom and design flexibility.

Common exportable formats for 3D models, such as `.obj` and `.mtl`, which are also used in the approaches reviewed, ensure broad compatibility. However, since our framework is implemented as a Blender add-on, users do not need to handle exporting, as the generated models are immediately accessible within Blender.

4.2 User Tests

Following implementation, user testing will be conducted to evaluate the application's usability and efficiency. Efficiency will be measured by the time each participant takes to complete the tasks involved in modelling a full plant, while usability will be assessed using the 10-question System Usability Scale (SUS). Participants will also be asked to provide demographic information (e.g., age, gender, and background) to support further analysis of the results.

The tests will be administered via a Google Forms questionnaire, which will include the add-on installation zip file, instructions, the modelling tasks, the SUS questionnaire, and the demographic questions.

The participant group is planned to consist of 40 individuals, divided into four categories: 1) 10 non-artistic users with a mouse, 2) 10 non-artistic users with a pen tablet, 3) 10 artistic users with a pen tablet, and 4) 10 game development users with a pen tablet.

[1] http://www.crazybump.com/ (accessed July 18, 2025).
[2] https://xnormal.net/ (accessed July 18, 2025).
[3] https://shadermap.com/home/ (accessed July 18, 2025).
[4] https://www.simplygon.com/ (accessed July 18, 2025).

5 Conclusion and Future Work

This project introduces a sketch-based modelling framework designed as a Blender add-on, to simplify and enhance the creation of diverse 3D plant models. Unlike previous methods that focus on specific plant categories, the proposed framework is general and flexible, enabling users to design a wide range of plant structures through intuitive 2D sketches.

By integrating principles from both single- and multi-sketch techniques and incorporating swept-surface branches, B-spline-based leaf generation, and optional features such as normal maps, level-of-detail (LoD) control, and model variations, the system provides users with greater creative control. Its interface is designed to align closely with the modelling workflow, ensuring efficiency and ease of use.

This work establishes the foundation for a full implementation and subsequent user testing with at least ten participants to evaluate usability and efficiency. Future developments may extend the interface to support additional plant components, such as flowers and fruits, and integrate external libraries of premade assets to broaden creative possibilities.

Given the rapid progress of Artificial Intelligence (AI) in creative domains, incorporating AI-based methods offers several promising directions. Techniques such as AI-driven sketch recognition [32,33] could automatically classify strokes as branches or leaves, streamlining the workflow and reducing manual mode switching. AI could also assist in completing partial sketches and provide adaptive modelling suggestions based on user preferences. Furthermore, AI may enhance technical aspects of the pipeline, including automated generation of normal maps and dynamic LoD adjustment based on performance or contextual criteria.

Acknowledgments. This work was supported by national funds through the Portuguese Foundation for Science and Technology (FCT) under the project UID/4524/2025.

Disclosure of Interests. The authors declare they have no competing interests.

References

1. Ijiri, T., Owada, S., Okabe, M., Igarashi, T.: Floral diagrams and inflorescences: interactive flower modeling using botanical structural constraints. ACM Trans. Graph. **24**, 720–726 (2005)
2. Ding, Z., Xu, S.C., Ye, X.Z., Zhang, Y., Zhang, S.Y.: Flower solid modeling based on sketches. J. Zhejiang Univ., Sci., A **9**, 481–488 (2008)
3. Okabe, M., Owada, S., Igarashi, T.: Interactive design of botanical trees using freehand sketches and example-based editing. In: ACM SIGGRAPH 2007 Courses, pp. 26–es (2007)
4. Mitsanis, C., Hurst, W., Tekinerdogan, B.: A 3D functional plant modelling framework for agricultural digital twins. Comput. Electron. Agric. **218**, 108733 (2024)

5. Zhang, Y., Teng, P., Aono, M., Shimizu, Y., Hosoi, F., Omasa, K.: 3D monitoring for plant growth parameters in field with a single camerby multi-view approach. J. Agric. Meteorol. **74**, 129–139 (2018)
6. Paturkar, A., Sen Gupta, G., Bailey, D.: Plant trait measurement in 3D for growth monitoring. Plant Methods **18**, 59 (2022)
7. Lin, Y., Hyyppä, J.: Towards 3D basic theories of plant forms. Commun. Biol. **5**, 1–6 (2022)
8. Liu, P., Liu, Y., Xu, X.: Three-Dimensional Modeling Technology of Virtual Plant in Digital Landscape, pp. 146–149. Atlantis Press (2016)
9. Muhar, A.: Three-dimensional modelling and visualisation of vegetation for landscape simulation. Landsc. Urban Plan. **54**, 5–17 (2001)
10. Xu, D., Yang, X., Wang, C., Xi, X., Fan, G.: Three-dimensional reconstruction of forest scenes with tree-shrub-grass structure using airborne LiDAR point cloud. Forests **15**, 1627 (2024)
11. Hu, A., Yabuki, N., Fukuda, T.: Generating 4D plant models for virtual reality environments using the instant neural graphics primitives and stable diffusion model (2024)
12. Prusinkiewicz, P., Lindenmayer, A.: The Algorithmic Beauty of Plants. Springer, Cham (1990)
13. Lu, C., Deng, L., Fei, M.: An improved visualization modelling method of greenhouse tomato plants based on L-system, pp. 480–485 (2015)
14. Nguyen, T.T., Slaughter, D.C., Max, N., Maloof, J.N., Sinha, N.: Structured light-based 3D reconstruction system for plants. Sensors **15**, 18587–18612 (2015)
15. Bailey, B.N., Ochoa, M.H.: Semi-direct tree reconstruction using terrestrial LiDAR point cloud data. Remote Sens. Environ. **208**, 133–144 (2018)
16. Xie, D., et al.: Reconstruction of single tree with leaves based on terrestrial LiDAR point cloud data **10**, 686
17. Li, D., Xu, L., Tan, C., Goodman, E.D., Fu, D., Xin, L.: Digitization and visualization of greenhouse tomato plants in indoor environments. Sensors **15**, 4019–4051 (2015)
18. Liu, Y., Yuan, H., Zhao, X., Fan, C., Cheng, M.: Fast reconstruction method of three-dimension model based on dual RGB-D cameras for peanut plant **19**, 17 (2023)
19. Okura, F.: 3D modeling and reconstruction of plants and trees: a cross-cutting review across computer graphics, vision, and plant phenotyping. Breed. Sci. **72**, 31–47 (2022)
20. Zamuda, A., Brest, J., Boskovic, B., Zumer, V.: Differential evolution for parameterized procedural woody plant models reconstruction. Appl. Soft Comput. **11**, 4904–4912 (2011)
21. Lopez, L.D., Ding, Y., Yu, J.: Modeling complex unfoliaged trees from a sparse set of images. Comput. Graph. Forum **29**, 2075–2082 (2010)
22. Zamuda, A., Brest, J.: Vectorized procedural models for animated trees reconstruction using differential evolution. Inf. Sci. **278**, 1–21 (2014)
23. Neubert, B., Franken, T., Deussen, O.: Approximate image-based tree-modeling using particle flows. ACM Trans. Graph. **26**, 88–es (2007)
24. Yang, M., Sheng, B., Wu, E., Sun, H.: Multi-level tree branch modeling and animation. In: 11th IEEE International Conference on Computer-Aided Design and Computer Graphics, pp. 96–99 (2009)
25. Teng, C.H., Chen, Y.S.: Image-based tree modeling from a few images with very narrow viewing range. Vis. Comput. **25**, 297–307 (2009)

26. Kuwahara, N., Shiwa, S., Kishino, F.: Three-dimensional tree shape reconstruction from multiviewpoint images based on fractal geometry. In: Proceedings of SPIE - The International Society for Optical Engineering, vol. 2501, pp. 1267–1278 (1995)
27. Kim, J., Jeong, I.K.: Single image-based 3d tree and growth models reconstruction. ETRI J. **36**, 450–459 (2014)
28. Liu, Z., Wu, K., Guo, J., Wang, Y., Deussen, O., Cheng, Z.: Single image tree reconstruction via adversarial network. Graph. Models, **117** (2021)
29. Tan, P., Fang, T., Xiao, J., Zhao, P., Quan, L.: Single image tree modeling. ACM Trans. Graph. **27**, 1–7 (2008)
30. Liu, J., Zhang, X., Li, H., Dai, M.: Creation of tree models from freehand sketches by building 3d skeleton point cloud. In: Entertainment for Education. Digital Techniques and Systems, pp. 621–632 (2010)
31. Liu, J., Jiang, Z., Li, H., Zhang, X.: Easy modeling of realistic trees from freehand sketches. Front. Comp. Sci. **6**, 756–768 (2012)
32. Li, L., Zou, C., Zheng, Y., Qingkun, S., Fu, H., Tai, C.L.: Sketch-R2CNN: an attentive network for vector sketch recognition (2018)
33. Yu, Q., Yang, Y., Liu, F., Song, Y.Z., Xiang, T., Hospedales, T.M.: Sketch-a-net: a deep neural network that beats humans. Int. J. Comput. Vis. **122**, 411–425 (2017)

In-Game Behaviour Expression Using Dynamic Key Bindings

Samuel Gomes[1,2](✉), Carlos Martinho[1,2], and João Dias[2,3,4]

[1] Instituto Superior Técnico, Universidade de Lisboa, Lisbon, Portugal
{samuel.gomes,carlos.martinho}@tecnico.ulisboa.pt
[2] INESC-ID, Lisbon, Portugal
jmdias@ualg.pt
[3] Faculdade de Ciências e Tecnologia, Universidade do Algarve, Faro, Portugal
[4] CISCA, Faro, Portugal

Abstract. This paper introduces an innovative way of allowing the expression of different in-game behaviours, with the use of key bindings (assigning specific in-game actions to keyboard keys). As such, a word-matching game called *CrossAnt* was transformed into a two-player game, such that some levels require simultaneous input from both players (dependent) and other levels can be completed by each player independently (independent). Multiple dyads played the modified *CrossAnt* side-by-side during an interactive showcase, while discovering the actions needed to succeed. Responses from 22 players revealed that perceived cooperation prevailed and was higher in dependent levels, and that perceived independence was higher in independent levels for experienced players.

Keywords: Social Interaction · Game Mechanic · Key Binding

1 Introduction

Over the years, videogames evolved into a highly successful industry in the entertainment segment. This success is mainly driven by their interactivity and how easily they can shape experiences and convey messages [4,14]. The interactive nature of videogames leveraged their application on different research domains, including preferences and personality profiling [3,8], personalization [8,11], persuasion and behaviour change [1,5], and generation of feedback [2,10]. Despite such a widespread videogame research, the influence game mechanics can have on players remains an active research issue [4,9,12], critical for diverse gameplay and effective individualization [8].

In order to convey certain behaviours, game developers and researchers often use mechanics and rewards [6,13], e.g., scores, experience points, and unlocking mechanisms. As far as we know, this paper introduces a less explored but creative way of expressing player interaction, with the use of a dynamic *key bindings*

R. Baptista et al. (Eds.): VJ 2025, CCIS 2988, pp. 101–106, 2027.
https://doi.org/10.1007/978-3-032-31642-4_9

system in which in-game actions may require keyboard input from players individually or in conjunction. Thus, it approaches *how different in-game behaviours can be expressed from dynamically adjusting key bindings.*

Following this goal, a game called *CrossAnt* was modified so that it became a two-player game in which key bindings are generated for each level, allowing the integration of dependent and independent gameplay levels. The game was then used to evaluate how the different gameplay styles affected the player's perception of cooperation, competition, and independence.

2 Related Work

Wendel and Konert [14] comment how player interaction can be profiled as competitive, cooperative, or collaborative. In competitive games, players (or teams) play against each other; in cooperative games they build teams and either the whole team wins or loses; and in collaborative games, players are usually dependent on other players (who may or may not build a common team) and need to help each other, that is, collaborate, in order to advance in the game.

Games often express different behaviour dynamics through the use of mechanics ranging from scores to experience points, collectibles, item granting systems, resources, achievement systems, badges, player dossiers, feedback messages, plot animations and pictures, and unlocking mechanisms [6,13]. Oksanen and Hämäläinen [7] present cooperative/collaborative techniques like the use of shared space and objects between players, complementary actions (actions which can only be triggered by a group), and indirect actions (situations where some of the players have a task that requires other player's action). Aligned with these techniques [7], the present study applies a creative mechanic aimed at expressing different behaviour styles: using a dynamic *key bindings* system in which in-game actions may require keyboard input from players individually or in conjunction.

3 CrossAnt

This work draws from the modification of a single-player word-matching game called *CrossAnt*, created using *Unity*[1] game engine during the marathon *Global Game Jam*[2]. Functionalities were added to allow two players to interact concurrently (local multi-player). The modified version of the game is depicted in Fig. 1. In the considered *CrossAnt* version, each player serves a *Queen Ant* (elements in A) the food it requests (displayed in B) in a limited amount of time (displayed in the top C box). In order to get some food, players use coloured stamps positioned at the bottom right side of the screen to select the letters of each request in a rolling letter soup (element D). Crucially, a system was added to dynamically generate key combinations for controlling the in-game stamps at each level. The system has two settings: **independent** (each player can find

[1] https://unity.com/ (accessed 2026-02-09).

[2] https://globalgamejam.org/2018/games/crossant (accessed 2026-02-09).

the key combinations for the game stamps using their own keys) and **dependent** (some stamps require simultaneous input from the two players). Figure 2 presents examples of generated bindings.

The last player to complete a key combination and select a letter earns 50 points (see the bottom C box) if the letter is the next one of the request (displayed in B), and if not, both players lose a life (see the top C box). The game continuously generates new levels, i.e., words for players to complete, and, when 50 lives are lost, the game ends. Thus, the game has an interesting mixture of cooperative word completion with competitive scoring, while integrating a dynamic *key bindings* mechanic that is able to express independent and interdependent gameplay.

Fig. 1. Screenshot of the modified version of *Cross Ant*, where relevant game elements are labelled: *Queen Ants* (A); request balloon (B); game metrics including scores, remaining lives, and time left to complete the level (C); letter track (D).

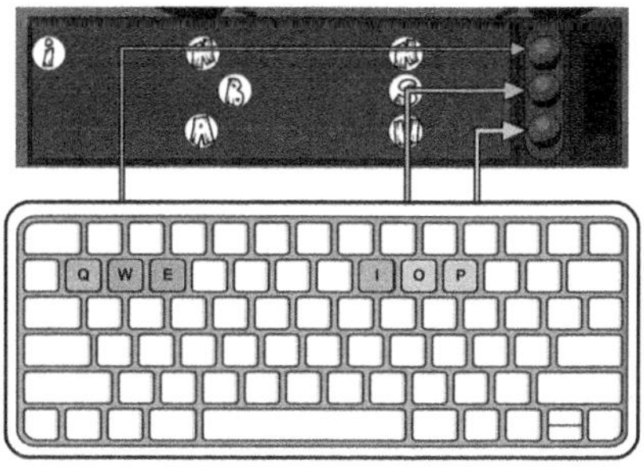

Fig. 2. Possible key bindings (represented with different colours). Assume that players use the keys {Q,W,E} and {I,O,P}. {W,E} and {O,P} are independent key combinations triggering the top and bottom stamps, respectively. {Q,I} is a dependent key combination triggering the middle stamp.

4 Evaluation

In order to assess the behaviour expression of independent and dependent key bindings, tests were conducted where several dyads played the game during an interactive showcase held at our university[3]. Overall, 22 valid questionnaires were obtained from participants who experienced both conditions.

Participants were asked to play a tutorial level to get familiarized with the game controls, and then informed they could play as many levels as they wanted. After playing each non-tutorial level, they were asked to rate their experience in

[3] https://tecnico.ulisboa.pt/pt/tag/mojo/ (accessed 2026-02-09).

a five-point Likert scale regarding how much they agreed with perceiving three behaviour types: *cooperation*; *competition*; and *behavioural independence.*

To analyse data, a factor *Key Binding Style* was considered, with values {*Independent, Dependent*}. Its influence was tested on participants' *cooperation*, *competition*, and *behavioural independence* ratings. Due to a reduced number of samples, (non-parametric) Wilcoxon Signed Ranks tests were performed. All data and statistical methods are available online[4].

The data distributions by *Key Binding Style* are plotted on Fig. 3. Because we expected that some distributions would vary to only one side, i.e., that the dependent key bindings would lead to higher *cooperation* ratings, and lower *behavioural independence* ratings, we considered one-tailed significance levels in these cases.

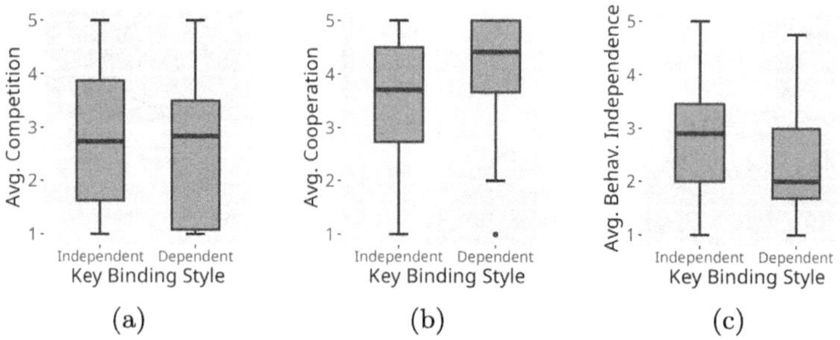

Fig. 3. Distributions of the players' average *competition* Fig. 3(a), *cooperation* Fig. 3(b), and *behavioural independence* Fig. 3(c) ratings for each *Key Binding Style.*

Indeed, the results indicate that, on average, participants perceived higher *cooperation* ($Z = -2.680, p = 0.003, r = 0.57$) and lower *behavioural independence* ($Z = -1.728, p = 0.043, r = 0.37$) when using the dependent bindings. Conversely, perceived *competition* did not change significantly between key binding settings. A predominance of average *cooperation* ratings can also be observed when comparing all distributions (see Fig. 3), possibly due to players always completing a word together during gameplay. Contrasting with the average ratings, no significant differences were verified between key binding strategies on the ratings given for the first recorded game level.

The fact that the first level did not present differences inspired the scrutiny of how players changed their perceptions throughout gameplay. This analysis focused on the dimensions that significantly influenced the average ratings: *cooperation* and *behavioural independence*, see Figs. 3(b) and 3(c). For this, heatmaps were constructed to express the frequency with which each rating was selected after a certain number of levels were played, see Fig. 4. Because subjects could play as many levels as they wanted, the rating frequencies (given by active players) diminished as the number of played levels increased.

[4] https://osf.io/u4axv/ (accessed 2026-02-09).

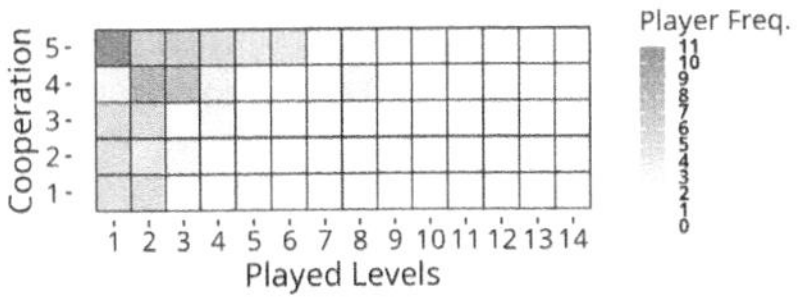

(a) Independent Key Bindings

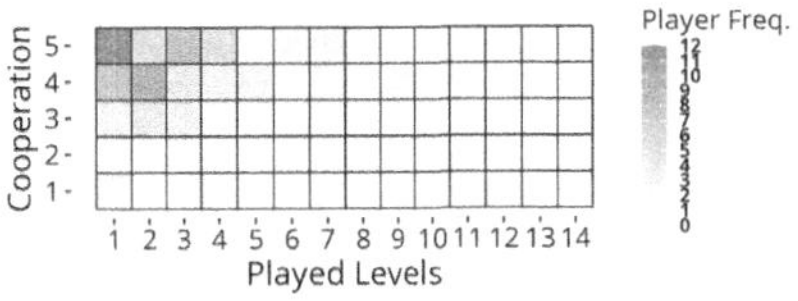

(b) Dependent Key Bindings

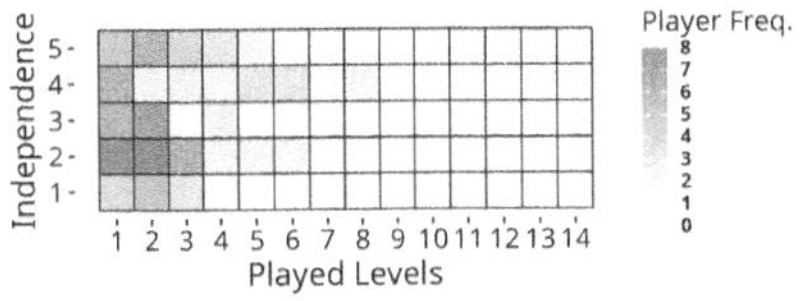

(c) Independent Key Bindings

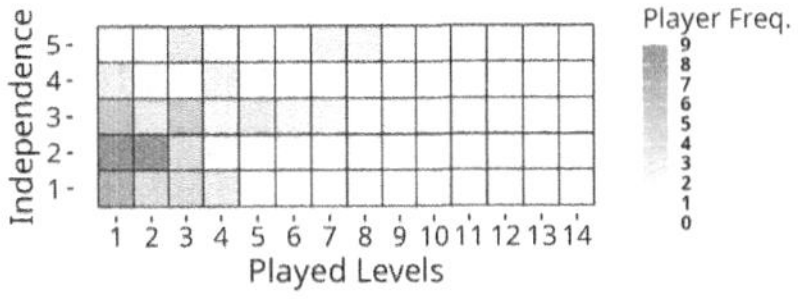

(d) Dependent Key Bindings

Fig. 4. Heatmaps representing the evolution of felt *cooperation* and *independence* by number of played levels, for independent and dependent key binding conditions.

Starting with the *cooperation* values, see Figs. 4(a) and 4(b), although high during the initial levels over the two conditions, they seem more sparse in the independent setting. More importantly, there is a considerable shift regarding the last played levels (although only a few participants played through these many levels). This can signify a period of lower felt cooperation after players understood the workings of the game using independent key bindings. Regarding the *behavioural independence* scores, see Figs. 4(c) and 4(d), while initially there is no clear distinction in independence, after several levels, players perceived independent key bindings as entailing higher behavioural independence.

5 Conclusion

This paper introduces an innovative and creative way of expressing different gameplay styles, with the use of key bindings (assigning specific in-game actions to keyboard keys). This was done through the transformation of a word-matching game called *CrossAnt* into a two-player game that can dynamically generate different key bindings, such that some levels can be completed by each player independently (independent key bindings) and other levels require simultaneous input from both players (dependent key bindings).

After several dyads played the game in an interactive showcase, tests measuring the impact that such control modifications had on players' interaction perceptions revealed that cooperation prevailed due to core gameplay, and was exacerbated when input was required from both players. Independent behaviour, on the other hand, was more strongly perceived when using independent key bindings. Furthermore, these differences were not present initially, as corroborated by some nuances verified in the evolution of player perceptions. This suggests that the consideration of a moment-by-moment analysis enables a more accurate study of the expression and emergence of social interaction.

Acknowledgments. Work supported by national funds through Fundação para a Ciência e a Tecnologia, I.P. (FCT) under projects UID/50021/2025 and UID/PRR/50021/2025.

References

1. Chow, C.Y., Riantiningtyas, R.R., Kanstrup, M.B., Papavasileiou, M., Liem, G.D., Olsen, A.: Can games change children's eating behaviour? A review of gamification and serious games. Food Qual. Prefer. **80**, 103823 (2019)
2. Gabelica, C., den Bossche, P.V., Segers, M., Gijselaers, W.: Feedback, a powerful lever in teams: a review. Educ. Res. Rev. **7**(2), 123–144 (2012)
3. Kuhlman, D.M., Marshello, A.F.: Individual differences in game motivation as moderators of preprogrammed strategy effects in prisoner's dilemma. J. Pers. Soc. Psychol. **32**(5), 922 (1975)
4. Martinho, C., Santos, P., Prada, R.: Design e Desenvolvimento de Jogos. Tecnologias de Informação, FCA (2014)
5. Masthoff, J., Vassileva, J.: 9 Personalized persuasion for behavior change, pp. 205–236. De Gruyter Oldenbourg, Berlin, Boston (2023). https://doi.org/10.1515/9783110988567-009
6. Medler, B.: Player dossiers: analyzing gameplay data as a reward. Game Stud. **11**(1) (2011)
7. Oksanen, K., Hämäläinen, R.: Game mechanics in the design of a collaborative 3D serious game. Simul. Gaming **45**(2), 255–278 (2014)
8. Sajjadi, P., Ewais, A., De Troyer, O.: Individualization in serious games: a systematic review of the literature on the aspects of the players to adapt to. Entertainment Comput. **41**, 100468 (2022)
9. Sicart, M.: Defining game mechanics. Game Stud. **8**(2) (2008)
10. Sudyana, A., Putri, A., Rosmansyah, Y.: Feedback system in educational games: a systematic literature review. J. Pendidikan Indonesia **5**(7) (2024)
11. Togelius, J., De Nardi, R., Lucas, S.M.: Towards automatic personalised content creation for racing games. In: IEEE Symposium on Computational Intelligence and Games, CIG 2007, pp. 252–259. IEEE (2007)
12. Vegt, N., Visch, V., Vermeeren, A., Ridder, H.D.: Player experiences and behaviors in a multiplayer game: designing game rules to change interdependent behavior. Int. J. Serious Games **3**(4), 69–85 (2016). https://doi.org/10.17083/ijsg.v3i4.150
13. Wang, H., Sun, C.T.: Game reward systems: gaming experiences and social meanings. In: DiGRA Conference, vol. 114 (2011)
14. Wendel, V., Konert, J.: Multiplayer serious games. In: Dörner, R., Göbel, S., Effelsberg, W., Wiemeyer, J. (eds.) Serious Games, pp. 211–241. Springer, Cham (2016). https://doi.org/10.1007/978-3-319-40612-1_8

Artificial Intelligence, Procedural Generation, and Computational Approaches to Play

Playing Hex and Counter Wargames Using Reinforcement Learning and Recurrent Neural Networks

Guilherme Palma[1,2], João Dias[2,3,4], and Pedro A. Santos[1,2](✉)

[1] Instituto Superior Técnico, Universidade de Lisboa, Lisbon, Portugal
pedro.santos@tecnico.ulisboa.pt
[2] INESC-ID, Lisbon, Portugal
[3] Faculdade de Ciências e Tecnologia, Universidade do Algarve, Faro, Portugal
[4] CISCA, Faro, Portugal
jmdias@ualg.pt

Abstract. Hex and Counter Wargames are adversarial two-player simulations of real military conflicts requiring complex strategic decision-making. Unlike classical board games, these games feature intricate terrain/unit interactions, unit stacking, large maps of varying sizes, and simultaneous move and combat decisions involving hundreds of units. This paper introduces a novel system designed to address the strategic complexity of Hex and Counter Wargames by integrating cutting-edge advancements in Recurrent Neural Networks with AlphaZero, a reliable modern Reinforcement Learning algorithm. The system utilizes a Neural Network architecture developed from existing research and incorporates innovative state and action representations tailored to these specific game environments. With minimal training, our solution has shown promising results in typical scenarios, demonstrating the ability to generalize across different terrain and tactical situations. Additionally, we explore the system's potential to scale to larger map sizes, establishing that there is a decrease in the network's performance. The developed system is openly accessible, facilitating continued research and exploration within this challenging domain.

1 Introduction

The pursuit of perfect or super-human proficiency in board games has long been a benchmark for assessing the capabilities of contemporary artificial intelligence. This paper explores the application of advanced AI techniques to Hex and Counter Wargames, a class of adversarial two-player simulations of real military conflicts that demand complex strategic decision-making. Unlike classical games such as Chess and Go, these games involve intricate terrain and unit interactions, unit stacking, large variable-sized maps, and simultaneous movement and combat decisions involving hundreds of units.

Our methodology is based on Alpha Zero [12], but with a substantially different Neural Network architecture, adapted to much lower computing requirements

R. Baptista et al. (Eds.): VJ 2025, CCIS 2988, pp. 109–122, 2027.
https://doi.org/10.1007/978-3-032-31642-4_10

and the specific needs of these types of games. The main contributions of our work are:

- **Network architecture** - A dual-head fully convolutional recurrent neural network architecture adaptable to varying board dimensions and reduced training resources.
- **State and action representations** - Novel state and action representations applicable across multiple Hex and Counter Wargames and extensible to specific game requirements.
- **Generalization results** - Significant results on the capacity of this type of architecture to generalize to different board and unit configurations serve as important groundwork for future research.
- **Game environment and AlphaZero implementation** - We developed an environment for Hex and Counter Wargames, and an asynchronous AlphaZero implementation, based on the original paper, with extra features adapted to these specific games.

1.1 Problem Setting

Hex and Counter Wargames are adversarial board games played on hexagonally tiled maps, using cardboard markers to represent units and resources. They often simulate historic military conflicts and typically feature large maps and extensive rule systems. All training and testing in this study were conducted under a subset of rules inspired by the Standard Combat Series ruleset [4].

The games are played on game boards that can be configured to have any desired dimensions. Each tile on the game board has a type of terrain with 3 attributes: attack modifier, defence modifier and movement cost. Additionally, certain tiles on the map yield victory points. Play lasts for a predetermined number of turns. After these turns, the player who controls the highest percentage of victory point tiles emerges victorious.

Throughout the game, players place units on the map that they receive as reinforcements. Units are characterized by their three features: attack strength, defence strength and movement allowance. Groups of units can stack in the same tile up to a predefined limit. Beyond that, there are no stacking group restrictions, meaning that all units can stack with each other.

Combat can be conducted between units on adjacent hexes. When a group of units attacks another, the total attack and defence strength of each group of units is calculated to determine the combat's result. For the attackers, each unit multiplies its attack strength by the terrain's attack modifier and adds it to the group's total. The same thing happens in the group of defending units, using the defence strength and modifiers. The group that obtains the lower combined strength loses their strongest unit. If a draw happens, both groups lose a unit.

Each player's turn consists of two distinct phases: the movement and combat phases. Both the movement and combat phases comprise two sub-phases, resulting in a total of four sub-phases throughout each player's turn. During the movement phase, players engage in the reinforcement and movement sub-phases, wherein they strategically place reinforcements and maneuver their units, respectively. Meanwhile, the combat phase entails sub-phases for: target selection (where the player chooses the tile to attack) and attacker selection (in which adjacent units are chosen to enter combat).

Each turn is characterized by both players engaging in both phases, with each player completing their turn before the other can proceed. The only exception to this rule happens at the beginning of the game, before the first turn, where both players place their initial reinforcements on the map, without going through any other phases.

2 Related Work

The Wargame landscape remains very diversified, despite attempts at unification and formalization [3], with environments ranging from realistic air combat simulation for pilot training [6] to simple family board games like Risk [7].

Several properties of these games make them particularly challenging for AI approaches [5], leading a lot of research to focus on human-crafted knowledge as a way to address these obstacles, either by directly enforcing optimal actions in certain board states [15], or by simplifying in-game features using hand-crafted functions [14]. More recently, however, [17] has demonstrated promising results, utilizing new methods and relying on human knowledge just to accelerate early training using Supervised Learning.

Other research has focused on the usage of Reinforcement Learning, such as the paper [2], which provided important contributions to the study of unit combat in wargames. This research was conducted on a 10×10 featureless map and demonstrated the impact of different combat models and policy optimization algorithms on the training of Reinforcement Learning agents.

On the other hand, in 2019, Glenn Moy and Slava Shekh published research [8] that proposed the use of AlphaZero in Wargaming. This paper showed that AlphaZero was capable of reaching optimal play in a simple 10×10 environment with two units and a single terrain type, but demonstrated that human-crafted heuristics were still needed in order to accelerate training.

Beyond Wargames, there have been other games where similar Reinforcement Learning techniques have been utilized, such as *FreeCiv* [16] and *Terra Mistica*. The research in [10] applied AlphaZero to the game of *Terra Mistica* and gives important insights into possible action and state space representations, since the game shares multiple characteristics with Wargames such as the adversarial nature, hexagon-based boards and multi-phased turns.

3 Methods

Due to the space available it was not possible to include detailed explanations for the design decisions. We opted for giving as much detail as possible of the actual architecture and choices to allow reproducibility of the work. Further details can be found in the thesis [9].

3.1 Training Strategy

The main concept of our solution is the combination of the techniques discussed in [1,11] with the learning algorithm of AlphaZero [12] (Fig. 1).

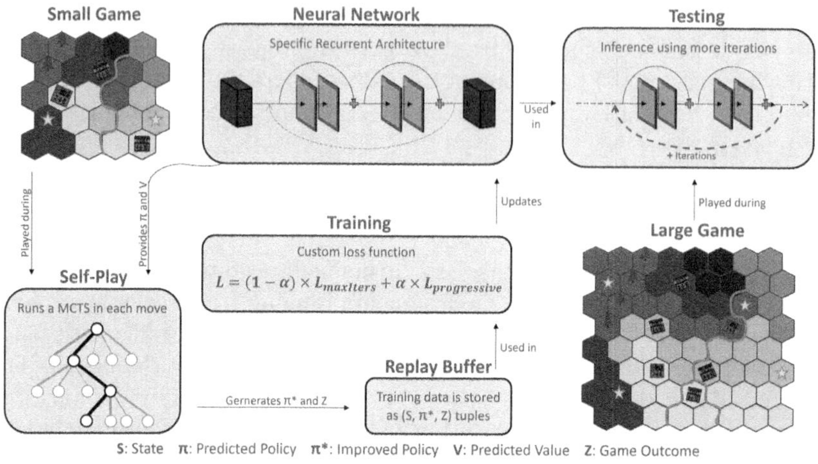

Fig. 1. Diagram of the designed solution

The first key aspect is the utilization of the recurrent neural network architecture described in [1]. This architecture, allows us to control how many times information goes through the recurrent module, before being passed to the output module (the number of recurrent iterations), while simultaneously being fully convolutional, which enables the use of different input sizes/resolutions.

Having this in mind, we use AlphaZero's algorithm to first train the network on a small game map, using a low number of recurrent iterations. This not only decreases training time but also allows the algorithm to train in a simple environment, with a smaller search space, where it can learn strategies with greater ease.

When training ends, we test that trained network on a larger map, but we use a larger number of recurrent iterations. This is the same methodology used in [1,11] and it should allow the network to extrapolate what it learned on the small map, to the larger one, simply by increasing the number of recurrent iterations. This process was designed with the intent of obtaining networks capable of playing on larger scenarios using the limited computational resources we had available.

3.2 Game State Representation and Network Input

The game state representation is a very important part of our solution since we wish to have a representation capable of encompassing a broad set of Hex and Counter Wargames, without requiring re-training of the network.

Since Hex and Counter Wargames are oftentimes highly asymmetric and will regularly have different win conditions for each player, we have decided to represent board positions statically for the two players instead of always using the perspective of the current player as in systems like AlphaGo.

The game state was represented using a feature stack with the same resolution as the board ($Height \times Width$) with different channels representing different properties of the game.

The following sections, explain how each of the game characteristics was represented. We start by outlining the features that are necessary for both players (win conditions, unit positioning and reinforcements), and then take a closer look at the remaining properties that are still required to fully represent the game.

Win Conditions. Players win through the control of victory point tiles. For each player, this is represented using 1 channel, that one-hot encodes the victory point locations on the board.

Unit Positioning. The units present on the board need to be represented taking in consideration their different attributes, statuses and also their position and stacking.

There is a group of planes for each of the 3 unit statuses: ready to move, already moved and already performed an attack. Within each status group, units are represented using 3 channels, one for each of their attributes (attack strength, defence strength and movement points). In each of these channels the respective unit attribute is marked at each unit's position. However, since there are S stacking levels, S groups of 3 planes are required instead, per status. This leads to $3 \times 3 \times S = 9S$ planes to represent units, for each player.

Reinforcements. Depicting the reinforcement schedule for the entire game would be too extensive. For this reason, we illustrate instead, the next R reinforcements to come into play. We represent these units by the order in which they will come into play, using two sets of planes: the first portrays the units themselves, while the second represents how long they take to arrive. In the first set each unit is represented using 3 planes (one for each unit attribute), in each of those planes the respective unit attribute is marked at its possible arrival locations, while the remaining locations are marked with zeros. On the second set, there is an equal number of planes for each unit but they instead contain: the total number of turns minus the number of turns until the unit arrives[1]. This representation results in a total of $(3 \times R) \times 2 = 6R$ channels, per player, to represent incoming reinforcements.

[1] Using the number of turns until the unit arrives directly, would lead to the need of representing an "infinite" number of turns at the end of the reinforcement schedule.

Other Features and Final Representation. Considering terrain as the first player-independent aspect, we chose to represent it using 3 planes: one for each terrain attribute (attack modifier, defence modifier and movement cost).

Due to its complexity, the combat phase also requires some special attention, since there is the need to distinguish between different states that occur during the combat itself. First, we need to represent the state where a player has decided to attack a tile. This is accomplished by using 1 channel where the position being attacked will be marked. We also need S more channels marking the position of each of the units that the attacker has chosen to use, considering their stacking level. This leads to $S + 1$ channels for state representation during combat.

Beyond combat and terrain, there are still some other features that are part of the game state: the current player, current turn and current sub-phase. To represent the sub-phases we add 4 more planes (one for each sub-phase). During each sub-phase the respective plane is filled with ones, while the remainder stays empty. For the current player, we add a plane filled with either 1 or -1, representing players 1 or 2 respectively. Finally, for the current turn we use one more plane filled with the current turn divided by the total number of turns, which can be interpreted as the percentage of the game played so far.

All the player-independent features just described amount to a total of $3 + S + 7 = S + 10$ input channels. The features required by both players, previously described require $2 \times (1 + 9S + 6R)$ more input channels. Putting everything together, we reach the final expression for the number of input channels of: $19S + 12(R + 1)$.

3.3 Action Space Representation

Actions were spatially represented using three dimensions, as we reasoned that such a representation might make the learning process for the neural network more direct, due to the adoption of convolutional layers in the neural network architecture. The three dimensional representation is achieved using several planes with the same resolution as the board ($Height \times Width$) stacked together.

We will start by considering the actions required for the movement sub-phase. Since pathing is such an important part of strategic planning, and movement plans are often complex, we have decided that movement decisions should be taken one tile at a time. Considering that we are moving over hexagonal tiles, each having 6 adjacent neighbours, there will be 6 groups of S planes used to represent the movement. Each group represents one of the possible directions of movement, and each plane within that group will be used to select the position and stacking level of the unit to be moved. This representation takes $6 \times S$ planes.

The fighting phase is perhaps the one that requires a more complex representation. Due to the different sub-phases, combats are executed using a sequence of several actions. First, to start an engagement the attacking player must choose the grid position he wants to attack. This is done using a single plane where the position is picked. Next, the player selects one by one, each of the adjacent units he wants to use in the attack. For this purpose, S planes are used so that the attacking player can select units according to both their position and stacking level. Finally, when the attacking player is ready, he must once again select the position he wishes to attack on yet another plane, in order to confirm the attack being made. All these sub-actions leave us with $1 + S + 1 = S + 2$ more planes (Fig. 2).

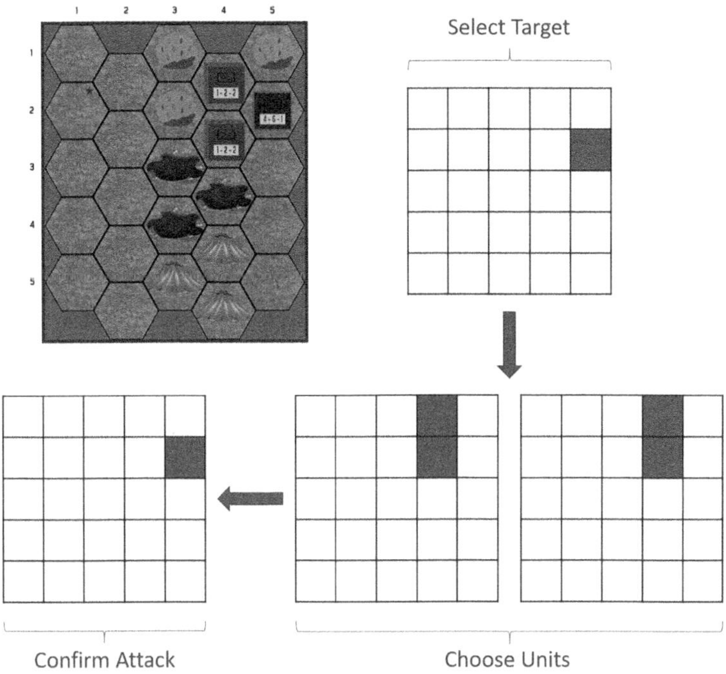

Fig. 2. Representation of an attack where all player one units (green) decide to target the enemy armour (red). Note that each action (blue square) would be taken sequentially. (Color figure online)

We are still missing the actions needed for reinforcements placement at the beginning of the movement phase. We can achieve this using a single plane where the player just needs to select a position to place the next incoming unit.

Lastly, we need to add S planes for the action of not moving a unit, and another S more planes for the action of not attacking with a unit, for the cases where the player wishes to declare that we will not move or attack with certain troops, in a given turn. S planes are used for each of these actions since there can be multiple units in the same location and we need to distinguish between stacking levels.

If we combine all the previously described planes we get an action space representation of size $(9S + 3) \times Height \times Width$.

3.4 Neural Network Architecture

The network architecture that was used is based on the *Recall* architecture from the paper [1]. Similar to the networks described there, our network can be divided into three sections: input module, recurrent module and output module. For the input and recurrent modules we maintained the original architecture, while for the output module we use two output heads (one for the value and another for the policy), instead of just one.

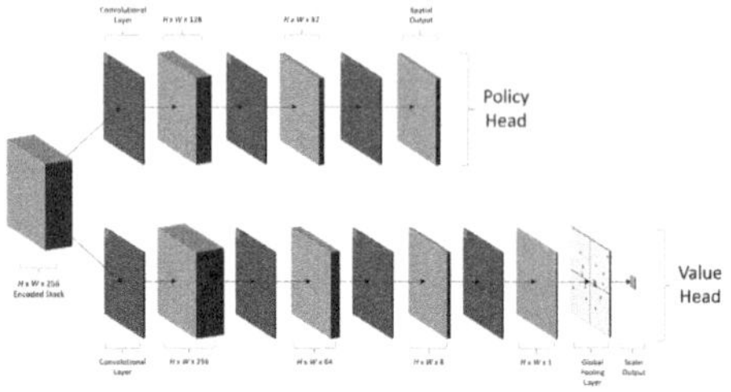

Fig. 3. Output module architecture

We maintain a latent space with 256 channels throughout the network by using 256 filters on all the convolutional layers until we reach the output module.

Both the policy and value heads of the output module we designed can be seen in Fig. 3. The value head consists of four convolutional layers that progressively reduce the number of filters, followed by an average pooling layer to reduce the output to a single scalar value. This value is then passed through a tanh activation function to give the final output.

The policy head contains three convolutional layers, each reducing the number of filters from the previous layer, with the final layer having as many filters as the number of action space channels.

Note that performing regular convolutions over hexagonally sampled data would deform the output of the operations. For this reason, since we are dealing with hexagonal tiles, all the convolutional layers in this network are hexagonal convolution layers, implemented using the Hexagdly library [13].

4 Results

In order to test the system, we created a symmetrical scenario and a randomized scenario. Afterwards, we analyse the network performance when extrapolating to larger game boards. All the networks presented used 6 recurrent iterations during training and a progressive loss α of 0.01.

The training for all the scenarios was done on a 5×5 game board, including two unit types and 4 possible terrain types. All the training and testing was performed using only CPU since, at the time of training, the system was not optimized to efficiently use GPU and took little advantage of the extra hardware.

To access the performance of our solution in all the different scenarios, using various opponents, four agents were created:

- *Policy* agent - An agent that selects the action which was given the highest probability by the network being used.
- *MCTS* agent - This agent runs AlphaZero's MCTS before each action and selects the action with the highest visit count. The MCTS uses 300 iterations.
- *Random* agent - The agent selects actions randomly amongst the possible actions in the current board state.
- *Goal Rush* agent - This agent places units randomly and tries to move each unit towards the closest victory point. If an enemy stands in the path of a unit to its victory point, it attacks the enemy with all available units.

In the scenarios where the *Goal Rush* agent was utilized 250 test games were played to determine each of the win rate values. On the other hand, in the extrapolation graphs presented at the end of the this section, each data point is the average of 3 runs with 100 test games in each.

4.1 Symmetric Scenario - Curriculum Learning

To test the effectiveness of curriculum learning, a scenario was created where both players have two infantry units and the board is symmetric. Each of the players received two extra reinforcements, one at turn 3 and another at turn 5. This effectively doubles the amount of units that come into play from 4 to 8 (Fig. 4).

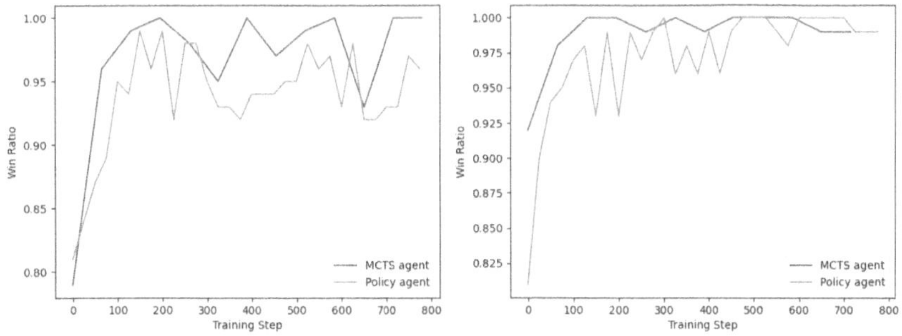

Fig. 4. Win rates obtained by player 1 (left) and player 2 (right), against the *Random* agent during training, on the curriculum learning extension of the symmetric scenario.

The training configuration used for this scenario did 32 network updates per training step, with a mini-batch size of 128. We started the training using the latest network from the original symmetric scenario and after a short number of training steps, it could already achieve very high win rates against the *Random* agent. These results demonstrate that curriculum learning could be used as an effective tool to increase the complexity, for game scenarios where there is already a well-trained network.

Finally, the network was tested against the *Goal Rush* agent (Table 1), where it obtained even better results than in the original scenario. The more units a player has compared to the opponent, the easier it is to overpower enemy units while taking fewer casualties. One of the reasons for the better performance in this scenario is the fact that, as the AI agent coordinates its units better, it can grow larger and larger leads and defeat the opponent with greater ease. The results also show that the *Policy* agent has a higher win rate when playing as player two. After analysing some of the games between the two agents, we found that this happens because the AI tends to have a more defensive strategy when playing with player two, which works much better against the attacks from the *Goal Rush* agent.

Table 1. Win rate results from testing against the *Goal Rush* agent in both variations of the symmetric scenario.

	Symmetric				Symmetric – Curriculum Learning			
	Player 1		Player 2		Player 1		Player 2	
	MCTS	Policy	MCTS	Policy	MCTS	Policy	MCTS	Policy
Win (%)	76,8	73,0	80,5	75,6	94,4	79,2	98,0	89,2
Draw (%)	23,2	27,0	19,5	24,4	5,6	19,2	2,0	9,2
Loss (%)	0	0	0	0	0	1,6	0	1,6

4.2 Randomized Scenario

For the final and most complex scenario, both players start with two infantry units, and they receive an extra armor unit at the beginning of the second turn. The map is fully randomly generated using a distribution over the four terrain types[2]. The objective of this scenario is to understand if the network can learn in a variety of different maps while managing different unit types.

The neural network used for this scenario had the longest training process, reaching a total of 3640 training steps with 32 weight updates within, each using a mini-batch of 256 positions (Fig. 5).

During training, the network managed to achieve approximately 100% win rate using the *MCTS* agent and roughly 80% with the *Policy* agent for both players, versus the *Random* agent. The performance against the *Random* agent, especially for the *Policy* agent, was slightly better on player two. This might have happened because, since the game always ends in player two's turn, it directly "sees" terminal states when using the MCTS during self-play, while player one always has to rely on the neural network predictions to evaluate the states.

[2] The exact distribution used, had probabilities of 0.1, 0.15, 0.65, and 0.1 for swamp, mountains, plains, and forest, respectively.

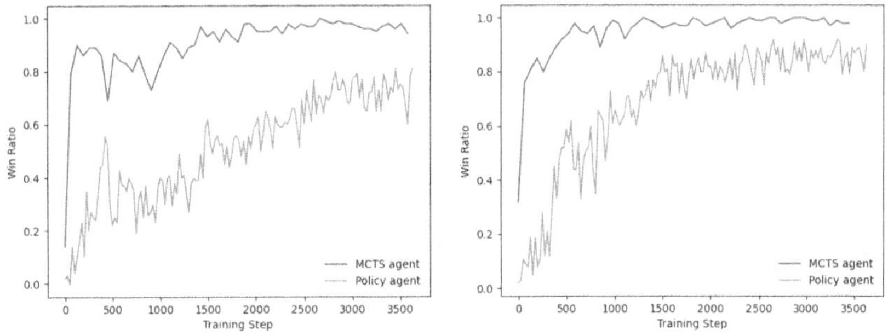

Fig. 5. Win rates obtained by player 1 (left) and player 2 (right), against the *Random* agent during training, on the randomized scenario.

Table 2. Win rate results from testing against the *Goal Rush* agent in the randomized scenario.

	Player 1		Player 2	
	MCTS	Policy	MCTS	Policy
Win (%)	92,8	60,4	80,4	59,2
Draw (%)	5,2	28,4	17,6	30,4
Loss (%)	2,0	11,2	2,0	10,4

The *Goal Rush* agent was also tested (Table 2). The *MCTS* agents managed to get above 92% and 80% win rates for players one and two, respectively. While the *Policy* agents had a drop in performance to about 60% win rate for both players. The difference found in *MCTS* agent's win ratios from 92.8% for player one to 80% in player two, can be explained by the fact that, when playing on a random map, using intelligent agents, the capacity to act first is a big advantage. Since player one always plays first, it can dictate what kind of engagements happen, while player two is forced to simply react. On top of that, this player also receives its reinforcements first, which provides a very strong offensive advantage and can make certain positions indefensible for the enemy. When analyzing games where the *Goal Rush* agent played as player one, we noticed that in many situations, it would use the extra reinforcement to overpower the enemy defense, and the best that the *MCTS* agent could do was counter-attack the enemy victory point and make a draw. Situations like these can explain the difference found in win rates, as we can see that the draw percentage increases in an equal amount to the win rate reduction. The randomized board and victory points from this last scenario, force the neural network to understand game strategy and not just "memorize" the best action in each state, leading to the display of more advanced strategic abilities.

4.3 Extrapolation to Larger Map Sizes

After training the system on the 5×5 map, several tests were done on larger maps to test the system's extrapolation capacity. We started by testing on a map made solely of plains tiles, using one unit and a victory point on a random location. We trained multiple networks using different hyper-parameters, such as the number of recurrent module iterations and the α value for the progressive loss. Afterwards, the networks were tested on maps of increasing size (between 5×5 and 12×12). To test the effectiveness of the recurrent architecture itself, a residual neural network was also trained to serve as a baseline. This network had 12 residual blocks, which is the same effective depth as a RNN using 6 recurrent iterations (the lowest that we tested). Effective depth is defined as the depth that the recurrent network would have if we unrolled the recurrent iterations.

Figure 6 presents the results obtained by the best performing recurrent network when compared to the baseline residual network. The best-performing recurrent network utilized 30 recurrent iterations (resulting in a much higher effective depth), and employed a progressive loss α value of 1, meaning that it only used progressive loss during training.

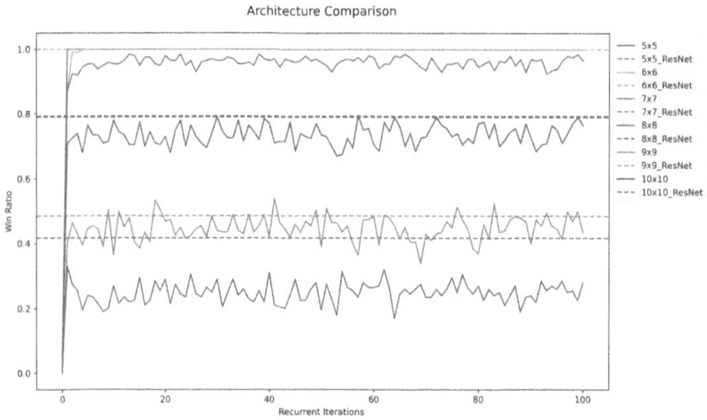

Fig. 6. Comparison between the win rates of the best performing recurrent network and the baseline residual network, using varying numbers of iterations and different map sizes.

The new architecture obtained inferior results to the baseline residual network. We can also observe that the network's performance significantly decreases with the map size and, unlike what was expected, larger numbers of iterations do not seem to have any impact on the network performance.

We believe the issues found may be related to the nature of the problem and the way the network attempts to solve larger problems with more iterations. When considering a maze-like problem, if we are trying to solve a large maze, possessing information about what paths are or not viable in a smaller version of that maze, gives us direct and valuable information on how to solve the larger problem. However, for other more complex problems such as chess or the games we studied, the translation of information from simpler problems to more complex ones might not be so direct.

Another possible explanation for the poor extrapolation capacity might be the total amount of training that the neural networks undertook. The networks trained for our extrapolation tests ran for 1100 training steps and the maximum number of games held in the replay buffer was 6000, due to memory constraints, which pales in comparison to AlphaZero's 700,000 training steps and 1 million games' replay buffer. It could be the case that additional training would be required for the networks to extrapolate to larger map sizes.

5 Conclusions and Future Work

We proposed a system to play Hex and Counter Wargames. Our approach used AlphaZero's training algorithm and a recurrent network architecture based on the previous research [1,11]. We obtained good results on several scenarios using small amounts of training and limited resources. We demonstrated, that the current methods (including curriculum learning) can generalize for variable terrain configurations and number of units in more complex scenarios, but are not enough to extrapolate well to larger map sizes.

Regarding the neural networks used in this work, we presented a value head architecture designed for fully convolutional networks and the task of attributing values to different board states. Our architecture proved capable of learning in the scenarios we trained it on, even with variable terrain. Still, we believe that the incorporation of different layer architectures such as depth-wise or separable convolutions, is worth investigating in future research, as they could be a better fit to the problem's requirements.

Acknowledgments. Work supported by national funds through Fundação para a Ciência e a Tecnologia, I.P. (FCT) under projects UID/50021/2025 and UID/PRR/50021/2025.

The authors dedicate this paper to the memory of Dean Essig (1961–2024).

References

1. Bansal, A., et al.: End-to-end algorithm synthesis with recurrent networks: logical extrapolation without overthinking. In: Advances in Neural Information Processing Systems (NeurIPS), vol. 35 (2022)
2. Boron, J., Darken, C.: Developing combat behavior through reinforcement learning in wargames and simulations. In: 2020 IEEE Conference on Games (CoG), pp. 728–731 (2020)
3. By, T.: Formalizing game-play. Simul. Gaming **43**, 157–187 (2012). https://api.semanticscholar.org/CorpusID:62324226
4. Essig, D.: Standard Combat Series: Series rules, ver 1.8 (2015). https://mmpgamers.com/support/gamersarchive/scs/SCS_Rules_v18_September_2015.pdf
5. Goodman, J., Risi, S., Lucas, S.M.M.: AI and wargaming. arXiv abs/2009.08922 (2020)

6. Källström, J., Heintz, F.: Agent coordination in air combat simulation using multi-agent deep reinforcement learning. In: 2020 IEEE International Conference on Systems, Man, and Cybernetics (SMC), pp. 2157–2164 (2020)
7. Lamorisse, A.: Risk. Board game published by Hasbro (1957). https://en.wikipedia.org/wiki/Risk_(game)
8. Moy, G., Shekh, S.: The application of AlphaZero to wargaming. In: AI 2019: Advances in Artificial Intelligence, 32nd Australasian Joint Conference on Artificial Intelligence, pp. 3–14. Springer, Cham (2019)
9. Palma, G.: AlphaSCS: playing hex and counter board games with reinforcement learning and recurrent neural networks. Master's thesis, Instituto Superior Técnico, Universidade de Lisboa (2024), Master's thesis, supervised by Pedro Alexandre Simões dos Santos and João Miguel de Sousa de Assis Dias
10. Perez, L.: Mastering Terra Mystica: applying self-play to multi-agent cooperative board games (2021). arXiv abs/2102.10540
11. Schwarzschild, A., et al.: Can you learn an algorithm? Generalizing from easy to hard problems with recurrent networks. In: Advances in Neural Information Processing Systems (NeurIPS) (2021)
12. Silver, D., et al.: A general reinforcement learning algorithm that masters chess, shogi, and go through self-play. Science **362**, 1140–1144 (2018)
13. Steppa, C., Holch, T.L.: Hexagdly: Processing hexagonally sampled data with CNNs in pytorch. SoftwareX **9** (2019)
14. Sun, Y., Yuan, B., Xue, Y., Zhou, J., Zhang, X., Zhou, X.: Method for making multi-attribute decisions in wargames by combining intuitionistic fuzzy numbers with reinforcement learning. arXiv abs/2109.02354 (2021)
15. Sun, Y., Yuan, B., Zhang, T., Tang, B., Zheng, W., Zhou, X.: Research and implementation of intelligent decision based on a priori knowledge and DQN algorithms in wargame environment. Electronics (2020). https://api.semanticscholar.org/CorpusID:225162040
16. Ulam, P., Jones, J.K., Goel, A.K.: Combining model-based meta-reasoning and reinforcement learning for adapting game-playing agents. In: Proceedings of the AAAI Conference on Artificial Intelligence and Interactive Digital Entertainment (2008). https://api.semanticscholar.org/CorpusID:14236438
17. Yu, S., Zhu, W., Wang, Y.: Research on wargame decision-making method based on multi-agent deep deterministic policy gradient. Appl. Sci. (2023). https://api.semanticscholar.org/CorpusID:257961484

Conditional Latent Diffusion Models for Controlled Terrain Generation

Margarida Amaro[1,2], João Dias[2,3,4(✉)], and Pedro A. Santos[1,2]

[1] Instituto Superior Técnico, Universidade de Lisboa, Lisbon, Portugal
pedro.santos@tecnico.ulisboa.pt
[2] INESC-ID, Lisbon, Portugal
jmdias@ualg.pt
[3] Faculdade de Ciências e Tecnologia, Universidade do Algarve, Faro, Portugal
[4] CISCA, Faro, Portugal

Abstract. Procedural terrain generation is essential in industries such as entertainment and education, where high fidelity and control over terrain design are critical. Recent approaches often use Deep Learning (DL) models, particularly Generative Adversarial Networks (GANs), for terrain generation. However, these approaches have limitations both in terrain quality and in the flexibility of user control. This work explores a novel approach using Latent Diffusion Models (LDMs) for terrain generation, offering simultaneous elevation and texture synthesis, and employing more mainstream control methods such as creating text descriptions and drawing semantic masks. Together, these complementary methods enhance the terrain authoring experience, enabling more dynamic terrain generation fit for different use cases and artistic processes. The proposed approach produces realistic terrain comparable to state-of-the-art methods while offering the added advantage of generating both terrain and texture, without compromising overall quality. These results are supported by quantitative metrics and a user survey, which also highlighted some ambiguity in the control methods. Despite this, the models successfully generate a diverse range of landforms and textures.

Keywords: Terrain generation · Diffusion Models

1 Introduction

The need for realistic and accurate terrain in digital media is the driving force behind the development of more efficient and advanced methods of terrain generation. In entertainment, the quality and realism of generated terrain significantly affect consumers' immersion and enjoyment,

Recently, there has been a widespread interest in using Deep Learning (DL) for the generation of terrain, spurred on by impressive advancements in the image synthesis field. The seminal work by Guerin et al. [11] introduced the use of Generative Adversarial Networks (GANs) to terrain generation, allowing users to control the terrain modeling process by drawing a high-level sketch defining

R. Baptista et al. (Eds.): VJ 2025, CCIS 2988, pp. 123–134, 2027.
https://doi.org/10.1007/978-3-032-31642-4_11

the location of ridges and valleys. This work highlighted the potential of DL for controlled and realistic terrain synthesis.

Since then, DL-based techniques for image synthesis have rapidly advanced, and Diffusion Models (DMs), in particular Latent Diffusion Models (LDM) [23], are now the backbone of the state-of-the-art approaches for tasks such as text-to-image generation [9] and semantic image synthesis [19]. More specifically, semantic synthesis involves generating images from a semantic mask, where subjects are spatially represented using color-coded labels, and text-to-image uses a text caption to generate an image. Despite these breakthroughs, the use of DMs in terrain synthesis remains under-explored.

Furthermore, generating terrain elevation is typically followed by a separate task of terrain texturing: the process of painting the terrain to achieve faithful and lifelike visuals. While there is DL-based research on terrain texture generation, few studies have attempted to generate both terrain elevation and texture simultaneously. Achieving this could significantly reduce the time and effort involved in terrain generation.

Therefore, this work aims to contribute to the existing body of knowledge on terrain generation, by addressing the following research question:

- Can conditional LDMs generate realistic textured terrain based on user input?

2 Related Work

In literature, the DL technology most used to produce terrain is the GAN (Generative Adversarial Network), and authors also focus on providing users with means to control the terrain generation process.

In literature, GANs (Generative Adversarial Networks) is the most used architecture with Deep Learning approaches, specifically the pix2pix [16] and the DCGAN [21] architectures, which are usually trained conditionally to allow for user-controlled input. Li et al. adapt pix2pix [17] to generate LDMs. Guerin et al. [11] adapt both architectures and build 4 cGANs: sketch-to-terrain, levelset-to-terrain GANs, which produce heightmaps. Cai et al. [5] also adapt both models but add self-attention. Ramos et al. [22] created the Dual Critic Conditional Wasserstein GAN, which adapts the Wasserstein GAN architecture and makes use of two discriminators: One to criticize the quality of the output, and another to evaluate the correspondence of the conditioning data to real terrain.

Diffusion models [13,24] accomplish image generation by adding noise to data and then learning how to reverse this process. More specifically, the model can iteratively remove noise from a noisy image, over T timesteps, until a clear image is obtained, because it has learned to predict the noise that was added at each timestep. Latent diffusion models [23] perform the diffusion process on a compressed latent space instead of the regular pixel space. This makes training less expensive and inference faster with a negligible effect on the output quality. LDMs are currently the model configuration used in state-of-the-art approaches in multiple tasks.

There are a small number of approaches using DMs for terrain generation. Lochner et al. [18], adapt the DM created by Dhariwal et al. [8] to generate terrain DEMs and employ this as part of a terrain modeling framework. Then, Hu et al. [14] follow the approach taken by [3] and train 3 models to denoise different timesteps of the denoising process, producing terrain DEMs with higher detail.

The most common way of providing control over the terrain modeling process is by having the user create a high-level sketch depicting features or properties of terrain. An example of a 2D image that can be drawn by a user is the **levelset image**. This image was also introduced by Guerin et al. [11], and is a binary image where a gray color denotes an area where the altitude is above the 60th percentile of the altitude distribution. These images are also used by Naik et al. [20], where the he combines the feature sketch and levelset image into one. Other approaches include that of Ramos et al. [22], where users draw a **hexagonal tile map** where each tile corresponds to a certain land type. Tang et al. [25], built a solution where a **segmentation map** can be drawn to generate terrain. The segmentation map uses colors to define areas belonging to a terrain category (Fig. 1).

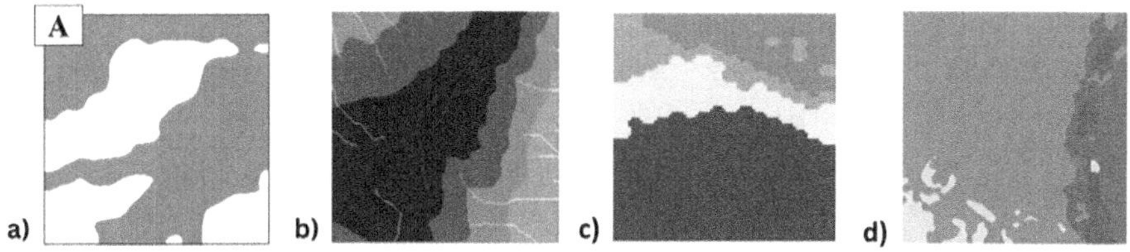

Fig. 1. 2D sketch types, where the sketch a) is from Guerin et al. [11], b) from Naik et al. [20], c) from Ramos et al. [22], d) from Tang et al. [25]

There are two very recent approaches published after our work started that are worth mentioning here. The first one, Trello3D, is a 3D general-purposed object-generator based on diffusion models, later extended to be capable of generating large 3D maps [6]. TRELLISWorld's approach focus on generating tiles with local geometry, and then blending the overlapping tiles using a 3D cosine-weighted averaging scheme and smoothing transitions. While very scalable and flexible, there are no guarantees regarding the realism of the generated maps, as the underlying generative models were not fine-tuned for the generation of realistic terrain.

The second approach, MESA [4], is similar to our approach but uses a single conditioned denoising model, where conditioning is based on a textual caption. In our approach we will train two conditioned models, one for text-based conditioning, and another for semantic mask conditioning. Their model was trained on a version of the Major TOM dataset extended with global digital elevation models from the Copernicus DSM [2], and they also used automatically generated captions describing 4 types of geospatial context: biome, geology, country and season. On the weak side, only a small qualitative evaluation is presented with examples of generated images showcasing the model's ability to generate realistic images conditioned on the given textual captions.

3 Dataset

In this work, we explore two forms of conditioning terrain generation, conditioning via textual descriptions/captions, and conditioning via a semantic mask. Here, we describe how the dataset used to train and validate the proposed models was created.

All terrain data was obtained from Google Earth Engine (GEE) datasets. These GEE datasets were processed and three datasets were created: textured terrain, textured terrain and semantic mask pairs, and textured terrain and terrain caption pairs.

Textured terrain is a 4-channel RGBA image where the Alpha channel contains elevation data, while the RGB channels represent the corresponding surface colors. The elevation information was obtained from the NASA SRTM [10] dataset with a precision of 30 m/pixel, and surface images were obtained from the Landsat 8 dataset [1], with the same precision. In total, 42,379 combination images were obtained, each with a resolution of 256×256.

On the other hand, semantic masks, also called semantic layout images, use color-coded labels to spatially represent subjects. In this context, semantic masks classify terrain landforms using color. The land information was obtained from a landform classification dataset based on the work of [26], in which landforms are classified based on local and global relief. The water information was obtained from the Copernicus Digital Surface Model (DSM) [2], which identifies permanent water bodies. The semantic masks dataset comprises a total of 22,175 pairs of semantic masks and combination terrain images, all with a resolution of 256×256.

Finally, a terrain caption is a textual description of the landforms present in a terrain image. The landform classes that can be included in a caption are mountain, hills, plain, valley, cliff, river, and water. The terrain caption is comprised of one or more of these keywords, in any order, separated by a comma. Examples are depicted in Fig. 2. It is important to point out that given the size of the dataset (22,175 images) it was not possible to manually label the images with a textual description. Instead, a multi-label classifier was trained and used to automatically generate captions from the semantic masks. The final dataset has 22,175 pairs of combination images and their corresponding terrain captions.

4 Conditional LDMs for Controlled Terrain Generation

As depicted in Fig. 3, the proposed Conditional LDM architecture is composed of 3 essential parts: the Auto-Encoder composed of an encoder (E) and decoder

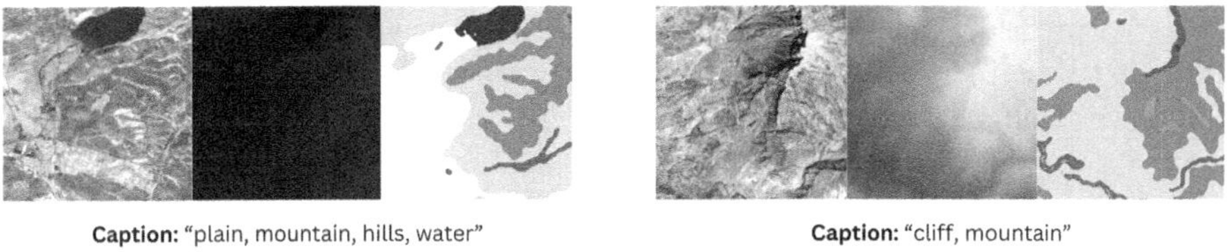

Fig. 2. Examples of terrain captions and the heightmap, texture and semantic mask associated.

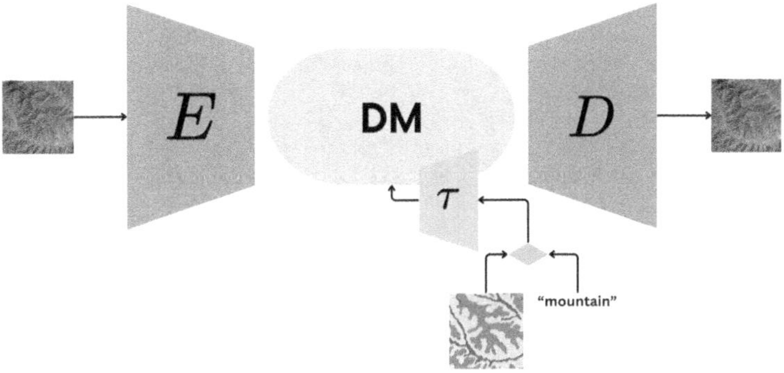

Fig. 3. Layout of Conditional LDMs.

(D) model, which provides a representative compressed space for training a diffusion model; the diffusion model itself (DM), which generates images; and the τ "expert" encoder, which processes the conditioning information.

In this work, two conditional LDMs were trained: a Text-to-image model, and a Semantic Synthesis model. The AE architecture used was a Variational AE (VAE) enhanced with an adversarial objective, adapted from [23]. Two VAEs were trained with the combination images, one for the Text-To-Image model and another for the Semantic Synthesis model. Then, using these VAEs, the diffusion models were trained.

The semantic synthesis model was trained conditionally with the semantic mask dataset. This makes it so that after being fully trained, a semantic mask can be used for generating textured terrain. The Text-To-Image model was trained conditionally with the terrain captions dataset. After being fully trained, the model can generate textured terrain using textual terrain descriptions. Both models used the training procedure and τ architecture of Rombach et al. [23]. The hyperparameters for both models are defined in Table 1.

The models were trained on a machine with an Intel Xeon W-2223 8 cores processor, with an RTX 3090 with 24 GB, with 16 GB of ram, and running a Linux Operating System. Training was conducted until convergence or until reaching epoch 100.

These two models complement each other, as they each explore a distinct user-guided technique for generating terrain. The semantic mask drawing allows users to precisely specify landforms and their spatial arrangement, while terrain text descriptions offer an effortless way to obtain specific landforms in an unknown configuration.

Table 1. LDM hyperparameters and configuration.

Task	Text-to-Image	Semantic Synthesis
Dataset	Terrain-Captions	Terrain-Mask
f	8	4
z-shape	$32 \times 32 \times 4$	$64 \times 64 \times 4$
Diffusion steps	1000	1000
Noise Schedule	linear	linear
Model Size	382M	291M
Channels	128	128
Depth	2	2
Channel Multiplier	1,2,4,4	1,4,8
Number of Heads	8	8
Dropout	–	–
Batch Size	2	4
Learning Rate	5.0e−05	1.0e−06
Conditioning	CA	concat
(C)A-resolutions	32, 16, 8	16
Embedding Dimension	640	–
Transformer Depth	1	–

5 Evaluation

To validate the results of the conditional LDMs for controlled terrain generation, we focused on two main forms of evaluation: a quantitative evaluation of the quality of generated images, and a qualitative evaluation with users.

5.1 Performance Metrics

For the quantitative evaluation, we used two metrics that are sometimes used to evaluate terrain generation approaches with Deep Learning models. The FID [12] metric evaluates the similarity between generated images and real images by comparing the latent features of a large pre-trained model, while LPIPS [27] evaluates the perceived quality of images using a NN fine-tuned on human perceptual judgments. In Table 2 the results for these metrics are presented, along with the scores obtained by other relevant works. StyleTerrain and TDN only used FID as an evaluation metrid. Furthermore, most related work only generates the heightmap and do not generate textures.

What can first be deduced from these results is that according to both metrics, the Text-to-Image model performs better than the Semantic Synthesis model, for both the texture and the elevation. With respect to other works, concerning the FID metrics, it has a better score than GAN approaches, and

Table 2. FID and LPIPS metric comparison of works on terrain generation. GAN and DM solutions are separated by a line. * denotes our models. The best scores are highlighted in **bold** while the second best are underlined.

	↓ LPIPS Elevation	↓ LPIPS Texture	↓ FID Elevation	↓ FID Texture
StyleTerrain [15]	–	–	5.67	–
Guerin et al. [11]	≈ 0.22	–	≈ 70	–
TDN [14]	–	–	**0.44**	–
Lochner et al. [18]	≈ **0.18**	–	≈ 25	–
Text-to-Image*	0.39	**0.58**	1.57	**7.88**
Semantic Synthesis*	0.34	0.57	2.92	11.68

the second-best score of DM approaches. The LPIPS score is not great, but the NN used to score was trained in regular images from Imagenet [7] and might not be the best approach for this domain. It is also important to point out that our models are the only ones that also produce textures.

5.2 User Evaluation

We conducted an evaluation with users with the goal of evaluating users' perceptions of 3 concepts:

- the **realism** of the terrains generated by the LDMs;
- the **quality of the conditioning data** (text or semantic mask) which is used to describe the terrain
- the **alignment** between the terrain generated and the conditioning data

The survey begins with a brief introduction to the theme to ensure consistency among participants regardless of knowledge background. This is followed by an explanation of the survey structure which recommended a completion time of around 10 min, meaning on average 30 s per question. This duration was deemed sufficient based on pre-testing results.

We used a *within-subject design*, where participants where shown a total of 20 different terrain patches. A terrain patch consists in an image of 3D terrain, along with the respective heightmap and color image. From these, 10 patches of terrain were real, 5 terrain patches were generated by the text-to-image model, and 5 terrain patches were generated by the semantic synthesis model. The different patches were presented to the participant in random order. After each patch, the participant was asked to rate the realism of the terrain, by rating their agreement to the statement "Based on the presented images, the depicted terrain is real", using a 7-point Likert scale. Additionally, for 5 of the 10 real patches and for the patches generated by the semantic synthesis, the participant was also presented with a semantic layout image for each patch and asked to rate if the semantic mask matched the terrain in the patch (also using a 7-point Likert scale). Alternatively, for the other 5 real patches, and the 5 patches generated by the text-to-image model, we presented the participant with a textual description of the terrain and asked if the description correctly defined the landforms depicted in the patch.

Results. We used the Prolific platform to conduct the survey, obtaining 76 responses, along the span of 1 days. Ages of participants range from 18 to 62 although 80% of participants are at most 34 years old. Gender representation has close to a 50/50 split between male and female.

Regarding perceived realism, we ended up with 4 sub-scales: (1.) realism for real terrain, (2.) realism for terrain generated by the Text-To-Image model, (3.) realism for terrain generated by the Semantic Synthesis model, and (4.) realism for all of the generated terrain combined. These constructs will be from here on referred to as **Real, T2I, SSynth** and **Generated**, respectively.

As a first step, we conducted a reliability analysis for each sub-scale to check if there was a strong consistency in the realism within each subgroup of patches. For the 10-item Real sub-scale, the results indicate an *acceptable* internal consistency (Cronbach's Alpha = .721). For the 10-item Generated sub-scale, the results indicate an *acceptable* internal consistency (Cronbach's Alpha = .73). For the 5-item T2I sub-scale, the results indicate a *questionable* internal consistency (Cronbach's Alpha = .0.663). For the 5-item SSynth sub-scale, the results indicate a *poor* internal consistency (Cronbach's Alpha = .515).

These scores suggest that the Real and Generated sub-scales reliably measure the construct of perceived realism for real terrain and generated terrain respectively. For this reason, the mean of the items will be used as a composite score in subsequent analysis. Even though the I2T and SSynth sub-scales do not score well, analysis will also be conducted on the composite scores of these.

Next the data was checked for normality, and a Shapiro-Wilk test indicated a deviation from normality for some sub-groups (e.g. W = .965, p = .033 for Generated). Therefore the non-parametric Wilcoxon signed-rank test was used to determine if there were any statistically significant differences between generated and real terrain patches. Figure 4 shows the boxplots for the results of perceived realism for the evaluated sub-scales.

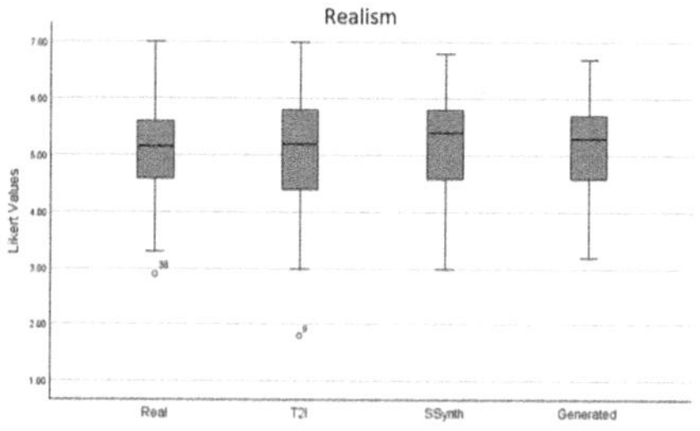

Fig. 4. Box plot of perceived realism for real and generated sub-scales.

The results of these tests showed that, for:

- Real and Generated, there was **no** statistically significant difference in perceived realism between real terrain and generated terrain, W = 1300.5, p = 0.435.

- Real and T2I, there was **no** statistically significant difference in perceived realism between real terrain and terrain generated via the Text-To-Image model, W = 1122, p = 0.48.
- Real and SSynth, there **was a** statistically significant difference in perceived realism between real terrain and terrain generated via the Semantic Synthesis model, W = 1693.5, p = .033. However, as can be seen by the Fig. 4, this is because the terrain generated by the Semantic Synthesis model is, overall, perceived as more realistic than real terrain. The effect size is $r = 0.2447$ which indicates a small to medium effect.

As both semantic masks and textual descriptions are automatically generated, we also want to evaluate the perceived quality of the generated conditioning information, both for the real patches and for the generated patches.

For evaluating the conditioning match, 4 sub-scales measure the following constructs: the (1.) match between real terrain and its terrain caption, (2.) match between generated terrain and its terrain caption. These concepts will be referred to as **Caption Real** and **Caption Generated**, respectively. For the semantic mask conditioning, there are 2 constructs: (3.) the match between real terrain and its semantic mask, and (4.) the match between generated terrain and its semantic mask. These concepts will be referred to as **Mask Real** and **Mask Generated**, respectively.

Then, to assess the **quality of the conditioning information**, box plots were created to display the statistics of each terrain patch regarding the match between *real* terrain and the conditioning information, depicted in Fig. 5.

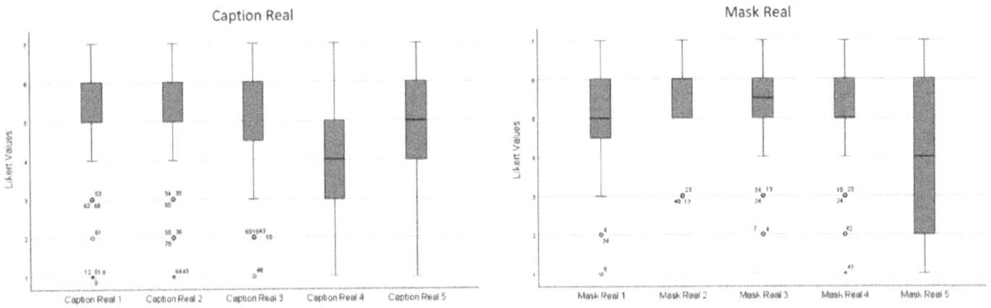

Fig. 5. Box plot of Caption Real and Mask real sub-scales.

From the box-plot, it is apparent that there was a lot of statistic variation between different terrain patches in each scale. For Caption Real, in some items the response was positive but contained many outliers, and in others, the overall response was more neutral but the variance was higher. Regarding Mask Real, four of the terrain patches had positive results and many outliers while the other patch had a neutral score, with a median of 4, and high variance. The internal consistency scores reflect these differences: Caption Real has a Cronbach's Alpha value of $\alpha = 0.359$ and Mask Real has a Cronbach's Alpha value of $\alpha = 0.611$.

The high variance in all items and the bad internal consistency for both sub-scales indicate that the conditioning is ambiguous, and therefore it is hard to generalize any findings. A similar story occurs when looking at the alignment between the conditioning information and the generated patches (see Fig. 6). There is a very high variance in the results across different terrain patches, with a low Cronbach's Alpha, which means that we cannot group patches and test a meaningful hypothesis. We can however gain some insights by analysing the boxplot. Overal, the results for the caption of generated patches seem to be worse than the semantic mask (e.g. patch #2).

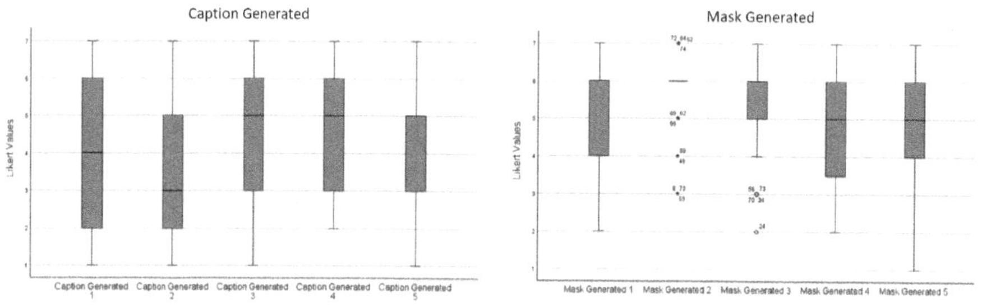

Fig. 6. Box plot of Caption Generated and Mask Generated sub-scales.

Although there is a high variability and many outliers the median for generated terrain is usually the same or higher than that of the real terrain, and in the case of Mask Generated for patch #2, the results were the most consistent among participants, with a median score of 6 (Agree) and a relatively low variance.

6 Conclusion

This study set out to explore the application of conditional LDMs for terrain generation, focusing on their ability to produce realistic textured terrain based on user input. Two distinct input modalities were investigated: text descriptions and semantic mask drawings.

The findings demonstrate that both trained models successfully generated realistic terrain textures. However, given the high variance in the alignment of the generated terrain to the conditioning information was unable to be methodologically evaluated. Nonetheless, the Semantic Synthesis LDM exhibited high potential for producing a diverse range of landforms due to its ability to spatially define the terrain layouts. The same is true for the text-based input method, although its descriptiveness is more constrained because of the caption formulation.

As a key contribution, this is one of the first works, together with MESA, to use diffusion models to generate realistic terrain elevation and texture simultaneously. But in addition to textual conditioning as supported by MESA, we also support semantic mask conditioning. We also provided an extensive evaluation of our model with both quantitative metrics and a qualitative user study.

In terms of limitations, the subjectivity of the user input methods - both text-based and semantic mask inputs - poses challenges, as precise and intuitive control is crucial for effective terrain generation. To address these, future work should focus on improving the quality of the terrain descriptions and semantic masks, by creating more expressive models (with more terrain classes), allowing for better control.

Acknowledgments. Work supported by national funds through Fundação para a Ciência e a Tecnologia, I.P. (FCT) under projects UID/50021/2025 and UID/PRR/50021/2025.

References

1. USGS Landsat 8 Level 2, Collection 2, Tier 1 courtesy of the U.S. Geological Survey. https://usgs.gov
2. Copernicus dem - global and european digital elevation model. https://dataspace.copernicus.eu/explore-data/data-collections/copernicus-contributing-missions/collections-description/COP-DEM. Accessed 14 Sept 2024
3. Balaji, Y., et al.: eDiff-I: text-to-image diffusion models with an ensemble of expert denoisers. arXiv preprint arXiv:2211.01324 (2022)
4. Borne-Pons, P., Czerkawski, M., Martin, R., Rouffet, R.: Mesa: text-driven terrain generation using latent diffusion and global copernicus data (2025). https://arxiv.org/abs/2504.07210
5. Cai, X., Xi, M., u, N., Yang, Z., Sun, H.: A terrain elevation map generation method based on self-attention mechanism and multifeature sketch. Comput. Intell. Neurosci. **2022** (2022)
6. Chen, H., Liu, Y., Li, M.: TrellisWorld: training-free world generation from object generators (2025). https://arxiv.org/abs/2510.23880
7. Deng, J., Dong, W., Socher, R., Li, L.J., Li, K., Fei-Fei, L.: ImageNet: a large-scale hierarchical image database. In: 2009 IEEE Conference on Computer Vision and Pattern Recognition, pp. 248–255. IEEE (2009)
8. Dhariwal, P., Nichol, A.: Diffusion models beat GANs on image synthesis. Adv. Neural. Inf. Process. Syst. **34**, 8780–8794 (2021)
9. Esser, P., et al.: Scaling rectified flow transformers for high-resolution image synthesis. In: Forty-First International Conference on Machine Learning (2024)
10. Farr, T.G., et al.: The shuttle radar topography mission. Rev. Geophys. **45**(2) (2007)
11. Guérin, É., et al.: Interactive example-based terrain authoring with conditional generative adversarial networks. ACM Trans. Graph. **36**(6), 228–1 (2017)
12. Heusel, M., Ramsauer, H., Unterthiner, T., Nessler, B., Hochreiter, S.: GANs trained by a two time-scale update rule converge to a local nash equilibrium. Advances in Neural Information Processing Systems, vol. 30 (2017)
13. Ho, J., Jain, A., Abbeel, P.: Denoising diffusion probabilistic models. Adv. Neural. Inf. Process. Syst. **33**, 6840–6851 (2020)

14. Hu, Z., Hu, K., Mo, C., Pan, L., Wang, Z.: Terrain diffusion network: climatic-aware terrain generation with geological sketch guidance. In: Proceedings of the AAAI Conference on Artificial Intelligence, vol. 38, pp. 12565–12573 (2024)
15. Huang, Y.L., Yuan, X.F.: StyleTerrain: a novel disentangled generative model for controllable high-quality procedural terrain generation. Comput. Graph. **116**, 373–382 (2023)
16. Isola, P., Zhu, J.Y., Zhou, T., Efros, A.A.: Image-to-image translation with conditional adversarial networks. In: Proceedings of the IEEE Conference on Computer Vision and Pattern Recognition, pp. 1125–1134 (2017)
17. Li, S., Li, K., Xiong, L., Tang, G.: Generating terrain data for geomorphological analysis by integrating topographical features and conditional generative adversarial networks. Remote Sens. **14**(5), 1166 (2022)
18. Lochner, J., Gain, J., Perche, S., Peytavie, A., Galin, E., Guérin, E.: Interactive authoring of terrain using diffusion models. In: Computer Graphics Forum, vol. 42, p. e14941. Wiley Online Library (2023)
19. Lv, Z., Wei, Y., Zuo, W., Wong, K.Y.K.: PLACE: adaptive layout-semantic fusion for semantic image synthesis. In: Proceedings of the IEEE/CVF Conference on Computer Vision and Pattern Recognition, pp. 9264–9274 (2024)
20. Naik, S., Jain, A., Sharma, A., Rajan, K.S.: Deep generative framework for interactive 3D terrain authoring and manipulation. In: IGARSS 2022-2022 IEEE International Geoscience and Remote Sensing Symposium, pp. 6410–6413 (2022)
21. Radford, A.: Unsupervised representation learning with deep convolutional generative adversarial networks. arXiv preprint arXiv:1511.06434 (2015)
22. Ramos, N., Santos, P., Dias, J.: Dual critic conditional Wasserstein GAN for height-map generation. In: Proceedings of the 18th International Conference on the Foundations of Digital Games, pp. 1–4 (2023)
23. Rombach, R., Blattmann, A., Lorenz, D., Esser, P., Ommer, B.: High-resolution image synthesis with latent diffusion models. In: Proceedings of the IEEE/CVF Conference on Computer Vision and Pattern Recognition, pp. 10684–10695 (2022)
24. Sohl-Dickstein, J., Weiss, E., Maheswaranathan, N., Ganguli, S.: Deep unsupervised learning using nonequilibrium thermodynamics. In: International Conference on Machine Learning, pp. 2256–2265. PMLR (2015)
25. Tang, R., Sweetser, P.: Multilayer map generation using attribute loss functions. In: Proceedings of the 18th International Conference on the Foundations of Digital Games, pp. 1–4 (2023)
26. Theobald, D.M., Harrison-Atlas, D., Monahan, W.B., Albano, C.M.: Ecologically-relevant maps of landforms and physiographic diversity for climate adaptation planning. PLoS ONE **10**(12), e0143619 (2015)
27. Zhang, R., Isola, P., Efros, A.A., Shechtman, E., Wang, O.: The unreasonable effectiveness of deep features as a perceptual metric. In: Proceedings of the IEEE Conference on Computer Vision and Pattern Recognition, pp. 586–595 (2018)

From Play to Plot: Sifting Emergent Stories Through Clustering Heuristics

Miguel Belbute(✉) and Carlos Martinho

INESC-ID, University of Lisbon - Instituto Superior Técnico, Lisbon, Portugal
{miguel.belbute,carlos.martinho}@tecnico.ulisboa.pt

Abstract. Emergent games are grounded on complex and unpredictable simulations, often incompatible with traditional narrative structures. This work explores how story sifting – the open design challenge of recognising gameplay event sequences as stories – can be implemented as a bottom-up approach of highlighting narrative value in emergent games through clustering heuristics. Log clustering is explored to identify gameplay sequences that are sufficiently relevant to formulate narratives. These sequences were extracted from simulated playthroughs of the emergent colony simulator RimWorld. Multiple clustering heuristics were considered (e.g., temporal/spatial distance, shared participants and verb importance), with two major overarching architectures being developed: clustering pipelines and voting ensembles. After a narratively relevant sequence is identified, the underlying logs are summarised by a Large Language Model (LLM), whose prompts were refined through iterative prompt engineering. When compared to clustering pipelines, voting ensembles present significantly better F1-score in identifying objective-specific stories from game logs (e.g., hunting, building, socialising). To evaluate the experience of utilising the story sifting system as a whole, two pilot studies were performed with distinct in-game tasks and session durations. Both players familiar and new to emergent games reported their experiences improved when in contact with narratives sifted from gameplay, especially considering shorter play sessions. Inherent noise from longer play sessions heavily impacts the system's accuracy, suggesting story sifting should be applied in shorter periods of gameplay. Study participants also mentioned the concept of story support, underlying their desire for the recognised stories to be naturally incorporated into gameplay.

Keywords: Story sifting · Game log clustering · LLM · Emergent narrative

1 Introduction

Emergent games are interactive systems which exploit their systemic nature to produce complex and unplanned behaviours from interactions grounded on simple rules. Despite emergence serving as a constant motor for engaging and

R. Baptista et al. (Eds.): VJ 2025, CCIS 2988, pp. 135–147, 2027.
https://doi.org/10.1007/978-3-032-31642-4_12

novel experiences, these games often showcase design issues which are under-represented in research [7,8,17]. One such challenge focuses on highlighting the narrative value of emergent games which, due to their bottom-up essence, are commonly incompatible with the top-down, storylike structures of most games. Sifting and supporting stories in a "play-driven" manner (as opposed to "author-driven") surfaces as a possible dynamic solution. By exploiting the rich event logging of emergent games, clustering heuristics can aid in identifying emerging narratives, which often go unnoticed by players or have their potential untapped [7,17]. These stories can then be employed to underline the narrative value of past events, with future prospects of exploiting them to populate in-game elements. In summary, this work addresses the following research question (**RQ**): How can "play-driven" story sifting, implemented through clustering heuristics, underline the narrative value of emergent games?

2 Related Work

2.1 Emergent Games and Emergent Narratives

Emergence in games can be defined as unpredictable complexity stemming from a simple set of rules which are applied to a limited group of entities [18]. This complexity derives from coupled relationships, with the context modifications to any given entity implying global transformations in the entire system [18]. Emergence has thus been characterised as a "bottom-up" phenomenon, since it implies simpler, local interactions originating larger, more complex patterns [18]. The value of emergence in games lies in unpredictability and novelty, as players remain engaged by exploring the possible interactions between game elements [18].

Specifically, emergence is also a central tool in generating storylike content. Such "emergent narratives" are valued because they arise organically from systemic interactions, rather than from pre-authored scripts, creating the impression of authentic events unfolding within the game world [15]. With emergence manifesting through system-driven behaviours (e.g., The Game of Life) and even social dynamics outside of formal systems (e.g., bluffing in Poker) [18], emergent games span multiple genres (notable examples include Dwarf Fortress and RimWorld [1,12]).

2.2 Story Sifting and Story Support Challenges of Emergent Games

While emergence enriches gameplay, it also introduces design challenges. Grounding themselves on examples both from academia and industry, Ryan et al. highlighted issues such as story sifting[1] – distinguishing meaningful event sequences from "mundane" occurrences, which may cause emergent stories to

[1] In [17], this challenge is referred to as "story recognition". However, the main author later claimed "story sifting" was a more appropriate term [15].

go unnoticed by players –, and story support – integrating and showcasing stories through gameplay [7,17]. Both of these open design problems have received relatively reduced attention from researchers [7,8,17].

Prior work regarding story sifting mostly relies on: tracing the player's actions [2,17]; matching designer-specified "relevant" event patterns [7–9,13,15,17]; and scoring events on particular metrics and their variance [4,6,10,11]. While a common approach to story sifting, designer specification of relevant event chains is not only resource-intensive in complex systems (such as Dwarf Fortress [1]), but also fundamentally misaligned with the bottom-up nature of emergent games, imposing a top-down perspective [8,14].

Story support often focuses on showcasing narrative value through natural language retellings [2,3] or the production of other artifacts (e.g., podcast) [15]. Nonetheless, these approaches generally depend on a prior sifting of simulation logs or gameplay traces. In fact, sifting has been perceived as a method to automatically populate in-game content (e.g., dialogue, statues) supporting unique, emergent stories [2]. Consequently, the present work focuses on story sifting – the foundation upon which story support can naturally develop.

3 Methodology

This work employs naïve heuristics to cluster events into story-worthy sequences, this bottom-up grouping allowing salient event patterns to surface without enforcing external story archetypes. This promotes each playthrough's unique interactions, bolstering "play-driven" story sifting and directly addressing **RQ**. The application of Large Language Models (LLMs) enables the prompt conversion of clustered event logs into natural language narratives, representing an initial step towards the integration of sifted stories in games.

For clarity, we distinguish the following terms: a *log* refers to a single entry of the game's logging system, an *event* denotes a gameplay phenomenon described by one or more logs, and a *cluster* consists of a group of logs identified as an event sequence.

3.1 Base Game: RimWorld

RimWorld [12] – a sci-fi colony management game[2] – was chosen as the testbed for story sifting due to its rich systemic simulation and vast modding community[3]. Some RimWorld mods have already explored the concept of story sifting. RimStory detects and retrospectively "honours" past events (e.g., deaths) through in-game ceremonies (e.g., funerals). RimSaga exploits an LLM to create narrative content based on the game's event logs, showcasing that story sifting and summarisation is viable and well-received by the community. However, both mods seemingly depend on designer-specification of relevant events. Building on this foundation, a new RimWorld mod was developed, leveraging existing modding tools (e.g., XML, dnSpy, Harmony).

[2] To get a glimpse of RimWorld gameplay, watch this tutorial video.

[3] Modding consists of modifying a game, resulting in a "mod".

3.2 Story Sifting Pipeline

This section outlines the overall structure of the story sifting pipeline (Fig. 1), demonstrating how raw gameplay logs are transformed into summarised narratives. Firstly, event logs are retrieved and formatted, being subsequently subjected to one of two overarching architectures managing the story sifting process: clustering pipeline or voting ensemble. These architectures are composed of different combinations of filtering and clustering heuristics. From the resulting clusters, a final decision heuristic selects the biggest cluster as the most complete event sequence (or story). The final cluster is later conveyed to a LLM, which generates a summarising narrative. The next sections describe each step in greater detail, with an in-game demonstration of the final result being available here.

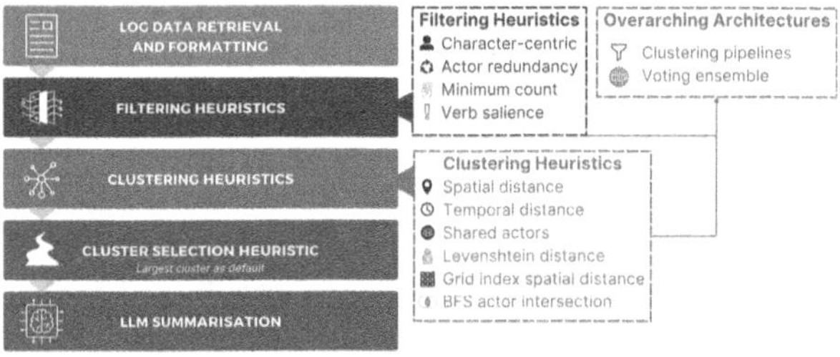

Fig. 1. The structure of the story sifting pipeline.

3.3 Log Data Retrieval and Formatting

With the quality and detail of the sifted story depending on the input data, it is important to collect event logs from multiple logging sources: combat encounters, social interactions, "notable" events (e.g., raids), health logs (e.g., wounds), and job orders (e.g., building roof). This data is subsequently formatted to include a timestamp, a location, identifiers, a list of participating actors, and a full event description, all of which are captured or generated at runtime. Both the unformatted and edited log data are stored in text files.

3.4 Event Sequence Sifting Filtering and Clustering Heuristics

This section presents the high-level heuristics that define how the system determines which gameplay moments are narratively meaningful among noisy event log data. The implemented heuristics either filter or cluster logs (Fig. 1), partially inspired by prior work on narrative modelling [4]. Filters remove less relevant logs (e.g., pertaining to redundant and frequent actions), whereas clustering heuristics group event logs by a metric of similarity (e.g., temporal proximity). Heuristics are combined into two overarching architectures: clustering pipelines (CPs), which apply heuristics sequentially to narrow down logs, and voting ensembles (VEs), where multiple heuristics vote on whether logs belong to the same cluster, generally achieving higher performance. The final cluster is selected based on size, assumed to represent the most complete story.

The following heuristics (Fig. 1), which guide the system's notion of narrative relevance, were developed and fine-tuned through a parameter grid search (Sect. 3.6):

- Character-centric - keeps logs whose participants are among the specified characters (e.g., main colonists);
- Actor redundancy - removes logs whose recent history already contains similar actions, reducing noise (e.g., wandering animals);
- Minimum count - only keeps clusters with a minimum of N event logs;
- Verb salience - logs are weighted by their main verbs' rarity (e.g., "died" is more salient than "wandering");
- Spatial distance - logs are clustered if the distance between their in-game sources falls below a specified threshold;
- Temporal distance - logs are clustered if the differences between associated timestamps fall below a specified threshold;
- Shared actors - groups logs that share participating actors or form contiguous actor chains;
- Levenshtein distance - logs are clustered considering the Levenshtein distance between their textual representations.[4]

Clustering Pipelines and Voting Ensembles. Two modular structures were implemented to account for the joint contributions of the heuristics (Fig. 1): CPs, which apply a heuristic on the output of the previous one; and VEs, in which heuristics "vote" on whether two event logs belong to the same cluster, having to reach a specified agreement threshold.

In practice, CPs sequentially narrow down the amount of event logs considered per cluster, funnelling information, whereas the VEs always consider the same initial set of event logs.

The results derived from both of these structures are stored in text files, with the clusters and their respective contents being separated – as shown in this example.

Selecting a Final Cluster. Currently, a single, final cluster is selected from the clusters outputted by the CPs and VEs. For the decision criteria, the largest cluster (number of logs) is identified as the most complete story and thus a sufficiently relevant event sequence.

[4] Two optimised heuristic variants were later developed (details in Sect. 4.1).

3.5 Summarisation of Sifted Event Sequences

After a relevant event sequence is identified, it is summarised and converted into a cohesive narrative structure. To pursue this objective, this work exploited a LLM API, since these artificial intelligence architectures are commonly employed in summarisation and creative writing for games [5]. After a filtering process which considered accessibility, instruction-following, efficiency and advanced language understanding, the Mistral 7B Instruct surfaced as the optimal candidate. Log data is fed into the selected LLM model, prompted to appropriately summarise the events described in the logs, without inferring information, creatively adding new content or compromising the game's setting.

3.6 Evaluating the Implemented Systems

The story sifting pipeline was separately evaluated considering its two main stages – event sequence sifting and LLM summarisation. The event sifting was quantitatively evaluated through F1-scores and comparison with "ground truth" sets, while the summarisation was qualitatively assessed based on the generated summaries. Additionally, the experience of utilising the story sifting pipeline was evaluated as a whole during the pilot studies.

Evaluating the Heuristics. The heuristics were evaluated quantitively through three case studies, derived from actual gameplay logs: a hunt story (colonists attack animals), a build story (colonists build a settlement), and a social story (colonists socialise with each other). The gameplay logs encompassing these case studies were extracted and formatted as mentioned in Sect. 3.3. Then, the logs were manually analysed to eliminate noisy entries, thus formulating a final cluster of relevant events – the evaluation's "ground truth".

The heuristics were applied on the logs composing each case study, with the clustering outputs being directly compared with the "ground truths" through F1-scores (e.g., a false positive occurs when a log is assigned by the heuristic to a story, though it is not included in the respective "ground truth"). The individual heuristics were evaluated in isolation and in combination with other heuristics, considering both overarching architectures (the VEs were only developed and tested after P1). This evaluation was pursued through an automatic evaluator script, which additionally performed a grid search of each heuristic's parameters.

The heuristic analysis' best results (over 300 combinations) are presented in Fig. 2 (detailed data can be accessed here). Overall, the F1-scores of Fig. 2 suggest that no single heuristic is sufficient: narratives can only be sifted considering the multi-dimensionality of gameplay (e.g., time, space, actors), reflecting the intricacy of emergence.

One of the best approaches for the CPs consisted of firstly having a filter heuristic to reduce noise, followed by a combination of clustering heuristics to group relevant event logs (e.g., *CP_Sal0.1_S10_T200*). The VEs generally perform better than the CPs, justifying further exploration. Despite this, some pipelines did achieve top scores regarding specific stories (e.g., *CP_Sal0.3_S20* for the hunt story).

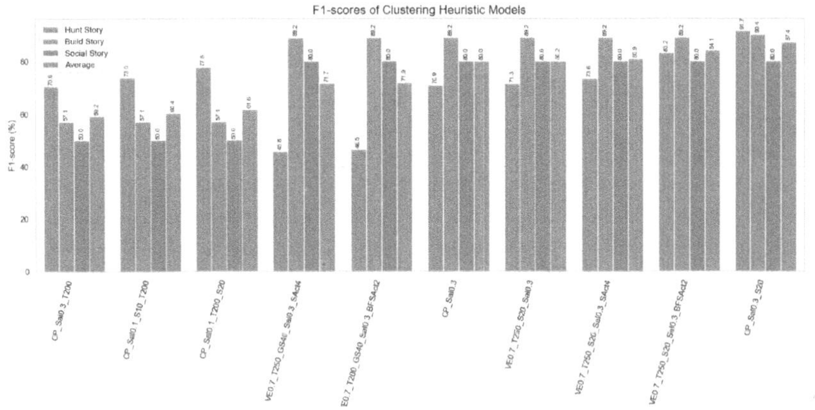

Fig. 2. F1-score comparison between story sifting models. The models are named after their heuristic components: "Sal" is verb salience, "S"/"T" are spatial/temporal distance, "GS" is the grid index spatial distance, "SA" is shared actors, and "BFSA" is BFS actor intersection. Following the heuristics' initialisms are the corresponding main parameters (e.g., "S20" represents spatial distance with a 20 units of distance of threshold). The models' initial letters – "CP"/"VE" –, indicate pipelines or voting ensembles, the latter being followed by their agreement threshold (e.g., "VE0.7").

Evaluating the LLM Prompts. The LLM prompts were qualitatively evaluated on the generated summaries' cohesion with the game setting and the accuracy of log integration. Immersion-breaking references to the game or the logs, unfounded subjective characterisations, wrongfully inferred information (e.g., a character's species), ambiguities, and other hallucinations led to an iterative prompt engineering process, which mitigated these issues.

4 Experimental Procedure

To evaluate the complete story sifting pipeline, two pilot studies were performed. It is relevant to underline that, due to their limited scope, these studies offer preliminary insights rather than definitive validation of the proposed system.

The studies followed a common structure: random participants were invited to supply demographic information about themselves and previous experiences with RimWorld [12] and similar emergent games. They were then invited to watch a RimWorld tutorial, and play a brief RimWorld [12] session with a specified goal.

The first pilot study (P1) had players control three colonists to hunt three different animals, after which they would press a button to execute the summary generation process. P1 was allocated a gameplay time limit of five minutes, with each session lasting approximately 20 min per participant.

The second pilot study (P2) had players control three colonists to freely interact with the game world and, after 10 min, the summary generation process was automatically executed. Each pilot session lasted approximately 30 min per participant.

In both pilots, players had access to miscellaneous items from a pre-defined pool of loot – some of these items were randomly selected (e.g., weapons) while others were always included in the scenario (e.g., survival meals, wood) –, ensuring diverse types of playthroughs. For each pilot study, the best combination of heuristics and LLM prompts (at the time of the experimental procedures) were exploited to generate the summaries – the *CP_Sal0.1_T200_S20* and *VE0.7_T250_S20_Sal0.3_BFSAct2* models (Fig. 2) were applied in P1 and P2, respectively, with the LLM prompts being accessible here. The summarised narratives were conveyed as in-game notifications, with participants being previously instructed to read them and subsequently return to the questionnaire to answer items about them. The studies' quantitative feedback can be visualised in Fig. 3.

The questionnaires' items (mostly 5-point Likert scale statements), the studies' game logs, the clustering results, and the generated narratives are accessible in the project's public OSF project. For the following analyses, participants are identified with "PYUX" – "Y" representing P1 or P2, and "X" the user's identifier.

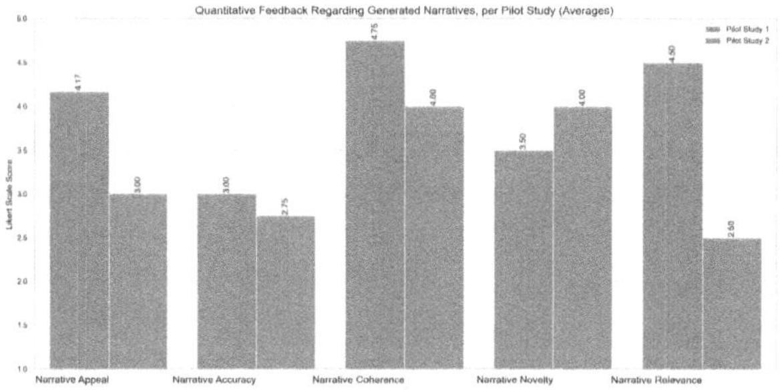

Fig. 3. Quantitative feedback regarding the generated narratives of both pilot studies.

4.1 Pilot Study 1 (P1)

Sample Characterisation. P1 included four Portuguese participants (three male, one female, aged 26–30). Only P1U1 was a regular RimWorld [12] player, showcasing high confidence regarding emergent games and claiming they were enjoyable. P1U2 had some experience with emergent games but lower confidence with them. P1U3 and P1U4 had no prior experience and negative attitudes toward such games. Only P1U1 and P1U2 fit the target demographic, though insights from all participants were valuable.

Narrative Feedback. Participants evaluated the generated narratives on appeal (NAp), accuracy (NAc), coherence with the game world (NC), novelty (NN) and relevance (NR) – Fig. 1 and Fig. 3. Overall, players found the narrative enjoyable and enhancing to their experience, even if their prior familiarity with the game varied and despite the story's fidelity to the actual gameplay not being fully convincing. The narrative did not violate the game's setting, being perceived as relevant and moderately introducing novelty, highlighting otherwise unnoticed gameplay events (Table 1).

Table 1. Quantitative feedback on the first (P1) and second (P2) pilot study's generated narrative across various evaluation criteria.

Criteria	P1U1	P1U2	P1U3	P1U4	Avg. P1	P2U1	P2U2	P2U3	P2U4	Avg. P2
Appeal (NAp)	4.00	4.67	3.67	5.00	4.17	2.67	3.00	3.67	2.67	3.00
Accuracy (NAc)	3.00	5.00	4.33	1.00	3.00	4.00	1.00	5.00	1.00	2.75
Coherence (NC)	4.00	5.00	2.00	5.00	4.75	4.00	2.00	5.00	5.00	4.00
Novelty (NN)	4.00	4.00	2.00	5.00	3.50	5.00	4.00	4.00	3.00	4.00
Relevance (NR)	5.00	5.00	5.00	3.00	4.50	4.00	1.00	4.00	1.00	2.50

Further Comments. Three out of four participants reported the story sifting system enhanced immersion, "player imagination"[5] and enjoyment, with one (P1U1) specifically noting that it effectively highlighted character interactions. Criticism focused on excessive text length (P1U1, P1U4) and the omission of notable events or characters (P1U2, P1U3, P1U4), making summaries seem incomplete (e.g., *"the animal was killed but the story stops at it is running away"*, P1U2). P1U1 suggested future improvements such as incorporating the narratives into dialogue that would additionally reflect character relationships and their personalities, hinting that story support – the future step in this work – is indeed a necessity felt by players.

Discussion (P1). The majority of participants, regardless of previous experience with emergent games, felt story sifting improved their experience, though this seems unrelated to the summaries faithfully reflecting gameplay (Fig. 3).

---

[5] This expression points to apophenia – the tendency to perceive patterns in randomness –, allowing players to imaginatively interpret the simulations and fill in the gaps to create narratives.

This seemingly implies that story sifting should prioritise structural clarity over exhaustive coverage of events. Limitations included missing characters or events, suggesting the need for more nuanced data sifting and further feedback questioning in P2.

Methodologically, strict reliance on combined temporal and spatial heuristics, which initially seemed like a necessity for a coherent story (hence why models like *CP_Sal0.3_S20* (Fig. 2) were not always pursued), proved too restrictive, motivating the development of VEs to capture broader narrative patterns (e.g., simultaneous but spatially distant events, or periodically recurring traditions). To verify whether VEs accomplished this goal, P2's in-game task was expanded to free-play, without a specific goal. For P2, the LLM prompts were refined by adding baseline character information to strengthen the LLM's knowledge of the game and reduce unfounded inferences.

Technical Optimisations. The shared actors and spatial distance heuristics proved computationally expensive so they were refactored into near-linear variants to improve performance while maintaining comparable accuracy, resulting in the BFS actor intersection and a grid index spatial distance heuristic.

4.2 Pilot Study 2 (P2)

Sample Characterisation. P2 included four Portuguese participants (2 male, 2 female, aged 23–30). Two users (P2U3, P2U4) had previously played RimWorld [12], though none were regular players. Only P2U4 showed a positive attitude toward RimWorld [12] and emergent games, while the remaining participants showed low engagement and confidence. No participant claimed to play or be confident in their knowledge of emergent games. No participants belonged to the target demographic, though their insights were still valuable.

Narrative Feedback. Participants evaluated the generated narratives on appeal (NAp), accuracy (NAc), coherence with the game world (NC), novelty (NN), and relevance (NR) – Fig. 1 and Fig. 3. Overall, players still found the narrative coherent with the game's setting, introducing a level of novelty into the game, despite its accuracy receiving mixed feedback. However, participants found the narratives less appealing and relevant than in the previous study. Further analysis showed that most of the presented narratives were based on final clusters containing few events (1–3), resulting in uninteresting stories.

Further Comments. The majority of participants once again appreciated the stories for enhancing their immersion and promoting creativity (e.g., *"As I'm reading it, I'm recalling or imagining those situations."*, P2U3). Similarly to P1, the importance of story support was mentioned (P2U1), with criticism focused on the text being too long (P2U2, P2U3), with P2U3 even suggesting accompanying images. Three out of four users also complained about the narrative lacking sufficient gameplay moments, aligning with lower ratings for NAc.

Discussion. In P2, the narratives generated with the VEs were rated lower in enjoyment and relevance than in P1. The mediocre scores of these dimensions suggest the system did not manage to properly recognise meaningful event sequences from gameplay. This decline appears linked to longer, less structured play sessions, which increased noise in the clustering task (verified by each final cluster only containing a handful of event logs). A further limitation may stem from a training bias, since the heuristics and their overarching architectures were tuned on short, goal-oriented sessions (hunt, build, socialise) – this could explain the poorer performance in P2, despite the perceived success in the supervised evaluation. These findings suggest the current story sifting approach is best applied incrementally to short spans of gameplay, rather than extended sessions, where noise is imminent and negatively hinders the appeal of such a system.

5 Conclusions

This work implemented a bottom-up story sifting system to highlight the narrative value of emergent games, exploiting heuristics to cluster gameplay events and an LLM to generate in-game summaries. Across two exploratory studies, players generally reported improved experiences, though omissions of relevant events limited narrative faithfulness. Results suggest that voting ensembles outperform clustering pipelines for short sessions, but longer play introduces excessive noise, indicating that incremental story sifting over shorter durations is more effective with the current implementation. While **RQ** has been partially addressed, experimentation is necessary to further substantiate the preliminary results. Research of new heuristics, final cluster selection criteria, and extended "ground truth" datasets is additionally planned. Future directions also include refining LLM prompts to integrate character traits and relationships ("focalization" [6]), and addressing story support by embedding the identified narratives into in-game content (e.g., dialogue, books). Given that imperfect summaries were still perceived as enjoyable, exploring uncertainty in story conveying (as [16] did with rumours) may prove worthwhile.

Acknowledgments. This work was supported by the EU Horizon 2021 project EMPOWER (GA No. 101060918), and by national funds through Fundação para a Ciência e Tecnologia, I.P. (FCT) under projects UID/50021/2025 and UID/PRR/50021/2025.

Disclosure of Interests. The authors have no competing interests to declare that are relevant to the content of this article.

References

1. Adams, T., Adams, Z.: Slaves to armok: god of blood chapter II: Dwarf fortress. http://www.bay12games.com/dwarves/. Bay 12 Games
2. Antoun, C., Antoun, M., Ryan, J.O., Samuel, B., Swanson, R., Walker, M.A.: Generating natural language retellings from prom week play traces. In: Proceedings of the FDG Workshop on Procedural Content Generation (2015)
3. Behrooz, M., Swanson, R., Jhala, A.: Remember that time? Telling interesting stories from past interactions. In: Schoenau-Fog, H., Bruni, L.E., Louchart, S., Baceviciute, S. (eds.) ICIDS 2015. LNCS, vol. 9445, pp. 93–104. Springer, Cham (2015). https://doi.org/10.1007/978-3-319-27036-4_9
4. Cardona-Rivera, R.E., Cassell, B.A., Ware, S.G., Young, R.M.: Indexter: a computational model of the event-indexing situation model for characterizing narratives. In: Proceedings of the 3rd Workshop on Computational Models of Narrative, pp. 34–43 (2012)
5. Gallotta, R., et al.: Large language models and games: a survey and roadmap. IEEE Trans. Games (2024)
6. Hassan, S., León, C., Gervás, P., Hervás, R.: A computer model that generates biography-like narratives. In: Proceedings of the 4th International Joint Workshop on Computational Creativity, pp. 5–12 (2007)
7. Johnson-Bey, S., Mateas, M.: Centrifuge: a visual tool for authoring sifting patterns for character-based simulationist storyworlds. In: AIIDE Workshops (2021)
8. Kreminski, M., Dickinson, M., Wardrip-Fruin, N.: Felt: a simple story sifter. In: Cardona-Rivera, R.E., Sullivan, A., Young, R.M. (eds.) ICIDS 2019. LNCS, vol. 11869, pp. 267–281. Springer, Cham (2019). https://doi.org/10.1007/978-3-030-33894-7_27
9. Kreminski, M., Dickinson, M., Wardrip-Fruin, N., Mateas, M.: Select the unexpected: a statistical heuristic for story sifting. In: Vosmeer, M., Holloway-Attaway, L. (eds.) ICIDS 2022. LNCS, vol. 13762, pp. 292–308. Springer, Cham (2022). https://doi.org/10.1007/978-3-031-22298-6_18
10. Lareau, F., Dras, M., Dale, R.: Detecting interesting event sequences for sports reporting. In: 13th European Workshop on Natural Language Generation, ENLG 2011. pp. 200–205. Association for Computational Linguistics (ACL) (2011)
11. León, C., Hassan, S., Gervás, P.: From the event log of a social simulation to narrative discourse: content planning in story generation. In: AISB Annual Convention, Newcastle University, Newcastle upon Tyne, UK, pp. 402–409 (2007)
12. Ludeon Studios: Rimworld (2013). https://rimworldgame.com/
13. Miller, C., Dighe, M., Martens, C., Jhala, A.: Stories of the town: balancing character autonomy and coherent narrative in procedurally generated worlds. In: Proceedings of the 14th International Conference on the Foundations of Digital Games, FDG 2019. Association for Computing Machinery, New York (2019). https://doi.org/10.1145/3337722.3341850
14. Osborn, J., Samuel, B., Mateas, M., Wardrip-Fruin, N.: Playspecs: regular expressions for game play traces. In: Proceedings of the AAAI Conference on Artificial Intelligence and Interactive Digital Entertainment, vol. 11, no. 1 (2021). https://doi.org/10.1609/aiide.v11i1.12803
15. Ryan, J.: Curating simulated storyworlds. Ph.D. thesis, UC Santa Cruz (2018)

16. Ryan, J., Mateas, M.: Simulating character knowledge phenomena in talk of the town. In: Game AI Pro 360, pp. 135–150. CRC Press (2019)
17. Ryan, J.O., Mateas, M., Wardrip-Fruin, N.: Open design challenges for interactive emergent narrative. In: International Conference on Interactive Digital Storytelling (2015). https://api.semanticscholar.org/CorpusID:16783879
18. Salen, K., Zimmerman, E.: Rules of Play: Game Design Fundamentals. The MIT Press (2003)

Wait, It's All Dynamical Systems? Always Has Been: Toward Precisely yet Intuitively Designing Ludonarrative Ergodicity

Pratama Wirya Atmaja[1,2,3](✉), Darlis Herumurti[1], Sylvester Arnab[1], Hadziq Fabroyir[1], and Petros Lameras[2]

[1] Institut Teknologi Sepuluh Nopember, Surabaya, Indonesia
7025251017@student.its.ac.id, {darlis,hadziq}@its.ac.id, aa8110@coventry.ac.uk
[2] Coventry University, Coventry, UK
ab3430@coventry.ac.uk
[3] University of Pembangunan Nasional "Veteran" Jawa Timur, Surabaya, Indonesia

Abstract. Ludonarrative systems, such as narrative games, are capable of accommodating fun, learning, reflection, and other human needs by virtue of being dynamical systems. However, designers typically conceptualize these systems in ways that pay little attention to their systemic qualities, leading to the concept's inefficient verification and validation (V&V) and other issues. To address this gap, we propose a general, precise, yet intuitive framework of ludonarrative systems as dynamical systems. Crucially, the framework integrates the notions of mechanics, dynamics, and player experience in the literature on ludonarrative systems with established theories of dynamical system *ergodicity* in physics, complex systems, and other sciences. We then outline how to use the framework to precisely yet intuitively design any ludonarrative system and conduct the design's V&V. We close this paper with our research plan to expand the framework into a domain-specific language (DSL) for early V&V of ludonarrative systems and use the DSL in the co-design of ludonarrative systems on a complex 21st-century issue.

Keywords: Ludonarrative systems · ergodicity · dynamical systems · verification and validation · design framework

1 Introduction

Across disciplines and industries, narrative games, interactive digital narratives, and other ludonarrative systems increasingly contribute their immense experiential potential to more and more use cases and scholarly investigations. Outside entertainment, the systems' capacity for providing engrossing, interactive, and highly malleable stories has myriad utilities in education [1], marketing [2], and even the military [3]. As established by the influential Mechanics-Dynamics-Aesthetics (MDA) framework [4] and Game Loop model [5], this capacity is the fruit of the systems' fundamental qualities as *dynamical systems*, i.e., those capable of producing dynamics. Thanks to these qualities,

R. Baptista et al. (Eds.): VJ 2025, CCIS 2988, pp. 148–165, 2027.
https://doi.org/10.1007/978-3-032-31642-4_13

the player can, as the gameplay progresses, experience exciting dynamics, which in some ways represent those in reality [6]. In turn, the dynamics let the player optimally yet safely apply their faculties for real-world benefits, such as cutting through the apparent hopelessness of sustainability crises or other complex issues [7].

However, despite this seemingly solid theoretical basis, the discourse on ludonarrative systems too often understates their systemic attributes [8]. The criticality of player experience, a very "soft" requirement [9], does make it a common practice, even among professional designers, to conceptualize ludonarrative systems with a vocabulary that accommodates creativity yet ambiguously aligns with that of systems [10]. Such vocabularies continue to be proposed, such as at the 2024 VideoJogos conference [11]. Unfortunately, regardless of the usefulness of such vocabularies, the resulting ambiguity is the Pandora's Box of all sorts of system development problems, from unstable requirements to misleading verification and validation (V&V) [12]. In particular, these problems severely affect socially impactful uses of ludonarrative systems, such as communicating complex issues to realize societal changes [6], due to their high stakes and costs, including those stemming from transdisciplinary co-design [13]. In the face of these problems, designers often choose to tread familiar ground, such as through genre-specific design patterns or domain-specific languages (DSLs) [14], a solution that, considering the ever-evolving catalog of ludonarrative genres [15] and possible uses of the systems in society [6], can only be short-term. Thus, there is an urgent need to ensure the design rigor of ludonarrative systems without constraining creativity or the systems' scopes.

We help fulfill the need by proposing a new design vocabulary: a genre-agnostic, precise, yet intuitive framework of dynamical ludonarrative systems. We achieve this goal by first identifying critical issues in the design of ludonarrative systems through an exploratory and cross-disciplinary literature review, followed by more targeted reviews on ludonarrative systems and dynamical systems in physics and other sciences. In particular, our review of the scientific literature reveals the precise yet intuitive essence of the systems: *ergodicity* [16]. Based on these reviews, we present our framework and outline its optimal use to address the aforementioned design issues. Lastly, we discuss our research plan to expand our framework into a DSL for early V&V of ludonarrative systems [17] and apply the DSL in a representative case study.

2 Literature Review

2.1 Current Issues Regarding Ludonarrative Design

On the one hand, system design increasingly strives for maximum efficiency by shortening the time between conceptualizing the system and the system's V&V through formal methods, DSLs, and such [17]. On the other hand, the open-ended process of translating requirements into the system's design requires more intuitive tools, such as non-canonical diagrams and free-form sketches, which can ease communication between team members and be a crucial body of design knowledge [18]. In software and system engineering, flexible modeling, which allows a gradual increase in design precision and standard conformity through automatic design disambiguation, is the state-of-the-art bridge between the two needs [19].

However, no such bridge exists yet in ludonarrative design. Despite the increasing maturity of the discipline [12], it remains plagued with ambiguity [9], which stems from its complex marriage of engineering and art [10]. The way this complexity manifests is at least twofold. Firstly, as the literature has long stated, ludonarrative design is an effort of a "second order" because it aims for player experience, for which the ludonarrative system is only a tool [5]. Thus, unlike in regular system design, soft requirements take center stage throughout ludonarrative design, complicating the specification of the ludonarrative system. Secondly, the ludonarrative system itself is but an abstract object on top of the actual system in development. The abstract system and the actual system require separate design vocabularies, which may require equally separate documents: the invaluable Game Design Document (GDD) [20] and the less essential Technical Design Document [9]. In turn, these vocabularies breed ambiguity thanks to their different degrees of precision, with that of the GDD being lower, and the lack of a standard for translating one into the other, primarily since the ludonarrative design vocabulary spans diverse genres and use contexts [20].

Ambiguity harms not only the system's design process but also the dissemination of the process's results [21]. Firstly, considering the myriad experiential and contextual factors in ludonarrative systems [22, 23], even minor ambiguity early on can snowball into significant flaws in the end product. Secondly, although modern V&V methods can produce detailed and quantitative data, design ambiguity complicates the interpretation of these data [24]. Pressured by a tight deadline, the development team often fails to address these problems promptly, leading to the accumulation of user experience (UX) debt [25], which in the long run severely affects the ludonarrative system. Lastly, as the endless GDD variations exemplify [20], it is often hard to mix and match imprecise designs across genres and contexts. Even when other actors are willing to reuse the designs, they may find that the designs' V&V results are not replicable, holding back the designs' applications in society [26].

Currently, only partial solutions to these problems are available. To design the ludonarrative system, the designer can either attack ambiguity head-on through genre-agnostic yet coldly mathematical vocabularies, such as Ceptre [27] and Ludii [28], or bypass it with intuitive yet genre-specific DSLs [14] or game engines [29], which can quickly turn the design into an executable, technology-specific system. Still, both sides ignore player experience, for which the designer must turn to emotion-oriented formal languages [30], DSLs [31], trigger maps [32], or other tools, which cannot easily integrate into system design. In conclusion, there is a lack of a solution that (1) offers generality, precision, and intuitiveness, and (2) covers both system design and experience design. This *middle-level vocabulary* should bridge informal requirements at the "upper layer" and the technical specification at the "bottom layer." Indeed, intermediary theories and methods affording both precision and intuitiveness are commonplace in sociotechnical fields [33–35]. Ludonarrative design, too, urgently needs to consolidate perspectives and support productive collaborations through such theories and methods [36]. Yet, although there have been intermediary ludonarrative design theories [37], none can serve as the interlayer bridge to solve design ambiguity and lack of reuse.

2.2 Ludonarrative Systems as Dynamical-Experiential Systems

As a dynamical system, a ludonarrative system interacts with the player within a loop of dynamics, which realizes, from the system's vast space of multifaceted ludonarrative potential [38], a linear narrative representing the player's current playthrough [39], which the player consumes for fun, wonder, curiosity, or other experiences [4]. Generally, the narrative potential requires ludonarrative mechanics, a ludonarrative world, and the world's entities [40], whereas the player's consumption of the realized narrative necessitates presentational assets and user interface (UI) [39].

As a critical aspect of the dynamics, ludonarrative mechanics mostly fall under one of two categories: *emergence* mechanics and *progression* mechanics [41]. The former is closer to the "ludic" part of a ludonarrative system, whereas the latter is essential to its "narrative" part. Although the term "mechanics" can confusingly mean multiple things [42], it is always associated with "rules." Notably, emergence mechanics, such as those for physics simulation and internal economy, encompass rules that operate within the logical borders of a ludonarrative world or its segments to govern entities, including the player's character, characters, combat units, etc. [43]. From these entities, whose behaviors and interactions the mechanics temporally and logically organize, emerge ludonarrative dynamics whose combinatorial complexity may surprise even the designer [38].

Indeed, very rarely is a ludonarrative world just one big chunk, especially nowadays. Instead, the world typically consists of segments representing spaces, such as dungeons and levels [44], or processes, such as quests and events [45]. Both the rules for the player's transitions between segments and those that *prevent* the player's character from leaving a segment constitute progression mechanics [41]. Examples of these mechanics are lock-and-key mechanisms, warp zones, and quest triggers, e.g., defeat n enemies to summon their leader. Just like the entities within each segment, the segments themselves can have a specific temporal organization [46], which determines whether two segments run sequentially or in parallel, which runs first, etc. Furthermore, segments can (1) have different ludonarrative mechanics, (2) influence each other through shared ludonarrative data, and (3) be non-interactive, such as for cutscenes [47].

Whether of emergence or of progression, ludonarrative mechanics can accommodate different degrees of the player's agency [48]. Design-wise, the degree of agency typically follows the role of the player's character. For example, playing as the struggling hero may allow the player to affect the hero's surroundings intimately yet limitedly, whereas taking on the role of the godly, immortal, and faceless leader of a millennia-old civilization quite likely confers far more gameplay freedom. Thus, on the one hand, high agency suits more cerebral ludonarrative systems, such as those of the strategy genre, which simulate or represent a complex issue to let the player explore its elusive mechanisms [6], such as the equilibrium between the issue's factors [49]. On the other hand, low agency can lead to more emotionally impactful experiences [50]. Furthermore, as previously discussed, it is entirely possible to mix degrees of agency within the same ludonarrative system by distributing different mechanics across the system's segments.

Lastly, another category of ludonarrative mechanics deals not with gameplay but with its presentation to the player. Prominent members of this category include mechanics for the camera system, which, system-wise, typically occupies a position between the ludonarrative world and the sensorimotor aspects, i.e., presentational assets and the UI [51, 52]. As before, different presentational mechanics, e.g., a manually rotatable camera and an automated one [53], may be suitable for different ludonarrative segments.

2.3 Ergodicity in Physics and Other Sciences

Ergodicity emerged from studies on dynamical physical systems. In this context, the term refers to how a system operates so dynamically that its behavior will eventually[1] encompass the full extent of the system's dynamics [16]. Not only that, but the system has a "time average" that equals its "ensemble average" [54], that is, running the system once for a long time and instantiating the system many times with different initial states both lead to or accumulate to essentially the same dynamics[2]. Mathematically, the dynamics' full extent typically takes the form of a *state space*, over which the system transitions between states to produce a *state space trajectory* that represents the system's ongoing behavior. Each "state" captures the values of all relevant variables of the system's dynamics at a given moment.

Ergodicity is invaluable in many sciences due to its role in crucial analyses [55], such as on a system's equilibrium [56] and group-individual generalizability [57]. This benefit has led scientists to search far and wide for ergodic systems [55], with classic examples including well-mixed fluids, gases, and hard balls [58]. However, ergodicity is an ideal attribute, meaning that finding it among real-world systems can be elusive [59]. In particular, complex systems, whose representative examples include the universe [60] and biological organisms [61], tend to be non-ergodic due to possessing a strongly idiosyncratic and segmented structure. Furthermore, a system may lose its ergodicity through various mechanisms of "ergodicity breaking" [62].

Yet, despite hindering factors to its applications, ergodicity has maintained its theoretical importance [58]. Since ergodicity and associated phenomena like equilibrium are undoubtedly natural, the problem becomes *where* to find them. Even when a system, which is no more than a construct, turns out not to be ergodic, some of its parts may be. For example, homeostasis or biological equilibrium indicates the existence of such ergodic subsystems within us [56], even if our whole body seems non-ergodic [61]. Furthermore, if the subsystems significantly influence each other through their interactions, they essentially operate as one ergodic whole [63]. This line of thinking implies that discussing a system's ergodicity or lack thereof makes little sense without first specifying the system's boundary or structure, aligning with our previous discussion on the segmented nature of ludonarrative systems [47].

2.4 Degrees of Ergodicity

Depending on its dynamics, a system may follow a specific manner in visiting all its states. Firstly, a system with highly uneven dynamics visits some of its states much more likely than others. Consequently, the system may complete its trajectory only with great

[1] Technically, the required time may approach infinity or be very long.

[2] This is reflected by the same distribution of state visitations, i.e., which states are often visited, which are visited the least, etc. [58].

difficulty after a very long time. A more dynamical system, such as a well-mixed fluid, may visit many of its states uniformly and thus need less effort to fulfill its ergodicity. Still, other systems may surpass it in being effortlessly ergodic, such as by transitioning freely between distant states. We can thus say that there is an *ergodic hierarchy* between these systems [16], which also serves as a hierarchy of behavioral unpredictability, culminating in the "coin-toss randomness" of Bernoulli systems [64].

Conversely, it is possible to relax the requirement for ergodicity to allow *weak ergodicity*. The human population exemplifies a weakly ergodic system: while its growth exhibits non-trivial and unpredictable dynamics, various external factors also inhibit these dynamics [65]. Such a system has a state transition trajectory that, while imperfect, does not disqualify the system from being ergodic. More specifically, although the trajectory never exactly visits some of the system's states, it at least passes arbitrarily close to them [58], requiring these unvisited states to spread randomly across the system's state space. Otherwise, if they clump together to form a significant "void," the system is unambiguously non-ergodic.

In reality, the ergodic hierarchy and the weak ergodicity are not mutually exclusive. A system can skip some of its states while visiting others with the freedom and intensity of a Bernoulli system [16]. Likewise, having a perfectly ergodic trajectory does not guarantee the system to be anything more than "minimally ergodic."

3 A General Framework of Dynamical Ludonarrative Systems

We will now distill the state-of-the-art understanding of dynamical ludonarrative systems and the notion of ergodicity in various sciences into a general, precise, yet intuitive framework. We will describe the framework, which specifically deals with three subjects of ludonarrative ergodicity, each aligning with one specific ergodicity principle in the sciences, before discussing how to use the framework in design in Sect. 4.

3.1 First Subject: Systemic Ludonarrative Structure

We will first discuss the first subject, which is the systemic structure of a ludonarrative system. As previously discussed, a ludonarrative system can comprise subsystems with various ludonarrative purposes, time frames, and interactional patterns. A subsystem can have sub-subsystems, which each break down into sub-sub-subsystems, and so on. This systemic organization can even expand along multiple dimensions, allowing a subsystem to contribute to distinct supersystems.

Subsystems represent the ludonarrative world's segments, different camera systems, and other components capable of producing dynamics. More precisely, any element of the ludonarrative system with a state space and a state transition trajectory within the space is a subsystem of the ludonarrative system, regardless of the state space's size or the trajectory's complexity. Thus, "subsystems" can include segments with no apparent mechanics, such as non-interactive story scenes, and fine-grained ludonarrative entities, if capable of actions and not merely a collection of attributes.

A system may trade ludonarrative data with its supersystem or subsystems. These data may or may not reflect the sender's inner dynamics, such as when it merely signals the completion of those dynamics. Incoming ludonarrative data affect the receiving system's state transition trajectory the same way the system's internal mechanisms do. Thus, from this input-output perspective, there is no functional difference between a system that distributes systemic processes among its subsystems and one that handles the same processes by itself. However, there can be a practical difference from the designer's perspective, which we will discuss in Sect. 4.

Lastly, the player themselves, or rather their faculties that are relevant to the ludonarrative dynamics, participate in the ludonarrative structure as a special system. Regardless of this system's configuration—a singular entity, a hierarchy of subsystems with nesting time frames, etc.—it always indirectly connects to ludonarrative world segments through subsystems for presentational mechanics, assets, and UI [51].

3.2 Second Subject: Ludonarrative State Space

The second design subject relates to the inner workings of the ludonarrative system and its subsystems. As previously discussed, every dynamical system is unquestionably ergodic within a limit. Instead, the question is: Given such a system, what is the limit to its ergodicity? A ludonarrative system can have not one but two ergodicity limits, starting from the system's state space, which emerges from the combinatorial explosion of the system's attributes. For example, a seemingly bare-bones set of ten story-characters and five binary character attributes can permutate into a vast array of more than one quadrillion possible ludonarrative states. These states establish a hard limit to the system's ergodicity since its run-time dynamics, across one very long playthrough or many shorter ones, can never traverse out of them.

Yet, some states may never contribute to actual gameplay. The hard limit may shrink thanks to the system's progression mechanics. Manifesting as invisible walls, teleporters, event triggers, or others, these mechanics direct the ongoing dynamics toward or away from specific states, sometimes permanently locking many states away from the player's reach. An example of a state space that is not entirely visitable is a game world bordered by an invisible wall that the player can bypass through cheat codes, glitches, or such to visit an "out-of-bounds" area. Progression mechanics can even create disjoint "subspaces" within an otherwise continuous state space. Similar to what we discussed in Subsect. 3.1, a system with disjoint subspaces of states is identical, function-wise, to multiple systems with the same set of mechanics but different state spaces that correspond to the subspaces.

Lastly, emergence mechanics impose a second limit by determining how player-controlled entities and non-player entities can traverse the state space through their combined behaviors and interactions, further narrowing the visitable part of the state space or each of its subspaces. Unlike the previous limit, this one is a soft limit due to the volatility of emergence mechanics. For example, the way the player character's moving body and attacks interact with those of enemies in an action-platformer level chaotically determines if exploring the whole level is possible or if some nooks and crannies are too dangerous. Even a minor change to the level, such as one additional enemy or ludonarrative inputs from a more experienced player, can radically reshape such no-go zones.

3.3 Third Subject: Dynamical Ludonarrative Topology

The framework's last subject is the *topology* of a ludonarrative system's state space, i.e., the pattern or shape of connections between the state space's nodes [66]. The topology stems from the *total* ergodicity degree of the system's mechanics, which typically aligns with a specific role that the player may take. For example, mechanics for minimal ergodicity, whose dynamics are sensitive to the system's configuration, realize an idiosyncratic topology over the system's state space, which suits roleplaying as the limitedly knowing and locally behaving denizens of a ludonarrative world. To these humble characters, traversing such a state space can be dangerous: one wrong turn at a branching point may drastically lengthen or altogether shut down their path toward their goal state. Moreover, any autonomous actions of non-player entities can increase the risk of making the wrong state transition trajectory.

Meanwhile, acting as a godly entity calls for more ergodicity, typically of the "strong mixing" level, which manifests in the system as so-called "god mechanics." Through these mechanics, the player can freely observe and mix up the system's entities, opening up many transition possibilities for each ludonarrative state [67]. This traversal freedom is not limitless since the player still cannot (1) transition between subspaces of the system's state space that are too far from each other, or (2) interfere with the inner workings of the system's entities. Yet, if the designer so wishes, they can grant the player Bernoulli-level ergodicity for true "god mode," which lets the player bypass any state space segmentation and entity-specific rules to jump between distant states, leading to a truly chaotic state transition trajectory. Such cheat-code-like mechanics are not without any recognized benefit to player experience [68], although indeed, ludonarrative systems most often reserve this "super-agency" for facilitators instead of regular players [69, 70].

We earlier mentioned the word "total." As with the soft state space limit, a system's ergodicity degree is a product of the interactions between the system's entities and mechanics, both of emergence and of progression. For example, despite having a jetpack-equipped protagonist that can initiate movement in any direction at any time, a capability of the strong-mixing degree, a platformer game ends up minimally ergodic if it limits this movement freedom with gravity, solid platforms, and deadly traps, leading to a state space topology riddled with lethal nodes and dead-end paths.

4 Using the Framework in Design

We will outline some practical considerations for designers wishing to apply our framework. These considerations help solve three urgent needs that our literature review uncovered: (1) translating informal requirements into precise systemic features, (2) optimizing component reuse, and (3) accommodating design revision through V&V.

4.1 Disambiguating Informal Requirements

Following the typical ludonarrative design workflow [51], the designer first gathers informal requirements for the ludonarrative system, such as the player's general profile, their preferred experiential patterns [71], the ludonarrative genre, and even real-world learning goals and contexts, and then translates these requirements into the system's design. As these requirements may lead to diverging systemic specifications, the designer should carefully decide which specification is most appropriate. Our framework allows the specifications to be precise while also staying intuitive with respect to their level of detail.

To specify a system's state space, the designer starts with the system's attributes, whose values permutate into the system's state space, followed by establishing the state space's hard limit by specifying progression mechanics to delineate the state space's visitable area—or areas, if there are disjoint subspaces. If needed, other progression mechanics, such as those for jumping between different subspaces, can also be specified.

While the complexity of emergence mechanics always explodes, planning the soft state space limit and the dynamical topology only requires dealing with crucial cases of interactions between entities. Essentially, the planning effort tries to identify (relatively small) subspaces of the (vast) state space that embody such cases. In the context of the soft state space limit, the cases are extreme outliers. For example, if the designer assumes the best, yet still legal, outcome at every branching point—enemies are far away, their attacks always miss, the player can swiftly control their character, etc.—will there be any path for the player character to reach the farthest corner of the level?

To design the system's dynamical topology, the designer can similarly deal with subspaces instead of individual states. However, in contrast to the soft state space limit, these subspaces represent *equilibria*: areas that entities most often visit for optimal gameplay benefits [72], such as "choke points" in the first-person shooting genre. Similar to the system's state space, the topology of the system's "space of subspaces" would follow the system's ergodicity degree. For example, the state space of a minimally ergodic ludonarrative system would likely host few and spread-out equilibria, which contrast with the more numerous and more evenly distributed equilibria in a well-mixed state space.

We will now discuss an example case of turning requirements into systemic specifications. Suppose a game's vague requirements are as follows: (1) *game mechanics:* the player should be able to move their character around and attack their enemies; (2) *camera system:* the player can look around at will while maintaining the narrative perspective; and (3) *player experience:* the player should be able to learn how to play the game—to use the mechanics and camera system—at a moderate pace. Starting with game mechanics, we find that two contrasting sets of exploration and combat mechanics from two different genres satisfy the requirements. The first genre is the real-time action adventure, which typically lets the player switch seamlessly between exploring and fighting, and even perform both at once. Thus, both activities have parallel and equally fast time scales and constitute minor subsystems of a much larger system that represents the currently played game level. Conversely, as systems, the real-time exploration and the turn-based combat of a Japanese role-playing game (JRPG) (1) cannot run simultaneously and thus have sequential time scales, one noticeably slower than the other, and (2) each can stand on its own, thus occupying a very significant portion of its supersystem. In fact, the supersystem is merely there to quietly handle general gameplay data, such as the player's hit points, and the two subsystems' marginal interactions, such as when the poison status from a battle carries over to the exploration segment.

State-space-wise, both sets of mechanics seem comparable in complexity, although their state spaces are structurally different. The state space of the real-time action-adventure one is bounded by the player character's position within the explorable level and the states of the player character and all enemies, e.g., alive, dead, or stunned. In contrast, the JRPG one has not one but *three* separate state spaces for the exploration segment, the combat segment, and the segments' supersystem. The exploration one resembles the action-adventure's state space, but with fewer states due to the absence of combat actions. On the other hand, due to the combat segment's discrete nature, the segment's state space is not "smooth" but comprises many disjoint subspaces for entity turns, combat phases, dramatic cutscenes, etc.

Regarding its dynamical topology, the action-adventure one exhibits, on average, ergodicity of a strong-mixing or moderate degree, which emerges from a relatively dense topology with many transition paths between neighboring states, creating a highly responsive feel. Regardless, the ergodicity level may sometimes rise, such as when the player character gains a temporary jetpack, or drop, such as in a game map with a labyrinthine layout. Equilibria form around areas where players naturally retreat to catch their breath or coordinate attacks, such as behind pillars or near health pickups.

The JRPG exhibits similar ergodicity in its exploration segment but not in its combat segment. At first, the combat segment's state-space topology is sparse and brittle: the player character either employs one of the few correct tactics or quickly dies. Yet, because the player character steadily gets stronger through new equipment, new abilities, and such, their combat options continuously widen, leading to more and more ergodicity—until it gets so high toward the game's completion that it trivializes combat.

Let us continue to the camera system. Applying our framework, the designer disambiguates its requirement by first identifying two relevant subsystems: the *view controller* and the *player-input interface*. Then, the designer considers at least two precise interpretations of the requirement. The first assumes *continuous control*, where the view controller runs instantly upon a signal from the player-input controller. Another assumes *context-sensitive control*, where the camera view updates with a varying speed to preserve narrative framing, i.e., the view controller sometimes operates at a slower time scale than the player-input interface.

Both camera systems have a state space emerging from the camera view's position and rotation. Yet, while the first system's state space is hard-limited only by the area in which the camera view may move around, the second system's state space is also replaced during a dramatic scene by a smaller subspace, which, together with the slowing down of the view's movement, maintains the player's focus on the scene. Topology-wise, both camera systems are moderately ergodic, although the second system is slightly less so due to its state space's movement-constraining subspace.

Lastly, let's consider how to translate the player experience requirement into precise player model systems. One possible model comprises three sequential subsystems: sensorimotor layer, cognitive layer, and strategic layer, an arrangement that follows the state-of-the-art theory of predictive processing [73]. Each subsystem operates at a different time scale, ranging from milliseconds for the sensorimotor layer to minutes for the strategic one, reflecting the nested time scales in the human brain [74]. This hierarchical state space represents several dimensions of the player's expertise, such as timing and resource management. The state space gradually expands as more dimensions become relevant throughout the game, ensuring that the player stays in a "flow state" [75].

Another potential player model offers a similar complexity progression, although by limiting game mechanics instead of expertise dimensions. Essentially, the model's state space expands over time as the player character, instead of the player themselves, gains more abilities, weapons, and other power upgrades. The state space gets more ergodic at a similar pace: its topology evolves from being sparse—mistakes are often fatal—to dense—many correct tactics have become available.

Not every combination of these precise specifications works equally well or even makes sense. One good combination involves the real-time mechanics, the continuous camera control, and the expertise-based player model, which together yield fluid yet tactical gameplay. Meanwhile, the JRPG mechanics are best combined with the context-sensitive camera and the power upgrade-based player model.

4.2 Modularity for Component Reuse (and Another Benefit)

To optimize component reuse, the designer should tap into systemic modularity. This principle is especially crucial to designing state spaces. While some of the system's attributes can be "loose," most should belong to reusable subsystems representing gameplay entities in the system. This modularity can keep the system's state space lean by ensuring that the system manages only attributes that it cannot entrust to its subsystems. Similarly, due to their reusability, several systems with small state spaces can be more efficient than one system with a large yet segmented state space.

While progression mechanics can work as stand-alone rules, e.g., "if the value of x is more than a, set x to b," they are more efficient when closely collaborating with entities. The lock-and-key pattern exemplifies a pair of a reusable entity and a progression rule. Through its interaction with the player, the entity can set off a progression rule for various purposes: changing the current state, informing the system's supersystem of the system's completion, or others. Likewise, the previous "invisible wall" is another entity that, besides serving as a hard state space limit, can be useful in other contexts.

More than their progression counterparts, emergence mechanics *necessitate* their distribution across the system's subsystems, or else what emerges from what would be too opaque. Any subsystem with emergence mechanics must also comprise sub-subsystems, and so on until the bottommost level of this hierarchy, where only progression mechanics remain. Only after completing this systemic decomposition may the designer roughly yet confidently plan the subsystem's soft state space limit and dynamical topology. Indeed, modularity's another benefit is simplifying the design of system dynamics by allowing the designer to ignore irrelevant states.

Let's consider the modularization of the example JRPG. It is straightforward to decompose the player character into subsystems for an "inventory entity," an "attribute entity," and an "ability entity." The last two can then be efficiently reused by each enemy entity. Similarly, it is a common practice to reuse the same non-player character (NPC) template for "town residents," "merchants," "quest givers," and many other NPCs. Meanwhile, as they are, the supersystem's global flags for the states of the storyline may unnecessarily explode into a ridiculously vast state space. When the flags are grouped, such as according to their story branches, the designer can avoid such a combinatorial explosion by focusing on only some groups in identifying the state space's soft limit, i.e., flags that are impractical to trigger, and equilibria, i.e., the most optimal flags to trigger. For example, a story branch whose activation requires strict timing is likely to contain the soft limit, while another branch related to the strongest abilities may hide the equilibria.

4.3 Design Verification and Validation

Upon turning the design into an executable system, the designer can proceed to the first part of V&V: verifying the system's correctness. The verification involves the system's structure and hard state space limits and entails running the system to check for critical issues. Major structural flaws include incorrect input-output data flows and process deadlocks, whereas illegal transitions to supposedly unreachable states indicate incorrectly designed progression mechanics. The mechanical nature of this process means that verification does not have to consider the player.

Let's briefly discuss the verification process of the example JRPG. Some of the game's input-output data exchanges are (1) *the supersystem's combat input:* whether the player character's inventory, strength attributes, and story-related state correctly inform combat initiation; (2) *combat's data output:* whether the previous data properly feed back into the supersystem before exploration starts again; and (3) *the player model's camera input:* whether this input, such as for rotating the view, correctly signal the camera's view controller. Meanwhile, verifying the temporal order between the exploration and the combat segment involves checking whether one segment's state transition always stops before that of the other segment begins.

Next is validation, in which the system's soft state space limit and dynamical topology take their turns. As it concerns the system's usefulness to the player, which itself concerns run-time dynamics and not static features or rules, validation is arguably the hardest of the two Vs. Due to the combinatorial explosion of the system's possible dynamics [38], statistical methods become the most practical way to validate the dynamics. In principle, the designer must gather enough *samples* of playthroughs, whether from playtests with human players or simulations with the player's model. For example, if we expected millions of playthroughs throughout the system's lifetime, it would require, at a minimum, around 400 random samples of the playthroughs to confidently validate the system's dynamics [76].

Specifically, the statistical validation process starts from the ludonarrative system's soft state space limit. The goal here is to prove that the system's actual state space matches, at least imperfectly, the system's designed state space. More precisely, the playthrough samples should combine into a state transition trajectory that is at least weakly ergodic relative to the designed state space. If instead the trajectory is non-ergodic, i.e., it leaves too many unvisited "voids" in the designed state space, then the design is due for revision.

Validating the system's dynamical topology follows the same ergodicity principle. However, the process is more thorough. Firstly, the playthrough samples must show, with sufficient confidence, that states in the designed subspaces for equilibria are indeed most frequently visited. Then, the samples should validate the *shapes* of the subspaces. Similar to validating the soft state space limit, does the state transition trajectory ergodically visit the subspaces? Or does it leave "voids" within each subspace?

We will close this section with examples of processes in the JRPG's validation. Validating the design of the story progression requires logging the values of the global story flags across playthroughs. Firstly, the soft limit should be revised when the log data show either too many activated story flags—let's say more than five percent of the game's total story flags—beyond the limit or too many inactivated flags clumping inside the limit. Afterward, the designer should revise their selection of the most beneficial flags—the equilibria among all flags—if the log data do not show these flags as the most frequently activated (let's say at least twice more often than the average).

5 Conclusion and Future Research

We have presented our general, precise, yet intuitive framework of dynamical ludonarrative systems, which integrates the concept of dynamical ludonarrative systems with theories of ergodicity in physics and other sciences. This integration allows the framework to serve as a middle-level vocabulary that bridges informal requirements with technical system specifications, potentially ensuring design rigor of socially impactful ludonarrative systems. More specifically, the framework shows how a ludonarrative system's precise yet intuitive design and verification and validation (V&V) critically depend on three factors: (1) the correctness of the systemic arrangement, ludonarrative data flow, and time frame within the system, (2) the appropriateness of the shape and size of the system's state space, and (3) the synergy between the system's entities and mechanics in realizing the intended dynamical topology. By paying attention to these factors, the designer can disambiguate requirements, optimize component reuse, and productively refine their design through V&V.

As we previously stated, we will expand our framework into a DSL, with which the designer can perform early V&V of their design [17]. The DSL will incorporate existing ludonarrative DSLs in the literature, including those for emotion modeling [31]. We will then apply the framework and the DSL in a representative case study of co-designing ludonarrative systems for learning about the complex issue of sustainability. Among the case study's potential research questions, we will investigate whether (1) the framework can indeed unite perspectives across disciplines and ease co-designers in mixing and matching components, and (2) the DSL can accommodate V&V that accurately reveals the design's flaws and is informative to the co-designers. Essentially, the framework and the DSL will help us participate in the co-design as the *technical communicator* [77], a role whose importance in ludonarrative design steadily rises.

Other research directions made possible by our framework include turning design patterns in the literature into systemic and dynamical patterns that are precise and easy to reuse. Some prominent examples of structural patterns are level designs [44], quest systems [78], and branching narrative graphs [79]. Meanwhile, reflective play [80], the stuck continuum [81], and types and patterns of betrayal in multiplayer games [11] exemplify patterns of dynamical topologies. To support the patterns' applications, future research should also explore practical design tools, both manual, such as GDD formats and visualization diagrams, and automatic, such as LLM-powered design assistants. In particular, these tools should ease the designer in planning soft state space limits and dynamical topologies.

Acknowledgments. The first author (Pratama Wirya Atmaja) would like to sincerely thank the Center for Higher Education Funding and Assessment of Indonesia's Ministry of Higher Education, Science, and Technology for funding his PhD study, which this paper is a part of, through *Beasiswa Program Doktor untuk Dosen Indonesia* (Doctoral Program Scholarship for Indonesian Lecturers).

References

1. Camingue, J., Melcer, E.F., Carstensdottir, E.: A (visual) novel route to learning: a taxonomy of teaching strategies in visual novels. In: FDG '20: Proceedings of the 15th International Conference on the Foundations of Digital Games, pp. 1–13. ACM, New York (2020). https://doi.org/10.1145/3402942.3403004
2. Chen, C., Yao, M.Z.: Strategic use of immersive media and narrative message in virtual marketing: understanding the roles of telepresence and transportation. Psychol. Mark. **39**, 524–542 (2022). https://doi.org/10.1002/mar.21630
3. Luo, L., Cai, W., Zhou, S., Lees, M., Yin, H.: A review of interactive narrative systems and technologies: a training perspective. Simulation **91**, 126–147 (2015). https://doi.org/10.1177/0037549714566722
4. Hunicke, R., Leblanc, M., Zubek, R.: MDA: a formal approach to game design and game research. In: AAAI Workshop - Technical Report (2004)
5. Deterding, S.: The lens of intrinsic skill atoms: a method for gameful design. Human-Comput. Interact. **30**, 294–335 (2015). https://doi.org/10.1080/07370024.2014.993471
6. Koenitz, H., Barbara, J., Eladhari, M.P.: Interactive digital narrative (IDN)—new ways to represent complexity and facilitate digitally empowered citizens. In:New Review of Hypermedia and Multimedia, pp. 1–21 (2023). https://doi.org/10.1080/13614568.2023.2181503
7. Kay, N., Baron, G., Vervoort, J., Armoudian, M.: Designing a toolkit for visualising desirable sustainable futures in video games. In: Conference Proceedings of DiGRA 2025: Games at the Crossroads (2025). https://doi.org/10.26503/dl.v2025i2.2459
8. Koenitz, H., Eladhari, M.P.: The paradigm of game system building. Trans. Digital Games Res. Assoc. **5**, 65–90 (2021). https://doi.org/10.26503/todigra.v5i3.123
9. Politowski, C., Petrillo, F., Ullmann, G.C., Guéhéneuc, Y.-G.: Game industry problems: an extensive analysis of the gray literature. Inf. Softw. Technol. **134**, 106538 (2021). https://doi.org/10.1016/j.infsof.2021.106538
10. Engström, H., Berg Marklund, B., Backlund, P., Toftedahl, M.: Game development from a software and creative product perspective: a quantitative literature review approach. Entertain. Comput. **27**, 10–22 (2018). https://doi.org/10.1016/j.entcom.2018.02.008
11. Valério, P., Cardoso, P.: Played like a damn fiddle: types and patterns of betrayal in multiplayer games. In: Marto, A., Prada, R., Gouveia, P., Espinosa, R.C.-, Gonçalves, A., Abrantes, E., Ribeiro, R. (eds.) Videogame Sciences and Arts. VJ 2024. CCIS, vol. 2324. pp. 3–20 (2025). https://doi.org/10.1007/978-3-031-81713-7_1
12. Chueca, J., Verón, J., Font, J., Pérez, F., Cetina, C.: The consolidation of game software engineering: a systematic literature review of software engineering for industry-scale computer games. Inf. Softw. Technol. **165**, 107330 (2024). https://doi.org/10.1016/j.infsof.2023.107330

13. Agusdinata, D.B., Lukosch, H.: Supporting interventions to reduce household greenhouse gas emissions: a transdisciplinary role-playing game development. Simul. Gaming **50**, 359–376 (2019). https://doi.org/10.1177/1046878119848135
14. van Rozen, R.: Languages of games and play: a systematic mapping study. ACM Comput. Surv. **53**, 1–37 (2021). https://doi.org/10.1145/3412843
15. Vargas-Iglesias, J.J.: Making sense of genre: the logic of video game genre organization. Games Cult. **15**, 158–178 (2020). https://doi.org/10.1177/1555412017751803
16. Frigg, R., Berkovitz, J., Kronz, F.: The ergodic hierarchy. In: Stanford Encyclopedia of Philosophy (2020)
17. Cederbladh, J., Cicchetti, A., Suryadevara, J.: Early validation and verification of system behaviour in model-based systems engineering: a systematic literature review. ACM Trans. Softw. Eng. Methodol. **33**, 1–67 (2024). https://doi.org/10.1145/3631976
18. Jongeling, R., Cicchetti, A., Ciccozzi, F.: How are informal diagrams used in software engineering? An exploratory study of open-source and industrial practices. Softw. Syst. Model. **24**, 601–613 (2025). https://doi.org/10.1007/s10270-024-01252-3
19. Jongeling, R., Ciccozzi, F.: Flexible modelling: a systematic literature review. J. Object Technol. **23**, 1–14 (2024). https://doi.org/10.5381/jot.2024.23.3.a3
20. Colby, R., Colby, R.S.: Game design documentation: four perspectives from independent game studios. Commun. Des. Q. **7**, 5–15 (2019). https://doi.org/10.1145/3321388.3321389
21. Bucchiarone, A.: Grand challenges in software engineering for games in serious contexts. In: Cooper, K.M.L., Bucchiarone, A. (eds.) Software Engineering for Games in Serious Contexts, pp. 291–300. Springer, Cham (2023). https://doi.org/10.1007/978-3-031-33338-5_13
22. Holm, S.K., Kaakinen, J.K., Forsström, S., Surakka, V.: Self-reported playing preferences resonate with emotion-related physiological reactions during playing and watching of first-person shooter videogames. Int. J. Hum Comput Stud. **155**, 102690 (2021). https://doi.org/10.1016/j.ijhcs.2021.102690
23. Huber, S., et al.: Addressing boundary conditions of cognitive and motivational effects of gamified learning. Front. Learn. Res. **13**, 53–82 (2025). https://doi.org/10.14786/flr.v13i3.1653
24. Su, Y., Backlund, P., Engström, H.: Comprehensive review and classification of game analytics. SOCA **15**, 141–156 (2021). https://doi.org/10.1007/s11761-020-00303-z
25. Rodriguez, A., Gardey, J.C., Grigera, J., Rossi, G., Garrido, A.: UX debt in an agile development process: evidence and characterization. Softw. Qual. J. **31**, 1467–1498 (2023). https://doi.org/10.1007/s11219-023-09652-2
26. Nosek, B.A., Errington, T.M.: What is replication? PLoS Biol. **18**, e3000691 (2020). https://doi.org/10.1371/journal.pbio.3000691
27. Martens, C., Card, A., Crain, H., Khatri, A.: Modeling game mechanics with ceptre. IEEE Trans. Games. **16**, 431–444 (2024). https://doi.org/10.1109/TG.2023.3292982
28. Soemers, D.J.N.J., Piette, É., Stephenson, M., Browne, C.: The ludii game description language is universal. In: 2024 IEEE Conference on Games (CoG), pp. 1–8. IEEE (2024). https://doi.org/10.1109/CoG60054.2024.10645550
29. Toftedahl, M., Engström, H.: A taxonomy of game engines and the tools that drive the industry. In: Proceedings of the 2019 DiGRA International Conference: Game, Play and the Emerging Ludo-Mix (2019)
30. Ansari, S.G., Prasetya, I.S.W.B., Dastani, M., Dignum, F., Keller, G.: EmoSTL: formal spatial-temporal verification of emotion specifications in computer games. In: 2024 IEEE Conference on Software Testing, Verification and Validation (ICST), pp. 13–24. IEEE (2024). https://doi.org/10.1109/ICST60714.2024.00011
31. Miguéis, G., Araujo, J., Moreira, A.: Towards a requirements language for modeling emotion in videogames. In: SAC '19: Proceedings of the 34th ACM/SIGAPP Symposium on Applied

Computing, pp. 1878–1880. ACM, New York (2019). https://doi.org/10.1145/3297280.3297614
32. Callele, D., Neufeld, E., Schneider, K.: Visualizing emotional requirements. In: 2009 Fourth International Workshop on Requirements Engineering Visualization, pp. 1–10. IEEE (2009). https://doi.org/10.1109/REV.2009.7
33. Cartwright, N.: Middle-range theory: without it what could anyone do? Theoria: Int. J. Theory Hist. Found. Sci. **35**, 269–323 (2020)
34. Wieringa, R.J.: What is design science? In: Design Science Methodology for Information Systems and Software Engineering, pp. 3–11. Springer, Heidelberg (2014). https://doi.org/10.1007/978-3-662-43839-8_1
35. Höök, K., Löwgren, J.: Strong concepts: intermediate-level knowledge in interaction design research. ACM Trans. Comput.-Hum. Interact. **19**, 1–18 (2012). https://doi.org/10.1145/2362364.2362371
36. Deterding, S.: The pyrrhic victory of game studies: assessing the past, present, and future of interdisciplinary game research. Games Cult. **12**, 521–543 (2017). https://doi.org/10.1177/1555412016665067
37. Schumacher, T., Festing, M., Bick, M.: Toward a mid-range design theory for developing pedagogically effective serious games. Inf. Syst. Manag. 1–37 (2023). https://doi.org/10.1080/10580530.2023.2267762
38. Dormans, J.: Engineering emergence: applied theory for game design. PhD thesis. Universiteit van Amsterdam (2012)
39. Koenitz, H.: SPP: a model and analytical framework for IDN. In: Understanding Interactive Digital Narrative: Immersive Expressions for a Complex Time, pp. 58–98. Routledge (2023)
40. Adams, E.: Fundamentals of Game Design. New Riders (2014)
41. Adams, E., Dormans, J.: Game Mechanics: Advanced Game Design. New Riders, Berkeley (2012)
42. Sicart, M.: Defining game mechanics. Game Stud. **8** (2008)
43. Smith, G., Cha, M., Whitehead, J.: A framework for analysis of 2D platformer levels. In: Sandbox '08: Proceedings of the 2008 ACM SIGGRAPH Symposium on Video Games, pp. 75–80 (2008). https://doi.org/10.1145/1401843.1401858
44. Khalifa, A., de Mesentier Silva, F., Togelius, J.: Level design patterns in 2D games. In: 2019 IEEE Conference on Games (CoG), pp. 1–8. IEEE (2019). https://doi.org/10.1109/CIG.2019.8847953
45. Yu, K.K., Sturtevant, N.R., Guzdial, M.: What is a quest? In: Proceedings of the Intelligent Narrative Technologies Workshop (2020)
46. Zagal, J.P., Mateas, M.: Time in video games: a survey and analysis. Simul. Gaming **41**, 844–868 (2010). https://doi.org/10.1177/1046878110375594
47. Newman, J.: The myth of the ergodic videogame: some thoughts on player-character relationships in videogames. Game Stud. **2** (2002)
48. Koenitz, H.: What game narrative are we talking about? An ontological mapping of the foundational canon of interactive narrative forms. Arts **7**, 51 (2018). https://doi.org/10.3390/arts7040051
49. Sušnik, J., et al.: Multi-Stakeholder development of a serious game to explore the water-energy-food-land-climate nexus: the SIM4NEXUS approach. Water **10**, 139 (2018). https://doi.org/10.3390/w10020139
50. Stang, S.: "This Action Will Have Consequences": interactivity and player agency. Game Stud. **19** (2019)
51. Atmaja, P.W., Sugiarto.: When information, narrative, and interactivity join forces: designing and co-designing interactive digital narratives for complex issues. In: Vosmeer, M., Holloway-Attaway, L. (eds.) Interactive Storytelling. ICIDS 2022. LNCS, vol. 13762, pp. 329–351. Springer, Cham (2022). https://doi.org/10.1007/978-3-031-22298-6_20

52. Ollsson, T., Toll, D., Wingkvist, A., Ericsson, M.: Evolution and evaluation of the model-view-controller architecture in games. In: 2015 IEEE/ACM 4th International Workshop on Games and Software Engineering, pp. 8–14. IEEE (2015). https://doi.org/10.1109/GAS.2015.10
53. Arsenault, D., Côté, P.-M., Larochelle, A.: The Game FAVR: a framework for the analysis of visual representation in video games. Loading… J. Canad. Game Stud. Assoc. **9**, 88–123 (2015)
54. Peters, O., Adamou, A.: The ergodicity solution of the cooperation puzzle. Phil. Trans. Royal Soc. A: Math. Phys. Eng. Sci. **380** (2022). https://doi.org/10.1098/rsta.2020.0425
55. Moore, C.C.: Ergodic theorem, ergodic theory, and statistical mechanics. Proc. Natl. Acad. Sci. **112**, 1907–1911 (2015). https://doi.org/10.1073/pnas.1421798112
56. Colombo, M., Palacios, P.: Non-equilibrium thermodynamics and the free energy principle in biology. Biol. Philos. **36**, 41 (2021). https://doi.org/10.1007/s10539-021-09818-x
57. Adolf, J.K., Fried, E.I.: Ergodicity is sufficient but not necessary for group-to-individual generalizability. Proc. Natl. Acad. Sci. **116**, 6540–6541 (2019). https://doi.org/10.1073/pnas.1818675116
58. Ashley, S.: Ergodic theory plays a key role in multiple fields. Proc. Natl. Acad. Sci. **112**, 1914 (2015). https://doi.org/10.1073/pnas.1500429112
59. Speelman, C.P., Parker, L., Rapley, B.J., McGann, M.: Most psychological researchers assume their samples are ergodic: evidence from a year of articles in three major journals. Collabra: Psychol. **10** (2024). https://doi.org/10.1525/collabra.92888
60. Kauffman, S.: Is there a fourth law for non-ergodic systems that do work to construct their expanding phase space? Entropy **24**, 1383 (2022). https://doi.org/10.3390/e24101383
61. Mangalam, M., Kelty-Stephen, D.G.: Ergodic descriptors of non-ergodic stochastic processes. J. Royal Soc. Interface. **19** (2022). https://doi.org/10.1098/rsif.2022.0095
62. Venkataraman, G., Sahoo, D., Balakrishnan, V.: Ergodicity breaking. In: Beyond the Crystalline State, pp. 117–124 (1989). https://doi.org/10.1007/978-3-642-83434-9_8
63. Landau, L., Lifshitz, E.M.: The fundamental principles of statistical physics. In: Statistical Physics, pp. 1–28. Pergamon Press (1969)
64. Berkovitz, J., Frigg, R., Kronz, F.: The ergodic hierarchy, randomness and Hamiltonian chaos. Stud. Hist. Phil. Sci. Part B: Stud. Hist. Phil. Mod. Phys. **37**, 661–691 (2006). https://doi.org/10.1016/j.shpsb.2006.02.003
65. Inaba, H.: Weak ergodicity of population evolution processes. Math. Biosci. **96**, 195–219 (1989). https://doi.org/10.1016/0025-5564(89)90059-X
66. Millán, A.P., et al.: Topology shapes dynamics of higher-order networks. Nat. Phys. (2025). https://doi.org/10.1038/s41567-024-02757-w
67. op de Beke, L.: Anthropocene Temporality in gaia games. KronoScope. 20, 239–259 (2020). https://doi.org/10.1163/15685241-12341470
68. Bainbridge, W.S.: Autonomy within rigid rule-based systems. In: Virtual Sociocultural Convergence, pp. 93–115. Springer, Cham (2016). https://doi.org/10.1007/978-3-319-33020-4_5
69. Christensen, E.L., Paasivaara, M.: Respond to change or die: an educational scrum simulation for distributed teams. In: ICSE-SEET '22: Proceedings of the ACM/IEEE 44th International Conference on Software Engineering: Software Engineering Education and Training, pp. 235–246. ACM, New York (2022). https://doi.org/10.1145/3510456.3514145
70. Spierling, U.: Conceptual models for interactive digital storytelling in knowledge media applications. In: Technologies for Interactive Digital Storytelling and Entertainment. TIDSE 2004. LNCS, vol. 3105, pp. 171–176 (2004). https://doi.org/10.1007/978-3-540-27797-2_23
71. Reagan, A.J., Mitchell, L., Kiley, D., Danforth, C.M., Dodds, P.S.: The emotional arcs of stories are dominated by six basic shapes. EPJ Data Sci. **5**, 31 (2016). https://doi.org/10.1140/epjds/s13688-016-0093-1

72. Papadimitriou, C., Piliouras, G.: Game dynamics as the meaning of a game. ACM SIGecom Exchang. **16**, 53–63 (2019). https://doi.org/10.1145/3331041.3331048
73. Deterding, S., Andersen, M.M., Kiverstein, J., Miller, M.: Mastering uncertainty: a predictive processing account of enjoying uncertain success in video game play. Front. Psychol. **13** (2022). https://doi.org/10.3389/fpsyg.2022.924953
74. Chang, C.H.C., Nastase, S.A., Hasson, U.: Information flow across the cortical timescale hierarchy during narrative construction. Proc. Natl. Acad. Sci. **119** (2022). https://doi.org/10.1073/pnas.2209307119
75. Pujol, M., Caroux, L., Lemercier, C.: Flow state requires effortful attentional control but is experienced effortlessly by video game players. Interact. Comput. (2024). https://doi.org/10.1093/iwc/iwae026
76. Hazra, A.: Using the confidence interval confidently. J. Thoracic Dis. **9**, 4124–4129 (2017). https://doi.org/10.21037/jtd.2017.09.14
77. Catá-Ross, A.: Surveying technical communicators in the video games industry: understanding the backgrounds, skills, content, and roles of TCs in the video games industry. In: SIGDOC '22: Proceedings of the 40th ACM International Conference on Design of Communication, pp. 173–174. ACM, New York (2022). https://doi.org/10.1145/3513130.3559003
78. Yu, K.K., Guzdial, M., Sturtevant, N.: The definition-context-purpose paradigm and other insights from industry professionals about the definition of a quest. In: Proceedings of the AAAI Conference on Artificial Intelligence and Interactive Digital Entertainment, vol. 17, no. 1, pp. 107–114 (2021)
79. Millard, D.E.: Strange patterns: structure and post-structure in interactive digital narratives. In: The Authoring Problem: Challenges in Supporting Authoring for Interactive Digital Narratives, pp. 147–169 (2022). https://doi.org/10.1007/978-3-031-05214-9_10
80. Miller, J.A., et al.: A design framework for reflective play. In: CHI '24: Proceedings of the CHI Conference on Human Factors in Computing Systems, pp. 1–21. ACM, New York (2024). https://doi.org/10.1145/3613904.3642455
81. Drey, T., Fischbach, F., Jansen, P., Frommel, J., Rietzler, M., Rukzio, E.: To be or not to be stuck, or is it a continuum?: a systematic literature review on the concept of being stuck in games. Proc. ACM Hum.-Comput. Interact. **5**, 1–35 (2021). https://doi.org/10.1145/3474656

Game Studies, Cultural Memory, and Critical Perspectives

Unveiling Hidden Pioneers: Carla Vieira Faria's Legacy in Portuguese Digital Game History

Luciana Lima[1(✉)] and Maria Júlia Vieira[2]

[1] Interactive Technologies Institute (ITI/LARSyS), University of Lisbon, Lisbon, Portugal
luciana.lima@tecnico.ulisboa.pt

[2] DigiMedia, Department of Communication and Arts, University of Aveiro, Aveiro, Portugal

Abstract. This paper examines the trajectory of Carla Vieira Faria, a pioneer in developing educational games for people with disabilities in Portugal during the 1990s and early 2000s. This case study employs a qualitative approach that combines online and archival research with an in-depth interview to illuminate Carla Faria's largely unacknowledged contributions to the history of Portuguese video games. Working in collaboration with her husband, Pedro Faria, she created several award-winning educational games, including *A Cabana do Papim* (1998), *O Meu Baú dos Brinquedos* (2000), *Aventura na Ilha das Cores* (2001), and the application Pocket Voice (2001). Despite receiving national and international recognition, her work remains largely invisible in local historical narratives and beyond. Her trajectory demonstrates how women have expanded the scope of video games beyond entertainment, highlighting their educational and inclusive potential, while simultaneously revealing mechanisms that continue to erase female participation in the history of creative computing. This research contributes to feminist critiques of technology history and advocates for more recovering and recognizing the contributions of individuals who have been marginalized or forgotten in video game history.

Keywords: Women in games · Local game history · Gender equality

1 Introduction

Video game history writing has been shaped by selective processes privileging certain protagonists, geographies, and products over others. The microprocesses of women's exclusion from the digital games industry become evident in how historical narratives are chosen and canonized. These narratives are often homogeneous, focusing predominantly on male programmers, developers, and companies, as well as hardware and software from countries such as the United States, the United Kingdom, and Japan. As Swalwell [2021] argues, this stems from an orthodox and biased mode of history-writing, frequently driven by individuals in positions of privilege who determine what from the past is deemed significant. This process contributes to hegemonic narratives that, as Nooney [2013] argues, constitute a "patrilineal chronicle," canonizing "founding fathers, hacker heroes, and game gods" while reinforcing women's invisibility. In this way, examining gender

R. Baptista et al. (Eds.): VJ 2025, CCIS 2988, pp. 169–183, 2027.
https://doi.org/10.1007/978-3-032-31642-4_14

in this perspective reveals how creative computing and video game developing practices, locally and globally, have been shaped, erased, or marginalized. This perspective exposes the mechanisms through which power operates in technological systems, highlighting which contributions are recognized or forgotten.

Historical and contemporary case studies draw attention to both the material infrastructures of computing and gaming technologies, as well as the situated cultural practices surrounding them. By connecting these practices to the lived experiences of marginalized groups, feminist approaches [3–5] have been helping us understand how creative computing and video game histories are not only technical achievements but also deeply social and political processes, emphasizing the need to recover overlooked narratives and foster more inclusive understandings of technology, creativity, and in-novation.

In the Portuguese context, these dynamics of invisibility are systematically reproduced, as some we have examined in recent works [6–9]. The privileging of engineering and programming fields, more readily associated with male domains, has obscured the intersection between video games and artistic practices, where women's contributions have been, and continue to be, particularly significant. Moreover, the agents responsible for producing and reproducing video game history in Portugal, such as journalists, curators, game enthusiasts, and scholars, have often not paid sufficient attention to issues of gender and intersectionality. As a result, the narratives of both cis and trans women who played central roles in this history have not been adequately recovered or integrated into dominant narratives.

This case study examines Carla Vieira Faria's trajectory, a pioneer in developing educational games for people with disabilities during the transition from the 1990s to 2000s. In collaboration with her husband Pedro Faria, she developed several computer games and other software (see Figure 1), including *A Cabana do Papim* (Papim's Cabin, 1998), *O Meu Baú dos Brinquedos* (My Toy Chest, 2000), *Aventura na Ilha das Cores* (Adventure on the Island of Colors, 2001), Pocket Voice (2001), *Aventura no Circo* (Adventure at the Circus, unfinished, 2002), and *Quero Ser Presidente* (I Want to Be President, 2006). Many received national and international recognition, with *A Cabana do Papim, O Meu Baú dos Brinquedos, Aventura na Ilha das Cores*, and Pocket Voice receiving the most prestigious national awards of the time.

Fig. 1. Timeline showing the games and projects led by Carla Faria (1998–2006).

Beyond this introduction, the paper first outlines the historical and cultural context of computer games in Portugal, then presents the methodological design of the case study, followed by results, and concludes with key findings and their implications for the history of digital games.

2 A Brief Context: Computer Games and Digital Culture in Portugal, 1980s–1990s

As in many European countries, electronic game development in Portugal dates back to the early 1980s, driven by the diffusion of home computers and the widespread circulation of pirated game cassettes. Conditions enabling computer consumption linked to rising household incomes, domestic production of Timex Sinclair and Timex Computer models, and highly publicized "Technology Revolution" debates [10].

The transition from the 1970s coincided with a decisive historical rupture. Until 1974, Portugal lived under one of twentieth-century Europe's longest authoritarian regimes, characterized by strict censorship, political repression, nationalist and Catholic-conservative values, and protracted colonial wars in African countries. The "Carnation Revolution" on April 25, 1974, was a peaceful military coup initiating a turbulent revolutionary period (1974–1976) marked by popular mobilization and profound institutional change. According to [11], ruptures with the dictatorial model after 1974 must be understood within broader global cultural transformation and modernization contexts. Portugal sought alignment with rapid social changes in other European countries, driven by urban cultures ascendancy, new media rise, cultural institutions creation, and novel entertainment and consumption forms diffusion.

It is within this environment of transition and modernization that the life of Carla Vieira Faria unfolds. Born in Angola in March 1965, she arrived in Portugal as a young child, at a moment when hundreds of thousands of people were leaving the former Portuguese colonies after the collapse of the colonial regime. This mass displacement, one of the largest in the country's recent history, reshaped family geographies and emotional landscapes. Carla, therefore, grew up amid profound geographical, political, and cultural transitions.

The 1980s in Portugal were marked by the country's accession to the European Economic Community (EEC), the expansion of the tertiary sector, including commerce, transportation, public administration, education, and healthcare, and resulting improvements in living standards, even as challenges such as widespread illiteracy, unemployment, and social inequalities persisted; in this context, the decline of revolutionary ideals and the emergence of modern individualist values increasingly emphasized the private sphere, domestic life, and personal fulfillment through the consumption of non-essential goods, such as home computers. It was within this evolving landscape that Carla, holding a degree in Applied Mathematics, entered the technology sector—a field still largely inaccessible to Portuguese women at the time—experiencing the dawn of the digital age with both fascination for emerging machines and the pressures of gendered expectations shaping domestic life. What set her apart was not merely the rarity of being a female programmer in 1980s Portugal, but the way she reimagined what it meant to "make technology" within a sociotechnical environment that seldom recognized women as creative agents.

The proliferation of narratives highlighting microcomputer advantages for the "modern man," eager to advance and maintain pace with the technological revolution, as well as for youth keen to master new information technologies and explore novel entertainment forms, played a central role in the emergence of Portugal's computer gaming community.

Media discourses framed playful computer use not merely as entertainment but also as strategies to attract new consumers, suggesting gaming proficiency could serve as early indicators of broader society informatization through "ludification of everyday life", as highlighted by [12].

The 1990s in Portugal marked a decade of profound technological, cultural, and educational transformation, establishing the groundwork for the widespread integration of information technologies. The introduction of the Internet during this period progressively reshaped modes of communication, learning, and entertainment, particularly among younger generations. Simultaneously, travel experiences such as Interrail journeys across Europe broadened youths' cultural and technological horizons, fostering contact with emerging digital practices and nurturing aspirations to engage with new forms of digital entertainment, as noted by the Portuguese scholar Patrícia Gouveia [13, 14]. Urban centers also emerged as vital sites of cultural convergence: international music bands performing in Portuguese cities attracted large audiences and cultivated cosmopolitan environments where leisure, music, and nascent digital cultures intersected [15].

During the 1990s, secondary schools, universities, and vocational programs in Portugal considerably expanded their offerings in computing and multimedia education. This institutional investment reflected a growing awareness of the strategic importance of digital technologies and contributed to the formation of a generation increasingly literate in multimedia and Internet practices. The year 1998 was particularly emblematic: the Lisbon World Exposition (Expo' 98) highlighted multimedia innovation on a global stage, while the same year was officially declared the National Year of Multimedia (see Fig. 2), marking a peak in CD-ROM production for educational, cultural, and entertainment purposes.

Within this sociotechnical and cultural landscape, game developers such as Carla and Pedro Faria developed their games, engaging with a context in which multimedia was politically and economically positioned as a strategic industry aligned with the ambitions of the emerging "Information Society". Despite its significance, this period of Portuguese multimedia and video game development remains largely underexplored in academic research. Future studies should engage more deeply with the 1990s to elucidate how the Portuguese video game industry developed and to recover the contributions of the many individuals and collectives that have been omitted from dominant historical narratives.

Fig. 2. National Year of Multimedia. Source: *Exame Informática* Magazine, August 1998.

3 Methodological Design

This research adopts a qualitative single-case study design focusing on the Portuguese game developer Carla Vieira Faria. The methodological approach combined source triangulation, drawing on online materials, an in-depth interview, and archival research.

3.1 Phase 1: Exploratory Web Mapping (April – May 2025)

Systematic online mapping aimed at recovering traces of Carla Faria's public visibility, works, critical reception, and institutional networks within which they circulated. Keywords were used in online search engines and digital press repositories, including the game developer's name and game titles. All retrieved items were evaluated according to the inclusion criteria, namely identifiable authorship, clear dating, and direct relevance to the case study. This exploratory resulted in the identification of seven press mentions and webpages, which served a dual purpose: contextualizing Carla Vieira Faria's historical trajectory and informing interview guide design.

3.2 Phase 2: Contact with Carla Faria (May–June 2025)

Establishing contact with Carla Faria required persistence and careful negotiation, as she is not active on social media platforms. Initial communication was facilitated through Pedro Faria via LinkedIn, which enabled the secure acquisition of Carla Faria's email address. Three formal email invitations were subsequently sent, each outlining the research objectives, ethical safeguards, confidentiality protocols, and scientific purposes of the study. Confirmation of participation was obtained following the third attempt.

3.3 Phase 3: Interview (July 3, 2025)

An in-depth, semi-structured interview lasting 1 hour and 16 minutes was conducted face-to-face in Lisbon at a shopping center chosen by the participant. Written informed consent was obtained following the conversation commencement. The interview guide was organized into seven thematic blocks: personal context and initial game development interest; project genesis and technical processes; circulation, reception, and social impact; accessibility and inclusion approaches; gender and power dynamics in the Portuguese game development ecosystem; recognition, awards, and institutional interactions; professional trajectory and final reflections. The session was audio-recorded with the participant's explicit consent, and field notes documented contextual details, including affective responses, emphasis, and the surrounding environment. The interview was fully transcribed with time codes using MAXQDA software, followed by familiarization processes involving repeated listening, first impression annotation, and reflexive fieldwork diary entries.

3.4 Phase 4: Archival Research (July–August 2025)

Archival research was a central component of this case study, aiming both to recover direct evidence of Carla Faria's professional activity and to situate her trajectory within the broader socio-cultural and technological contexts of Portugal in the 1990s and early 2000s. Systematic consultation was conducted at the Lisbon Newspaper Library (Hemeroteca Municipal), with particular attention to both generalist and specialized press sources.

In this phase, additional efforts were made to trace further mentions of Carla Faria's work, including leads she herself suggested during the in-depth interview. The archival investigation thus pursued dual objectives: identifying explicit references to Faria and her projects, verifying their circulation and reception in local media, and reconstructing the political, cultural, and economic landscapes of the period, alongside the evolution of information and communication technologies (ICTs) in Portugal. The primary sources consulted included general newspapers such as *Tal & Qual* and *Público*, as well as the specialized technology magazine *Exame Informática* (1998–2001).

3.5 Phase 5: Data Analysis (September 2025)

The analytical strategy combined deductive and inductive dimensions through reflexive thematic analysis [16]. This approach was chosen because it foregrounds reflexivity and the situated nature of interpretation rather than treating themes as objectively "discovered" entities. Deductive categories were informed by feminist critiques of women's erasure in design, media, and technology histories [5, 17–21], focusing on recurring themes such as invisibility, patrilinear historiography [2], and gendered exclusions. Simultaneously, inductive categories emerged organically through close data engagement.

The MAXQDA software managed the corpus and conducted thematic coding. Codes were progressively refined iteratively, moving between data and theory to ensure analytical rigor and openness to emergent insights. Throughout this process, particular care was taken to preserve the participant's voice, retaining relevant oral expression features in transcripts to capture tone, emphasis, and affective dimensions.

4 Results

4.1 Web-based Sources

The exploratory web mapping revealed a diverse set of digital traces documenting Carla Faria's professional activities and the circulation of her work. Several web pages were identified, some of which are now inactive but can still be retrieved through the Internet Archive (https://archive.org/).

Among these were two significant websites directly linked to Carla and Pedro Faria: (i) www.papim.com, created as a dissemination platform for their educational game "*A Cabana do Papim*" and other games (see Fig. 3); (ii) www.ajudas.pt, a project that, according to Carla Faria, "emerged to address a gap in the field of rehabilitation and disability support, aiming to provide a bridge between those in need of solutions and those who may be able to offer them."

Fig. 3. Screenshots of the inactive website www.papim.com. Source: https://archive.org/

Beyond these websites, seven press articles and online features were identified, where Carla Faria typically appeared as the main interviewee, presenting her work, and reflecting on the broader aims of her projects, namely:

1. "*A Cabana do Papim*", Público Newspaper, May 28, 2000.
2. "Falar a partir de um Pocket", Público Newspaper, September 16, 2002.
3. "*Bem-vindo à Cabana do Papim*", Tek Sapo, October 26, 2003.
4. "*Ajudar a comunicar*", Jornal de Notícias, June 13, 2004.
5. "*Transformei a deficiência em competência*", Lerparaver blog, October 15, 2006.
6. "*Carla Faria: A necessidade faz o engenho*", Activa Magazine, March 2007.
7. "*Jogos: O Baú dos Brinquedos e Aventura na Ilha das Cores*", Retroarquivo blog, March 01, 2024.

The analysis of the online media coverage of Carla Vieira Faria's career identified seven recurrent themes: (i) the family-based and collaborative nature of game production, (ii) the framing of her work as a solidarity project, (iii) the emphasis on accessibility for children with special needs, (iv) references to motherhood, (v) institutional recognition and awards, (vi) technical skills, and (vii) financial constraints and eco-nomic precarity.

(i) **Family-Based Collaborative Game Production** - Appeared in all media except Activa Magazine, 2007. Media consistently portrayed Carla and Pedro Faria as a couple whose technological practice was rooted in domestic and family collaboration. Game development was situated within a household where partnership, care, and creativity roles converged. Children, especially the eldest son, Diogo, were positioned not only as beneficiaries of educational software but also as contributors to the creative process, acting as testers, voice actors, and co-experimenters. Media discourses highlighted the artisanal and home-based nature of the production process, depicting the household as a creative workshop where diverse knowledge forms (such as design, programming, music, and storytelling) were interwoven into game development.

(ii) **Solidarity Project** - Appeared in five sources, positioning the couple's work as solidarity-driven initiatives explicitly contrasting their sharing and accessibility ethos with educational toy and technology market profit-driven logics. Media emphasized their refusal to align with market logics, foregrounding generosity and social compromise practices. However, while solidarity framing was consistently presented as joint endeavors between Carla and Pedro Faria, media representations privileged Carla's voice as the one giving interviews and embodying an altruistic ethos. Across these portrayals, Carla—who became the public face of the small family business, *CamiSoft*—occupied this position because her husband, the games' co-creator, did not like giving interviews, as she explained to me.

(iii) **Accessibility** - Appeared in five sources. The ludic software developed by Carla and Pedro Faria was portrayed as adaptable to diverse users and needs. The online me-dia highlighted features such as multiple difficulty levels, redesigns of popular games for alternative input devices, and the creation of assistive tools. For example, Pocket Voice enabled communication through pictorial language, symbols, or text (*Público*, 2002), while *Aventura no Circo* incorporated accessibility features including sign language and interfaces for children with severe motor difficulties (*Jornal de Notícias*, 2004). *A Cabana do Papim* was noted for offering technology-based activities that stimulated memory and reasoning skills.

(iv) **Motherhood** - Appeared in four sources, with public framing frequently anchored in Carla's personal biography, especially her role as mother of a child with cerebral palsy. Media highlighted work origins and motivations through motherhood lenses, framing maternal identity as central driving force behind game development practice. Even when her professional IT background was acknowledged, it was quickly redirected toward affective and domestic spheres, conflating technical ingenuity with ma-ternal devotion.

(v) **Institutional Recognition and Awards** - Appeared in six sources, underscoring institutional recognition and awards roles in legitimizing Carla and Pedro Faria's contributions to educational and inclusive game development. Media framing highlighted how state and corporate institutions provided resources enabling project continuity, with prizes from Ministry of Education and Microsoft presented as key educational and technical merit indicators.

(vi) **Technical Skills** - Appeared in three sources, foregrounding references to Carla Vieira Faria's academic background in Applied Mathematics. Although less frequent across media coverage, these few references positioned Carla Faria as technically competent and innovative professional capable of strategically mobilizing expertise in educational and assistive technology development. However, accounts often reframed technical knowledge through maternal lenses.

(vii) **Constraints and Economic Precarity** - Appeared in three sources, highlighting how financial hardship and unemployment were not merely background conditions but relevant factors in Carla and Pedro Faria's game developer trajectory. Media situated family creativity within structural fragility contexts, emphasizing how necessity drove innovation while financial constraints shaped dissemination strategies.

4.2 Isolated Echoes: Other Findings

The Retroarquivo blog (2024) emphasized that its post on the games of Carla and Pedro Faria was developed in collaboration with Yuri, a Ukrainian critic operating under the pseudonym UKA. In the same year, Yuri published reviews, written in Russian, of three titles: *A Cabana do Papim*, *O Meu Baú dos Brinquedos*, and *Aventura na Ilha das Cores*.

Yuri's reviews demonstrate that the games continued to resonate internationally decades after their original release. Retrogaming communities play a crucial role in reviving and disseminating forgotten or marginalized digital artifacts, often preventing them from fading into local oblivion [10]. Nonetheless, this resurgence of attention should be interpreted with caution. The case remains singular, driven by the initiative of one individual rather than indicative of sustained global engagement. Circulation, in this context, is sporadic and shaped by personal enthusiasm, not by a broader or institutionalized pattern of dissemination.

In addition to online media coverage, we also identified an academic work that directly examined *A Cabana do Papim* within the broader ecosystem of Portuguese educational software. This was the master's dissertation by Alexandra da Paz, entitled "Multimedia educational software in kindergarten: activities preferred by children aged 3 to 5" [22].

4.3 Interview Results

Carla Vieira Faria's trajectory as a game developer originates from dual motivation: providing cognitive stimulation for her eldest son and navigating financial constraints after her first childbirth. *A Cabana do Papim* (1998) creation, her first game developed in collaboration with Pedro Faria, did not arise from commercial ambition or recreational experimentation but from urgent domestic contexts: designing cognitive and motor stimulation strategies for her son Diogo, who was born with cerebral palsy.

Traditional analog games soon proved inadequate in stimulating Diogo, largely because of his exceptional memory and spasticity described as "disproportionate muscular strength."

These limitations, combined with financial constraints that prevented regular toy acquisition, prompted the couple to adopt technological solutions using household objects, such as metal pencil cases equipped with micro-switches, as interactive devices. The computer emerged as privileged cognitive and sensory stimulation medium, with assistive technological adaptations like simplified four-button keyboards acting as accessible mediators reducing motor interaction demands while creating opportunities more closely aligned with Diogo's abilities.

4.3.1 Academic background and Self-education

Carla situated her initial technology training within "the older courses" completed in the 1980s. While providing solid foundations, she emphasized limited applicability to rapidly changing 1990s digital environments. She and Pedro began experimenting with emerging Microsoft tools, particularly Visual Basic, forcing improvisation when software lacked animation functions. Her narrative highlighted how technical innovation often arises from formal training and informal, situated learning intersections.

Crucially, Carla's account highlighted her strong autodidactic learning disposition, which played a decisive role in shaping both pedagogical strategies and technological experimentation. Her enduring fascination with psychology provided conceptual frameworks for understanding cognitive and affective play dimensions, and she actively sought child development resources across different age groups.

4.3.2 External Validation Importance

Equally significant was her recollection of the first moments of external validation. She recounted how an *Exame Informática* magazine journalist noticed their first game when she still felt insecure about aesthetic quality. The journalist's encouragement to submit games to competitions consolidated recognition, situating their work within broader evaluation and recognition ecosystems. Archival research confirms this trajectory through the journalist's assessment published in *Exame Informática* in May 1998 (Fig. 4).

Fig. 4. Review of the game "A Cabana do Papim" (Papim's Cabin). Source: Exame Informática magazine, May 1998, p. 118. Image digitized by the Lisbon Municipal Newspaper Library.

4.3.3 Early Game Distribution Stages

Carla Faria recalled the early stages of game distribution as particularly difficult, marked by both financial precarity and the absence of infrastructures supporting small-scale, independent production. Games were initially recorded on CD-ROMs when large-scale CD printing technologies were first being explored, presenting immediate obstacles due to the limited resources available for professional production. The couple improvised domestic solutions, personally designing CD-ROM labels, covers, and packaging at home, then attempting direct "door-to-door" street promotion. However, people often misinterpreted efforts, assuming charity requests rather than innovative product presentations. Only after these challenges did Carla Faria approach *Instituto de Inovação Educacional* for game evaluation, noting the improbable nature of such support since "they did not usually fund individuals, only companies," but the institution eventually provided modest funding.

4.3.4 Economic Precarity and Awards

Financial hardship emerged not merely as a backdrop but as a structuring condition, shaping both couple dissemination strategies and terms under which innovation was acknowledged. The modest *Instituto de Inovação Educacional* funding (500,000 Portuguese escudos) was particularly significant, opening pathways toward new opportunities, including Microsoft competitions where they competed successfully against established publishers.

When asked directly about the significance of awards, Carla offered strikingly pragmatic perspectives: "Prizes only matter when we know what they are worth. And what they were worth for our software was a free evaluation." This account highlighted how, in contexts of financial precarity, recognition was valued less as symbolic capital than as a practical validation and legitimacy mechanism. Awards functioned not as prestige markers but as cost-free certification processes conferring credibility without additional financial burden.

4.3.5 Lack of Sustained Support and Gender Discrimination

When asked whether she and Pedro had considered seeking entrepreneurial training or establishing companies, Carla's response was unequivocal: "No. The doors all closed when they saw me." This statement encapsulates not only the gendered legitimacy dynamics that marked her trajectory but also the broader structural barriers shaping the trajectories of independent game producers in late 1990s and early 2000s Portugal.

Despite insisting presentations were "fully realized products and solutions," Carla recalls consistent dismissal. She reflects candidly on field gendered dynamics: "Being a woman in this environment is terrible, it is very bad." Yet resistance encountered was not solely about gender but tied to her accessibility and early stimulation work's disruptive nature for children with disabilities, challenging entrenched assumptions about disability when children with impairments were often hidden in institutions.

4.3.6 Software Piracy Problem

Carla's piracy recollections exposed yet another precarious condition layer shaping independent game development in 1990s and early 2000s Portugal. After Microsoft awards, games quickly became unauthorized copying targets through practices both blatant and socially normalized. Schools and institutions contacted her directly, asking if they could install single copies across multiple machines, conceding her response was immaterial: "We are going to copy it anyway." Without resources for anti-piracy software and with "strange and vague" legal protections, she found herself effectively defenseless.

4.3.7 Family-Based Collaborative Game Production

Carla's account highlighted a deeply familiar and collaborative game production process. What began as a limitation—her self-professed inability to draw—became a catalyst for Pedro's deeper creative involvement.

The couple's collaboration blurred conventional professional boundaries, with the family unit collectively substituting for formal development team specialized roles. This mode contrasted sharply with industrial game development models. Carla recalled competing in Microsoft contests against university research groups with dozen or more members, each responsible for narrow project aspects. By comparison, she and Pedro could speak to every game aspect, embodying holistic "whole package" knowledge that became strength sources, allowing them to defend work with authority and coherence.

5 Conclusion

Carla Vieira Faria's trajectory illustrates the pivotal role of women in expanding video games beyond mere entertainment, emphasizing their educational and inclusive potential. Her work, however, remains largely invisible in mainstream historical accounts of Portuguese video game development, revealing persistent mechanisms of marginalization that systematically subordinate or erase female contributions to creative computing. Despite institutional recognition and awards, her achievements often occupy the margins of official narratives, underscoring the limitations of formal validation in ensuring lasting visibility for women innovators. Faria's experience highlights how gendered assumptions, combined with the domestic and collaborative contexts in which many women operate, influence the recognition and historiography of technological creativity. This study contributes to feminist critiques of technology history and digital game studies, and future publications are planned to further explore this case study, advancing inclusive documentation practices that foreground the agency, innovation, and labor of women in shaping interactive media.

Future work will focus on disseminating this case study across multiple platforms and formats, including its integration into the Open Educational Resources (OER) on Women and Minorities in Creative Computing, developed within COST Action Grass-roots of Digital Europe: from Historic to Contemporary Cultures of Creative Compu-ting.

Acknowledgments. This case study would not have been possible without the generosity, clarity, and trust of Carla Vieira Faria, who agreed to share her story, her concerns, and the intimate archive of a life shaped by challenges and creativity with the first author. We are profoundly grateful for the time she devoted to us, for the honesty with which she revisited difficult moments, and for her willingness to open the doors to a memory that had, until now, remained almost entirely outside the historical record. We are also indebted to Maria Garda and Natalija Majsova, coordinators of the Open Call for Case Studies of COST Action 21141 – Grassroots of Digital Europe: from Historic to Contemporary Cultures of Creative Computing (costgrade.eu). This call, dedicated to identifying and documenting women, minorities, and other historically marginalized groups in European cultures of creative computing, provided not only the institutional framework but also the intellectual impetus that made this case study possible.

References

1. Swalwell, M.: Introduction: game history and the local, em game history and the local. Swalwell, M. (ed.), pp. 1–15. Springer Cham (2021.) https://doi.org/10.1007/978-3-030-66422-0_1

2. Nooney, L.: A pedestal, a table, a love letter: Archaeologies of gender in videogame history **13** (2013)
3. Jennings, S.C.: CHAPTER 8 The Horrors Of Transcendent Knowledge A Feminist- Epistemological Approach to Video Games, em Woke Gaming. In: Gray, K.L., Leonard, D.J. (eds.), pp. 155–172. University of Washington Press (2018). https://doi.org/10.1515/9780295744193-010
4. Phillips, A.: Gamer trouble: feminist confrontations in digital culture. New York University Press, New York (2020)
5. Rhody, L.M., Schreibman, S. (eds.) Feminist digital humanities: intersections in practice. em Topics in the digital humanities. Urbana: University of Illinois Press (2025)
6. Gouveia, P., Lima, L.: Convergent feminism, gaming, digital transition, and equity, em Techno-feminism: multi and transdisciplinary contemporary views of women in technology, pp. 125–143. UA Editora (2023). http://hdl.handle.net/10773/37656
7. Lima, L., Pinto, C., Martilla, T., Gouveia, P.: Home computing and digital game piracy in the 1980s in Portugal. In: Conference Proceedings of DiGRA 2023 Conference: Limits and Margins of Games Settings (2023). https://doi.org/10.26503/dl.v2023i1.1939
8. Lima, L., Gouveia, P., Ramos, L., Marttila, T., Correia, S., Costa, I., Gouveia, M.: (In)Visible Women: Multidisciplinary Creation and Collaborative Research in Transmedia Art and Gaming in Portugal. In: Proceedings of the 29th International Symposium on Electronic Arts: ISEA2024 Everywhen Proceedings. Vol. 1: Academic Papers pp. 451– 458 (2024). https://doi.org/10.5204/book.eprints.256296
9. Lima, L.: Pensar o Género a partir dos jogos digitais: uma análise sobre as assimetrias de género na indústria portuguesa de jogos digitais., 1st Edn., Porto, Portugal: Editora BAND. (2023). ISBN: 978–989–33–4234–3. https://doi.org/10.57859/ulisboa-istiti.000057
10. Lima, L., Mota, A.T.: Memory void: digital games preservation in Portugal, em Anais Estendidos do XXII Simpósio Brasileiro de Jogos e Entretenimento Digital (SBGames Estendido 2023), Brasil: Sociedade Brasileira de Computação, pp. 1403–1409 (2023). https://doi.org/10.5753/sbgames_es-tendido.2023.235624
11. Trindade, L.: O "Gosto" do Se7e-Uma história cultural do semanário Se7e, lerhistoria, no 67, pp. 45–61 (2014), https://doi.org/10.4000/lerhistoria.829
12. Lima, L., Pinto, C., Gouveia, P.: Genesis of a Gaming Culture: a Historical Analysis Based on the Computer Press in Portugal, apresentado na Proceedings of DiGRA 2022 Conference: Bringing Worlds Together (2022). https://doi.org/10.26503/dl.v2022i1.1326
13. Gouveia, P.: The Digital Playful River, a River Out of Eden: How the Internet Shaped my Planetary Perception, em Challenges of the Technological Mind. In: Alexandre, P., Castro, E.: (eds.) em New Directions in Philosophy and Cognitive Science, pp. 139–158. Springer, Cham (2024). https://doi.org/10.1007/978-3-031-55333-2_9
14. Gouveia, P.: My Journey Through the 1980s and 1990s as an Art Student and Young Artist, RAE, vol. 2024, no. 1 (2024). https://doi.org/10.54916/rae.142299
15. Pappámikail, L.: Juventude: Entre a Fase da Vida e o Tempo de Viver., em História da Vida Pri-vada em Portugal: Os Nossos Dias. Coordenação de Anna Nunes de Almeida., Lisboa: Temas e Debates/Círculo de Leitores, pp. 208–241 (2011)
16. Braun, V., Clarke, V.: Reflecting on reflexive thematic analysis. Qual. Res. Sport Exerc. Health **11**(4), 589–597 (2019). https://doi.org/10.1080/2159676X.2019.1628806
17. Buckley, C.: Made in patriarchy: toward a feminist analysis of women and design. Des. Issues **3**(2), 3 (1986). https://doi.org/10.2307/1511480
18. Ernst, W.: Gender in science and technology: interdisciplinary approaches. em Gender Studies. Bie-lefeld: Transcript (2014)
19. Young, E., Wajcman, J., Sprejer, L.: Where are the Women? Mapping the Gender Job Gap in AI, Policy Briefing: Full Report. The Alan Turing Institute (2021). https://www.turing.ac.uk/sites/default/files/2021-03/where-are-the-women_public-policy_full-re-port.pdf

20. Wajcman, J., Technology as a Site of Feminist Politics, em Recodierungen des Wissens: Stand und Perspektiven der Geschlechterforschung in Naturwissenschaft und Technik (Broschiert), 1st ed., vol. 1, pp. 87–101. Frankfurt: Petra Lucht, Tanja Paulitz (2008)
21. Wajcman, J.: Feminist theories of technology. Cambridge J. Econ. **34**(1), 143–152 (2010). https://doi.org/10.1093/cje/ben057
22. da Paz, A.M.S.M.: Software educativo multimédia no jardim de infância: actividades preferidas pelas crianças dos 3 aos 5 anos. Universidade do Minho, Braga, Portugal (2004)

From Pitch to Pixel: Portuguese Football, Identity, and the Microhistory of *Elifoot*

Ivan Barroso and Filipe Luz(✉)

University Lusófona, Lisbon, Portugal
ivanflow@gmail.com

Abstract. This article examines *Elifoot* (ZX Spectrum, 1987), one of Portugal's earliest football management simulations, as a cultural artefact reflecting national identity, technological modernisation, and social change in late twentieth-century Portugal. Moving beyond mainstream Game Studies' industrial focus, it situates *Elifoot* within local football and computing histories to show how video games embody specific socio-cultural dynamics.

Using an interdisciplinary framework of microhistory and Media Archaeology, the study explores the individual trajectory of creator André Elias, highlighting how his creative practice intersected with technological access, family influence, and football fandom. Media Archaeology situates the game within 1980s Portuguese infrastructures, including the Timex computing industry, home coding culture, and informal software networks.

Through this lens, *Elifoot* emerges as a historically situated narrative encoding Portuguese notions of rationality, competition, and national belonging. Its minimalist interface, numerical abstraction, and turn-based design reflect both technical constraints and contemporary ideals of efficiency. The game also demonstrates the creative agency of amateur developers in peripheral technological contexts, connecting grassroots production to broader European media transformations.

The study concludes that *Elifoot* provides a microhistorical lens for understanding the convergence of sport, identity, and digital modernity in Portugal. It argues that local, small-scale games serve as valuable historical documents, inscribing national aspirations and cultural imaginaries into code and play. This research contributes to the localisation of Game Studies and underscores the importance of preserving regional media artefacts within the global history of digital culture.

Keywords: Game Studies · Elifoot · Microhistory · Media Archaeology

1 Introduction

The study of video games as cultural artefacts has steadily grown; nevertheless, it often prioritises commercially dominant productions from major industrial centres in the United States, Europe and Japan. This focus risks overlooking localised, small-scale software, frequently offering richer, more nuanced insights into specific national identities, technological constraints, and social dynamics. For Portugal, where football has long

R. Baptista et al. (Eds.): VJ 2025, CCIS 2988, pp. 184–195, 2027.
https://doi.org/10.1007/978-3-032-31642-4_15

functioned as a primary marker of collective identity, intertwining passion, local politics, and social meaning, this local production proves particularly insightful. The immense cultural significance of sport, often serving national dreams and collective imagination, finds a unique parallel expression in the country's early 1980s digital culture.

This article presents a microhistorical and media-archaeological analysis of Elifoot (Elias, 1987), one of the earliest and most influential Portuguese football management simulation games. Developed during the formative years of the 1980s microcomputer age, which can be characterised by amateur programming, limited technological resources, and a growing domestic enthusiasm for digital creation, *Elifoot* is far more than a pastime. It constitutes a technological and cultural echo of its time, encapsulating the aspirations and constraints of small-scale Portuguese software development.

By examining *Elifoot,* this study interprets the game as both a product and a reflection of the social imaginaries of modernity in Portuguese society in the late twentieth century. Based on minimalist aesthetics, numerical management systems, and turn-based competition, the game's design mirrors contemporary ideals of rationalisation, efficiency, and organisation associated with sport and technology [1]. Through its abstract, data-driven representation of football management, *Elifoot* transforms the collective experience of club administration into a digital model of control and progress, resonating with the broader discourses of modernisation that shaped Portuguese cultural life in the 1980s.

At the same time, *Elifoot* embodies the creative agency of the local bedroom coder, revealing how individual experimentation with accessible computing tools could produce artefacts that express and share cultural meanings. In translating the local football expressions - arguably a central component of Portuguese identity - into a digital system governed by numbers, probabilities, and competition, *Elifoot* bridges players' passions and digital rationalities, capturing the tensions of an era in which national culture, technology, and play converged. Employing Microhistory [2, 3] and Media Archaeology [4, 5] as critical frameworks, this study asks, "How did *Elifoot* (ZX Spectrum, 1987), as a locally produced software artefact, embody and articulate the specific socio-cultural dynamics, technological constraints, and collective identity in 1980s Portugal?".

This analysis aims to demonstrate that video games function as historically situated narratives that inscribe national identities, values, and aspirations in code and play. Thus, they contribute to game history, emphasising local productions' socio-cultural reflection.

2 Methodology

This study adopts an interdisciplinary methodological framework that combines Microhistory [2, 3]) and Media Archaeology [4, 5] to examine *Elifoot* (ZX Spectrum, 1987) as both a cultural artefact and a technological product of its time. Microhistory provides a means of analysing small-scale phenomena (such as the work of a single developer or a locally produced game) to uncover broader social, cultural, and historical dynamics that might otherwise remain invisible in broader analyses. This method allows the study to focus on *Elifoot's* creator, André Elias, and his social and technological environment, tracing how individual agency and everyday practices intersected with wider processes of digital literacy, economic change, and national identity formation in late-twentieth-century Portugal.

Media Archaeology complements this perspective by situating *Elifoot* within the material and discursive layers of media history. Rather than treating the game merely as software, Media Archaeology encourages an exploration of the technological infrastructures, practices, and discourses that shaped its creation and circulation (ranging from the ZX Spectrum's local production and affordability to informal networks of software distribution and the role of computer magazines in fostering a culture of experimentation). This approach emphasises continuities and ruptures in how media technologies evolve and acquire meaning across time.

These two perspectives enable a multi-scalar analysis that bridges the micro (individual experience and creative practice) with the macro (national and technological contexts). By combining the interpretive depth of Microhistory with the critical excavation of Media Archaeology, this study situates *Elifoot* not simply as a nostalgic object or isolated game but as a historically situated expression of Portuguese modernity, reflecting how local forms of digital creativity engaged with broader European media and cultural transformations.

2.1 Microhistorical Approach

Following the principles of microhistory, this research privileges the *small scale*, focusing on the individual story of *Elifoot's* creation by André Elias as a lens through which broader cultural and technological processes can be understood. Instead of approaching representativeness or generic statistical data, this analysis focuses on the "exceptional normal" [2]. In other words, this investigation identifies a singular event that can help us reveal the social structures surrounding it.

Primary data for this microhistory derive from interviews with André Elias[1] [6], supplemented by contemporaneous press materials such as *MicroSe7e* and *Pokes & Dicas* magazines, as well as historical and sociological studies of Portuguese football and computing [7–9]. A comparative reading of these sources allows us to reconstruct the personal circumstances of production and the broader social meaning of amateur programming and football culture in 1980s Portugal.

[1] The primary source material for this study was a single, semi-structured interview conducted by the author with André Elias, the original developer of the Elifoot game series. The interview was executed via the online video conferencing service Zoom to secure primary source material and direct insight into the game's genesis and developmental philosophy. The interview was conducted in a private setting, and the full video recording is publicly available (URL provided in the references). To prepare the data for analysis, the author performed a Verbatim transcription into a text processor, deliberately omitting non-verbal cues to prioritise the semantic content of the discussion. As the interview was conducted in Portuguese, an AI-assisted translation service was employed to generate the English transcript, which was then carefully reviewed and finalised by the author to ensure conceptual fidelity. The analysis was conducted using Thematic Analysis, in which the entire transcript was line-by-line coded. This coding was performed in two stages: initially on the original Portuguese text to capture language-specific nuances and subsequently verified against the final English transcript. The analysis was partially deductive, as the research explicitly aimed to validate or disconfirm preliminary analytical findings against the developer's firsthand account, thereby enhancing the trustworthiness and resonance of the study's interpretations.

2.2 Media Archaeological Framework

To complement this microhistorical focus, Media Archaeology was elected to provide tools to analyse *Elifoot* as a media object embedded within its time's technological and aesthetic conditions. This framework resists common narratives of technological progress, instead emphasising ruptures, forgotten practices, and the materiality of media artefacts [4]. Through this approach, *Elifoot* is not examined as a precursor to later commercial football management games, but instead, as an artefact reflecting local infrastructures (such as the Timex of Portugal microcomputer local manufacturing and the ZX Spectrum's accessibility) that shaped Portugal's 1980s computing culture.

2.3 Analytical Procedure

The analysis proceeds in three stages: a) *Contextual Reconstruction* which situates *Elifoot* within the socio-historical background of Portuguese football and computing culture of the 1980s; b) *Microhistorical Narrative*, tracing the individual trajectory of André Elias and his creative process, linking his biography to the domestic and educational conditions that made bedroom coding possible in Portugal; and c) *Media Archaeological Interpretation*, examining the game's design features, distribution networks, and technical limitations to understand how they encode local technological and cultural meanings.

Through this hybrid methodology, the study demonstrates how a small-scale, locally produced game can illuminate national identity formation and digital modernity. It reveals how cultural values, technological access, and everyday creativity intersected in Portugal's transition to a networked media society.

3 Portuguese Football as Social and Cultural Context

Football's trajectory in Portugal from the late 19th century to the 1980s illustrates how the sport became embedded not only in everyday life but also in the Portuguese national imaginary. Introduced by English workers and Portuguese students returning from the United Kingdom [10, 11], football rapidly spread from elite circles into working-class neighbourhoods, becoming the country's dominant sport throughout the 20th century [12]. This expansion aligns with Benedict Anderson's [13] description of the emergence of "imagined communities," in which shared cultural practices (such as newspapers in his example or football in this case) enable individuals to imagine themselves as belonging to a collective national body.

By the 1930s, football occupied an ambiguous position within the Estado Novo dictatorship (1932–1974). While many European authoritarian regimes directly mobilised football for propaganda, the Portuguese state initially invested more heavily in mass gymnastics and physical education [14, 15]. Even though the national team played against Mussolini's Italy, Franco's Spain, and Hitler's Germany during this period [16], these matches were not publicly framed as political spectacles. Football nevertheless functioned as a widespread cultural activity capable of symbolising Portuguese modernity and international presence, even when not explicitly used by the regime.

It was only in the 1950s and 1960s, when clubs such as S.L. Benfica and Sporting C.P. achieved international visibility, that Estado Novo began to symbolically appropriate football. The 1966 World Cup became especially significant: the government interpreted the team's success as proof of the vitality of the colonial empire, framing racial mixture as a national asset [12]. Here, football, for the state, acted as what Eric Hobsbawm calls an "invented tradition", a shared ritual that naturalises specific narratives of national identity.

The collapse of the dictatorship following the 1974 Carnation Revolution saw football temporarily recede from cultural centrality amid widespread political upheaval. Crucially, however, by the 1980s, the sport re-emerged as, in Telo's words, "a universal social topic" that transcended traditional divisions of class, geography, and ideology [18]. Through football, citizens imagined a nationalistic imaginary, functioning as a symbolic space onto which the Portuguese could project collective hopes, frustrations, and narratives. Matches thus became key occasions for the nation to interpret and debate broader social realities through the lens of sporting competition. The complex mechanics of club organisation, governance hierarchies, player transfers, and league competition became subjects of intense public opinion, effectively mirroring the structures of a socio-political system. In this sense, football operated as a cultural shorthand (or even a paradigmatic cultural state) through which national performance, order, and aspiration were constantly negotiated and articulated [3].

This cultural backdrop gives *Elifoot* its distinctive resonance. Rather than being merely a managerial game, *Elifoot* digitised core elements of the Portuguese football imaginary: club organisation, league systems, transfers, and competitive hierarchies. Its minimalist design allowed players to reenact, in domestic spaces, the rationalised and statistical logic through which football was increasingly interpreted in public discourse. By abstracting the sport into tables, budgets, and results, *Elifoot* echoed a broader cultural move toward interpreting football (and, symbolically, the nation) as a system to be managed, optimised, and narrated. For Portuguese players, the game became a simulation not only of football administration but also of a familiar cultural framework through which national belonging, order, and collective identity were habitually imagined.

4 Portuguese Computing and the 1980s Digital Context

In parallel with football's growing cultural prominence, Portugal experienced the micro-historical rise of digital technology during the late twentieth century. Although the Estado Novo's isolationist economic policies limited technological exchange [18], the country's accession to the European Free Trade Association (EFTA) in the 1960s laid the groundwork for industrial and technological collaboration. One tangible result was the establishment of the Timex factory near Lisbon, which would later play a pivotal role in the domestic manufacture of microcomputers.

Following the 1974 Carnation Revolution, Portugal gradually opened its markets and aligned with broader European technological trends. The 1980s witnessed a surge in home computing, primarily through the proliferation of affordable 8-bit microcomputers. This expansion was significantly aided by Timex's local production of ZX Spectrum–compatible systems [8, 19], which democratized access to computing across middle-class households. By 1985, approximately 100,000 ZX Spectrums had been sold in Portugal [18], signalling the emergence of a new digital public.

Across Europe, the microcomputer became a symbol of modernity, progress, and education. Portugal mirrored this transformation. Government initiatives such as the MINERVA programme promoted digital literacy in schools. At the same time, a growing popular press, including magazines like *MicroSe7e* and *Pokes & Dicas*, nurtured a culture of experimentation by publishing programming tutorials, "type-ins," and interviews with amateur developers [9]. This convergence of media, education, and accessibility, in microhistorical terms, fostered a network of everyday digital creativity.

Within this ecosystem, the figure of the "bedroom coder" emerged, young enthusiasts learning BASIC or Assembly in domestic settings, producing games, demos, and utilities that circulated informally through schools, clubs, and copy networks. These practices were not merely technical exercises; they constituted early forms of cultural authorship, transforming computing into both entertainment and self-expression. The games produced during this period functioned as microhistorical artefacts of a transitional society negotiating between analogue pasts and digital futures.

It was within this environment that *Elifoot* emerged as a product of Portugal's local technological conditions and its deeply embedded football culture. Its creator, André Elias, epitomises the bedroom coder of the 1980s: a Lisbon teenager with access to the affordable ZX Spectrum ecosystem, shaped by both domestic encouragement and public enthusiasm for football. His personal trajectory illustrates how individual creativity intersected with national processes of technological modernisation and cultural identity formation. Through this intersection, *Elifoot* encapsulates the convergence of two key Portuguese passions, football and innovation, translating them into the language of code and play (Fig. 1).

Fig. 1. The Timex of Portugal factory, which produced microcomputers.

5 The Portuguese Microhistory of Elifoot

At the age of 17, André Elias developed *Elifoot* in 1987 using BASIC on the ZX Spectrum. Coming from a middle-class family, Elias benefited from early access to computers through his father, who worked with technology and saw its future potential. His father introduced him to BASIC programming on systems such as the ZX81 and the Tektronix computers, and by 1986, Elias had his own ZX Spectrum+.

> «My parents always believed that early technological access was crucial. So, they provided it so their children could access technology as early as possible. They always made sacrifices, especially regarding computers and internet access, so that we could have that» [6].

In the collected interviews, Elias recalls how football provided stability and joy in a politically unstable decade. He merged his love for football with programming experiments, generating random match results, building league tables, and simulating seasons. From these experiments came *Elifoot*:

> «Using the football theme, I sorted the results and organised the standings to display them in order. Perhaps... ah, and then there was also the concept of randomness, which I found extraordinary. It was about generating random numbers...This "random" concept is the name of the command in English, so I was drawing lots for the teams to play against each other. Eventually, I started assigning some weight to certain results so that they weren't completely random. Then I would organise and begin to sort the standings, number of points, goals, wins, losses, etc. It was data management. This was the beginning.» [6].

Fig. 2. This is a recreated splash page from the ZX Spectrum version of *Elifoot* (Elias, 1987), done with Elias's permission and approval.

Created as an experience and primarily for leisure with his friends, the first version of the game allowed up to eight players to manage teams across four divisions. Human players took turns managing their clubs and buying and selling players.[2] Matches were simulated off-screen, with only results displayed, through an auction system and by watching their progress in league tables. This reflected both technological limitations and the abstraction of management. The game ended when a human-controlled team

[2] The players' names would be made-up, with the teenager references emerging, such as having characters from comic books as football players.

won the Primeira Divisão. The final project name was a combination of Elias' name plus the word football (Elifoot) [6] (Fig. 2).

This early ZX Spectrum version was distributed locally only among his close network.[3]. However, in 1990, during his university years, Elias recreated the game for PC with no significant upgrades, keeping the same core gameplay loop. Even the visuals and graphics were still black and white. Once again, distribution was informal: friends copied and shared the game, and no commercial release occurred. Written in Pascal, the PC version spread further through university networks and piracy.

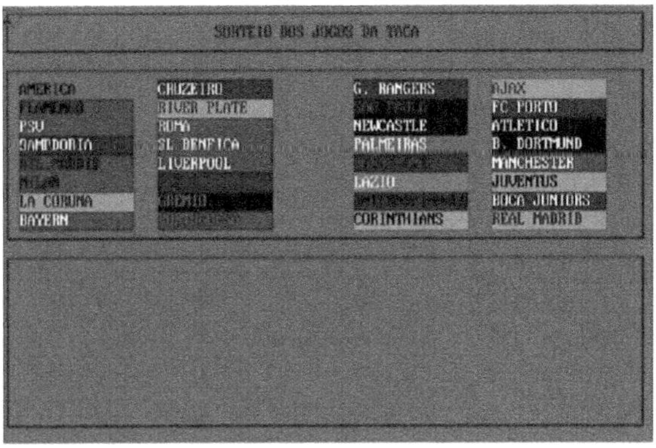

Fig. 3. *Elifoot II* (Elias, 1992).

Popularity was growing, and colleagues asked if he could (finally) update the game to add more features [6]. From here, in 1992, emerged *Elifoot II* (Fig. 3), which expanded the formula with improved graphics and new features, cementing its reputation as a cult classic of Portuguese computing. Two more updates would follow, and by 1998, Elias released *Elifoot 98*, the first commercial title of the series and the last major release of the twentieth century[4].

[3] It should be pointed out that the first versions of *Elifoot*, developed for the ZX Spectrum (1987) and MS-DOS (1990), are currently considered lost media. The games were initially distributed in minimal numbers without a formal commercial release, and a stable, working copy has not been located (reportedly, not even the original creator, André Elias, possesses a functional version). However, references to the first ZX Spectrum game are common in online communities, where users frequently share their recollections of playing it. Besides the author, other sources, such as Zagalo [21] and Leão [22], also acknowledge the existence of a ZX Spectrum version.

[4] *Elifoot 98* would receive two minor updates before the end of the century, fixing minor bugs and adding national teams.

6 *Elifoot*, Portuguese Culture and Computer Games

From a cultural perspective, *Elifoot* encapsulates the intertwining of football and Portuguese identity. It mirrors the widespread practice of fans acting as "treinadores de bancada" (stands managers), debating coaching decisions and imagining alternative outcomes [23]. By giving players direct control over clubs, budgets, and squads, *Elifoot* microhistory translated this cultural practice into interactive form.

The game also reflects the broader rationalisation processes evident in modern sport [1]. Specifically, its reliance on numerical data, statistics, and performance analytics fundamentally abstracted the game of football into quantifiable systems, thereby aligning with contemporary managerial discourses. Even when compared to contemporary football manager games, Elifoot remains notably simplified and minimal. This contrasts with titles released across Europe during the same period, such as the British-developed *Football Manager* (Addictive Games, 1982) and *Brian Clough's Football Fortunes* (CDS Micro Systems, 1987), the German *Profi-Fußball* (Purple-Soft, 1986), the Italian *Mexico '86* (Gruppo Editoriale Jackson, 1986), the Norwegian *Fotball-Ligaen* (Datacompaniet, 1985) or the Hungarian *Random Champ 8* (SV Matias, 1988). Many of these contemporary titles offered expansive features, including stadium improvements, staff hiring, and granular control over tactics and strategy (and even colour visuals or graphics). In stark contrast, *Elifoot* provided a more basic experience focused almost exclusively on the transactional mechanics of hiring and selling players, followed by simple, minimal-input match simulations. This focus on simple, quantifiable metrics effectively distilled the football experience, favouring a minimal approach that prioritised the core mechanics of competition and squad management over the complexity of the wider football environment. Consequently, the game serves as an early example of the purely statistics-based managerial abstraction, efficiency and organisation prevalent in contemporary titles. This lineage can be traced to modern simplified managers such as the browser-based *Hattrick* (Hattrick Limited), the mobile-focused *Football Manager 26 Touch* (Sport Interactive, 2025), and *Be the Manager 2025: Soccer* (Mobisoca, 2025). Furthermore, it is documented as a direct conceptual influence on later simplified titles, such as *Brasfoot* (Santos, 2025).

While the first version is considered lost media, the subsequent release is not. *Elifoot II* (1992) featured a visually minimal interface characterised by modest colours and tabular data. This visual approach is often interpreted as a deliberate aesthetic refinement when contrasted with accounts of the original, suggesting the inaugural release may have been even more rudimentary in its design.

It is also in these simple origins, informal circulation, and humorous naming (e.g., parody player names) that it is firmly grounded in local, small-scale Portuguese digital culture.

Importantly, *Elifoot* demonstrates how games function as historically situated narratives. Emerging in 1987 during Portugal's transition from an isolated dictatorship to membership in the European Economic Community (later known as the European Union), the game embodies the microhistory of local computer literacy while retaining grassroots values of DIY quality and nationalistic themes. It represents a step towards European digital culture and reflects (uniquely) Portuguese experiences and expressions through football and computing.

7 Conclusions

This study, employing Microhistory and Media Archaeology, demonstrates that *Elifoot* (ZX Spectrum, 1987) functions as a culturally saturated artefact that reflects the socio-technical dynamics and collective identities of 1980s Portugal. Through Microhistory, the game reveals the power of small, seemingly marginal productions to illuminate broader cultural processes [2]. Examining a game developed by a Portuguese teenager opens a window onto the world of national sport, the popularisation of the microcomputer through television and printed media, family dynamics, technological literacy, the EFTA agreements that led to local computer production, and the informal circulation networks that characterised local software cultures. What was initially seen as a minor DIY title now emerges as a window for understanding how Portuguese society imagined technology, nationhood, and sport during this period.

Media Archaeology deepens this perspective by locating *Elifoot* within the European microcomputer production. It underscores that both canonical titles and locally produced, DIY games are necessary to reconstruct how gaming cultures were lived and shared outside dominant European markets, countries and territories [4]. Elifoot's significance lies not in commercial reach but in its cultural embeddedness, reflecting how players appropriated digital media to re-enact familiar social worlds.

Crucially, a brief comparison with contemporaneous football management games highlights *Elifoot's* distinctiveness. British titles such as *Football Manager* series (Addictive Games), *Soccer Boss* (1984), or *Brian Clough's Football Fortunes* (CDS Micro Systems, 1987) pursued increasingly complex managerial realism: scouting systems, financial modelling, match commentary, and expanded user interfaces made possible by professional studios and established commercial distribution. *Elifoot*, by contrast, emerged from the technological and social constraints of the Portuguese microcomputer scene. Its radical abstraction, such as the single-screen tables, immediate match results, and minimal narrative mediation, mirrored the DIY mentality of local "bedroom coding" and the informal tape-copying economy in which it circulated. Most importantly, while British management games encoded the structures and logic of English football institutions, *Elifoot* translated the Portuguese football imaginary into code: the hierarchical league system, the centrality of small regional clubs, and the cultural perception of football as a space of success projection and rationalised aspiration. It does, however, without being a complex managerial realism, showcasing even some humour through introducing comic book characters as football players. These differences underscore *Elifoot's* status as a uniquely situated cultural expression rather than a derivative simulation.

Our analysis, therefore, reveals that *Elifoot* operates as a technological and cultural echo of 1980s Portugal. By distilling the deeply rooted football imaginary into a structured, numerical form, it enabled players to rehearse national dreams of sporting glory within the intimate space of their homes. Its aesthetic simplicity and technical limitations register the realities of small-scale Portuguese software development and the broader DIY European microcomputer ecosystem.

This study contributes to game history and microhistory by affirming that local, DIY productions encode historically specific narratives and values and are essential for understanding global media cultures. After all, knowing about game development techniques might not be enough to understand this medium. To fully comprehend the history of games, we must examine these marginalised local productions and how the economic, political, and social contexts around them inscribe national aspirations, technological imagination, and cultural identity into code and play.

8 Future Research and Limitations

Future research on *Elifoot* and its cultural and historical significance could expand in several directions, offering more profound insights into the game and the broader context of early Portuguese game development. One promising avenue for future exploration would be a comparative analysis between *Elifoot* microhistory and similar football management games from other countries during the same period. By examining how different technological, cultural, and economic contexts shaped game development across regions, researchers could highlight the unique aspects of *Elifoot* tied to Portugal's specific circumstances and understand local considerations in game development. This comparison would help identify how regional production trends influenced the Portuguese game and its international counterparts when approaching the same theme, features and genre. Therefore, collaborating with other researchers in European game studies could provide a better understanding of *Elifoot* and its period counterparts.

Acknowledgments. This study was funded by national funds through the Fundação para a Ciência e Tecnologia (FCT), under HEI-Lab Research and Development Unit (UIDB/05380/2020, https://doi.org/https://doi.org/10.54499/UIDB/05380/2020).

Disclosure of Interests. The authors declare no potential competing interests on the scope of this research. This article was proofread and edited for language clarity using Grammarly and Generative AI tools. These tools were employed solely for linguistic enhancement, without impacting the content, arguments, or conclusions. The authors, for whom English is not the primary language, retain full responsibility for the work's intellectual integrity.

References

1. Guttmann, A.: From ritual to record: The nature of modern sports (Updated ed.). Columbia University Press (2004). http://www.jstor.org/stable/10.7312/gutt13340
2. Ginzburg, C.: Microhistory: Two or three things that I know about it. Crit. Inq. **20**(1), 10–35 (1993). https://doi.org/10.1086/448696
3. Levi, G.: On microhistory. In: Burke, P. (ed.) New perspectives on historical writing, pp. 93–113. Polity Press (1991)
4. Huhtamo, E., Parikka, J. (eds.): Media archaeology: Approaches, applications, and implications. University of California Press (2011). https://doi.org/10.2307/jj.23689317
5. Parikka, J.: What is media archaeology? Polity Press (2012)
6. Elias, A.: Interview 3. Interview by Ivan Barroso. Lisbon, Portugal (2024). https://youtu.be/v31InP5x_Nc?si=anTsaA4MLE4_ILZo
7. Coelho, J.N.: Paixão FC, a equipa de todos nós: Futebol, identidades, significados e representações sociais. Oficina do CES, 161, 1–24. Universidade de Coimbra (2000). https://ces.uc.pt/publicacoes/oficina/ficheiros/161.pdf
8. Dias Figueiredo, A.: Engenharia Informática, Informação e Comunicações. In: Heitor, M., Brandão de Brito, J.M., Rolo, M.F. (ed.). A Engenharia em Portugal no séc. XX, Vol. III, D. Quixote, pp. 551–573 (2004). ISBN 927-20-2792-1

9. Lima, L., Pinto, C., Gouveia, P.: Genesis of a Gaming Culture: a Historical Analysis Based on the Computer Press in Portugal. DiGRA (2022). https://doi.org/10.26503/dl.v2022i1.1326
10. Simões, A.C.: Desporto com política: nos 100 anos da República. Imprensa nacional-Casa da moeda (2011)
11. Nunes, A.B., Valério, N.: Contribuição para a História do Futebol em Portugal. Universidade de Lisboa (1996). http://hdl.handle.net/10400.5/907
12. Pinheiro, F.: Futebol e política na Ditadura: factos e mitos. In: Tiesler, N.C., Domingos, N. (eds.) Futebol Português-Política, género e movimento, pp. 47–82 (2012)
13. Anderson, B.: Imagined communities: Reflections on the origin and spread of nationalism (Revised ed.). Verso (2006)
14. Hobsbawm, E.J.: Nations and nationalism since 1780: Programme, myth, reality. Cambridge University Press (1990)
15. Serrado, R.: O jogo de Salazar: A política e o futebol no Estado Novo. Casa das Letras (2009)
16. Costa, J.P.O.: Portugal na História: Uma Identidade. Lisboa: Temas e debates: Círculo de Leitores (2022)
17. Sobral, F.: Futebol, O Estádio Total. Lisboa, Fundação Francisco Manuel dos Santos (2017)
18. Telo, A.J.: História contemporânea de Portugal: do 25 de Abril à actualidade (Vol. 1). Editorial Presença (2007)
19. Barroso, I.: História dos Videojogos (4.ª Edição), Holland, Blurb (2012)
20. Antunes, F.: Na intimidade do microcomputador o futuro invade o presente: A ludificação da vida quotidiana. Seminário Sete (Micro Se7e), pp. 1–2 (1988)
21. Zagalo, N.: Videojogos em Portugal: História, tecnología e arte. Lisboa: FCA Editora referencial de educação para os media (2013)
22. Leão, A.: Os Programadores Portugueses. Cantanhede: Museu Load ZX Spectrum (2022)
23. Coelho, J.N.: "Paião FC, A Equipa de Todos Nós": FUTEBOL, IDENTIDADES, SIGNIFICADOS E REPRESENTAÇÕES SOCIAIS. Comunicação apresentada no IV Congresso Português de Sociologia, Coimbra (2000)

Aloy's Challenge to Gender Stereotypes in Contemporary Video-Game Narratives

Maria Júlia Vieira[1(✉)], Dalila Martins[1], Pedro Cardoso[2], and Luciana Lima[3]

[1] DigiMedia, Department of Communication and Arts, University of Aveiro, Aveiro, Portugal
mjlvc26@ua.pt

[2] i2ADS / Faculty of Fine Arts, University of Porto, Porto, Portugal

[3] Interactive Technologies Institute (ITI/LARSyS), University of Lisbon, Lisbon, Portugal

Abstract. This study examines the representation of women in video games through a qualitative analysis of player perceptions of Aloy, the protagonist of *Horizon Zero Dawn* (2017). Semi-structured interviews with ten video-game-development students investigate three dimensions central to gender studies: stereotypes and physical appearance, female positioning in social contexts and leadership, and reflections on gender inequality in videogames. Findings reveal that Aloy marks a paradigmatic shift in female character design, transcending the hyper-sexualized stereotypes prevalent in the industry. Participants describe Aloy's leadership as collaborative and empathetic, contrasting sharply with the authoritarian models typically assigned to male protagonists; the game's moral-choice system further disrupts expectations that female characters must embody nurturing stereotypes. Interviewees also report that playing as Aloy reshapes their perceptions of gender roles, enabling cross-gender identification and encouraging reflection on cultural norms embedded in virtual environments. The study concludes that Aloy establishes new expectations for female protagonists, demonstrating that compelling characters can embody strength, agency, and complexity without relying on stereotypical gender markers, thereby fostering a more inclusive and reflective gaming culture.

Keywords: Gender studies · Horizon Zero Dawn · Inclusion · Videogames · Women Representation

1 Introduction

Video games have become a significant cultural phenomenon and an integral part of contemporary society [1]. A 2023 study by [2], a leading research and market analysis company in the gaming sector, found that approximately 46% of those surveyed identified themselves as women [3]. These figures represent about 2.2 billion active women gamers, a number close to that of men players [4]. Despite this, men still dominate the professional sphere of game development, with women comprising only 30% of the workforce in Europe [5]. Gender issues and the inclusion of women in video games, whether as players or developers, have therefore attracted increasing scholarly attention [6, 7]. Patriarchal norms in the industry have led to gender imbalances in character

R. Baptista et al. (Eds.): VJ 2025, CCIS 2988, pp. 196–209, 2027.
https://doi.org/10.1007/978-3-032-31642-4_16

representation, influencing both the quantity and portrayal of female characters, who are often confined to stereotypes, objectified, and hypersexualized [8, 9]. In this sense, the literature shows that this objectification is a cultural legacy that affects the way the public consumes and perceives female characters, keeping the industry geared towards a mostly male audience [7, 10, 11]. Historically, video games have mostly been designed, developed and marketed for a male audience [12]. An example of this is Lara Croft in *Tomb Raider* (1996), who became a sexualized icon [13], in which "female characters remained underrepresented and sexually objectified" [14], p.567. In recent years, the growing presence of women in the industry has led to progress in creating more inclusive characters and narratives [15, 16]. According to [17] this inclusion is enabling the emergence of new stories and characters shaped by female perspectives, promoting more balanced gender representation. Though challenges persist, the movement toward fairer, more diverse portrayals signals a promising future—one in which female characters take central roles, reflecting the depth and complexity of human experience [18, 19]. This is evident in *Horizon Zero Dawn* (2017) and *Hellblade: Senua's Sacrifice* (2017) in which previously marginalized female protagonists have been given a voice [20, 21]; as well as in *The Last of Us* (2013). The main character of *Horizon Zero Dawn*, Aloy, was considered by her publisher, Sony, the icon of the future of the Playstation [22]. Since then, Aloy has indeed become an image of representation of fluid genders in video games [23, 24]. But how does she represent the player? This paper explores how men and women players – video game development students – perceive how they feel or don't feel represented by the character Aloy in *Horizon Zero Dawn*. The paper begins by contextualizing the importance of female representation in games and introducing *Horizon Zero Dawn*. It then details the thematic analysis methodology applied to semi-structured interviews. Finally, it presents and discusses the interview results and concludes with reflections and future research directions.

2 Literature Review

2.1 A Brief Overview of Women Representation in Video Game Characters

Historically, video games were mostly targeted at male audiences, reinforcing gender stereotypes through male protagonists, violence-centered plots, and marketing aimed at men [16]. Over time the industry began to face challenges of misrepresentation and lack of inclusion [25]. Hayes [26, 27], argues there are no biological reasons for gendered game preferences; rather, games have been socially framed as a male domain, alienating women from gaming culture. Gendered technology labels further reinforce stereotypes, marginalizing diverse identities [28]. An example is *Barbie Fashion Designer* (1996), a game about dressing dolls and designing fashion, which epitomized "games for girls" and entrenched market divisions. These portrayals suggest women lack competitive skills—an idea not supported by evidence [10] and reinforce stereotypes that limit choices and overlook individual preferences [28]. Since the 1990s, the number of women involved in video games has grown significantly, now representing almost half of the gamer population. This shift led the industry to start addressing gender-related concerns, working to challenge misogynistic norms and promote the value of women. As a result, female representation evolved, with more women portrayed as autonomous and even taking on protagonist roles [29]. Although these changes were significant, especially compared to the state of the art in the 1980s and the 1990s, there are still today numerous cases of female stereotyping and objectification. This type of narrative continues to reinforce the stereotype that women are the "weaker sex", which makes them unsuitable to take on prominent roles in environments traditionally seen as masculine, such as war and conflict scenarios [16. 10] state that female gamers who show frequent interest in video games traditionally considered "masculine", such as those with themes of fighting, competition and war, are often seen by the gamer community as "nerds" or "geeks", being considered masculinized or lesbian, because they don't fit the standards of games intended for women. This kind of prejudice alienates and intimidates women, discouraging them from taking on the role of active players in the community, and reinforces a macho and exclusionary culture.[1]

2.2 Social Impact of Gender Stereotyping on the Design of Female Characters

As video games continue to grow towards a mainstream of entertainment, it becomes crucial to understand the social implications of how female characters are portrayed and to push for inclusive representations that can foster healthier gender dynamics. Early examples, such as Princess Peach, from *Super Mario Bros* (1985), and Princess Zelda, from *The Legend of Zelda* series (1986–2024), epitomized the damsel in distress trope, wherein female characters were relegated to passive roles, awaiting rescue by male protagonists[2]. The 1990s introduced stronger female leads, such as Lara Croft (*Tomb Raider*, 1996), yet these characters remained hypersexualized, reflecting more fantasy than empowerment [30]. This construction of the female figure as an object of digital entertainment reflects corporate values, influencing the socialization of players [10, 27]. This approach ends up promoting values that range from the objectification of the female body to the normalization of behaviors such as violence, prostitution and humiliation [10, 27]. Such portrayals shape perceptions of women from childhood, both virtually and in real life [11, 31]. Although there have been significant changes in recent years, there is still a strong presence of stereotypes and female objectification in many contemporary games. The design of female characters continues to be based on fertility symbols and concepts of inferiority, in which women are often portrayed as sexual objects or mere instruments for satisfying male desires [16]. [28] point out that, although there has been an increase in the representation of female characters, there is still a significant gap between this representation and reality, highlighting the persistence of gaps in the production and development of video games. Historically male-dominated development teams have created characters reflecting male fantasies [32]. Perpetuating stereotypes

[1] It is important to point out that, when discussing gender relations, the article emphasizes that gender relations also involve historical power dynamics between men and women, which have developed unequally and under patriarchal domination. This context perpetuates the notion that women are less capable than men, often leaving their achievements and abilities unrecognized [29].

[2] On September 26, 2024, the first main Legend of Zelda game featuring Princess Zelda as the main playable character was released (Carpenter, 2024) – *The Legend of Zelda: Echoes of Wisdom (2024).*

like the *femme fatale*, the hypersexualized heroine, or the nurturing caregiver [33]. This reinforces the notion that women are less capable or important within the context of gaming worlds, mirroring societal views that diminish women's roles in leadership and decision-making [34]. Such portrayals also influence how female players view themselves and their place in gaming, potentially discouraging participation in certain genres or competitive play [35]. In the context of video games, prolonged exposure to virtual stereotypes can shape players' beliefs and behaviors [36]. Moreover, the objectification and hypersexualization of female characters in games can contribute to the normalization of sexism and gender discrimination within gaming communities. [37] found that male players exposed to hypersexualized female characters are more likely to express sexist attitudes in real life. These portrayals reinforce discrimination in gaming culture and influence broader gender perceptions, reinforcing traditional views on how women should look or behave [35, 36]. The evolution of female characters in video games mirrors wider societal shifts in gender representation. While often constrained by stereotypes, these characters have also challenged dominant norms, reflecting ongoing tensions around women's roles in society.

2.3 ALOY: A Turning Point for Female Characters in Computer Games

Horizon Zero Dawn (2017) is an open-world narrative game developed by Guerrila Games and published by Sony Interactive Entertainment [23]. Released in February 2017 [38], the game has won several awards and also sold more than 2.6 units in the first two weeks after its release [39]. The game opens with the player controlling a young girl from a third-person perspective, without context of the story or setting. She soon discovers a device granting augmented-reality insights, contrasting sharply with the primitive surroundings [40]. Set in the 31st century, *Horizon* unfolds in a post-apocalyptic world where humans, after a mysterious extinction event, have regressed to tribal societies [24, 40]. These include the matriarchal Nora, the monarchic Carja, the metallurgic Oseram, and the nomadic Banuk [4]. The world is overrun by corrupted robotic creatures, originally military machines from the "Old Ones," now driven by a phenomenon called "The Derangement." Players control Aloy, a Nora outcast raised by Rost. The story revolves around Aloy's search for her origins and the mystery behind the apocalypse, centered on Elisabet Sobeck, a 99% DNA match and the mind behind the "Zero Dawn" project meant to save the planet [24, 41]. Aloy exists in a realm entirely ruled by nature [41].

Characterized by being an expert hunter and possessing the unusual ability to control "machines", Aloy is also agile, skilled and trained in combat, using bows, traps and other types of weaponry to support her survival as shown in Fig. 1. The player is free to choose how to shape Aloy's personality by selecting her responses to specific situations through "moral choices" story-centered moments, influencing specific aspects of the game along their traversal [42]. Aloy is an exiled character and hostile to others, which means that she doesn't have much experience in social relationships.

Fig. 1. Characterizations of Aloy in the video game Horizon Zero Dawn (2017).

Despite her lack of experience, Aloy maintains a close relationship with Rost [4] – one of the most influential characters in Aloy's life, having adopted and raised her since she was a baby. Being empathetic, Aloy grows and builds bonds with other characters throughout the game, strong enough for her to receive their help when she needs it most [4]. Despite the residual literature on Aloy and female representation in *Horizon Zero Dawn*, according to Harley Williams [40], Aloy is a feminist character who, contrary to what is expected, is a strong female characters who have to prove their worth in a patriarchal society, does what she wants within the game without repeatedly drawing attention to her femininity. She has been designed so that players can see her as a complete and complex character and not just a woman. Her portrayal is praised for being more than a female character, Aloy is a non-sexualized heroine female character [23]. According to [24], she is not seen as a "Ms. Male Character" or a female version of a male character. She has been conceived with a complexity that goes beyond the rigid gender stereotypes still present in the video game industry.

3 Methodology

Through a qualitative study, we analyze how male and female players, particularly video game development students, perceive how they feel or don't feel represented by Aloy in *Horizon Zero Dawn* (2017). The aim was to understand how (and if) this construction contributes to the promotion of gender equality in video games. This study was conducted through interview surveys, as they allow the researcher to obtain information about the participants' perspectives and experiences. [43] also highlight the main advantages of this technique: in-depth exploration of the analyzed elements and flexibility for gathering testimonies and interpretations from interviewees. To carry out the study, non-probabilistic convenience sampling was used. We gathered 10 interviewees (5 women and 5 men) studying at the University of Aveiro, in Portugal, all enrolled in video game development programs or related courses. The interviews were conducted online and included 15 questions. Participants were required to have completed *Horizon: Zero Dawn* to answer the semi-structured questionnaire, divided into three sections with specific objectives: **(1) Stereotypes and physical appearance:** The aim of this section was to explore the perception of the construction of the character Aloy in terms of the character's coherence and originality; the specific characteristics that represent the audience and the comparative content in relation to other genders. **(2) Female positioning in the social context and leadership:** In this section, the intention was to critically deepen the female character in terms of the comparative content on leadership in relation to other genders; the influence of the female character in the social context and the evaluation of leadership and the need for support in this context. **(3) Reflection on gender inequality in videogames:** In this section, we planned to understand the evolution of videogames in terms of gender representation; how character design can promote gender equality and what the participants' expectations are in terms of the context of gender equality in videogames. Thematic Analysis (TA) was used to examine the results, defined as a set of qualitative methods for exploring and interpreting patterned meaning across datasets [43]. It involves identifying, analyzing, and reporting recurring themes in the data. TA is a descriptive and flexible method that can be combined with other analytical approaches [44, 45].

4 Data Analysis and Discussion

This section presents a thematic analysis of the interviewees' perceptions regarding the character Aloy. The semi-structured interviews conducted with video game development students allowed for the identification of significant patterns in the areas of character construction, gender representation, and leadership. The three main themes are discussed based on the responses obtained (see Tables 1, 2, and 3).

4.1 Construction and Evolution of Aloy's Character

Participants recognize Aloy as a credible and complex character. The protagonist's narrative progression is considered realistic, considering her training from childhood and her emotional development throughout the story. The absence of hypersexualized stereotypes is noted and valued, with particular emphasis on her physical representation, which aligns with the hostile environment and the functional demands of being a hunter. The character's design—featuring no makeup, functional clothing, and diverse phenotypic traits, as shown in Fig. 2—was cited as a distinguishing element that upholds narrative coherence.

Fig. 2. Detailed screenshot of the character Aloy's face at three different moments in the game, without the use of makeup and/or hypersexualization devices.

Furthermore, Aloy is consistently described by all interviewees—regardless of gender—as a "neutral" character in an overwhelmingly positive sense. Both male and female participants unanimously agreed that she is not reduced to restrictive gender archetypes or stereotypical feminine tropes but is instead presented as a genuinely multifaceted human being with plausible motivations, complex internal dilemmas, and authentic emotions that resonate across the gender spectrum. This universal perception among respondents reinforces the characterization of Aloy as a "normal superheroine"—a compelling figure whose struggles, triumphs, and personal growth transcend traditional gender boundaries, enabling players of any gender to empathize with her journey and identify with her experiences on a deeply human level. The remarkable consensus across all participants, both men and women alike, suggests that Aloy's character design successfully achieves a form of inclusive relatability that avoids pandering to any single demographic while simultaneously appealing to diverse audiences. Her strength is portrayed not as exceptional because she is female, but as extraordinary because she is fully realized as a character, making her heroism feel earned, accessible, and genuinely inspirational to players regardless of their own gender identity.

The analysis of interview responses revealed several recurring themes regarding participants' perceptions of Aloy's character construction and development throughout the Horizon series. Table 1 synthesizes these key themes, organizing them into distinct categories that emerged consistently across all respondents, regardless of gender. This thematic overview demonstrates the multidimensional nature of Aloy's characterization and highlights the specific narrative and design elements that contributed to her reception as a well-rounded protagonist. The table encapsulates both the structural components of her character design and the emotional resonance these elements generated among players, providing a comprehensive framework for understanding how Aloy's portrayal successfully transcended traditional gender stereotypes while maintaining broad audience appeal.

Table 1. Summary of Themes Related to the Construction and Evolution of Aloy's Character.

Credibility and Realism	There is consensus that Aloy is a well-constructed and convincing character. One interviewee mentions her "realistic" progression over time, particularly in leadership and trust in others, despite the inherent unreality of combat levels in video games. The concept that she trained from childhood is identified as a factor that supports her skill development
Non-Stereotypical and Non-Sexualized Representation	Several respondents highlight the absence of sexualization in Aloy's design. Her physical appearance (clothing, hair) is viewed as consistent with the environment in which she lives, prioritizing comfort and functionality—characteristics befitting a hunter. One interviewee praises the "extensive phenotypic diversity" in the game overall, and Aloy is perceived as a character who is "neutral in all respects" and not "extremely sexualized, curvaceous, or unrealistic." The representation of her skin and the absence of makeup are also noted
Character Development	It is emphasized that Aloy is not a "flat" or "shallow" character. Her journey includes the loss of a father and interactions with diverse individuals, which contributes to her depth. The evolution of her leadership and her capacity to learn to trust others are important aspects of her development
Personality Traits and Identification	Notable traits include her resilience and her ability to be a "superheroine" while remaining a "normal person." The possibility for players to identify with her, regardless of gender, is mentioned as a significant strength

4.2 Aloy's Leadership and Social Interactions

Aloy's leadership style is consistently highlighted by all interviewees—both men and women—as fundamentally collaborative, empathetic, and grounded in active listening, standing in marked contrast to the more authoritarian, top-down leadership models traditionally and predominantly attributed to male characters in video games. Respondents universally noted that the game actively fosters interactions based on trust, mutual respect, and reciprocal support, qualities that are particularly evident in the strategic alliances and meaningful relationships Aloy builds throughout the narrative arc. The presence of nuanced moral decisions embedded within the game's dialogue system—offering multiple viable approaches such as empathetic, rational, or assertive responses—was also emphasized across all participant accounts. Although several interviewees acknowledged an implicit social expectation for female protagonists to consistently choose more affectionate or nurturing approaches (a reflection of persistent traditional gender roles in media), they praised the game for allowing these gendered expectations to be deliberately subverted by offering players genuine freedom of choice without narrative penalty or judgment.

This design decision was viewed as particularly significant, as it reinforces not only the narrative autonomy of the character but also validates diverse player preferences and moral frameworks. By decoupling Aloy's effectiveness as a leader from stereotypically feminine behavioral expectations, the game presents leadership as a flexible, situational skill rather than a gendered trait, further cementing her status as a character defined by competence and agency rather than gender conformity.

Table 2. Summary of Themes Related to Aloy's Leadership and Social Interactions.

Collaborative Leadership vs. Command Authority	Aloy's leadership is consistently praised as collaborative and empathetic, in opposition to a "boss" or authoritarian stance observed in other games (e.g., reference to Red Dead Redemption 2010). Her capacity to listen to others' problems, interact, and even change the course of events at the grassroots level is highlighted as an example of genuine leadership
Influence of Interaction	Aloy's presence as protagonist significantly influences interaction with other characters. The game appears to promote collaboration, with gameplay elements that corroborate the necessity of having allies to accomplish the final mission. Aloy's decisions are described as "sound and well-considered," "reasonable," and "more thoughtful than average," while also exhibiting moments of impulsiveness
Multiple Decision-Making Approaches	It is noted that Aloy employs different approaches to her decisions: cerebral, affectionate/ empathetic, and aggressive. Although there exists an expectation that she should be more affectionate/ empathetic (which raises the question of whether this is expected of the feminine role), the game offers the possibility of distinct behaviors with narrative consequences
Importance of Secondary Support	The concept of Aloy having secondary support characters is viewed as consistent with her collaborative logic and thoughtful behavior, rather than as a necessity dictated by her gender

4.3 Gender Representation and Influence in Video Games

Aloy's representation is unanimously valued as a model for overcoming gender stereotypes. The absence of hypersexualization, coupled with a robust narrative protagonism, grants her a status as a reference point in the evolution of female representation in video games. Aloy is viewed as a successor to figures like Lara Croft but constructed with significantly more depth and humanity. Participants reported that the experience of playing as Aloy impacts their own perceptions of gender roles, prompting reflection on the cultural norms that shape virtual worlds. This identification and narrative immersion were highlighted as one of the character's greatest strengths, with the potential to influence attitudes beyond the game itself. Ultimately, the protagonist is recognized as an active promoter of gender equality—not only through her design, but through the way the narrative values her personal journey, her agency, and her humanity.

Table 3. Summary of Themes Related to Gender Representation and Influence in Video Games.

Evolution in Gender Representation	There is a clear perception that video games have evolved in their gender representation. The transition of Lara Croft from a stereotypical character to one more focused on story and development is cited as a precursor. Aloy is viewed as taking this "even further," consolidating this evolution with physical and personality traits never before seen in female protagonists
Influence on Player Perception	Aloy's construction, by being a character that allows the player to "put themselves in her life," can influence perceptions about gender roles. Her complexity and journey of questioning enable the player to experience it "firsthand," which is considered her "greatest merit."
Promotion of Gender Equality	Aloy is regarded as a character who promotes the advancement of gender equality in video games. Her "more credible" representation, featuring extensive dialogue and strong positioning, distances itself from stereotypes. The possibility of identifying her as "just a redhead, freckled, a more common person" in cosplay, in contrast to the sexualized exuberance of other characters, is a relevant point
Future Expectations	Aloy's representation raises expectations for future players regarding gender equality in video games. She establishes a new standard for female protagonists, demonstrating that it is possible to have a "superheroine" who is also a "normal person," focused on her story and development, without resorting to stereotypes

The analysis demonstrates that Aloy transcends traditional female representation in video games by presenting a protagonist who simultaneously challenges the binaries of gender-function and form-content. While the industry continues to exhibit recurring cases of sexualized or secondary portrayals of female characters, *Horizon Zero*

Dawn offers a tangible and effective alternative: the inclusion of a main character whose protagonism is not justified by her physical appearance. This character model can be examined through the lens of postfeminist theory, which acknowledges the importance of representation characterized by full agency, without the constant need to underscore the "woman" condition as a narrative distinction. The neutrality expressed by some interviewees, who stated that they identify with Aloy regardless of her gender, reveals an important conceptual advancement: the transition from a "gendered" representation to a "human" representation. In this regard, Aloy's case invites both the industry and academia to reconsider what constitutes a "hero" in contemporary video games. The answer seems to point toward protagonists who embody emotional depth, identity diversity, and narrative agency—fundamental values for a more inclusive and reflective gaming culture.

5 Conclusion

Based on the findings of the research on Aloy's representation in Horizon Zero Dawn, this study reveals significant insights into the purpose of this research: to understand how players—video game development students—perceive how they feel represented or not by the character Aloy and the influence of this character on gender inclusion and representation in the video game industry. Regarding stereotypes and physical appearance, Aloy represents a fundamental departure from traditional hypersexualized female video game characters. Her design prioritizes narrative coherence and functional authenticity, featuring practical clothing, absence of makeup, and diverse phenotypic traits that align with her role as a hunter in a hostile post-apocalyptic environment. This deliberate design choice challenges the industry's longstanding tendency to prioritize visual appeal over narrative consistency, allowing players to engage with Aloy as a complex human being rather than a gendered archetype. The research participants consistently emphasized how this non-stereotypical representation enhances the character's credibility and enables cross-gender identification.

Concerning female positioning in social contexts and leadership, Aloy's approach represents a paradigmatic shift from traditional masculine leadership models. Her collaborative, empathetic leadership style, grounded in active listening, contrasts sharply with authoritarian approaches typically associated with male protagonists. The game's moral choice system provides multiple decision-making approaches—empathetic, rational, or assertive—thereby subverting expectations that female characters must conform to nurturing stereotypes while reinforcing narrative autonomy. This demonstrates that effective leadership transcends gender boundaries and challenges traditional power dynamics within gaming narratives.

The broader reflection on gender inequality in video on industry representation standards. Participants recognized her as a successor to previous female gaming icons like Lara Croft, but with significantly enhanced depth and humanity. The research demonstrates that playing as Aloy influences participants' perceptions of gender roles, prompting critical reflection on cultural norms within virtual environments. This transformative potential extends beyond gaming, with participants noting how the character's complexity fosters identification regardless of player gender. Ultimately, Aloy establishes new expectations for female protagonists, demonstrating that compelling characters can embody strength, agency, and complexity without relying on stereotypical gender markers, thereby fostering a more inclusive gaming culture.

Acknowledgments. This work is financially supported by national funds through the FCT – Foundation for Science and Technology, I.P., within the scope of project UID/05460 – Research Centre in Digital Media and Interaction and supported by project reference UI/BD/154590/2022 and DOI identifier: https://doi.org/10.54499/UI/BD/154590/2022. Additionally, supported by project reference UI/BD/154590/2022 and DOI identifier: https://doi.org/https://doi.org/10.54499/UI/BD/154590/2022.

References

1. Grizzard, M., Tamborini, R., Lewis, R., Wang, L., Prabhu, S.: Being Bad in a video game can make us morally sensitive. Cyberpsychol. Behav. Soc. Netw. **17** (2014). https://doi.org/10.1089/cyber.2013.0658
2. Ngoc, M.: Spotlighting women gamers and how they play and spend on video games, Newzoo. Acedido: 8 de novembro de (2024). https://newzoo.com/resources/blog/spotlighting-women-gamers-and-how-they-play-and-spend-on-video-games
3. Clement, Distribution of video gamers in the United States from 2006 to 2023, by gender, Statista. Acedido: 8 de novembro de 2024. https://www.statista.com/statistics/232383/gender-split-of-us-computer-and-video-gamers/
4. Vieira, P.P., Mota, R.: A Representacao Feminina em Horizon Zero Dawn. In: SBC – Proceedings of SBGames, pp. 694–703 (2018)
5. Chen, V.: Leveling Up The Gaming Gender Gap, Forbes. Acedido: 8 de novembro de 2024. https://www.forbes.com/councils/forbesbusinesscouncil/2023/08/24/leveling-up-the-gaming-gender-gap/
6. Paaßen, B., Morgenroth, T., Stratemeyer, M.: What is a True Gamer? The Male Gamer Stereotype and the Marginalization of Women in Video Game Culture. Sex Roles **76**(7–8), 421–435 (2017). https://doi.org/10.1007/s11199-016-0678-y
7. Vieira, M.J., Cardoso, P.: A systematic literature review of inclusion and representativity of women in videogame live streaming between 2017–2023. em Springer Series in Design and Innovation, vol. 35, pp. 357–370. Springer, Cham (2024). https://doi.org/10.1007/978-3-031-47281-7_29
8. Lima, L.: Pensar o Género a partir dos jogos digitais: uma análise sobre as assimetrias de género na indústria portuguesa de jogos digitais (2023). Porto: Editora BAND. ISBN:978–989–33–4234–3
9. Luo, L.: The evolution of female character representations in video games from a feminism perspective. In: 2nd International Conference on Interdiscip. Humanit. Commun. Stud., vol. 30, no 1, Art. no 1 (2023), https://doi.org/10.54254/2753-7048/30/20231605
10. Gasoto, A.C.G., Vaz, T.R.D.: A mulher gamer: uma análise da presença das mulheres nos jogos virtuais, II Encontro Internacional de Gestão, Desenvolvimento e Inovação, Naviraí, MS, novembro de 2018. Acedido: 21 de novembro de 2022. https://periodicos.ufms.br/index.php/EIGEDIN/article/view/7116
11. Cote, A.C.: Gaming sexism: gender and identity in the era of casual video games. New York University Press, New York (2020)
12. Kline, S., Dyer-Witherford, N., Peuter, G.: Digital Play: The Interaction of Technology, Culture, and Marketing. McGill-Queen's University Press (2003)

13. Levenee, R.: Grand thieves & Tomb Raiders: How British video games conquered the world. Aurum Press Ltd. (2012)
14. Dietz, T.L.: An examination of violence and gender role portrayals in video games: Implications for gender socialization and aggressive behavior. Sex Roles J. Res. **38**(5–6), 5–6 (1998)
15. Rocha, I.L.A., Fantini, L.M.C.: A representação contemporânea da mulher nos jogos AAA: por que Abby causou incômodo? In: SBC – Proceedings of SBGames, pp. 430–437 (2020)
16. Santos, K.P., de Lima, E.S., Cunha, A.: A Evolução da Representação da Figura Feminina nos Jogos : Um Estudo de Caso das Séries Bayonetta , Tomb Raider e The Witcher, SBC – Proceedings of SBGames, pp. 458–466 (2020)
17. Chess, S.: Play Like a Feminist, vol. 1. The MIT Press, Cambridge, Massachusetts (2020)
18. Condis, M.A.: Gaming Masculinity - Trolls, Fake Geeks, and the Gendered Battle for Online Culture, vol. 1. University of Lowa Press, Lowa City (2018)
19. Gray, K.L., Voorhees, G., Vossen, E.: Feminism in Play, vol. 1. Springer, Cham (2018). http://www.palgrave.com/gp/series/16027
20. Kennedy, V.P.: How The Last Of Us Elevates Women In Gaming, ScreenRant. Acedido: 11 de novembro de 2024. https://screenrant.com/last-us-ellie-abby-tlou2-female-main-characters/
21. Reed, A., Hartup, A.: The 25 most inspirational female characters in games, gamesradar. Acedido: 11 de novembro de 2024. https://www.gamesradar.com/20-most-inspirational-female-characters-games/
22. Makuch, E.: Horizon Zero Dawn's Aloy Is A "PlayStation Icon Of The Future," Sony Says, GameSpot. Acedido: 8 de novembro de 2024. https://www.gamespot.com/articles/horizon-zero-dawns-aloy-is-a-playstation-icon-of-t/1100-6447839/
23. Forni, D.: Horizon zero dawn: the educational influence of video games in counteracting gender stereotypes. Digit. Games Res. Assoc. **5**(1), 1 (2019). https://doi.org/10.26503/todigra.v5i1.111
24. Solska, D.: The evolving female narrative in dystopian video games: the case of bioshck infinite, the last of us, and horizon: zero dawn. J. Young Engl. Philol. Thought Rev. **7–8**, 191–213 (2022)
25. Seoane, A., Sanmartín, M.: As mulheres que amavam os videojogos. Santiago de Compostela, Galiza: Através Editora (2019)
26. Hayes, E.: Gendered identities at play: Case studies of two women playing morrowind. Games Cult. **2**(1), 23–48, (2007). https://doi.org/10.1177/1555412006294768
27. Hayes, E.: Women, video gaming and learning: beyond stereotypes. TechTrends **49**(5), 23–28 (2005). https://doi.org/10.1007/BF02763686
28. Saláfia, J., Ferreira, N., Nesteriuk, S.: Os estereótipos em jogos de luta: da indumentária à hipersexualização de personagens femininas. SBGames 225–232 (2018)
29. Pereira, C., Detoni, A.: Reação patriarcal à nova mulher: de Cesário Verde ao Gamergate, Sbgames.Org, pp. 999–1002 (2018)
30. Cassel, J., Jenkins, H.: From Barbie to Mortal Kombat: Gender and Computer Games, The MIT Press (2000)
31. Friman, U., Baltazar, P., Ståhl, M.: Diversity, Equity, and Inclusion in Esports., em Routledge Handbook of Esports. In: Jenny, E.S., Besombes, N., Brock, T., Cote, C.A., Scholz, M.T. (eds.), pp. 540–550. New York: Routledge (2024) https://doi.org/10.4324/9781003410591
32. Williams, D., Consalvo, M., Caplan, S., Yee, N.: Looking for gender: gender roles and behaviors among Online Gamers, J. Commun. **59**(4), 4 (2009). https://doi.org/10.1111/j.1460-2466.2009.01453.x
33. Behm-Morawitz, E., Mastro, D.: The Effects of the sexualization of female video game characters on gender stereotyping and female self-concept. Sex Roles **61**(11–12), 11–12 (2009). https://doi.org/10.1007/s11199-009-9683-8

34. Ivory, J.D.: Still a man's game: gender representation in online reviews of video games. Mass Commun. Soc. **9**(1), 1 (2006). https://doi.org/10.1207/s15327825mcs0901_6
35. Shaw, A.: Gaming at the edge: sexuality and gender at the margins of gamer culture. University of Minnesota Press, Minneapolis, MN (2015)
36. Martins, N., Williams, D.C., Harrison, K., Ratan, R.A.: A content analysis of female body imagery in video games. Sex Roles **61**(11–12), 11–12 (2009). https://doi.org/10.1007/s11199-009-9682-9
37. Fox, J., Tang, W.Y.: Women's experiences with general and sexual harassment in online video games: Rumination, organizational responsiveness, withdrawal, and coping strategies. New Media Soc. **19**(8), 1290–1307 (2017). https://doi.org/10.1177/1461444816635778
38. IMDb, Horizon Zero Dawn (Video Game 2017) - Awards - IMDb, IMDb: Awards. Acedido: 11 de novembro de 2024. https://www.imdb.com/title/tt4044024/awards/
39. Sony Interactive Entertainment, Horizon Zero Dawn Global Sales Exceed 2.6 Million - Sony Interactive Entertainment, Sony Interactive Entertainment. Acedido: 11 de novembro de 2024. https://sonyinteractive.com/en/press-releases/2017/horizon-zero-dawn-global-sales-exceed-26-million/
40. Woolbright, L.: Ecofeminism and Gaia Theory in Horizon Zero Dawn, TRACE: A Journal of Writing, Media, and Ecology, 24 de outubro de 2018. Acedido: 11 de novembro de 2024. http://tracejournal.net/trace-issues/issue2/02-Woolbright.html
41. Falkenhayner, N.: Futurity as an Effect of Playing Horizon: Zero Dawn (2017). Humanities **10**(2), 2 (2021). https://doi.org/10.3390/h10020072
42. Brotherson, C.: The creation of Horizon Zero Dawn's Aloy, as told by Guerrilla Games, PlayStation.Blog. Acedido: 11 de novembro de 2024. https://blog.playstation.com/archive/2017/02/13/the-creation-of-horizon-zero-dawns-aloy-as-told-by-guerrilla-games
43. Nieman, S.: Thematic analysis: a practical guide. Qual. Soc. Work **22**(3), 3 (2023). https://doi.org/10.1177/14733250231170275
44. Vaismoradi, M., Turunen, H., Bondas, T.: Content analysis and thematic analysis: Implications for conducting a qualitative descriptive study. Nurs. Health Sci. **15**(3), 3 (2013)
45. Braun, V., Clarke, V.: Using thematic analysis in psychology. Qual. Res. Psychol. **3**(2), 2 (2006)

The Rhetoric of Contagion in Digital Games: Depiction, Symptomatology, and Social Measures Across 16 Games

Liliana Vale Costa(✉) and Nelson Zagalo

Dep. Comunicação e Arte – DigiMedia, Universidade de Aveiro, Aveiro, Portugal
{lilianavale,nzagalo}@ua.pt

Abstract. In light of the growing global attention to animal and human infections, there is an increasing need to understand how popular media frame the idea of contagion. While digital games have been extensively used for health education, representations of contagion remain underexplored. This paper analyses sixteen widely disseminated digital games through three dimensions—depiction, symptomology, and health and social measures. The study finds that pathogens are commonly portrayed as bioweapons or experimental accidents; symptoms are dramatized through visual and behavioural distortions associated with madness or violence; and social responses often revolve around fear, control, and survival. Together, these patterns reveal a distinctive rhetoric of contagion in which digital games blend scientific imagery with cultural anxieties, shaping how players imagine infection, risk, and collective response.

Keywords: Digital Games · Viral infections · Outbreaks · Media Representation · Rhetoric of Contagion · Health Literacy · Content Analysis · Misinformation

1 Introduction

The popular use of digital games in different domains that go beyond entertainment (e.g., education, history, architecture) has led to increasing interest in its media to simulate or fictionally recreate worlds that often result from artistic self-expression experiences and depiction of different bio-psycho-socio-cultural contexts – e.g., technoscience portrayals [1]; sex and gender [2]; marginalized identities [3]; mental illness [4]; genetic manipulations [5]; concerns with animal rights [6, 7]; or construction of social imaginaries [8], among others.

Some current market-driven games have even been exploring the richness of our ethos within a society – e.g., *Humankind* (Amplitude Studios, 2021); being 'testemonials' of our past – e.g., *Assassin's Creed* (Ubisoft, 2007–2020); or future – e.g., *Deus Ex: Mankind Divided* (Eidos Montréal, 2016).

Although extensive research [9, 10] has been carried out on the use of digital games as sources of identity, self-expression, and representations, detailed investigations of textual and visual references to crisis scenarios in gameplay [11] are still limited, and to

R. Baptista et al. (Eds.): VJ 2025, CCIS 2988, pp. 210–225, 2027.
https://doi.org/10.1007/978-3-032-31642-4_17

the best of our knowledge, coverage in contagion has been scarce – e.g., Mitchell and Hamilton [12].

In addition, the changes experienced during an outbreak crisis over the past years have also led to the increasing of media coverage amplifying one's emotions, sense of surprise, and fears. Consequently, such content representation and misrepresentation may provoke sense of confusion, mistrust, skepticism, and conspiracy theories. While contagion has been used as background in media outlets, its portrayal in such media that blends reality and fictional information as games, posit a greater challenge to distinguish between accurate information and misinformation.

Various infections and outbreaks have been portrayed in media throughout the history and games are not an exception – e.g., *Malaria in Far Cry 2* (Ubisoft, 2008), *The Plague in A Plague Tale: Innocence* (Asobo Studio, 2019), Smallpox in *Tom Clancy's The Division 2* (Ubisoft, 2019), and Yellow Fever in *Railroad Corporation Yellow Fever* (Corbie Games, 2020). Additional infections and diseases but fictional have also been covered in game-playing – e.g., *Necromorph Infection in Dead Space* (Visceral Games et al., 2011–2013), FOXDIE infection in *Metal Gear* (Konami et al., 2013–2018) or t-virus, g-virus or uroboros in *Resident Evil* games (Capcom, 2002–2021), or even the speculative role of infections based on existent data and transitioned to a fictional scenario – e.g., Cordyceps infection in human-beings in *The Last of Us* (Naughty Dog, 2013–2020). In these examples, not only the infection characterization or symptomology are presented but also psychological perceptions, and dilemmas in frequent post-apocalyptic scenarios are found.

The purpose of this paper is to pave the way into the analysis of the portrayal of contagion in current popular digital games. While reviewing both the representations and misrepresentations of contagion in terms of depiction, symptomology, and health and social measures, a comprehensive analysis of all games portraying contagion would be unfeasible and, as such, the corpus of texts identified is based on the most disseminated games, allowing us to expand the understanding of how contagion is portrayed. The analysis includes: (a) discussion of infection-themed digital games; (b) symptomology classification; and (c) health and social measures adopted and context coverage. Data for this study were collected searching videogame databases and official wikis, scanning the keywords 'infection' or 'outbreak.'

2 Coverage of Infections in Digital Games

According to the Interactive Software Federation of Europe [13], the game-playing activity has been very popular among all age groups, and its usage has intensified during the COVID-19 pandemic extending its purpose of entertaining to educating and socializing. In addition, the potential use of games in the health domain has been explored – e.g., neurorehabilitation [14, 15], therapeutics [16] or health education [17], but still research is necessary to get further insight into the use of digital games to raise health awareness [18] namely in healthcare-associated infection prevention, interventions and control [19].

Indeed, emerging infectious disease outbreaks and necessary preparedness to respond to health crises have also heightened the importance of media and, especially digital games, to convey messages about infection prevention and control [19, 20], avoiding self-contamination (e.g., [21]), infection transmission, and ensuring biosecurity, and nosocomial infection safety measures (e.g., [22, 23]). The following are some examples in which games have been designed to create awareness to infections or/ and encourage the involvement of citizens in scientific practices:

- Digital games to role-play (e.g., patient-doctor) and make different decisions based on the scenarios which relevant information is presented, i.e., symptomology, transmission, treatment, outbreak prevention, or hygiene precautions (hand hygiene, respiratory etiquette, or exposure to blood or body fluid). Examples include Flu.0 [24]; I.Control [25]; or the location-based game MeetDurian [26];
- Digital games to educate to safe sex and prevent sexually transmitted infections. Examples include The Secret of Seven Stones [27]; Viral Combat [28]; PlayForward [29]; and Epic allies [30];
- Digital games to create awareness of the epidemiological impact resulting from social distancing measures, i.e., measures to lower the risk of infection spread, vaccination, testing, and immunity. Some game examples include Infection Detective [31], Infection Defender [32], CovidCampus [33], among others. In a broader sense, such games as Micro-combat [34], or Plague Inc. [35] cover these measures as a strategic management challenge to fight pathogens or/and control epidemics;
- Digital games to learn about microbiology, specifically bacteriology, virology, diagnosis, and prevention of infectious diseases. Examples include MedMicroFunWithFacts game (MMFWF) [36] and Body busters [37], in which players collect antibiotics to kill bacteria while learning about types of microbes and use of antibiotics; and
- Digital games relative to hygiene education to prevent healthcare-associated infections. SureWash from Glanta Ltd in Dublin is an example of its use in handwashing education [38].

Given that many discoveries in the health field rely on pattern detection and a large quantity of data is needed to be processed, extracted, and analyzed, some games like "Play to Cure: Genes in Space" [39], "Foldit" [40], and "Fraxinus" [41] involve the player in these practices. In "Play to Cure: Genes in Space", players help to analyze scientific genetic data and detect DNA errors that may cause cancer. Foldit uses protein puzzles to understand its structure, whereas the Fraxinus game helps to decipher the genetic code of the disease Ash dieback affecting ash tree and understand immunity to the fungus.

Digital games to simulate the patterns of spreading an infectious disease have also been used. The most cited case of a "Virtual Plague" is the World of Warcraft's fictional corrupted blood disease spread in 2005, which reached different game areas with the character's possibility of teleporting and use of pets as 'disease reservoirs' [42]. Another example of a virtual plague was the virtual guinea pig mod that occurs in The Sims [43], which seems to be a reference to the zoonotic Salmonella infections as guinea pigs may be bacteria carriers.

Few studies, however, have investigated the infection coverage in digital games. In "*There is no cure: Paratexts as remediations of agency in Red Redemption 2,*" Ruffino [44] refers to the use of textual readings relative to the contagion of Arthur's Morgan's tuberculosis covered both in the narrative and game space, translating into the character's heavy fatigue, coughing, pale color, and less agility. This bacteria-caused infection commonly targets the lungs among other areas and considering that the era of the game was the 19th century, there is neither a cure nor treatment.

Another publication that covers the narrative of contagion is "*The Reconstruction of Morality and the Evolution of Naturalism in The Last of Us*" [45], in which a cordyceps pandemic infection has affected human population. Although the cordyceps fungus exist in daily life, these do not affect humans but insects or other arthropods. In these two examples, the merge between physical reality and fiction is part of a fantasy that is played and cultural representations, advancing our knowledge about living in times of pandemics, i.e., behavioral epidemiology including self-quarantining, social distancing, hygiene, and avoidance of surface contamination, among other measures.

The next sections cover how contagion is portrayed in the visual and textual references on digital games, considering the dimensions of depiction, symptomology, and health and social measures.

3 Materials and Methods

A considerable amount of attention was given to infection transmission and bio-psychosocial measures in media press and social media coverage (e.g., newspapers, television, radio, and social networks). However, its representation in digital games has been understudied. This study employed content analysis to understand the way contagion is portrayed in current popular digital games. Understanding how current popular digital games cover contagion is, therefore, important to demystify possible misconceptions that may impact the player's perception towards societal lived crisis events, create awareness and foster public discussion towards infections.

Sample Characteristics and Content Analysis. In a first iteration, we started to select games by searching the Internet Game Database, and top sellers' lists covering contagion in PlayStation/Nintendo/Microsoft and Steam. Although the IMDB database enlists rankings of video games, refining those by a set of pre-determined keywords instead of closed game types did not demonstrate to be feasible within the assigned classification and time constraints, and as such, it was excluded.

Also, it is worth noting that the use of the terms 'infections' and 'outbreaks' in search engine optimization has not revealed to be effective considering that many popular games portraying contagion have not the terms 'infection' or 'outbreak' in the metadata. Hence, game articles about the coverage of outbreaks and diseases – e.g., [46–49], and the wikis [50, 51] were also gathered and some of the popular digital games featuring infections and how these are portrayed during gameplay were enlisted (see Appendix 1) and from that list, those mentioned in the Imagine Games Network - IGN Top Leading 100 games (https://www.ign.com/articles/the-best-100-video-games-of-all-time) were selected owing to the fact that understanding the representation of these infections should consider its popularity in gaming community and, as such, selection was refined.

These games are: Bioshock, Bloodborne, Dishonored2, Fallout: New Vegas, Halo: Combat Evolved, Hollow Knight, Mass Effect 2, Metal Gear Solid, Metroid Prime, Monster Hunter: World, Red Dead Redemption, Resident Evil 2 (Remake), Resident

Evil 4, StarCraft, The Last of Us Part 2, and World of Warcraft. It is worth noting that the games Mega Man 3, Pokémon Yellow, and The Elder Scrolls V: Skyrim were excluded for not sufficient coverage of contagion in the narrative, gameplay mechanics or world-building scenarios and Left4Dead 2 owe to the lack of playthrough material that adequately portrayed Green Flu beyond gameplay mechanics.

Qualitative Content Analysis. We employed three content categories to analyze the essential components of the portrayal of contagion: depiction, symptomology, and health and social measures. Considering that pathogens are microorganisms that may cause diseases and induce symptoms to likely generate infection, one of the categories pre-determined was symptomology. Each unit of analysis described included Depiction: *The way a pathogen is represented—structure, transmission, replication, and infection*; Symptomology: *References to patients' symptoms and medical conditions.* It is worth mentioning this category is essential to understand the risk factor for the emergence and spread of infections and, subsequently, prevention, and diagnosis; and Health and social measures: *Public health and social measures that are used to prevent or delay the spread of infectious diseases.*

These units of analysis are based on the topics often covered to introduce modern virology (e.g., [52]) in which the nature of infections, classifications, evolution, and cell interactions are presented at the basis, then virus interactions with the organism, and symptomology of diseases are explored followed by the wider impact in a wider context. A qualitative content analysis was selected owing to the need of gathering an in-depth analysis portrayal of contagion in games and assessing both the content and context of information to support the meaning interpretation [53].

Following the initial deductive coding of the three categories—depiction, symptomology, and health and social measures—an additional interpretive layer was developed through axial coding. This stage sought to identify recurrent intersections among the categories that consistently generated higher-order meanings about the representation of contagion. These emergent patterns were then grouped into thematic functions, which capture how portrayals of infection, embodied experience, and social response combine to produce overarching interpretive frames of contagion. The resulting functions, presented in Sect. 4.4, do not constitute a separate coding category but rather a synthesis produced through triangulation across the three original dimensions.

4 Finding Analysis

Across the sixteen selected games, contagion is integrated into narrative and mechanics through recurring design patterns. To move beyond enumeration, we organized the results into three sub-sections—depiction, symptomology, and health and social measures—followed by a comparative synthesis that articulates how these dimensions co-determine one another in play.

4.1 Depiction of Infections in Games

We observe four dominant narrative framings of infection: **(Bio)weapon/experimental accident** (e.g., *Resident Evil 2 [Remake], Resident Evil 4, Metal Gear Solid: The Twin*

Snakes, BioShock, Metroid Prime, MassEffect2), where the pathogen functions as an instrument of power or technoscientific failure; **Hyperbolised natural agent** (e.g., cordyceps in *The Last of Us Part II*; the "infection" in *Hollow Knight*), channeling bio-ecological anxiety; **Xeno-organic/parasitic threat** (e.g., the Flood in *Halo: Combat Evolved*; the Frenzy in *Monster Hunter: World*; "Ashen Blood" in *Bloodborne*; reference to parasitic infections in *Fallout*), foregrounding loss of bodily integrity; and **Historically grounded disease** (e.g., tuberculosis in *Red Dead Redemption,* allegorical plague in *Dishonored* 2), aligning with a naturalist ethos.

These modalities are not neutral: these structure player agency (what one can do, why, and at what cost) and encode cultural interpretations of contagion (moral punishment, human error, natural selection, population control). In terms of procedural rhetoric, the pathogen operates both as a game trigger (shaping rules, resources, pacing) and as a social metaphor (risk, responsibility, governance).

4.2 Symptomology and Affective Representation

Beyond clinical lists (fever, cough, dyspnoea, mutation), games make the infection felt through an embodied aesthetic: **Sensory–motor feedback**: blur, vignettes, colour shifts, audio artefacts, input latency and reduced precision signal delirium, fatigue, or intoxication (e.g., *Red Dead Redemption*; *Fallout: New Vegas, Bloodborne*); **Cognitive/behavioural distortion**: "madness," aggression and impulsivity rendered via hostile AI, frenzied attack patterns, or berserk states (e.g., *Hollow Knight, Monster Hunter: World, Starcraft*)**;** and **Depersonalisation/body horror**: metamorphoses and hybridisations dramatise dissolution of the self (e.g., *Resident Evil*; *Halo, Starcraft*), emphasising ontological threat over pathology per se. Thus, symptomology functions as an aesthetics of contagion: players do not only observe symptoms; they experience constraints, which intensifies perceived risk and urgency.

4.3 Health and Social Measures in Play

Public health and social responses appear on three levels: **Crisis infrastructures and logistics**: scarcity, looting, supply chains, checklists, and crafting as proxies for rationing (e.g., *The Last of Us Part-TLoU II*); **Governance and discipline**: quarantines, checkpoints, martial law, surveillance—frequently coded as antagonistic (regulators vs. survivors), aligning with biopolitical readings; and **Collective behaviours**: ignorance, rumour, disbelief (e.g., failure to distinguish "plague" from "cough" in *Mass Effect 2*), but also cooperation, incubation periods, sacrifice, and the pursuit of cures/vaccines as mission drivers.

Crucially, many titles implicate the player in these measures (obey/defy orders, allocate treatment, and prioritise who to save), turning public-health policy into decision mechanics with moral and systemic consequences.

4.4 Comparative Synthesis

The three analytical categories—**depiction, symptomology**, and **health and social measures**—are deeply interconnected. Specific representational choices in each category coalesce into broader narrative and ideological patterns that we identify here as **thematic functions**. Each theme emerges from the intersection between *what is represented* (depiction), *how it is felt* (symptomology), and *how societies respond* (measures). Table 1 shows a comparative synthesis of depiction, symptomology, health and social measures, and thematic function across five digital games, that illustrate the dominant contagion ecologies identified across the corpus.

Table 1. Comparative synthesis

Game	Depiction	Symptomology	Measures	Thematic function
TLoU Part II	Naturalistic fungal	Loss of humanity, ferocity	Isolation, survival, rationing	Ethics of care/ resilience
Resident Evil 2 (Remake)	Laboratory bioweapon	Mutation, body horror	Military security, containment	Technoscientific fear/control
Dishonored 2	Allegorical plague	Madness, violence	Class segregation, repression	Moral corruption and power
RDR	Historical disease	Fatigue, cough, decline	No cure, fatalism	Tragic naturalism of illness
Halo: Combat Evolved	Xeno-parasitic	Bodily invasion	Total military response	Existential threat/ escalation

The five cases presented in Table 1 were selected as paradigmatic instances of the dominant contagion ecologies identified across the corpus. Their comparison highlights how the three analytical dimensions—depiction, symptomology, and health and social measures—converge into distinct thematic functions, derived through iterative cross-analysis of all coded categories. Each function represents a specific cultural framing of contagion, shaped by the interplay between representation, experience, and response.

For instance, in *Resident Evil 2* the alignment between a laboratory-origin virus (depiction), mutational embodiment of fear (symptomology), and militarised containment (measures) converges into a discourse of technoscientific hubris—a morality tale of human overreach. In contrast, *The Last of Us* links a naturalistic infection with affective disintegration and care ethics, translating contagion into an emotional drama of empathy. *Dishonored 2* integrates plague, delirium, and repression into a social critique of inequality and biopolitical control. *Red Dead Redemption*'s realistic illness and lack of cure foreground a fatalistic view of life and mortality, while *Halo* amplifies the logic of infection into a cosmic allegory of total war.

Across these titles, the rhetoric of contagion oscillates between instrumental and allegorical functions: it sustains mechanical tension and simultaneously expresses cultural anxieties about power, vulnerability, and the limits of human agency. Recognising these layered meanings allows us to move from taxonomic description to interpretive insight—revealing how digital games, intentionally or not, shape popular understandings of infection, health crisis, and survival ethics.

Overall, the analysis indicates that the rhetoric of contagion in games operates on two complementary levels: instrumentally, by sustaining mechanical tension and urgency, and allegorically, by staging collective anxieties about science, power, and vulnerability. These rhetorical patterns shape how players interpret infection, control, and agency.

5 Conclusion

This study analysed how contagion is represented across sixteen popular digital games, revealing a consistent tension between instrumental game design and allegorical world-building. Infections are frequently portrayed as human-made or weaponised, symptoms are dramatised through embodied mechanics that simulate loss of control, and public health measures are translated into gameplay systems of regulation, scarcity, and moral choice. Together, these findings demonstrate how digital games construct a distinctive *rhetoric of contagion* that blends scientific motifs with cultural fears of power, vulnerability, and contamination.

Understanding these representational patterns is relevant not only for media scholars but also for designers seeking to integrate health-related themes responsibly. Rather than prescribing medical accuracy, our analysis suggests the value of multi-layered design approaches that connect bio-chemical realism with experiential embodiment and socio-political awareness. Such integration can foster empathy and reflection, enabling players to engage with infection scenarios as spaces of ethical and collective decision-making rather than mere survival.

Future work should extend this analysis through developer-centered inquiry, including interviews with design teams to explore the intentionality behind these portrayals, and through broader corpus analysis combining critical coding with player reception data (e.g., reviews and ratings from the Metacritic database). This could help clarify how the interplay between fiction, realism, and affect shapes public understanding of contagion and preparedness in health crisis contexts.

Acknowledgments. This research was conducted in the scope of project PLAYMUTATION from the Digital Media and Interaction Research Center (DigiMedia), funded by Foundation for Science and Technology (FCT) in the scope of project [UIDB/05460/2025].

Appendix

Appendix 1. List of digital games covering viral infections

Digital Game	Game Type	Infection portrayal
.hack game series	Action role-play	Virus Cores (PC infection)
112 Operator: Pandemic Outbreak	Management Game	Coronavirus Pandemics
2013: Infected Wars	Third Person Shooter	Scourge, an engineered virus

(*continued*)

(*continued*)

Digital Game	Game Type	Infection portrayal
A Cure for Jessica	First Person Shooter	"A Deadly Virus"
A Plague Tale: Innocence	Action-adventure Stealth Game	Prima Macula (Bubonic Plague)
Abomination: The Nemesis Project	Real Time Strategy	"The Virus" (Fictional)
Advance Wars: Days of Ruin	Turn-based Strategy,	The Creeping Derengea/ Endoflorescence terribilis
Arknights	Role-Playing Game	Oripathy
Assassins Creed Odyssey	Role-Playing Game	Ref. to Plague of Athens 430 BC
Back 4 Blood	First Person Shooter	Devil Worm
BattleTanx Series	Action Game	X2 Virus - A double-X chromosome Virus
Bio-Hazard Battle	Shooter	A retrovirus
Bioshock	First Person Shooter	Adam chemical substances, Plasmids (Non-ethical steam cell experiments)
Bloodborne	Role-Playing Game	Ashen Blood Disease (reference to bloodborne diseases)
Bubonic: OutBreak	Adventure	Reference to Bubonic Plague?
Call of Duty: Black Ops III	First-person shooter	Infected Player – "Patient Zero"
Civilization VI	Strategy Game	The Black Death
Command & Conquer	Real-time Strategy	Viruses - Bioweapon
Contagion VR: Outbreak	First-person shooter	Virus Outbreaks (Zombie Apocalypse)
COVID: The Outbreak	Real-time Strategy	Coronavirus
Crackdown Series	Action-adventure	Freak virus
Cradle	Adventure	Outbreak (Backstory)
Crisis on the Planet of the Apes	VR Person-shooter	Simian Flu
Crysis Series	First-Person Shooter	Manhattan Virus
Danganronpa Series	Visual Novel Adventure Game	Despair Disease
DANGER! Escape Lab	Adventure	"Lab leak" virus
Dark Sector	Third-Person Shooter	Technocyte Virus – T-Cyte
Day of the Infected	Online Role-Playing	Unidentified virus

(*continued*)

(continued)

Digital Game	Game Type	Infection portrayal
Daymare: 1998	Survival Horror	Pollux viral agente / Zombie-creating contagion
Days Gone	Action-Adventure	Freaker Virus
Dead Age	Survival-RPG	Zombie Infection
Dead Cells	Roguelike	Malaise
Dead Island Series	Role-Playing Game	Pathogen HK (Infectious Protein – Kuru Disease)
Dead Rising Series	Action-adventure	Zombie Virus from genetically modified wasps
Dead Space Series	Horror FPS	Necromorph infection
Deadlight	Survival Horror	Dead-reanimating Virus
Deus Ex Series	Role-Playing Game	Nano-virus Gray Death
Devo Presents Adventure of the Small Patrol	Adventure game	Osso Bucco Myelitis
Digital Devil Saga	Role-Playing Game	The Mystical Virus Atma
Dishonored Series	Action-adventure game	The Rat Plague (1835 Bubonic Plague)
Dragon Age	Role-playing Game	Red Lyrium – Infected Giant
Dying Light Series	Survival Horror	Harran Virus (rabies variation)
Epidemic	First-person shooter	Gigari virus
Epidemic!	Strategic simulation	Deadly
EPIDEMIC	Adventure	Coronavirus
Escape Dead Island	Survival Horror	Zombie virus
Fallen Earth	Multiplayer RPG	Shiva Virus
Fallout Series	Role-playing Game	Anthrax, Pneumonia, Tuberculosis, Smallpox, Syphilis, Forced Evolutionary Virus, Ebola, Cholera, Chicken Pox, Brain fever, Black Plague, Troglodyte Degeneration Contagion, New Plague, Tetanus, Influenza, Rabies, Scorched Plague, Dysentery Sepsis, Gamma Cyclotronic Virus, Phase Shifting Virus
Far Cry Series	First-person shooter	Malaria
Gears of War series	Third-person shooter	Parasitic fungus Imulsion

(continued)

(*continued*)

Digital Game	Game Type	Infection portrayal
Global Outbreak: Doomsday Edition	Strategy Game	(Not specified)
Guild Wars Series	Online Reality Games	The Canthan Plague, Vampiric Infection
Gunmetal	First-Person Shooter	The Keller Virus
Halo	First Person Shooter	Zombie infection, Flood infection (Halo 4)
Hollow Knight	Indie Game	"The infection"
Horde: Zombie Outbreak	Action Game	Zombie Outbreak
Infect and Destroy	Action Game	Player (Self-aware virus)
Infected: The Twin Vaccine	Adventure Game	"A new breed of virus"
Infected	Third-person shooter	Virus
Infection: Humanity's Last Gasp	Strategy Game	Various Virus – Random, Reoviridae, Picornaviridae Astroviridae, Floviridae…
Infectious	Action Game	Bacteriophage, Influenza virus, Unidentified Extraterrestrial
Infectonator Series	Strategy Game	Deadly Virus
Kabuki: Quantum Fighter	Platform game	Computer virus
Killing Floor 2	First-person Shooter	Not specific -'Infected Soldier'
Last Message	Adventure Game	Not specific -'Infected World'
Left4Dead Series	Survival Game	Green Flu
Madworld	Beat'em up	A deadly contagion
Mass Effect Series	Role-playing Game	Asari Cyanophage, Ayalon B, Blood Plague, Chickenpox, Ebola, Fortinbras Plague, Genophage, H7N7 Flu, Hunno Plague, Marburg virus, Omega Plague, Sangelian hemorrhagic fever, Scale-Itch, Shingles, Simian Bacterial Fever, Teukrian flu, TH-314, Yoqtan
Mega Man Series	Action Game	Roboenza, Zero Virus, Nightmare Virus
Metal Gear Solid Series	Action-adventure	FOXDIE
Metroid Prime	Action-adventure	Rezbit Virus, Miteralis
Michigan: Report from Hell	Survival Horror	"The virus"
Mist Survival	Adventure Game	Virus Outbreak

(*continued*)

(*continued*)

Digital Game	Game Type	Infection portrayal
Monster Hunter Series	Role-play Game	Frenzy Virus
Neverwinter Nights	RPG	Bubonic-like plague
Nightmare creatures	Survival Horror	Hecate virus
Ninja Blade	Action Game	Alpha Worms
1000xResist	Sci-fi Adventure	Virus of extraterrestrial origin
Outpost 2: Divided Destiny	Real-time Strategy	The Blight
Pathologic	Survival Horror RPG	The Plague
Plague Inc	Strategy game	Plague Bacteria, Virus, Fungus, Parasite, Prion, Nano-Virus…
POD: Planets of Death	Racing	A fungus
Pokémon	RPG	Pokérus
Project Zomboid	Survival game	Knox Infection
Prototype	Action-Adventure	Blacklight Virus
Puchi Puchi Virus	Puzzle	Linking viruses
Quarantine	First-person shooter	Outbreak
Red Dead Redemption	Adventure game	Tuberculosis
Resident Evil Series	Survival Horror	Progenitor Virus, T-Veronics vírus, Ancient vírus, C-Virus, G-Virus, Las Plagas, Nemesis Alpha, NE-Beta Parasite, T-Abyss Virus, T-Virus, Uroboros
Resistance: Fall of Man	First Person Shooter	Chimeran Virus
Scurge: Hive	Action-adventure	Scurge
Shadowrun: Dragonfall	RPG	Grey Virus
StarCraft	Real-time strategy	Hyper-evolutionary virus
Sunset Overdrive	Third-person game	OverChange Drinkers
Syphon Filter	Third-person game	Icosahedral retrovirus
Tales of Monkey Island	Adventure	Pox of LeChuck
Tales of Symphonia	RPG	Chronic Angelus Crystallus
Terranigma	RPG	Virus Asmodeus
The Amazing Spider-Man (2012 video game)	Adventure game	Cross-species virus
The Black Death	Survival MMORPG	Plague
The Callisto Protocol	Survival Horror	Biophage Pathogen
The Division 2	Survival Game	Green Poison, Ourbreak

(*continued*)

(*continued*)

Digital Game	Game Type	Infection portrayal
The Elder Scrolls III	RPG	Corprus
The Elder Scrolls IV	RPG	Porphyric Hemophilia
The Last of Us	Adventure game	Cordyceps
The 7th Guest: Infection	Puzzle Game	Infection
The Walking Dead	Adventure game	Wildfire Virus
Time Splitters 2	Third-person game	Virus
Trauma Center	Simulation	Ganglia Utrophin Immuno Latency Toxin (GUILT)
Trauma Team	Simulation game	Variation of viral hemorrhagic fever; Rosalinda Virus
Unforseen Incidents	Adventure game	Deadly Viral Outbreak
V2000	Action-adventure	Virus
Vampyr	RPG	Vampyr infection
Warcraft III	RPG	The Plague of Undeath
Warhammer	Wargame	Yellow Death
Warframe	Third-person game	Infestation
Winnie's Hole	Roguelike	Symbiotic virus
World of Warcraft	MMORPG	Corrupted Blood
World War Z	First-person game	Solanum
Zero Escape: Virtue's Last Reward	Adventure	Radical-6
Zero Time Dilemma	Adventure game	Infection Radical-6 virus
Day Z	Survival Game	Unknown Pathogen

References

1. Dudo, A., Cicchirillo, V., Atkinson, L., Marx, S.: Portrayals of technoscience in video games: a potential avenue for informal science learning. Sci. Commun. **36**(2), 219–247 (2014). https://doi.org/10.1177/1075547013520240
2. Burgess, M.C., Stermer, S.P., Burgess, S.R.: Sex, lies, and video games: the portrayal of male and female characters on video game covers. Sex Roles **57**(5), 419–433 (2007). https://doi.org/10.1007/s11199-007-9250-0
3. Hammar, E.L.: Counter-hegemonic commemorative play: marginalized pasts and the politics of memory in the digital game Assassin's Creed: freedom cry. Rethink. Hist. **21**(3), 372–395 (2016). https://doi.org/10.1080/13642529.2016.1256622
4. Shapiro, S., Rotter, M.: Graphic depictions: portrayals of mental illness in video games. J. Forensic Sci. **61**(6), 1592–1595 (2016). https://doi.org/10.1111/1556-4029.13214

5. Attebery, S.: Coshaping digital and biological animals: companion species encounters and biopower in the video games Pikmin and Pokémon. Humanimalia **6**(2), 56–84 (2015). https://doi.org/10.52537/humanimalia.9912
6. Fothergill, B.T., Flick, C.: The ethics of human-chicken relationships in video games. ACM SIGCAS Comput. Soc. **45**(3), 100–108 (2016). https://doi.org/10.1145/2874239.2874254
7. Van Ooijen, E.: On the brink of virtual extinction: hunting and killing animals in open world video games. Eludamos: J. Comput. Game Cult. **9**(1), 33–45 (2018). https://doi.org/10.7557/23.6164
8. Pérez-Latorre, Ó., Navarro-Remesal, V., Planells de la Maza, A.J., Sánchez-Serradilla, C.: Recessionary games: video games and the social imaginary of the Great Recession (2009–2015). Convergence **25**(5–6), 884–900 (2019). https://doi.org/10.1177/1354856517744489
9. Abrudan, E., Prundaru, G.: Social representations and ideologies in digital games. J. Media Res. **5**, 31–41 (2009)
10. Bogost, I., Poremba, C.: Can games get real? A closer look at 'documentary' digital games. In: Jahn-Sudmann, A., Stockmann, R. (eds.) Computer Games as a Sociocultural Phenomenon. Palgrave Macmillan, London (2008). https://doi.org/10.1057/9780230583306_2
11. Pérez-Latorre, Ó.: Post-apocalyptic games, heroism and the Great Recession. Game Stud. **19**(3) (2019). http://gamestudies.org/1903/articles/perezlatorre
12. Mitchell, S., Hamilton, S.N.: Playing at apocalypse: reading Plague Inc. in pandemic culture. Convergence **24**(6), 587–606 (2018). https://doi.org/10.1177/1354856516687235
13. ISFE – Europe's Video Games Industry. Key Facts 2020 [Report] (2021). https://www.isfe.eu/wp-content/uploads/2020/08/ISFE-final-1.pdf
14. Deutsch, J.E., Westcott McCoy, S.: Virtual reality and serious games in neurorehabilitation of children and adults: prevention, plasticity, and participation. Pediatr. Phys. Ther.: Off. Publ. Sect. Pediatr. Am. Phys. Ther. Assoc. **29**(Suppl 3 IV STEP 2016 Conference Proc-), S23–S36 (2017). https://doi.org/10.1097/PEP.0000000000000387
15. Iosa, M., Verrelli, C.M., Gentile, A.E., Ruggieri, M., Polizzi, A.: Gaming technology for pediatric neurorehabilitation: a systematic review. Front. Pediatr. **10** (2022). https://doi.org/10.3389/fped.2022.775356
16. Colder Carras, M., et al.: Commercial video games as therapy: a new research agenda to unlock the potential of a global pastime. Front. Psych. **8**, 300 (2018). https://doi.org/10.3389/fpsyt.2017.00300
17. Dorman, S.M.: Video and computer games: Effect on children and implications for health education. J. Sch. Health **67**(4), 133–138 (1997). https://doi.org/10.1111/j.1746-1561.1997.tb03432.x
18. Sharifzadeh, N., et al.: Health education serious games targeting health care providers, patients, and public health users: scoping review. JMIR Serious Games **8**(1), e13459 (2020). https://doi.org/10.2196/13459
19. Castro-Sánchez, E., Kyratsis, Y., Iwami, M., Rawson, T.M., Holmes, A.H.: Serious electronic games as behavioural change interventions in healthcare-associated infections and infection prevention and control: a scoping review of the literature and future directions. Antimicrob. Resist. Infect. Control **5**(1), 1–7 (2016)
20. Suppan, L., et al.: Impact of a serious game on the intention to change infection prevention and control practices in nursing homes during the COVID-19 pandemic: protocol for a web-based randomized controlled trial. JMIR Res. Protocols **9**(12), e25595 (2020). https://doi.org/10.2196/25595
21. Tyerman, J., Luctkar-Flude, M., Baker, C.: Rapid development of a COVID-19 assessment and PPE virtual simulation game. Clin. Simul. Nurs. **56**, 125–132 (2021). https://doi.org/10.1016/j.ecns.2021.03.002

22. Atack, L., Luke, R.: Impact of an online course on infection control and prevention competencies. J. Adv. Nurs. **63**(2), 175–180 (2008). https://doi.org/10.1111/j.1365-2648.2008.04660.x
23. Calik, A., Cakmak, B., Kapucu, S., Inkaya, B.: The effectiveness of serious games designed for infection prevention and promotion of safe behaviors of senior nursing students during the COVID-19 pandemic. Am. J. Infect. Control (2022). https://doi.org/10.1016/j.ajic.2022.02.025
24. Venier, A.-G., Marie, S., Duroux, T., Bervas, C., & Parneix, P. Teaching good infection control practices with fun: impact of the serious game Flu.0. Antimicrob. Resistance Infect. Control **4**(S1) (2015). https://doi.org/10.1186/2047-2994-4-s1-i10
25. CPIAS Nouvelle-Aquitaine I.control. Centre d'appui pour la Prévention des Infections Associées aux Soins de Nouvelle-Aquitaine (2022). https://www.cpias-nouvelle-aquitaine.fr/serious_games/
26. Chen, D., Bucchiarone, A., Lv, Z.: MeetDurian: can location-based games be used to improve COVID-19 hygiene habits? Games and Culture 1–24 (2022). https://doi.org/10.1177/15554120211049578
27. Shegog, R., et al.: A web-based game for young adolescents to improve parental communication and prevent unintended pregnancy and sexually transmitted infections (the secret of seven stones): development and feasibility study. JMIR Serious Games **9**(1), e23088 (2021). https://doi.org/10.2196/23088
28. Whiteley, L., Mena, L., Craker, L.K., Healy, M.G., Brown, L.K.: Creating a theoretically grounded gaming app to increase adherence to pre-exposure prophylaxis: lessons from the development of the viral combat mobile phone game. JMIR Serious Games **7**(1), e11861 (2019). https://doi.org/10.2196/11861
29. Fiellin, L.E., et al.: The design and implementation of a randomized controlled trial of a risk reduction and human immunodeficiency virus prevention videogame intervention in minority adolescents: PlayForward: Elm City stories. Clin. Trials **13**(4), 400–408 (2016). https://doi.org/10.1177/1740774516637871
30. LeGrand, S., et al.: Epic allies: development of a gaming app to improve antiretroviral therapy adherence among young HIV-positive men who have sex with men. JMIR Serious Games **4**(1), e6 (2016). https://doi.org/10.2196/games.5687
31. Hougaard, B.I., Knoche, H., Grunfeld, M.: Pandemic as game mechanic: simulation of infection spread for the classroom. In: 2021 International Conference on Advanced Learning Technologies (ICALT) (2021). https://doi.org/10.1109/icalt52272.2021.00075
32. Nikolov, I., Madsen, C.: Initial development of "infection defender": a children's educational game for pandemic prevention measurements. In: Proceedings of the 16th International Joint Conference on Computer Vision, Imaging and Computer Graphics Theory and Applications (2021). https://doi.org/10.5220/0010284102530260
33. Johnson-Glenberg, M.C., et al.: Interactive CovidCampus simulation game: genesis, design, and outcomes. Front. Commun. **6** (2021). https://doi.org/10.3389/fcomm.2021.657756
34. Instituto de Salud Global Barcelona - ISGlobal Protect the Health of The Citizens (2018). https://microcombat.eu/
35. Ndemic Creations. Plague Inc. (2022). https://www.ndemiccreations.com/en/22-plague-inc
36. Beylefeld, A.A., Struwig, M.C.: A gaming approach to learning medical microbiology: students' experiences of flow. Med. Teach. **29**(9–10), 933–940 (2007). https://doi.org/10.1080/01421590701601550
37. Eley, C.V., Young, V.L., Hayes, C.V., Verlander, N.Q., McNulty, C.A.M.: Young people's knowledge of antibiotics and vaccinations and increasing this knowledge through gaming: mixed-methods study using e-bug. JMIR Serious Games **7**(1), e10915 (2019). https://doi.org/10.2196/10915

38. Higgins, A., Hannan, M.M.: Improved hand hygiene technique and compliance in healthcare workers using gaming technology. J. Hosp. Infect. **84**(1), 32–37 (2013). https://doi.org/10.1016/j.jhin.2013.02.004
39. Coburn, C.: Play to cure: genes in space. Lancet Oncol. **15**(7), 688 (2014). https://doi.org/10.1016/s1470-2045(14)70259-1
40. Curtis, V.: Motivation to participate in an online citizen science game: a study of Foldit. Sci. Commun. **37**(6), 723–746 (2015)
41. Rallapalli, G., et al.: Lessons from Fraxinus, a crowd-sourced citizen science game in genomics. eLife **4** (2015). https://doi.org/10.7554/elife.07460
42. Balicer, R.D.: Modeling infectious diseases dissemination through online role-playing games. Epidemiology **18**(2), 260–261 (2007). https://doi.org/10.1097/01.ede.0000254692.80550.60
43. Boman, M., Johansson, S.J.: Modeling epidemic spread in synthetic populations-virtual plagues in massively multiplayer online games. In: Situated Play, Proceedings of DiGRA 2007 Conference, pp. 1–5 (2007). arXiv preprint arXiv:0705.4584, https://doi.org/10.48550/arXiv.0705.4584
44. Ruffino, P.: There is no cure: paratexts as remediations of agency in red dead redemption 2. Converg.: Int. J. Res. New Media Technol. 135485652210810 (2022). https://doi.org/10.1177/13548565221081062
45. Green, A.M.: The reconstruction of morality and the evolution of naturalism in the last of us. Games Cult. **11**(7–8), 745–763 (2016). https://doi.org/10.1177/1555412015579489
46. Bowen, T. 10 video game outbreaks that are actually terrifying. Gamerant (2020). https://gamerant.com/video-game-outbreaks-actually-terrifying/
47. Jensen, K.T.: The 10 deadliest video game diseases (2020). https://www.pcmag.com/news/the-10-deadliest-video-game-diseases
48. Gordon, L. How Viral Video Games Model Pandemics Frieze (2020). https://www.frieze.com/article/how-viral-video-games-model-pandemics
49. Sneddon, C.: The 10 best games about viruses, outbreaks, & diseases. The Gamer (2020). https://www.thegamer.com/games-best-about-viruses-outbreaks-diseases/. Accessed 15 May 2022
50. List of fictional diseases In Wikipedia (2022). https://en.wikipedia.org/wiki/List_of_fictional_diseases
51. Video games about viral outbreaks. In Wikipedia (2019). https://en.wikipedia.org/wiki/Category:Video_games_about_viral_outbreaks
52. Dimmock, N.J., Easton, A.J., Leppard, K.N.: Introduction to Modern Virology. Wiley (2016)
53. Drisko, J.W., Maschi, T.: Content Analysis. Oxford University Press (2016)

Video Games as Mirrors, Refuges, and Stages: A Reflexive Thematic Analysis of Self-image in the Digital Era

Carla Sousa[1(✉)], Mustafa Can Gursesli[4], Amanda Cei Santos Pirola[2], Ana Filipa Oliveira[3], Juho Hamari[4], and Mirko Duradoni[5]

[1] Laboratory of Distance Education and eLearning, Universidade Aberta, Lisbon, Portugal
carla.mira@uab.pt
[2] EPCV, Lusófona University, Lisbon/Porto, Portugal
amandacei.psi@gmail.com
[3] CICANT, Lusófona University, Lisbon/Porto, Portugal
[4] Faculty of Information Technology and Communication Sciences, Gamification Group, Research Centre of Gameful Realities, Tampere University, Tampere, Finland
[5] Department of Human and Social Sciences, Mercatorum University, Rome, Italy

Abstract. Video games have evolved into a cultural and technological ecosystem, in which there are blurred boundaries between "playing", "socialising" and "presenting oneself to others", creating environments where identity is continuously performed and negotiated. However, prior literature on gaming has focused on behavioural effects and on dimensions of social interaction, lacking more socio-critical readings. Considering this, the present study aims to explore the potential role of different experiences with video games in the processes of constructing self-image and personal identity. A sample of 627 frequent Portuguese speakers was included through non-probabilistic sampling to answer an open question: "How do video games and your interaction with the digital world influence the way you see yourself?". Reflexive Thematic Analysis (RTA) was adopted to approach the collected answers, through a bottom-up coding process that allowed the creation of a model based on five main emerging themes: (1) games as mirrors of the self; (2) escape and emotional regulation; (3) social connection and community; (4) digital identity and representation; and (5) detachment and resistance. Broadly, the results of this study suggest that the relationship between video games, digital interaction, and self-image is multifaceted, situated, and reflective, framing the notion that the contemporary self is constructed in dialogue with technological and social contexts.

Keywords: Video Games · Self-Image · Reflexive Thematic Analysis · Digital Identity · Social Interaction

R. Baptista et al. (Eds.): VJ 2025, CCIS 2988, pp. 226–241, 2027.
https://doi.org/10.1007/978-3-032-31642-4_18

1 Introduction

Video games are no longer a niche activity for young people, but have become a cultural and technological ecosystem that transcends age, gender and socio-cultural contexts [1]. At the same time, digital interaction, including social networks, streaming platforms, forums and voice services, blurs the boundaries between "playing", "socialising" and "presenting oneself to others", creating environments where identity is continuously performed and negotiated [2]. This ubiquity makes it pertinent to ask how these experiences influence self-image, that is, the beliefs, evaluations and narratives that a person holds about themselves.

The literature on gaming has predominantly focused on behavioural effects, including cognitive skills, learning, emotional regulation, well-being or problematic uses, and on dimensions of social interaction such as cooperation, belonging, or toxicity. However, it has less frequently addressed the reflective construction of self-image based on concrete experiences of gaming and related sociability [4,5], especially with in-depth qualitative approaches [6,7]. Additionally, socio-critical readings that problematise representation, inclusion/exclusion, agency, and power within gaming ecosystems remain scarce, as well as reflections on how these structures shape players' identities and self-perceptions in gaming contexts.

Thus, the present study is organised around a range of complex concepts, of which three fundamental ones can be highlighted:

- Self-image refers to how a person views themselves, encompassing beliefs, attitudes, and emotional evaluations about their own attributes, abilities, and worth. It is dynamic and can evolve as a result of new experiences and changing social contexts [8,9].
- Digital identity is not simply a digital version of physical identity; it is a dynamic and multi-layered concept shaped by technological, social, legal, and psychological factors [10,11].
- Game experience refers to the overall subjective perception and emotional response a player has while interacting with a game. It encompasses a wide range of elements, including multi-dimensionality, varying significantly among individuals due to differences in preferences, play styles, expectations, and others. For the purpose of this study, only the digital game experience was considered [13–15].

Considering this context, this study aims to explore how experiences with video games and other forms of digital interaction impact self-image, identifying significant moments and the psychosocial and sociotechnical mechanisms involved. Thus, it aims to list potential answers to the question: How do experiences with video games and digital interaction influence the processes of constructing self-image and personal identity? More specifically, it focuses on two sub-questions (SQs):

- SQ1. What meanings do participants attribute to their experiences in digital gaming regarding their self-perceptions?

- SQ2. What episodes or significant moments do participants recognise as having contributed to transformations or reaffirmations of their self-image and identity through gaming?

2 Method

2.1 Participants

A non-probabilistic sampling was adopted for this study, with the online questionnaire being disseminated with the support of higher education undergraduate students enrolled in a research methods course. Inclusion criteria were: being of legal age, frequently playing video games of any genre and on any platform, and understanding written Portuguese.

Six hundred and twenty-seven participants took part in the study, comprising 390 males (62.20%), 222 females (35.41%), one trans male (0.16%), two trans females (0.32%), and 12 persons opting not to disclose their gender (1.91%). The average age of the sample was 27.09 years ($SD = 11.84$). In terms of daily gaming behaviours, they were categorised by duration: 49 individuals (7.81%) reported approximately one hour per day, 111 (17.71%) engaged for roughly 2–3 h, and 59 (9.41%) dedicated 4–5 h daily. A lesser percentage indicated elevated involvement levels, with 11 people (1.75%) gaming for 6–7 h every day and 13 (2.07%) gaming for eight or more hours each day.

2.2 Data Gathering Tools and Procedure

This study was part of a broader mixed-methods survey developed to explore the relationships between gaming practices, digital-offline balance, motivations, and subjective experiences associated with interaction with digital games. Nevertheless, and considering its complexity and extension, the present study only analysed one open-ended qualitative question: "How do video games or your interaction with the digital world influence the way you see yourself? Describe a moment when this influence was particularly striking". This question was designed to encourage self-reflection and the description of significant episodes, providing insights into how participants interpret and attribute meaning to their digital experiences and subsequent impact on identity. Besides this aspect, demographic questions (age, gender and others) were also analysed to critically interpret the findings.

Data collection was flexible and inclusive, allowing the completion of the questionnaire in both digital (via *Google Forms*) and paper format to accommodate different levels of digital literacy. All data were subsequently digitised and integrated into a single database, ensuring consistency, anonymity and confidentiality according to current ethical standards [16]. The study adhered to the *Declaration of Helsinki* (and later amendments), the ethical guidelines of the American Psychological Association (APA) and the *Internet Research: Ethical Guidelines* 3.0 from the Association of Internet Researchers (AoIR). Based on national privacy and informed consent regulations, formal IRB approval was not required.

2.3 Data Analysis

Methodologically, Reflexive Thematic Analysis (RTA) as proposed by Braun and Clarke [21,22] was adopted. This approach allows for flexible, theoretical, and critical reading of the data, in line with understanding how gaming experiences are lived, narrated, and signified within specific sociocultural conditions. The most recent approach to RTA [26] emphasises the role of the researcher as an active interpreter and co-author of meaning, highlighting the relevance of continuous reflexivity and transparency in analytical decisions.

The analytical process followed the six phases defined by Braun and Clarke [21], adapted to the study context. The process favoured thick interpretation over code quantification, valuing the contextual meaning and subjective complexity of the narratives. Besides continuous reflexivity, validity was also approached through the adoption of Journal Article Reporting Standards (JARS) for qualitative designs [47].

3 Results

The reflexive thematic analysis generated a picture of how participants articulate the relationship between their engagement with video games and their self-perception. Rather than describing games simply as sources of entertainment, respondents tended to position them as meaning-making environments, particularly spaces where emotions, values, and identities are explored, challenged, and/or reaffirmed. Across the dataset, participants moved fluidly between narratives of empowerment and struggle, suggesting that video games serve simultaneously as mirrors, refuges, and boundaries of the contemporary self.

This interpretative process led to the identification of five interrelated themes, represented in Fig. 1: (1) Games as mirrors of the self; (2) Escape and emotional regulation; (3) Social connection and community; (4) Digital identity and representation; and (5) Detachment and resistance.

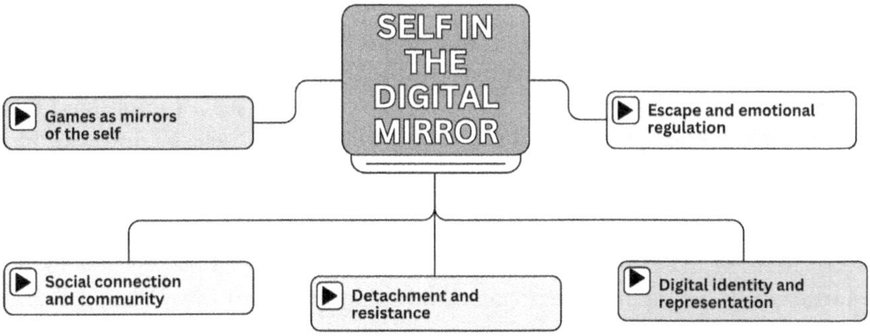

Fig. 1. Conceptual reflexive thematic map about the influence of video games on self-perception. Source: Authors' elaboration.

Together, these themes form a conceptual map of what we term "Self-Image in the Digital Mirror" (Fig. 1). Each captures a distinct yet interconnected way in which participants make sense of how digital play influences their understanding of who they are, whether through mastery and reflection, emotional coping, belonging and recognition, symbolic representation, or conscious disengagement. The following subsections present these themes in detail, supported by illustrative extracts that highlight the depth and diversity of participants' experiences.

3.1 Games as Mirrors of the Self

Participants tended to describe video games as a mirror through which they recognise traits of their personality, skills and values. In several narratives, memorable moments in the game led to reflections about themselves, revealing both positive qualities and perceived limitations. For example, in-game challenges and achievements helped some individuals realise their persistence, creativity, or problem-solving skills, attributes that they came to value in themselves outside the game. One participant mentioned a difficult puzzle in a narrative horror game (*Fran Bow*[1] that made them recognise how persistent and determined they can be in the face of complex obstacles, reinforcing their self-image as someone creative in finding solutions:

> " ...I realised how persistent I am, even when something seems difficult or confusing. This experience reinforced my self-perception as someone who faces difficulties with creativity and determination, characteristics that I carry with me outside the digital world."

These testimonials illustrate how performance in video games can reveal personality traits, which may include persistence, competitiveness, or quick thinking, that participants later recognise as part of their self. In some cases, the gaming experience even served as a test of personal values. One player described the difficult moral decision they faced in a game (*Hogwarts Legacy*[2]), in this case, whether to use a forbidden spell to progress or not, and how it made her reflect on her principles in the real world. Their response shows that they tried to resist making the "wrong" decision in the game, feeling that this virtual choice conflicted with their real values. In the end, they gave in to move forward, but remained uneasy, until they realised that "it was just a game and that it didn't change who I am in real life". That moment led them to understand how much they are true to personal values, even in a digital environment, revealing continuity between their own ethics and in-game behaviour:

> "...it seemed like more than just a decision within a game – it was as if I had to reflect on something that could happen in real life. When I finally

[1] Developed and produced by *Killmonday Games* (available at https://store.steampowered.com/app/362680/Fran_Bow/.

[2] Developed by *Avalanche Software* and published by *Warner Bros. Games*. More at: https://www.hogwartslegacy.com/en-us.

gave in, I felt a certain uneasiness, but I quickly realised that it was just a game and that it didn't change who I am in real life. That moment made me realise how much I get involved in the stories I play and how, even in a digital environment, I try to stay true to my own values."

This reflective integration posits that virtual situations, particularly video games, can serve as ethical or personal simulations where participants experience reactions akin to real life. Video games act as identity laboratories for testing intrinsic characteristics and limits. While the experiences can yield positive outcomes, such as enhanced self-esteem and perceived self-efficacy through overcoming challenges, they may also provoke negative feelings like frustration and self-doubt, particularly in the face of difficulties.

In general, this theme demonstrates that video games can catalyse self-reflection by confronting participants with goals, choices, and obstacles. In this sense, players discover or confirm aspects of themselves through gameplay, transposing these perceptions onto their broader identity outside the game.

However, significant tensions and contrasts also emerge. Not all social experiences mediated by games were inclusive. Some participants shared feelings of exclusion or isolation related to their gaming experience. One participant of younger age reported difficulty relating to colleagues because he spent "more time gaming than his classmates". This perceived difference seemed to result in feelings of insecurity and exclusion from face-to-face social interactions. Another participant admitted to losing friends due to excessive gaming, indicating that it can, paradoxically, erode social ties if it becomes disproportionate. These reports warn of a phenomenon of self-imposed isolation: by investing too much in the virtual world, some gamers seem to find themselves distanced from face-to-face socialisation. These participants frequently described themselves as "addicted/anti-social" or experiencing guilt and regret over deteriorating of friendships.

3.2 Escape and Emotional Regulation

A second recurring theme highlighted the use of video games as a strategy for escape or emotional relief, allowing players to "switch off" from real-world problems. This virtual immersion seems to positively influence subjective well-being, providing psychological respite, although it does not significantly alter self-esteem or identity.

For example, one respondent explicitly stated that video games do not have a major impact on their self-esteem or self-image, serving mainly to distract the mind and relieve everyday stress. During the COVID-19 pandemic, this person found in gaming an escape route to cope with anxiety and isolation, managing to "switch off" from their preoccupations:

"Video games don't have a big impact on my self-esteem, but they help distract me from problems and "switch off" thoughts about everyday worries. When I'm playing, I can think only about the game and not about

> my worries. One moment was during the pandemic... I started playing to occupy my free time and rest my mind without feeling like I'm constantly dealing with the real world... Games are a form of escape and entertainment for me."

This testimony illustrates a common attitude: games as an escape from stress, with no reported influence on self-perception. The experience of flowing in playful activity, as being "absorbed" by the game and as defined by Csikszentmihalyi [23], allows external pressures and negative emotions to be temporarily suspended, promoting a state of relief. In this sense, it is possible to note that some participants see themselves as people who know how to strategically switch-off when necessary, using gaming as a tool for self-care.

However, this theme also brings to light ambivalences and socio-psychological risks. While moderate escapism offers benefits, several participants recognised the danger of excessive reliance on games as a refuge, leading them to avoid confronting real-world problems. Some warned of the possibility of addiction and alienation. One offered a socio-critical analysis:

> "there are those who use games as an escape from everyday frustrations... this can end up increasing feelings of violence, frustration and, in more serious cases, even lead to suicide."

While this comment extends personal experience (representing a general social concern), it demonstrates critical awareness that digital escape fails to solve the underlying dilemmas.

Some individuals reported realising escapism's limits. An older adult (above 65) described playing as "filling in downtime" since retirement, suggesting gaming attempts to fill emptiness without providing identity meaning. Others experienced bittersweet realisations after extended gaming sessions since time had "slipped away", while real-world responsibilities persisted. One notable case involved someone spending hours gaming, "disconnected from the outside world", not noticing time passing or failing to carry out basic routines. Though not directly addressing self-image, this account suggests a subsequent awareness and recognition of deep absorption capacity, generating discomfort or self-criticism upon returning to reality. In this sense, some participants may see themselves as occasional "escapists", aware of needing moderate escape.

The use of video games as emotional refuge is complex, with participants oscillating between valuing temporary relief and recognising the pitfalls of prolonged escapism. From an identity perspective, many claim escape does not redefine who they are, yet the need for escape reveals something about the contemporary self - a self subjected to stress seeking suspension and comfort in games. The socio-critical discussion also points to a perceived need for Digital-Life Balance (DLB) [45,46].

3.3 Social Connection and Community

The third emerging theme concerns the influence of social experiences mediated by video games on how participants perceive themselves, namely, feelings of belonging, inclusion or, in contrast, social isolation. The responses show that playing with others (close friends or online communities) not only changes the individual's social context but can also affect how they see themselves within a relationship network.

Several participants pointed out that video games acted as a social bridge, strengthening existing friendships or enabling new connections, which had a positive impact on their relational self-esteem (e.g., their view of themselves as a friend, teammate, or group member).

A relevant testimony comes from a participant who went through the pandemic period by keeping in touch with their group of friends exclusively through online games. They describe how the joint gaming sessions on Friday and Saturday nights recreated a sense of "normal" socialisation amid confinement, making them feel less alone, through the promotion of a certain sense of belonging:

> "...at times I even forgot I was alone in my room... Gaming allowed me to continue socialising "normally" with my friends during COVID and made me realise the importance of my relationships. I started to appreciate the little things much more. ... When we started playing, that [loneliness] ended. I think that's when I realised how important it was to have friends. After feeling so alone, having fun with my friends again was incredible."

This excerpt highlights the inclusive and perhaps almost therapeutic dimension of online gaming: participants reposition themselves from isolated to socially connected, reinforcing their identity as a "friend" and re-signifying their own loneliness. At the same time, other participants emphasised that playing as a team or with friends helped them develop communication, cooperation and leadership skills, which impacted how they see themselves in a group context. One participant reported the experience of strategically coordinating a group of friends in an online tournament, which made them realise their leadership and team management skills. These experiences might help individuals see themselves as effective members of a collective, building identity aspects within gaming environments that translates into greater confidence in offline collaborative contexts (e.g., at work or in group studies).

Additionally, the quality of online social environments also influences identity experience. Though not heavily emphasised, some participants mentioned toxicity and hate speech in certain gaming communities, particularly against minority groups. Such hostile environments impact how players from targeted communities feel (included or valued). In this qualitative dataset, the focus was primarily on positive community experiences (friendship, mutual support, shared intimacy) rather than on negative ones; yet indirect mentions of "toxic environments" suggest that inclusion is not universal and that some subjects experience identity tensions in these spaces, particularly women or LGBTQIAP+ people.

A relevant example of self-exploration in a digital social context came from a participant who described the freedom with which they shared intimate aspects with strangers in a game lobby:

"...I found myself talking about relatively intimate topics with [strangers in the game], which I probably don't even share with close friends, and it really dawned on me that this was a side of me that brought me closeness with others and that I was going to start trying to bring it more into my everyday life. In that respect, it changed how I saw myself.

This example illustrates social identity experimentation in the digital world: behind the veil of anonymity (or at least the distance provided by the screen), the subject felt less constrained by the expectations of others. The experience prompted them to re-evaluate their self-image and motivated them to integrate this facet into real life. This represents reflective agency: individuals use online gaming spaces to experiment with behaviours and social identities, and by validating themselves in that environment they may transform their conduct through relational skills transfer.

In conclusion, the social impact of video games on participants seems to be two-fold. For many, games were a vehicle for inclusion, strengthening social ties and building community, which fostered a more positive self-image (feeling like better friends, valuable teammates, less alone in the world). On the other hand, warnings of exclusion and isolation emerged, factors that can lead to negative self-perception, as feeling like an outsider or an addict, whether due to excessive dedication to digital at the expense of face-to-face interaction, or due to the toxicity found in certain online environments.

3.4 Digital Identity and Representation

This emergent theme explores how participants experience identities and see themselves through characters, avatars, or virtual narratives, highlighting issues of representation and self-acceptance. The data reveals that some individuals understand video games as a safe space to explore different aspects of the self, project aspirations, or see their characteristics reflected in fictional characters, creating space to rethink their own identity.

A notable case is that of a transgender participant who described the importance of finding characters in games with similar experiences to their own. They specifically mention the game Celeste[3], whose storyline and engaging community helped them to better accept themselves. Seeing this representation in a virtual avatar and interacting online with welcoming fandoms seemed to provide them with identity comfort and a sense of inclusion:

"I think that, as a trans person, being able to see and play with characters who have been through situations similar to mine, as in the game *Celeste*, helped me to look at my problems differently... it helped me to accept myself better and get through more difficult times."

[3] Developed and published by indie studio *Maddy Makes Games*. Available at: https://store.steampowered.com/app/504230/Celeste/.

This testimony seems to highlight the affirmative dimension of representation. Through empathising with the experiences of a transgender character, the participant validated their own story, acquiring more emotional resources to embrace their identity. Moreover, engagement with "diverse and tolerant" online forums triggered their perception of not being isolated, which can be seen as an essential part of their well-being.

3.5 Detachment and Resistance

Finally, a cross-cutting theme emerged: some participants adopted critical distance, denying or minimising video games' influence on their self-image. These respondents described games solely as leisure, hobbies or pastimes without any deeper implications. This perspective reflects active resistance to digital domination of the self, with individuals positioning themselves as agents controlling the experience and emphasising clear boundaries between game world and "real life".

A quote illustrates this position well:

> "Video games have no influence on how I see myself, I just play to relieve stress or to distract myself."

Here, the participant is assertive about separating the self (self-image) from the recreational activity, attributing to it only entertainment and relaxation value. Another similar statement reinforced the idea of limits:

> "Gaming is not my life, and I cannot in any way become addicted to it."

The participant limits the game influence by resisting excessive involvement ("I can't become addicted"), while acknowledging learning from games (faster, more thoughtful decisions). This combination suggests they admit functional effects but resist impacts on their essential identity or priorities.

These dissenting voices provide an important counterpoint, as they reveal that not all players identify as "gamers" or attribute transformative meaning to digital experiences. For some, gaming is "just gaming", and the self "that matters" is constructed elsewhere. This distance may reflect differences in investment (sporadic play with little emotional involvement), but more significantly, may represent a conscious strategy to avoid becoming diluted in the virtual world. In fact, testimonials express pride in maintaining control, for example, when stated: "I don't invest myself", "it's not my life". Participants establish identities distinct from video gaming, viewing themselves as balanced, self-directed and resistant to cultural currents.

From a socio-critical perspective, this resistance responds to ubiquitous life digitisation. Subjects defend their agency against digital colonisation of identity stating that "It's just a game". Several explicitly mention social media as having a greater impact on self-image than games, distinguishing between digital interaction types and perhaps seeing video games as less personal or identity-driven.

Still, even those denying influence recognise instrumental benefits: they learned English, History, or improved reflexes and strategies thanks to games. They simply do not attribute identity value to them. As an example, one participant said they had no memorable moments, but acknowledged that

> "through *The Sims 4*[4] game, I learned to decorate and learned what I would like to have in my home."

This means they acquired knowledge and preferences, although maintaining that none of this "influenced" their sense of self. This apparent contradiction between learning something about oneself and not being influenced possibly indicates that participants define "influence on the way I see myself" more strictly, perhaps reserving it for profound changes in identity or self-esteem, rather than learnings seen as minor.

In short, this last topic highlights a diversity of reflective positions among participants: not everyone welcomes the idea that video games transform them. Some draw firm lines between themselves and the game, exercising a kind of protective scepticism. This scepticism, however, is also part of the spectrum of experiences and should be included in the overall understanding of the phenomenon.

4 Discussion

The results show that the relationship between video games and self-image can be multifaceted, situated, and reflective, underlining that the contemporary self is constructed in dialogue with technological and social contexts and experiences. RTA identified five interconnected dimensions - mirror of self, emotional regulation, community, representation, and resistance -, which outline the proposal of "self-image in the digital mirror" as an interpretative framework.

Many participants reported self-discovery and reaffirmation of personal values through gaming, suggesting that video games function as symbolic and emotional environments for identity experimentation [5]. These findings align with evidence on self-efficacy and flow states associated with overcoming challenges [26] and narrative identity [28]. At the same time, gaming functions as a regulatory refuge: a legitimate coping and stress-relief strategy, especially during periods of isolation, provided it is accompanied by DLB, as explored by Wang et al. [30] and Soylu and Bruning [31]. Awareness of excessive escapism risks (e.g. interference with daily functioning, problematic use) reinforces that the difference between adaptive and dysfunctional use might depend on player reflexivity, as addressed by Kiatsakared and Chen [32], Wang et al. [33], and Lee et al. [34]. The analysis also extends Meriläinen and Ruotsalainen [35]'s works, regarding gaming's complexity, where "a multitude of factors come together to produce a

[4] Developed by *Maxis* and published by *Electronic Arts*. More at: https://www.ea.com/games/the-sims/the-sims-4

personal, complex, and sometimes conflicted relationship with the social world of digital gaming".

The analysis frames the social dimension as structuring: community belonging, cooperation, and peer recognition seem to function as pillars of identity and predictors of relational self-esteem in this context. However, the same ecology can generate exclusion, frustration, or isolation when participation is surrounded by toxic dynamics, time/life imbalances, or non-inclusive community norms. These results align with previous interpretations that emphasise that the impact of games on identity depends less on content and more on the quality of relationships and conditions of participation (moderation, norms, accessibility) in each ecosystem [37].

Digital representation in games emerges as central to symbolic inclusion. Recognising oneself in game characters and communities, coupled with access to welcoming spaces, seems to facilitate self-acceptance and belonging, especially among historically marginalised groups (e.g., trans people, women, neurodivergent players), as explored by Bowling et al. [38], Jin [39], or Seijo et al. [40]. This connects with research on avatars [41], possible selves [42], and the so-called Proteus effect [43,44], while demanding socio-critical reading of who is represented, with what stereotypes, and with what identity consequences. In parallel, the theme "it's just a game" reveals resistance positions: for some, maintaining real/digital boundaries is an act of agency and critical literacy.

Theoretically, the "digital mirror self-image" proposes a model where video games mediate identity as mirrors (recognition), refuges (regulation), stages (expression/rehearsal of the self) and boundaries (resistance/limits), traversed by psychosocial mechanisms (agency, values, recognition, coping) and conditioned by socio-technical structures. From a practical point of view, this evidence can inform design, development and policies promoting diverse representation, community safety and accessibility, as well as educational/therapeutic interventions mobilising gaming's reflective potential for personal development and well-being.

4.1 Limitations and Future Directions

The study's limitations mainly concern its design, context, and analytical scope, which should be considered when interpreting the results. First, despite the sample size ($N = 627$), the responses analysed are based on voluntary and retrospective self-reports, subject to memory bias and social desirability. Therefore, future research may benefit from methodological triangulation to enrich the understanding of subjective experience.

Secondly, the study focused on a single open-ended question; although adequate for mapping the diversity of meanings in such a large sample, this option limits detailed exploration of the narrative and evolutionary trajectories of self-image over time. In the future, it could be beneficial to adopt longitudinal or life story-based designs to understand how engagement with video games resonates with lasting identity transformations.

Conceptually, the "digital mirror self-image" notion introduced in this article requires further theoretical validation. Better operationalisation could link this construct to narrative identity [28,29] or possible selves [42]. Future research could expand the focus to different game genres and formats, as well as other hybrid interaction spaces (social networks, streaming, participatory platforms), to understand how different forms of digital mediation can shape self-image and psychological well-being.

Acknowledgments. This research was funded by *Fundação para a Ciência e a Tecnologia* (FCT), under CICANT R&D Unit, grant UIDB/05260/2020. Ana Filipa Oliveira's participation in this work was funded by FCT under the Programme Scientific Employment Stimulus—Individual Call (Project byCitizens - Building Youth Citizenship Through Intergenerational approaches and digital media), financed by national funds (2023.07889.CEECIND).

References

1. Boyle, E.A., Connolly, T.M., Hainey, T., Boyle, J.M.: Engagement in digital entertainment games: a systematic review. Comput. Hum. Behav. **28**(3), 771–780 (2012). https://doi.org/10.1016/j.chb.2011.11.020
2. Granic, I., Morita, H., Scholten, H.: Beyond screen time: identity development in the digital age. Psychol. Inq. **31**(3), 195–223 (2020). https://doi.org/10.1080/1047840X.2020.1820214
3. Lüders, A., Dinkelberg, A., Quayle, M.: Becoming "us" in digital spaces: how online users creatively and strategically exploit social media affordances to build up social identity. Acta Physiol. (Oxf.) **228**, 103643 (2022). https://doi.org/10.1016/j.actpsy.2022.103643
4. Sharma, T.G., Hamari, J., Kesharwani, A., Tak, P.: Understanding continuance intention to play online games: roles of self-expressiveness, self-congruity, self-efficacy, and perceived risk. Behav. Inf. Technol. **41**(2), 348–364 (2022). https://doi.org/10.1080/0144929X.2020.1811770
5. Gabarnet, A., Feixas, G., Montesano, A.: Who am I inside the screen? Construction of virtual identity in multiplayer online videogames and its psychological functions. Cyberpsychol. Behav. Soc. Netw. **28**(1), 52–59 (2025). https://doi.org/10.1089/cyber.2024.0231
6. Kuruca Ozdemir, E., Dinc, L.: Game-based learning in undergraduate nursing education: a systematic review of mixed-method studies. Nurse Educ. Pract. **62**, 103375 (2022). https://doi.org/10.1016/j.nepr.2022.103375
7. Rienzo, A., Cubillos, C.: Playability and player experience in digital games for elderly: a systematic literature review. Sensors **20**(14), 3958 (2020). https://doi.org/10.3390/s20143958
8. Bailey, J.A.: Self-image, self-concept, and self-identity revisited. J. Natl. Med. Assoc. **95**(5), 383–386 (2003)
9. Cast, A.D., Burke, P.J.: A theory of self-esteem. Soc. Forces **80**(3), 1041–1068 (2002). https://doi.org/10.1353/sof.2002.0003
10. Robles-Carrillo, M.: Digital identity: an approach to its nature, concept, and functionalities. Int. J. Law Inf. Technol. **32**, eaae019 (2024). https://doi.org/10.1093/ijlit/eaae019

11. Rowland, J., Estevens, J.: "What is your digital identity?" Unpacking users' understandings of an evolving concept in datafied societies. Media Cult. Soc. **47**(2), 336–353 (2025). https://doi.org/10.1177/01634437241282240
12. Nagy, P., Koles, B.: The digital transformation of human identity: towards a conceptual model of virtual identity in virtual worlds. Converg.: Int. J. Res. New Media Technol. **20**(3), 276–292 (2014). https://doi.org/10.1177/1354856514531532
13. Blašković, L., Žužić, A., Orehovački, T.: Evaluating a conceptual model for measuring gaming experience: a case study of Stranded Away platformer game. Information **14**(6), 350 (2023). https://doi.org/10.3390/info14060350
14. IJsselsteijn, W.: Identification and categorization of digital game experiences: a qualitative study integrating theoretical insights and player perspectives. Westminster Pap. Commun. Cult. **9**(1) (2017). https://doi.org/10.16997/wpcc.153
15. Vahlo, J., Tuuri, K.: Eight types of video game experience. Entertain. Comput. **52**, 100882 (2025). https://doi.org/10.1016/j.entcom.2024.100882
16. Association of Internet Researchers: Internet Research: Ethical Guidelines 3.0. Association of Internet Researchers (2020). https://aoir.org/reports/ethics3.pdf
17. Creswell, J.W., Creswell, J.D.: Research Design: Qualitative, Quantitative, and Mixed Methods Approaches, 5th edn. SAGE, Los Angeles (2018)
18. Angermuller, J.: Accumulating discursive capital, valuating subject positions: from Marx to Foucault. Crit. Discourse Stud. **15**(4), 414–425 (2018). https://doi.org/10.1080/17405904.2018.1457551
19. Raessens, J.: Playful identities, or the ludification of culture. Games Cult. **1**(1), 52–57 (2006). https://doi.org/10.1177/1555412005281779
20. Christoph, W.: On the anthropology of play. PhIJ **5**(3) (2022). https://doi.org/10.23880/PhIJ-16000257
21. Braun, V., Clarke, V.: Using thematic analysis in psychology. Qual. Res. Psychol. **3**(2), 77–101 (2006). https://doi.org/10.1191/1478088706qp063oa
22. Braun, V., Clarke, V.: Reflecting on reflexive thematic analysis. Qual. Res. Sport Exercise Health **11**(4), 589–597 (2019). https://doi.org/10.1080/2159676X.2019.1628806
23. Csikszentmihalyi, M.: Flow: The Psychology of Optimal Experience. Harper and Row, New York (2009)
24. Sachan, T., Chhabra, D., Abraham, B.: Social capital in online gaming communities: a systematic review examining the role of virtual identities. Cyberpsychol. Behav. Soc. Netw. **28**(3), 147–161 (2025). https://doi.org/10.1089/cyber.2024.0375
25. Hong, J., Tai, T., Liang, F.: English vocabulary learning through gamification with Tic-Tac-Toe in Flippity-Connecto: The prediction of gameplay self-efficacy to anxiety, interest and flow experience. Br. J. Educ. Technol. bjet.13577 (2025). https://doi.org/10.1111/bjet.13577
26. Hung, C.-Y., Sun, J.C.-Y., Yu, P.-T.: The benefits of a challenge: student motivation and flow experience in tablet-PC-game-based learning. Interact. Learn. Environ. **23**(2), 172–190 (2015). https://doi.org/10.1080/10494820.2014.997248
27. Power, J., Lynch, R., McGarr, O.: Difficulty and self-efficacy: an exploratory study. Br. J. Edu. Technol. **51**(1), 281–296 (2020). https://doi.org/10.1111/bjet.12755
28. McAdams, D.P.: "First we invented stories, then they changed us": the evolution of narrative identity. Evol. Stud. Imaginative Cult. **3**(1), 1–18 (2019). https://doi.org/10.26613/esic.3.1.110
29. McAdams, D.P.: Narrative identity and the redemptive self: an intellectual autobiography, with occasional critique. Narrative Works **11**, 47–55 (2024). https://doi.org/10.7202/1108951ar

30. Wang, Z., Parnandi, A., Gutierrez-Osuna, R.: BioPad: leveraging off-the-shelf video games for stress self-regulation. IEEE J. Biomed. Health Inform. **22**(1), 47–55 (2018). https://doi.org/10.1109/JBHI.2017.2671788
31. Yilmaz Soylu, M., Bruning, R.H.: Exploring self-regulation of more or less expert college-age video game players: a sequential explanatory design. Front. Psychol. **7** (2016). https://doi.org/10.3389/fpsyg.2016.01441
32. Kiatsakared, P., Chen, K.-Y.: The effect of flow experience on online game addiction during the COVID-19 pandemic: the moderating effect of activity passion. Sustainability **14**(19), 12364 (2022). https://doi.org/10.3390/su141912364
33. Wang, X., Abdelhamid, M., Sanders, G.L.: Exploring the effects of psychological ownership, gaming motivations, and primary/secondary control on online game addiction. Decis. Support Syst. **144**, 113512 (2021). https://doi.org/10.1016/j.dss.2021.113512
34. Lee, Z.W.Y., Cheung, C.M.K., Chan, T.K.H.: Understanding massively multiplayer online role-playing game addiction: a hedonic management perspective. Inf. Syst. J. **31**(1), 33–61 (2021). https://doi.org/10.1111/isj.12292
35. Meriläinen, M., Ruotsalainen, M.: The light, the dark, and everything else: making sense of young people's digital gaming. Front. Psychol. **14**, 1164992 (2023). https://doi.org/10.3389/fpsyg.2023.1164992
36. Ai, J., Cross, B., Bignell, C.: The construction of gamer identity in narratives about video game playing and formal education learning experiences. Res. Learn. Technol. **31** (2023). https://doi.org/10.25304/rlt.v31.2852
37. Sachan, T., Chhabra, D., Abraham, B.: Social networking or social isolation? A systematic review on socio-relational outcomes for members of online gaming communities. Games Cult. **20**(3), 355–383 (2025). https://doi.org/10.1177/15554120231201760
38. Bowling, J., Barker, J., Gunn, L.H., Lace, T.: "It just feels right": perceptions of the effects of community connectedness among trans individuals. PLoS ONE **15**(10), e0240295 (2020). https://doi.org/10.1371/journal.pone.0240295
39. Jin, Y.: Media representation and social identity: a study of public discourse construction and the empowerment of marginalised groups in the digital age. IJEH **19**(2), 134–139 (2025). https://doi.org/10.54097/jq9t4b14
40. Seijo, D., Vázquez, M.J., Novo, M., Fariña, F.: Studying the effects of sense of belonging to virtual communities in psychological well-being and adjustment to academic setting. Educ. XX1 **26**(1), 229–247 (2023). https://doi.org/10.5944/educxx1.31818
41. Szolin, K., Kuss, D.J., Nuyens, F.M., Griffiths, M.D.: "I am the character, the character is me": a thematic analysis of the user-avatar relationship in videogames. Comput. Hum. Behav. **143**, 107694 (2023). https://doi.org/10.1016/j.chb.2023.107694
42. Erikson, M.G.: The meaning of the future: toward a more specific definition of possible selves. Rev. Gen. Psychol. **11**(4), 348–358 (2007). https://doi.org/10.26613/esic.3.1.110
43. Liu, Y.: The Proteus effect: overview, reflection, and recommendations. Games Cult. **20**(3), 384–400 (2025). https://doi.org/10.1177/15554120231202175
44. Szolin, K., Kuss, D.J., Nuyens, F.M., Griffiths, M.D.: Exploring the user-avatar relationship in videogames: a systematic review of the Proteus effect. Hum.-Comput. Interact. **38**(5–6), 374–399 (2023). https://doi.org/10.1080/07370024.2022.2103419

45. Lima-Costa, A.R., Tosti, A.E., Bonfá-Araujo, B., Duradoni, M.: Digital life balance and need for online social feedback: cross-cultural psychometric analysis in Brazil. Hum. Behav. Emerg. Technol. **1**(1), 1–8 (2024). https://doi.org/10.1155/2024/1179740
46. Soysal, F.S., Kosar, E., Gursesli, M.C., Guazzini, A., Duradoni, M.: Digital life balance scale: validity and reliability in the Turkish context. Hum. Behav. Emerg. Technol. **1**(1), 1–9 (2024). https://doi.org/10.1155/2024/9454784
47. APA.: Information Recommended for Inclusion in Manuscripts That Report Primary Qualitative Research. APA Style JARS, Washington, D.C. (2018)

Gamified Labubu: Exploring the Psychological Factors of Adult Play in Brazil and Finland

Katriina Heljakka[1(✉)], Letícia Hara Takahama Tagliacollo[2], and Jorge Luís Ferreira Abrão[2]

[1] Turku School of Economics, University of Turku, Pori, Finland
katriina.heljakka@utu.fi
[2] Sao Paulo State University (Unesp), Assis, Brazil

Abstract. This study investigates the recent global and viral Labubu toy phenomenon through the lens of gamification. We conduct a two-step qualitative analysis by exploring the phenomenon through the inspection of related media materials in Brazil and Finland. We aim first to identify adult play patterns around the acquisition and consumption of the toy, and second to interpret findings from gamified play by focusing on the underlying psychological factors. The contribution of the foundational study lies in unpacking the various dimensions of adult play and the psychological reasons that challenge narrow understandings of adult toy collecting.

Keywords: Labubu · Character Toys · Gamification · Adult Toy Play · Object Play · Psychological Factors

1 Introduction

In recent years, the popularity of collectible toys aimed at adults has increased significantly. Phenomena such as Funko Pop, Ugly Dolls, and, more recently, Labubu, demonstrate how the world of play extends far beyond childhood, taking on new emotional, social, and cultural meanings. As reported in the news media, such toy phenomena are linked to *kidultism*, a phenomenon in which adults engage in play with toys and games. We have observed that this phenomenon exhibits gamification tendencies, using game-like elements in non-game contexts to motivate, engage, or shape behavior.

Labubu, a line of uniquely designed collectible figures distributed by the Chinese company Pop Mart, has become a global craze, inspiring passionate collectors, fostering online communities, and sparking a race for rare and limited-edition pieces. This movement is fueled by nostalgia, the "ugly-cute" aesthetic (which is simultaneously cute and strange), and FOMO (Fear of Missing Out), which drives rapid purchasing behavior and fuels the cycle of trend-based collecting around viral toy phenomena.

Our study takes an interest in these *gamified* dimensions of adult object play around the Labubu phenomenon, linking contemporary object play with character toys with play patterns associated with goals, competition, and achievements motivated by intrapersonal and interpersonal reasons to acquire, collect, and play with Labubus through

R. Baptista et al. (Eds.): VJ 2025, CCIS 2988, pp. 242–254, 2027.
https://doi.org/10.1007/978-3-032-31642-4_19

engagement that simultaneously happens in physical space and digital platforms. The primary goal of this study is to explore the psychological factors underlying adult collecting behavior around Labubu, based on a literature review and online content analysis, with a focus on comparing perspectives between Brazil and Finland to reveal the similarities and differences in contemporary toy cultures between the two countries and continents where the researchers reside. This comparison aims to demonstrate how cultural—and global—contexts influence perceptions of the phenomenon, particularly with respect to motivation, consumption, and emotional engagement. To achieve this, a two-step qualitative analysis will be conducted by: 1) Collecting, categorizing, and consulting relevant articles, academic studies, and online materials, which form the data of this study, and: 2) Analyzing the content of data through thematic analysis to identify common themes, and interpreting the findings to identify patterns and cross-cultural similarities and differences between Labubu-related themes associated with gamification in the contexts of Brazilian and Finnish media materials. The contribution of our study is to contextualize the Labubu phenomenon within the broader landscape of global, commercially driven adult toy play in the post-digital era [1, 2] and, more specifically, to situate it as a gamified practice with psychological motivations. This study analyzes, identifies, and discusses these issues through cross-comparative research conducted using online media materials collected in Brazil and Finland in August and October 2025, a timeframe within which the Labubu trend peaked in global media. Before delving into our analysis of consumerist play employing Labubu, we first look at the dominant way of framing adult toy play, namely, toy collecting, and consider its positive effects and adverse consequences within psychological explanations.

2 Psychological Factors in Adult Collecting

Previous research positions adult collecting as a multidimensional activity with playful dimensions. Collecting, often associated with the hoarding of objects, extends to more nuanced forms of behaviour, namely engagement beyond compulsive consumption, and is understood as a form of play [3]. Indeed, adult collecting is a multifaceted phenomenon, particularly in the context of toys [4]. As a goal-driven play activity, we connect toy collection to *gamified toy play*.

Adult collecting can be understood through both psychological and psychoanalytic lenses. Toys, even in adulthood, serve as symbolic objects that carry deep personal meanings. From a psychoanalytic perspective, Sigmund Freud, Melanie Klein, and Donald Winnicott emphasize the therapeutic significance of play and toys. Winnicott [5] explicitly argues that toys can serve as transitional objects, helping children cope with anxiety or providing comfort, and that these objects can resurface later in life. We believe these explanations also apply to adult toy play. Ignacio and Cupchik [6] support this view, suggesting that adult collectors of, e.g., Ball-Jointed Dolls may also use them for comfort and security during periods of distress, or as aesthetic objects for creative and artistic expression during times of well-being.

Toy collecting, and character toy collecting in particular, may have both positive and negative effects on the adult toy enthusiast. Although collecting often carries an obsessive trait, involving the urge to organize and acquire more items, it can be beneficial as long as it is kept under control and does not harm the individual's physical or mental health. Engaging with toys in adulthood provides a meaningful way to maintain a sense of playfulness, allowing the characteristics of childhood play to be preserved and reinterpreted in adult life [7]. According to the *DSM-5* of the American Psychiatric Association, Hoarding Disorder differs from normal collecting in that collecting is systematic and organized and does not cause obstruction, distress, or harm to the collector or those around them [8]. Heljakka [9] notes that "collecting is playful as long as it does not become a compulsive activity in which the collector is interested only in accumulating objects for their monetary value" (p. 103). Thus, it is essential to recognize when an activity that began as fun and playful—encouraging both solitary and social play—begins to reflect a lack of ego organization, evolving into a harmful cycle of collecting, buying, and stockpiling objects. This phenomenon, in humorous terms, has been referred to as the "pile of shame" in association with the collecting of miniatures—a revealing example of consumer overaccumulation, often driven by impulse buying, nostalgia, or social pressures. Yet, as Meriläinen et al. point out, some collectors may experience joy in collecting miniatures. In contrast, others may feel burdened by unused figures, mirroring the duality of shame/pride associated with the activity [10] and 'childlike vs. childish' behaviors that can be associated with adult play [11].

As stated by Silva [12], low frustration tolerance can drive compulsive buying, leading individuals to lose control over how much money they invest in their collections, especially during stressful periods or as a way to cope with internal suffering. Farina, Toledo, and Corrêa [13] note that collecting can have a darker side, sometimes comparable to addictions such as alcohol, drugs, or gambling. Supporting this perspective, McIntosh and Schmeidel [14] explain that "Attaining the desired goal will result in a wave of positive affect, a 'rush' that is one of the motivations of collecting, and has also been the impetus for some to discuss collecting in terms of addictive behavior" [p. 92], also associated with playing with "The Internet's Favourite Monster" [15]. Earlier research analyzed the following psychological factors linked to adult toy collecting [16], which can be categorized into the following perspectives: a) *Rediscovery of playfulness*: The adult tendency of maintaining the capacity to play as a form of stress relief and creativity, b) *Affection and nostalgia*: Adults connecting present experiences with childhood memories, c) *Gamification*: Adults (both in the toy industry and toy cultures) structuring collecting as a game, with goals, rewards, and progression, and d) *Compulsive consumption*: Describing a state when the urge to complete collections becomes overwhelming or uncontrolled in adults. These factors build a foundational understanding for exploring the Labubu phenomenon.

3 Contextualization: The Labubu Phenomenon

Labubu was created by an asian designer Kasing Lung, who sought to combine cuteness and strangeness, evoking both empathy and curiosity. Its design features hybrid creatures with delicate yet grotesque traits, creating a unique aesthetic appeal. initially aimed at a niche market, Labubu gained international popularity thanks to social media exposure, limited-edition releases, and narrative marketing that encourages collecting behaviour. With its identifiable "character", face, backstory, and pre-described "personality", Labubu as a recognizable character fulfills the criteria of a character toy. "character

Fig. 1. (left) In Finland, original Labubu's in 'mint' condition were sold on the street for 65€ during the festival season of summer 2025. *Lafufus* (or unofficial copies of the toys are often sold in street markets without packaging). Photographed by Heljakka.

Fig. 2. (right) In Brazil, counterfeits (R$50 = €8,00) are widely sold in Brazilian stores because the prices of the originals are very high (R$400 = €65,00). Photographed by Hara Takahama Tagliacollo.

toys are toys identifiable by name, personality, and visual traits" [17]. Labubu has an expressive face with wide, staring eyes and a grin that shows its teeth – the character, in its most popular manifestations, does not smile in a "friendly" manner but appears mischievous to many (see Figs. 1 and 2).

The aesthetic and physiognomy of Labubu characters are reminiscent of former character toys, such as Monchichi and Trollz, and, due to their grins, also resemble the Gloomy Bear, a character created by Japanese designer Mori Chack. Due to this unconventional, "ugly-cute" appearance, we associate the mass-marketed versions of Labubu with the lineage of designer toys, or urban vinyl—collectible art objects in toy form [18]. Labubus belong to the *viral toy* category [17], as their popularity was significantly driven by and supported by social media posts on TikTok and Instagram by celebrity singers such as Lisa from the pop band Blackpink and Dua Lipa.

Gamification, an established field of research within not only games scholarship but also cultural, consumerist, and organizational behavior more broadly, offers a fitting lens for exploring contemporary toy consumption and play. In toy play, gamification is related to both toy marketing and consumer behavior. For example, many toys are sold in blind boxes to add excitement and drive repeated buying behavior, which is typical of toy collectors.

While research on toy play practices through the lens of gamification is limited, some studies have identified repetitive, goal-driven play patterns in doll play [19]. However, the academic literature on toy sales and marketing with gamified elements is scarce. In our study, we aim to address both areas related to adult engagement with character toys—specifically, collecting behaviors with Labubu—the business side—and gamification, as observed in player behavior. In our study, we lean on previous work on (digital game-based) gamification [20] to build our understanding of *toy-based gamification* through three perspectives recognized in association with digital gaming:

1. *Blind Box XP system* (progression mechanics and variable rewards): Players are motivated to make repeat purchases to "level up" or unlock exclusive content. Similarly,

for collectible toys, the marketing logic of blind boxes leverages collectors' need for a sense of completion, encouraging repeat purchases until the collection is considered complete.

2. *Time-limited events* (FOMO mechanics): Temporal scarcity, loss aversion, and event-based engagement cycles in gamified systems. Limited-time offers increase purchase urgency by creating psychological pressure for players through FOMO and perceived scarcity. For toys, similar mechanics are evident in limited releases paired with blind-box packaging and socially shared unboxing content, which drive the need to hunt for toys both online and offline, across first- and second-hand markets.
3. *Collection leaderboards* (status mechanics): Players are driven to buy more to climb leaderboards and signal expertise, wealth, and cultural literacy. In toy cultures, the concept of Bourdieu's cultural capital [21] aligns with non-economic forms of knowledge expressed through taste-making and lifestyle signaling. Here, toy collections function as a site of distinction, where aesthetic literacy translates into social recognition.

We identify a missing direction in scholarly contributions on adult play with character toys linked to gamification, as understood in relation to digital games. We aim to address this gap by investigating the Labubu phenomenon of 2025 from the perspective of collecting as a gamified type of object consumption and play. Simultaneously, our interest turns to investigating the psychological factors behind "Gamified Labubu."

4 Study Description

The study follows four structured steps: 1) *Material collection*: gathering of media articles, blog posts, forums, and social media content related to Labubu. 2) *Idea extraction*: identifying key arguments and findings from each source. 3) *Categorization*: grouping findings under themes such as nostalgia, FOMO, compulsive buying, gamification, and emotional bonding. And, 4) *Cross-cultural comparison*: highlighting similarities and differences between Brazil and Finland. These steps are explained in more detail in the following sections, and a comparative analysis of findings from Brazil and Finland is presented in a separate section.

Material Collection: The data for this study consists of articles, blog posts, forum posts, and social media content. The analysis drew on publicly accessible content from multiple social media platforms and online communities. We examined Facebook (Labubu Suomi), TikTok (user-generated unboxing videos, e.g., Niko Saarinen), Instagram (photoplay posts with #labubu #popmart), and WhatsApp (collector group interactions in Brazil). Additionally, we reviewed Finnish and Brazilian online news portals and blogs (e.g., Wilska 2025) that interpret platform-mediated consumption. The corpus comprises public content relevant to documenting the emergence, circulation, and interpretation of the Labubu trend in both countries. In total, 15 articles from Brazil and 10 from Finland (retrieved online between August and early October 2025) were based on searching materials with the terms "Labubu", "Labubu collection" (*coleção* in Portuguese), "Labubu and blog", and "Labubu and forum." The range of media materials published between June and October 2025 illustrates a broad perspective on the phenomenon, as journalistic media encompass various formats and social media posts are published in numerous online outlets, as tabulated below. It is notable that for some media articles (n = 8), journalists have observed or interviewed Labubu buyers, including both children and adults. Additionally, the TikTok posts are generated by the Labubu customers themselves. This multidimensional approach to the phenomenon supports the researchers' interpretations in the study, which did not gather data directly from players (Table 1).

Table 1. Media materials gathered as data.

Media materials from Brazil and Finland	Names of media outlets	Observations and interviews with Labubu customers
Brazil (n = 15)	Media articles (9), blog posts (2), social media content (4)	(n = 4)
Finland (n = 10)	Media articles (7), blog posts (1), forums (1) social media content (1)	(n = 4)

Idea Extraction: We used qualitative thematic analysis. During the study, the media materials were classified into two main categories: Category A, focusing on positive emotional aspects such as nostalgia, affection, and social bonding; and Category B, addressing complex emotions, including anxiety, FOMO, and compulsive behavior.

Categorization: The categories of nostalgia, community bonding, collectability, and scarcity were distilled from recurring themes in the Finnish and Brazilian materials and aligned with established concepts in consumer culture and toy research, capturing the forces driving the Labubu phenomenon. Based on the media materials gathered for this study, several traces of toy cultures and gamification were identified, which can be linked to the positive and negative effects of adult toy play. Based on the categorization, we saw examples of claims that demonstrate the views of both expert and toy customers on "Gamified Labubu", discussed in more detail in the following:

Nostalgia and Emotional Connection: Toys serve as both symbolic links to childhood memories and current affective states. According to Professor of Sociology and Consumer Researcher Terhi-Anna Wiska in Finland, "There may also be nostalgia and a longing for childhood behind it. In the right amounts, play and fantasy can be good for a person." [22]. "Pop consumerism" [23] in the current world's crises links Labubu to the "lipstick effect", a consumer behavior theory that suggests individuals shift their spending toward small, emotionally satisfying luxury items [24] during periods of economic uncertainty or psychological stress. Brazilian social media posts exemplify this perspective: There's nothing wrong with wanting to buy something trendy, as long as it comes from genuine desire and mindful consumption. Playing in adulthood can and should serve as a healthy form of escape, rather than a harmful regression into childish behavior [25–27]. Therefore, following Ignacio and Cupchik [11], collecting Labubu in adulthood illustrates a tendency toward childlikeness rather than childishness.

Community Bonding: Collectors engage online to share their experiences. For example, in June 2025, approximately 1.5 million videos related to Labubu were posted on TikTok, and some young consumers of the toy report seeing the toy first on this platform [28]. In Finland, social media influencers are showcasing their toy unboxings and sharing their opinions with their communities about Labubu. One toy customer said: "It's important to me that I can create interesting content for social media, and sometimes it's good to jump on a trend" [28].

To further illustrate, one influencer said he did not like Labubu before buying three of them, which he then unboxed in a video. After seeing the first of his toys, he uttered ambiguously, "This is the worst-looking thing in the world, but this is (also) the cutest thing in the world" [29].

Collectibility and Scarcity: Limited series create competition and desire among toy customers. In one media article, an interviewee said: "It's also nice to have something rare, because not everyone has access to them" [28]. Another article reported: "Screams of joy filled a Helsinki toy store on the first of July as the clock struck midnight. Dozens of children and adults had come to the store, eager to get their hands on the Labubu trend doll, which is rarely available in Finland." [28].

FOMO: The Fear of Missing Out encourages quick, even aggressive, purchasing decisions, leading toy customers to fight over limited Labubu sets. Some stores have pulled Labubu from sale because it is no longer safe to keep them on display [28].

5 Findings Based on the Comparative Analysis

5.1 Labubu in Brazil

In Brazil, the Labubu craze has spread beyond a single age group, gaining popularity among both children and adults. Until a few years ago, toy ads were allowed on children's and free-to-air TV channels. After the ban, advertising shifted to social media platforms like Instagram and TikTok, which now play a significant role in creating hype and influencing purchases, even though these platforms are officially restricted to users under 18 [30]. Among children, the toy's popularity is apparent: they constantly talk about Labubus and proudly share the rare figures they've collected. Adults, meanwhile, often use them as bag charms and post about their finds online. Since there is no official Pop Mart store in Brazil, fans must rely on local retailers that resell authentic figures or buy directly from international platforms like AliExpress [31–33].

Some playful nicknames for fake Labubus include *Lafufu* and *Tribufu* [34]. There's even a Brazilian parody version called *Lalulu*, featuring the face of the current president, Lula [36]. In São Paulo, popular commercial hubs like Brás and 25 de Março are the main places to find counterfeit versions of the toy, offering a cheaper, more accessible option for the public. Since the originals are sold in U.S. dollars and the Brazilian real is weak against the U.S. dollar, and given high import taxes and fees, many players turn to these knockoffs as a more affordable way to join the trend [35, 36].

Earlier in 2025, Reborn dolls mimicking real babies caused a stir in Brazil [37], but Labubus have been better received as a new way for adults to engage with toys. There's still limited material on the topic in the country, with most discussions taking place on social media or in news outlets reporting on the surge in sales and popularity. According to G1 [38], an important Brazilian news portal, "Other trends easily found in the largest shopping hub in Latin America—such as 'Reborn dolls' and coloring books—suggest that the phenomenon of adults willing to invest in the escapism and nostalgia that toys can provide is not new".

In online communities on Facebook and WhatsApp, where enthusiasts of other collectible niches gather, Labubus have been well received despite their high price. Much of the debate centers around prejudice against these figures, particularly since both Labubus and Bobbie Goods are marketed mainly toward women [39, 40]. There is also growing concern about conscious consumption and the role of FOMO—the fear of missing out—in influencing purchasing decisions [41]. Many reflect on how major companies exploit feelings of nostalgia and security, encouraging people to purchase items that evoke childhood memories amid global and domestic instability [42].

5.2 Labubu in Finland

The Labubu phenomenon in Finland exemplifies the convergence of global toy culture, platform-driven consumption, and affective relationships with toys. Media materials indicate that adult and child consumers alike are drawn to Labubu figures because of their limited availability, aesthetic appeal, and social media virality [22, 43]. In times of crisis, people often turn to toys for comfort, to escape reality, and for a sense of childhood nostalgia. However, addictive sales play a key role. Labubu is distinguished from previous hit toys, such as Squishmallows, by its clearly higher price [44]. In Finland (October 2025), Labubus in "mint condition" are sold in some stores for 59,99€. Again, on the Labubu Facebook group, the toys, sometimes already unboxed, are sold for 30 euros and up. Prices in Asian markets are significantly lower, ranging from 11 to 14€ [43]. Queuing for hours to purchase a Labubu [28] reflects a ritualized consumer performance, driven by FOMO intensified by algorithmic visibility on platforms like TikTok [29]. This scarcity-based desirability is further reinforced by collector culture, in which figures can resell for high prices. Critical voices have emerged and gone online. Wilska [43] argues that the Labubu craze exemplifies "the foolishness of social media-driven consumption", in which "psychological illusions are used to get people to pay" [22]. In toy cultures, symbolic value often outweighs utility, being primarily linked to playability and play value, as well as their relation to perceived resale value, as seen in online communities such as the Facebook group Labubu Suomi [44].

5.3 Comparison Between the Two Countries

Nostalgia and Emotional Connection: In Finland, Labubu's appeal is rooted in aesthetic appreciation intertwined with identity expression and playful lifestyle-related consumption. In Brazil, nostalgia manifests in equally playful ways. Still, there are also populist (and political) ways that remind us of how toys can be used for activist causes: adults use Labubus as bag charms, mascots, and humorous cultural references—evidenced by the parody figure "Lalulu", which features the president's face.

Blind Box System: The blind box system, in which buyers don't know which figure they receive, fuels emotional highs and lows in both countries. In Finland, this system is seen as a collector's gamified ritual—a mix of chance, scarcity, and potential resale value. The randomness enhances the symbolic value of rare figures, which encourages repeat purchases. In Brazil, the blind box system is complicated by economic limitations. Due to the weak Brazilian currency (real), high import taxes, and the dollar-based pricing of authentic Labubus, many consumers resort to knockoffs or gray-market imports. While the surprise element remains appealing, economic barriers push consumers towards fake Lafufus. Thus, the XP system in Brazil is more financially exclusionary, yet consumers creatively subvert it.

FOMO (Fear of Missing Out): FOMO is a significant driving force in both contexts. In Finland, FOMO is amplified by social media visibility and limited-edition drops, which trigger long queues and rapid sell-outs. In Brazil, children and adults are exposed to social media images of what they are missing. This creates aspirational pressure, particularly among lower-income groups who can't afford originals, leading to purchases of fake Lafufus.

Community Bonding: In both countries, Labubu fosters community bonds. In Finland, bonding occurs through interactions around toy shop releases and online groups focused on toy resale. In Brazil, community bonding occurs equally online and offline, particularly in WhatsApp groups, local fairs, and neighborhood commerce. Adult play with Labubu includes humor and resource-sharing (such as distinguishing between real and fake Labubu), but also a gendered critique: discussions often highlight how Labubu and similar products face dismissive attitudes for being "feminized" forms of toy fandom, reflecting broader prejudices against women-centered consumption. This finding closely aligns with an observation outside the gamification theme: According to media materials from both countries, the Labubu phenomenon in adult toy cultures exemplifies a predominantly feminine pastime. Curiously, a Finnish media article notes that all Labubus themselves represent "girls" [42]. Similarly, the articles from Finnish broadcasters are all written by women.

6 Discussion

This study represents a first-hand attempt to shed more light on the Labubu phenomenon from the perspectives of gamification and underlying psychological factors. Alongside the understanding that adults mainly collect toys and do not interact with their playthings as children do is the dominant rhetoric, combined with the presence of adult toy players [1]. Yet, research in this field evidences the broad spectrum of activities undertaken, for example, with character-type toys [17], such as the Labubu analyzed in this paper. The "nostalgia explanation" is often applied to video games [45], but, as illustrated by our study, the link between toy and game worlds can be accounted for by other factors as well. A limitation of the study is its focus on national and local media materials only. However, many materials cross-reference international media coverage, indicating the global reach of this viral toy phenomenon. In the next phase of research, the study could be expanded by interviewing adult toy enthusiasts who have acquired their own Labubus and exploring their motivations for participating in the phenomenon. To find a new, more inclusive angle for the study, the interviews should not limit themselves to female fans and Labubu players. Avenues for future research could also include consideration of the longevity of play with viral toys, as well as the consequences of adult collecting activities on toy lifecycles—including the possible preservation, cultivation, and end-of-life of toys (or players). Additionally, future work could investigate whether gamified play patterns support or limit sustainability in toy cultures. We speculate that gamification may shorten toy lifecycles by accelerating consumption through FOMO, unboxing rituals, and reward-driven collecting, which encourage rapid turnover rather than long-term use. With a visualization of the *Gamified dimensions of the Labubu collecting experience* below (Fig. 3), we hope to have contributed to an understanding of key perspectives on what gamification means in the context of adult toy collecting and play linked to the dimensions of materiality, functionality, fictionality, affectivity, sociality, and most significantly, temporality [17].

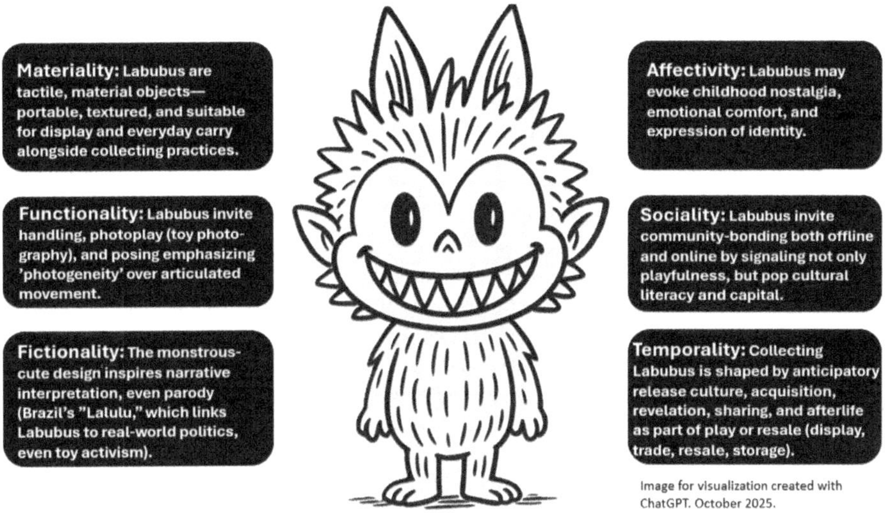

Fig. 3. Gamified dimensions of the Labubu collecting experience summarized by the authors.

7 Conclusions

Toys can act as sublimators, channeling desires, processing anxieties, and reconnecting with past emotional experiences. Moreover, collecting stimulates intrinsic motivation by offering pleasure through the game-oriented hunt-and-collect dynamic, progress tracking, and social interaction. The Labubu phenomenon demonstrates how toys can transcend childhood, playing complex emotional and social roles in adult life. By combining gamification, nostalgia, and competition, brands like Labubu create experiences that transcend material consumption, transforming collecting into an interactive and emotionally charged activity that is childlike rather than childish.

Our study contributes to a broader understanding of how gamification influences contemporary toy consumption patterns and highlights opportunities for future research into the boundaries between playing, collecting, and consuming toys as a lifelong practice, shaped by both negative and positive psychological factors.

According to a recent news article, toy designers are interested in recreating the Labubu phenomenon with new character toys; Chinese artist Runyu, 24, wants to create a new Labubu [46]. While the toy industry is fashion- and trend-driven, we speculate that, as the world becomes saturated with Labubu, a similar 'viral toy' craze is unlikely to spread as rapidly. Nevertheless, it will be interesting to see whether the gamified and globally emerging dimensions of toy acquisition and consumption persist as a significant aspect of adult toy collecting and play.

Disclosure of Interests. The first author was interviewed about the phenomenon for both international and national news media. The outcomes of these publications were excluded from the data collection and analysis.

References

1. Heljakka, K.: Principles of adult play(fulness) in contemporary toy cultures. From wow to flow to glow. Doctoral thesis. Aalto University, Helsinki (2013)
2. Heljakka, K: How play moves us: toys, technologies, and mobility in a digital world. Doctoral thesis. University of Turku (2024)
3. Rogan, B.: On collecting as play, creativity and aesthetic practice. Etnofoor **11**(1), 40–54 (1998)
4. Heljakka, K.: Toy fandom, adulthood, and the ludic age. In: Fandom: Identities and Communities in a Mediated World, pp. 91–105 (2017)
5. Winnicott, D.W.: O brincar e a realidade. Ubu Editora (1971/2020)
6. Ignacio, A., Cupchik, G.C.: Therapeutic benefits of adult doll play. Imagin. Cogn. Pers. **41**(1), 5–30 (2021)
7. Tagliacollo, L.H.T., Abrão, J.L.F., Heljakka, K.: A psicologia por trás do colecionismo de brinquedos na fase adulta: Compreendendo os benefícios emocionais e sociais do brincar. In: de Almeida, M.T.P. et al. (eds.) A cultura lúdica: O jogo, a brincadeira e o brinquedo, 1st edn., pp. 58–71. Instituto Nexos (2025)
8. American Psychiatric Association: Manual diagnóstico e estatístico de transtornos mentais: DSM-5. M. I. C. Nascimento, Trad.; 5th edn., pp. 277–281. Artmed (2014)
9. Heljakka, K.: From toys to television and back: My Little Pony appropriated in adult toy play. J. Popular Telev. **3**(1), 99–109 (2015)
10. Meriläinen, M., Stenros, J., Heljakka, K.: The pile of shame: the personal and social sustainability of collecting and hoarding miniatures. In: Muthu, S.S. (ed.) Toys and Sustainability, pp. 57–77. Springer, Singapore (2022)
11. Ignacio, A., Cupchik, G.C.: Understanding fantasy and adult doll play through regression in service of the self. Imagin. Cogn. Pers. **40**(3), 290–324 (2021)
12. Silva, A.B.B.: Mentes consumistas: do consumismo à compulsão por compras, 1st edn. Principium (2014)
13. Farina, M.C., Toledo, G.L., Corrêa, G.B.: Colecionismo: uma perspectiva abrangente sobre o comportamento do consumidor. Seminários Administração FEA-USP **9**, 1–15 (2006)
14. McIntosh, W.D., Schmeidel, B.: Collectors and collecting: a social psychological perspective. Leis. Sci. **26**(1), 85–97 (2004)
15. The Art Gorgeous: Kasing Lung: The Artist Behind the Internet's Favourite Monster, Labubu (2025)
16. Tagliacollo, L., Abraõ, J. L: Brincando de colecionar: uma análise do significado do brinquedo na vida adulta (2025)

17. Heljakka, K.: Adult play with character toys. Encyclopedia **5**(3) (2025)
18. Steinberg, M.: A vinyl platform for dissent: designer toys and character merchandising. J. Vis. Cult. **9**(2), 209–228 (2010)
19. Heljakka, K., Tuomi, P.: Gamified doll-dramas: provocations, playbor and participatory play practices in the age of iTV. 21st International Conference on Intelligent Games and Simulation, GAME-ON, pp. 67–70 (2020)
20. Hamari, J., Koivisto, J., Sarsa, H.: Does gamification work? A literature review of empirical studies on gamification. In: 2014 The 47th Hawaii International Conference on System Sciences, pp. 3025–3034. IEEE (2014)
21. Bourdieu, P.: Distinction: A Social Critique of the Judgement of Taste. Harvard University Press. (1984)
22. Hyttinen, N.: Miksi Labubu-trendilelut villitsevät lapsista aikuisiin? Massiivinen FOMO-ilmiö. MTVUutiset (2025)
23. Arias, A.M.: The Labubu mystery box revolution: what tech startups can learn from a $22.7B Toy Craze | The Current Thing #7 (2025)
24. Hill, S.E., Rodeheffer, C.D., Griskevicius, V., Durante, K., White, A.E.: Boosting beauty in an economic decline: mating, spending, and the lipstick effect. J. Pers. Soc. Psychol. **103**(2), 275 (2012)
25. Frazão, G.: Você precisa de um Labubu? O consumismo nas redes sociais. Startups (2025)
26. @psico_emily: Você não precisa, mas pode querer. Instagram post (2025)
27. SBT Brasil: Brinquedos para adultos impulsionam vendas com nostalgia e influência do cinema [Video]. YouTube (2025)
28. Littow Putkonen, I.: Viisi tuntia jonossa pehmolelun takia—näin maailman valloittanut Labubu-ilmiö näkyy Suomessa. YLE (2025)
29. Saarinen, N.: Labubun avaus-144€ yllätyksiä. [Video] TikTok (2025)
30. Lima, C. F.: De Labubu a Bobbie Goods: as tendências de consumo na infância. Lunetas (2025)
31. Band Jornalismo: Boneco chinês Labubu é febre mundial (2025)
32. Record Balanço G.: Conheça os 'labubus', bonecos que viraram febre e podem custar até R$1000 [Video] (2025)
33. Camargo, M. E.: O que significa Labubu? Brinquedo chinês que virou febre no Brasil. Estadão-MSN (2025)
34. Ferreira, C.B.: Labubu perdeu a vez? "Lafufu" é nova tendência em popularidade. Último Segundo – iG (2025)
35. Miranda, K.: Lalulu: versão do Labubu com rosto de Lula viraliza nas redes. Folha Vitória (2025)
36. SBT News: Bonecos Labubu se tornam febre mundial e ganham versões brasileiras. YouTube (2025)
37. Maraccini, G.: Bebês reborn: entenda o que são e por que chamam atenção. CNN Brasil (2025)
38. Fernandes, N.: Labubu: o monstrinho ostentação invade comércio popular; se tendência for boneca sem cabeça, a gente vende. G1 – Globo (2025)
39. @ataliestudio: Você imaginava que o Labubu faz parte de uma tendência microeconômica real? Instagram (2025)
40. @clubdaterapia: Você nem gosta tanto assim…Instagram (2025)
41. @academiadasfundadoras: Instagram. (Account no longer available in February 2026)
42. Airasvirta, E.: Mikä on Labubu ja miksi se on niin suosittu? Tästä on kyse. TalousSanomat (2025)
43. Wilska, T.-A.: Labubu-villityksessä tiivistyy somevälitteisen kulutuksen tyhmyys (2025)
44. Facebook: Labubu Suomi Ryhmä (Julkinen) 379 jäsentä. https://www.facebook.com/groups/1204930704450456/

45. Bowman, N.D., Wulf, T.: Nostalgia in video games. Curr. Opin. Psychol. **49**, 101544 (2023)
46. Virranniemi, G.: "Uskon, että Labubu-ilmiö voi todella tapahtua uudelleen jollekin toiselle" – Runyo haluaa luoda uuden hittifiguurin. YLE (2025). https://yle.fi/a/74-20185763

Game Consumption in Ludic Spaces: A Chronotopic Approach

Lizbeth Kanyat(✉)

Adventist University of Sao Paulo, Engenheiro Coelho, SP 13448-900, Brazil
lizbeth.kanyat@unasp.edu.br

Abstract. This paper presents an expanded version of the *Chronotope of Reception*, a methodological protocol originally developed by the author for research on the reception of serialized fiction and now adapted to the study of board game consumption in ludic spaces. Inspired by Mikhail Bakhtin's concept of the chronotope and articulated with Reception and Consumption Studies, the approach seeks to understand how time and space intertwine in the construction of meaning during ludic experiences. The protocol is structured into three analytical blocks —conditions of experience, consumption processes, and meaning-making— applied to three empirical axes: place, activities, and people. Drawing on data from an ethnographic study conducted in Tokyo's Board Game Cafés, the paper illustrates the applicability of this updated framework. The aim is to contribute an integrative model for qualitative investigations in the fields of Game Studies.

Keywords: Qualitative Methodology · Data Collection · Chronotope of Reception

1 Introduction

In recent years, the analog game market, particularly board games, has gained relevance as both an economic sector and a cultural phenomenon. During the COVID-19 pandemic, sales increased: in the United States, overall toy industry retail sales rose 19% in the first three quarters of 2020, and within this performance the Games & Puzzles supercategory grew 42% in the cumulative period January–September 2020, compared with January–September 2019 [1]. Beyond the pandemic period, Euromonitor reports continued demand for traditional toys and games in the "new normal," supported by adult hobbyists and at-home leisure patterns [2]. Consistently, Statista's Digital Market Insights projects growth for the global Board Games segment through 2029 [3]. This dynamism reflects not only the rise in game sales but also the proliferation of physical consumption spaces, such as board game cafés, which have consolidated as venues of sociability and belonging. In Japan, for example, the popularity of board game cafés has grown as a form of in-person leisure in response to rising social isolation and technological dependency [4, 5].

The development of Game Studies over the past decades has established a diverse methodological repertoire for understanding player experiences. Works such as *Game*

R. Baptista et al. (Eds.): VJ 2025, CCIS 2988, pp. 255–270, 2027.
https://doi.org/10.1007/978-3-032-31642-4_20

Research Methods [6], *Ethnography and Virtual Worlds* [7], *Games User Research* [8], and qualitative toolkits for analyzing games as cultural texts [9] offer critical reflections on the application of techniques such as ethnography, interviews, focus groups, participant observation, and player-experience protocols. While these approaches have advanced the analysis of specific aspects of ludic practice, there remains room for approaches that systematically articulate space, time, and consumption as central investigative categories.

It is at this juncture that the proposal of the Chronotope of Reception is situated. Inspired by Bakhtin's concept of the chronotope [10] and articulated with Reception Studies [11–13] and Consumption Studies [14, 16], this methodology is organized into three analytical blocks—conditions of experience, consumption processes, and meaning-making—applied to three empirical axes: place, people, and activities. The aim is to understand how ludic experiences are appropriated, lived, and re-signified in spaces of social interaction, such as game cafés and other urban environments of cultural consumption.

The Chronotope of Reception was originally developed by the author for research on the reception of serialized fiction. In a subsequent stage, the author and Allan Novaes collaboratively adapted the protocol to the study of ludic consumption spaces and applied it in ethnographic fieldwork conducted in nine board game cafés in Tokyo in 2024. The results of that study were published in co-authorship [15]. In this paper, the methodology is presented in its updated and expanded form; in order to exemplify its applicability, the data from the Tokyo research are reorganized according to the revised matrix. In this way, the protocol demonstrates applicability across different contexts, contributing to the expansion of qualitative research possibilities in the fields of Game Studies, Reception Studies, and Cultural Consumption.

2 Theoretical Framework

This section presents the conceptual references that underpin the methodological proposal of the Chronotope of Reception: the concept of the chronotope in the work of Mikhail Bakhtin, contributions from Reception Studies, and inputs from Consumption Studies. These references are articulated here and subsequently related to the consolidated methodological debate in Game Studies.

2.1 The Chronotope in Bakhtin

For Bakhtin [10], the chronotope is the essential connection between time and space in narrative construction. In literature, each genre organizes its own relations among temporality, spatiality, and characters, generating singular forms of aesthetic and social experience. Although originally conceived for the analysis of novels, the concept has been extended across different fields to think through social, cultural, and media practices.

In this work, the chronotope is transposed to the study of games as lived narratives, in which time and space are not merely external frames but constitutive conditions of the ludic experience. Thus, the Chronotope of Reception seeks to capture the ways in which players inhabit and ascribe meaning to concrete ludic spaces, such as game cafés and board game libraries, and how such experiences are articulated with individual and collective temporalities.

2.2 Reception Studies

Reception Studies shifted the focus from the message to the subjects and their contexts of appropriation. Authors such as Hans Robert Jauss [13] and Jesús Martín-Barbero [12] showed that reception is traversed by horizons of expectation, cultural mediations, and social practices. In the Brazilian field of communication, authors such as Roseli Fígaro [11] have also emphasized the situated dimension of reception, understood as an active process of meaning-making.

Applied to games, this perspective allows for the investigation not only of rules and mechanics, but also of how players interpret, negotiate, and incorporate such experiences into their everyday lives. By proposing analytical questions about who plays, when and where, how play unfolds, and which meanings are attributed, the Chronotope of Reception aligns with this tradition that understands reception as a complex cultural practice.

2.3 Consumption Studies

Consumption Studies contribute by highlighting that consuming is, above all, the attribution of social and symbolic meanings. For Douglas and Isherwood [14], goods function as systems of communication; for McCracken [16], they transport cultural meanings across contexts. From this perspective, the consumption of games is not limited to acquisition or the act of playing, but involves processes of distinction, belonging, and identity construction.

By integrating this dimension, the Chronotope of Reception makes it possible to understand games as cultural goods that are actualized in situated ludic experience, in which time and space structure both consumption practices and the meanings produced by players.

2.4 Methodologies in Game Studies

The Game Studies literature has already consolidated a substantial set of methods for investigating player experience. Among them are ethnography in virtual worlds (Boellstorff et al. [7]), games user research protocols oriented toward usability and user experience (Drachen, Mirza-Babaei & Nacke [8]), in-depth interviews, focus groups, and stimulated recall techniques (Lankoski & Björk [6]), as well as qualitative analyses of games as cultural texts (Consalvo & Dutton [9]). Each of these approaches sheds light on different dimensions of the ludic phenomenon—interactional, experiential, symbolic, or material—and together they form a robust methodological repertoire for the field.

Because these approaches organize their analytical focus in distinct ways, researchers studying physical ludic spaces may need to decide how to combine methods, which dimensions to prioritize, and how to structure an investigation that involves intertwined spatial, temporal, social, and symbolic elements. The Chronotope of Reception is situated in this methodological landscape. Rather than proposing a replacement for existing techniques, it offers a didactic and organizational resource that groups them into a visual matrix articulating place, people, and activities with the blocks of conditions of experience, consumption processes, and meaning-making.

Its contribution lies in making the analytical possibilities of well-established methods more visible, comparable, and adaptable, helping researchers select, combine, or sequence techniques according to the specific demands of each study. Based on these references, we present below the methodological proposal of the Chronotope of Reception.

3 Methodological Proposal: The *Chronotope of Reception* for Game Studies

The methodological proposal of the Chronotope of Reception is organized into two complementary layers. To help visualize these layers, Table 1, presented later in this section, summarizes their structure. The first defines the fundamental axes of the consumption of ludic spaces—place, activities, and people—which orient what to observe in the field. The second layer corresponds to a set of analytical questions, distributed across three chronotopic blocks—conditions of experience, consumption processes, and meaning-making—which serve as a guide for how to observe and analyze. The articulation between these two dimensions results in a protocol that can be read horizontally (by axes), vertically (by blocks), or crosswise (exploring relations among cells), offering a flexible and integrated interpretive framework.

3.1 Axes of the Consumption of Ludic Spaces

The consumption of games in social venues is not reducible to the act of playing. It involves an ecology of material, symbolic, and social elements that structure the ludic experience. To capture this, the Chronotope of Reception proposes three axes of analysis:

Place: Refers to the physical and symbolic space in which the experience unfolds. It includes urban location, architecture, sensory ambiance (light, sound, smells, furnishings), as well as the ways in which the space is appropriated and re-signified by patrons.

Activities: Concerns the practices carried out in the space, which go beyond game sessions. It includes rituals of playing, eating and drinking, buying and selling, studying, and hosting events or workshops. These are actions that structure sociability and build collective narratives among players and other participants.

People: Encompasses the subjects who frequent the spaces, their biographical trajectories, roles, and identities at play. It also considers forms of interaction (alone, in groups, with mediation), staff mediation, and the social and affective bonds cultivated by participants.

These three axes shift the focus from the game itself to the experience of situated consumption, foregrounding the articulation among materiality, practice, and subjectivity.

3.2 Analytical Questions

The chronotopic questions are not presented as a closed questionnaire but as a script for observation and interpretation. Their function is to organize data collection and analysis according to a processual logic. Unlike Lasswell's classical model, which describes communication in linear terms, the protocol emphasizes the temporal and spatial dimensions of reception and the performative, re-signifying nature of ludic consumption.

The questions are distributed across three chronotopic blocks:

Conditions of Experience: When and Where Does it Occur? Who Participates? This section examines the structural and relational contexts that enable the board game café experience. Temporally, it investigates when users frequent board game cafés, whether as part of daily routines, weekend leisure, or transitional life stages, situating these visits within broader social rhythms, such as post-pandemic reconnection or digital fatigue.

Spatially, it explores how material and symbolic configurations shape user perception. These configurations include elements such as interior design, location, lighting, and ambient aesthetics, which influence the types of activities the space affords and the user perception. Board game cafés function not only as sites of play but as multifunctional social environments, where a variety of practices unfold:

Eating and drinking, integrated into social rituals that enhance gameplay;

Studying and working, especially during off-peak hours, reinforcing their role as flexible third places [17];

Events and workshops, including beginner nights, themed gatherings, and design sessions;

Tournaments, typically on weekends, introducing structured interaction and competitive dynamics.

Relationally, the café ecosystem includes regular patrons, newcomers, staff, and owners. The interactions among these actors, shaped by roles, familiarity, and social codes, constitute a dynamic social fabric. These conditions are not neutral backdrops but active contexts for meaning-making, influencing how people perceive and engage with the space.

Consumption Processes: What is Received? How is it Practiced? This section shifts to the practice of consumption itself, understood as a sequence of interactions with goods, services, and experiences mediated by the BGC environment.

Consumption at board game cafés is neither purely transactional nor individual. It unfolds through a ritualized interplay between ludic activity, hospitality services, and spatial routines. Institutional elements such as game libraries, reservation systems, table time limits, and pricing models structure how users access and navigate the space. These features regulate the rhythm of interaction, shaping when, where, and how people engage with games, food, and each other.

Users typically follow informal sequences, beginning with lightweight games, pausing for food or drinks, and moving on to more complex or strategic titles. Events and tournaments introduce alternate temporalities: timed rounds, rule enforcement, and public scoring add performative layers to the act of playing.

Modes of participation also vary. Visitors may come alone, in pairs, or in open/closed groups, adapting their experience based on available tables, social comfort, or familiarity with games. Staff involvement is crucial: explaining rules, recommending games, or helping organize groups becomes part of the consumption narrative.

In this sense, consumption is not a singular act but a spatial-temporal performance, through which users pursue goals like relaxation, sociability, or skill development.

Meaning-Making: What Meanings Emerge? How are They Appropriated and Projected Beyond the Space?

The final block investigates the dimensions that emerge from the experience and are extended beyond the café. It addresses how users interpret and assign meaning to their practices, how they articulate these meanings in discourse, and how the BGC becomes a site of personal or collective transformation.

This block examines the discursive outputs generated by users: the ways they talk about the space, the feelings they associate with it, the memories they build, and the stories they tell about their participation. These meanings are often anchored in affective responses (feelings of welcome, challenge, inclusion, or nostalgia) and may include reflections on identity, community, and well-being.

Importantly, meaning-making is not confined to the moment of consumption. We explore how these experiences reverberate in the users' broader life narratives. For some, the café might become a space of belonging, a symbolic place that marks an era, a transition, or a healing process. For others, it offers a microcosm of social experimentation, where roles and relationships can be tested in a low-stakes, ludic environment.

This block also attends to the circulation of meanings in broader cultural and digital spheres. How are BGC experiences shared on social media? How do users appropriate the identity of a "gamer", "regular", or "community member"? What are the ideological implications of portraying board game cafés as alternatives to digital entertainment?

In sum, this block captures the symbolic productivity of the BGC experience: how people make sense of what they do, feel, and experience, and how these meanings are mobilized across time and space.

These blocks intersect with the three axes of consumption (place, activities, and people), forming an interpretive matrix. Table 1 should be read transversally: each cell corresponds to a focal point that can be explored using different techniques (participant observation, interviews, focus groups, field diaries, or questionnaires). In this way, the protocol functions as an integrative framework capable of guiding qualitative studies.

As a disclosure, it is important to note that, while the matrix may be applicable to different contexts, its analytical categories should be carefully evaluated and adapted to local cultural ontologies, and any generalizations must be made with caution to avoid imposing Western theoretical assumptions onto distinct sociocultural settings.

The following section outlines the research findings, organized into these analytical categories to demonstrate the applicability of the proposed protocol.

Table 1. Chronotopic Matrix—Axes × Blocks.

Axes × Blocks	Conditions of Experience	Consumption Processes	Meaning-Making
Place	**What space is this?** Where is it located within the urban and social fabric? How is it materially configured (architecture, furnishings, design) and sensorially arranged (light, sounds, smells, temperature)? When is it open or frequented (hours, seasonality, flow)? **Techniques:** systematic observation of the venue and descriptive field diary/fieldnotes	**What consumption processes does the space structure?** Which rules, devices, and dispositions (table time, reservations, game shelves, menu, payment system) orient use? How does the spatial configuration organize circulation, dwelling, and the sequence of activities? **Techniques:** systematic observation of space usage and semi-structured interviews with those responsible for the venue	**What meanings are attributed to the space?** Is it perceived as a refuge, meeting point, space of belonging, prestige, or community? How does it acquire symbolic value over time (memories, events, recurring appropriations)? **Techniques:** photo-elicitation interviews and semi-structured in-depth interviews
Activities	**What activities take place in this space, beyond play?** (eating, drinking, studying, events, workshops, tournaments). When do they occur and in what formats (schedule, frequency, duration)? **Techniques:** participant observation of everyday practices, field diary focused on routines, and structured interview	**How are the activities practiced?** What rituals and sequences structure consumption (order of games chosen, meal breaks, ordering and purchasing dynamics, tournament formats)? How are these routines organized over the course of one's stay in the space? **Techniques:** participant observation and semi-structured interview	**What meanings are associated with the activities?** Is playing, eating, competing, or participating in events perceived as fun, challenge, welcome, learning, distinction? How do certain practices come to be seen as emblematic experiences of the space? **Techniques:** focus group and episodic semi-structured interview (i.e., episodic interview)
People	**Who frequents the space?** What profiles, trajectories, or motives bring them there? Do they arrive alone or accompanied, for the first time or recurrently? Who assumes roles in organizing or conducting the experience (staff, monitors, hosts, experienced players)? **Techniques:** topical life history and structured interviews (sociodemographic profile)	**How do people participate in ludic practices?** Do they play solo, in pairs, or in open/closed groups? In what ways do they interact with rules, with staff, or among themselves during the experience? What personal narratives do they mobilize in the act of participating? **Techniques:** semi-structured interview	**What identities and relationships emerge from participation?** Does the player recognize themselves as friend, competitor, learner, host? What social and affective bonds are built among patrons? Which aspects of the experience are carried beyond the venue and become part of participants' social or subjective lives? **Techniques:** semi-structured interview

4 Empirical Application: Board Game Cafés in Tokyo

This section applies the Chronotope of Reception to empirical material from an ethnographic study conducted in nine board game cafés in Tokyo. Fieldwork took place between February and March 2024 and combined structured observation, participant observation, interviews, and fieldnotes. Data collection was concluded upon reaching empirical saturation, defined as the point at which additional interviews no longer produced new or relevant information (Pires, 2018). The venues visited included: Dear Spiele, Dyce, Jelly Jelly (Shibuya 2nd store), Jelly Jelly (Shinjuku), Korokoro Dou, Little Cave, U Café, Gotta2Cafe, and 10 Billion Point (visited twice).

To enrich the corpus and gain a nuanced understanding of board game café consumption, 36 interviews were conducted: 24 structured interviews with users (survey format), 3 in-depth interviews with users, and 9 in-depth interviews with owners and staff. Additional details on locations, visit dates, and photo documentation are available in Appendix 1.

The aim of this research was to understand how these venues function both as environments of ludic consumption and as sites of community building. The data are reorganized here using the updated matrix, allowing the protocol's analytical structure to be illustrated through concrete field examples. The following subsections present the findings according to the axes and chronotopic blocks that compose the proposed framework.

4.1 Place

Conditions: All board game cafés were located in central districts of Tokyo, close to train stations and universities. Entry fees ranged from ¥400 to ¥600 per hour, and most venues allowed free reentry within the time block paid.

Processes: Spatial organization played a key role in shaping the flow of activities. Game shelves were curated and categorized (party games, strategy, cooperative, etc.), and signage explained house rules. Furniture layout favored small groups, promoting both intimacy and rotation of tables.

Meanings: Patrons repeatedly described a board game café as urban refuges. In interviews, several used terms aligning with *ibasho* [18], expressing feelings of comfort, safety, and acceptance. Staff members emphasized creating "a place where people feel they can come even if they're alone," mirroring government discourse on combating loneliness.

We observed that board game cafés in Tokyo operate as spaces of social inclusion and belonging, closely aligned with the concept of *ibasho*. They respond to a growing demand for conviviality in a society marked by high levels of loneliness and urban isolation, particularly among young adults [4, 5]. In this context, board game cafés offer semi-public environments that encourage light and spontaneous social interaction. Their physical layout—including well-lit interiors, tables arranged for various group sizes, freedom to select games, and clearly defined rules for time use—facilitates extended and comfortable stays. These spatial elements invite patrons to linger, turning the café into a recurring site of social encounter. The primary focus is not the game itself; rather, the environment is intentionally designed to support being together, even among strangers. Beyond the play areas, there are living room-style spaces for conversation, as well as a bar area where guests can enjoy drinks and snacks. More than games, what is consumed in these spaces are social relations.

4.2 Activities

Conditions: Besides board games, most board game cafés organized events: tournaments, game nights, workshops, and "ladies-only" sessions. Events were promoted via social media and displayed on in-store calendars.

Processes: A common ritual observed was the collective selection of games, often mediated by staff suggestions. Food and drinks were typically ordered between sessions, contributing to a convivial rhythm. Some patrons maintained personal records of games played, especially during tournaments.

Meanings: Activities fostered shared experiences and symbolic memory. Participants described "coming back for the people and the feeling," indicating a temporal continuity of belonging. For many, these practices were less about the game itself and more about the social experience, reinforcing the *ibasho* dimension.

Playing unfolds as a social ritual composed of distinct but interconnected phases. First, groups are often formed upon arrival, a process facilitated by the café host who helps connect solo visitors or newcomers with others. Once a group is established, participants typically begin with light, casual party games to break the ice. These games serve to lower social barriers and create a relaxed atmosphere.

The second phase involves collectively selecting the next game, often guided by group interest, familiarity, and the level of challenge desired. One participant, usually more experienced, takes on the role of explaining the rules—a key moment of the ritual that fosters attention, patience, and mutual support.

Finally, the gameplay itself provides a structured environment where interaction follows a shared logic, enabling communication and cooperation. Across these phases, board games become tools for building trust and comfort, supporting a type of interaction that feels both meaningful and accessible. These practices transform the café into a setting where social connection is not only possible but intentionally cultivated.

4.3 People

Conditions: The demographic profile was consistent across venues: mostly young adults aged 20–35, with a balance between students and professionals. A notable portion of visitors came alone, particularly men in their early 30s.

Processes: Staff were central to the mediation of social interaction. They greet newcomers, suggesting suitable games, and facilitating rule explanations. This role was not only operational but performative, often cited by patrons as crucial to their decision to return.

Meanings: Beyond entertainment, board games function as tools for social connection, helping participants form new friendships and adopt different social roles. These dynamics foster meaningful interactions during gameplay that often extend beyond the café. Conversations continue over meals, and participants reported engaging in shared activities outside the venue, such as fishing trips, picnics, or walks. One notable case involved a couple who met at a board game café and eventually married, inviting other patrons and the café owner to their wedding. This is an example of the long-term bonds that can emerge in these settings.

Rather than selecting cafés based on geographic proximity, users prioritize qualities such as atmosphere, staff interaction, and accessibility. The user base is diverse, ranging from casual players to hardcore hobbyists, solo visitors to organized groups, and language learners to nightlife seekers. This variety contributes to distinct social dynamics in each café, allowing individuals to explore different identities depending on the establishment and the group they engage with.

5 Conclusions

This paper introduced the Chronotope of Reception as a methodological proposal for studying the consumption of games in urban ludic spaces. Inspired by the Bakhtinian concept of the chronotope and articulated with Reception Studies and Consumption Studies, the methodology organizes the investigation around three axes—place, activities, and people—observed through three chronotopic blocks: conditions of experience, consumption processes, and meaning-making.

The proposal structures the inquiry as an integrative framework capable of guiding both data collection and interpretive analysis. Unlike approaches that privilege dimensions of the game, the player, or design, the protocol emphasizes the interlacing of space, practices, and subjects, enabling an understanding of ludic consumption as a cultural practice situated in time and space.

The illustration with data from research conducted in Tokyo's board game cafés demonstrated how the protocol can be operationalized in the field. The matrix made it possible to organize multiple data-collection techniques to study the elements that mediate the processes of consumption and reception of games in ludic environments. Originating in the study of the reception of serialized fiction, this protocol can be applied to the consumption of other cultural goods, and it can also be expanded, within the framework of Game Studies, to the consumption of other analog or digital ludic spaces.

We conclude that the Chronotope of Reception constitutes a methodological tool adaptable to different cultural contexts and types of ludic spaces, such as eSports bars, game libraries, themed bars, or even metaverses. By systematizing the investigation in multiple layers, the protocol broadens the possibilities of analysis in Game Studies and Consumption Studies, contributing to an understanding of how play is inscribed in the fabric of contemporary social life.

Acknowledgments. The author thanks Allan Novaes for his collaboration in the research conducted in Tokyo's board game cafés, from which empirical data are drawn to illustrate the applicability of the revised methodology presented in this paper.

Disclosure of Interests. The author has no competing interests to declare that are relevant to the content of this article.

Appendix

1. Jelly Jelly Cafe 新宿店
Data: 29/02/24
Endereąo: Japão, 〒151-0051 Tokyo, Shibuya City, Sendagaya, 5 Chome−33−1, Coopinfield, １F

2. Little Cave
Data: 19/02
Japão, 〒166-0003 Tokyo, Suginami City, Koenjiminami, 4 Chome−26−16 芦野ビル ２階

3. Dear Spiel
Data: 20/02/24
Endereço: Japão, 〒164-0003 Tokyo, Nakano City, Higashinakano, 4 Chome−9−1 第一元太ビル 4-A 第一元太ビル

4. U Cafe
Data: 22/02
Endereço: Japão, 〒110-0005 Tokyo, Taito City, Ueno, 1 Chome−2−6 長谷川ビル 2F

5. Korokoro dou
Data: 22/02
Endereąo: Japão, 〒110-0005 Tokyo, Taito City, Ueno, 1 Chome−9−3 日向ビル 1階

6. Gotta2Cafe
Data: 25/02/24
Endereąo: Japão, 〒169-0051 Tokyo, Shinjuku City, Nishiwaseda, 2 Chome−16−17 NKビル 2F

7. 10 billion point
Data: 25/02/24
Endereąo: Japão, 〒162-0808 Tokyo, Shinjuku City, Tenjincho, ６８−3 橋本ビル 2F

8. DyCE Global Board Game Cafe
Data: 29/02/24
Endereąo: Japão, 〒150-0002 Tokyo, Shibuya City, Shibuya, 1-chōme−6−4 The Neat 青山 5階

9. Jelly Jelly Cafe Shibuya 2 Goten
Data: 29/02/24
Endereąo: Japão, 〒150-0002 Tokyo, Shibuya City, Shibuya, 1 Chome−13−5, Daikyo Shibuya Bldg., 11階

References

1. NPD Group: U.S. Toy Industry Retail Sales Grew 16% in 2020. https://www.prweb.com/releases/the-npd-group-u-s-toy-industry-retail-sales-grew-16-in-2020-810329175.html. Accessed 26 Sept 2025
2. Euromonitor International: Strong Demand for Toys and Games to Continue in the New Normal. https://www.euromonitor.com/article/strong-demand-for-toys-and-games-to-continue-in-the-new-normal. Accessed 29 Sept 2025
3. Statista: Board Games – Worldwide. https://www.statista.com/outlook/dmo/toys-hobby/board-games/worldwide. Accessed 29 Sept 2025
4. DiJulio, B., Hamel, L., Muñana, C., Brodie, M.: Loneliness and social isolation in the United States, the United Kingdom, and Japan: An international survey. KFF (2018). https://www.kff.org/other/report/loneliness-and-social-isolation-in-the-united-states-the-united-kingdom-and-japan-an-international-survey. Accessed 26 Sept 2025
5. Headquarters for Advancement of Measures to Address Loneliness and Isolation: Priority plan to facilitate the promotion of the policies regarding measures to address loneliness and isolation. Cabinet Office, Government of Japan (2024). https://www.cao.go.jp/kodoku_koritsu/pdf/jutenkeikaku_english.pdf. Accessed 26 Sept 2025
6. Lankoski, P., Björk, S.: Game Research Methods: An Overview. ETC Press, Pittsburgh (2015)
7. Boellstorff, T., Nardi, B., Pearce, C., Taylor, T.L.: Ethnography and Virtual Worlds: A Handbook of Method. Princeton University Press, Princeton (2012)
8. Drachen, A., Mirza-Babaei, P., Nacke, L.E. (eds.): Games User Research: A Case Study Approach. Oxford University Press, New York (2018)

9. Consalvo, M., Dutton, N.: Game analysis: Developing a methodological toolkit for the qualitative study of games. Game Stud. **6**(1) (2006)
10. Bakhtin, M.: The Dialogic Imagination: Four Essays. University of Texas Press, Austin (1981)
11. Fígaro, R., Grohmann, R.: A recepção serve para pensar: um "lugar" de embates. Palabra Clave **20**(1), 142–161 (2017). https://doi.org/10.5294/pacla.2017.20.1.7
12. Martín-Barbero, J.: De los medios a las mediaciones: comunicación, cultura y hegemonía. Gustavo Gili, Barcelona (1987)
13. Jauss, H.R.: A estética da recepção: leituras e perspectivas. Ática, São Paulo (1994)
14. Douglas, M., Isherwood, B.: The World of Goods: Towards an Anthropology of Consumption. Basic Books, New York (1979)
15. Novaes, A., Kanyat, L.: From play to belonging: board game cafes as mediators for social wellness and community building in Japan. Acta Ludol. **8**(1), 78–97 (2025), https://doi.org/10.34135/actaludologica.2025-8-1.78-97, https://actaludologica.com/wp-content/uploads/2025/06/AL_2025-8-1_Study-6_Novaes-Kanyat.pdf. Accessed 26 Sept 2025
16. McCracken, G.: Culture and Consumption: New Approaches to the Symbolic Character of Consumer Goods and Activities. Indiana University Press, Bloomington (1988)
17. Oldenburg, R.: The Great Good Place. Paragon House, New York (1989)
18. Tanaka, H.: Development of the "Ibasho" concept in Japanese education and youth work: "Ibasho" as a place of refuge and empowerment for excluded people. Educ. Stud. Jpn.: Int. Yearb. **15**(1), 3–15 (2021), https://eric.ed.gov/?id=EJ1324199. Accessed 26 Sept 2025

GPSR Compliance

The European Union's (EU) General Product Safety Regulation (GPSR) is a set of rules that requires consumer products to be safe and our obligations to ensure this.

If you have any concerns about our products, you can contact us on ProductSafety@springernature.com

In case Publisher is established outside the EU, the EU authorized representative is:

Springer Nature Customer Service Center GmbH
Europaplatz 3
69115 Heidelberg, Germany

Batch number: 10860630

Printed by Printforce, the Netherlands